D1615872

VISA The Power of an Idea

Bell Mobility
COREL
The fastest in graphics!

VISA

Maquedano
SIERPES, 40 - SEVILLA
Maquedano
SIERPES, 40 - SEVILLA
3400
LODEN VERDE
3400
LODEN GRIS
Maquedano
SIERPES, 40
VISA

D O'SHEA
SEVEN DAYS LICENCE TO
SELL BEER WINE & SPIRITS.
VISA

VISA TRIPLE CROWN

Kentucky Derby - Preakness Stakes
Belmont Stakes
VISA

4:59
RACE 9
TRACK
SLOPPY
VISA
TRIPLE CROWN
CHALLENGE

VISA The Power of an Idea

by Paul Chutkow

design by Yumiko Nakagawa

original photography by Matthew Klein

printing by Toppan Printing Co.

Harcourt
111West Jackson Boulevard
Seventh Floor
Chicago, IL 60604

©2001 Visa International

All rights reserved. No part of this publication may be reproduced, stored in a retrieval system or transmitted, in any form, or by any means, electronic, mechanical, photocopying, recording or otherwise, without the prior permission of Visa International

ISBN 0159004799
Library of Congress Card Number: 00-106354

Written by Paul Chutkow
Design by Yumiko Nakagawa Design
Printed in Japan by Toppan Printing Co., Tokyo, Japan
Typesetting and Production by Command Z

First published 2001
First Edition

Dedication

For Dee Hock,
and for the Visa member banks
and financial institutions which
embraced his ideals and helped
turn his vision into a reality.

The Vision

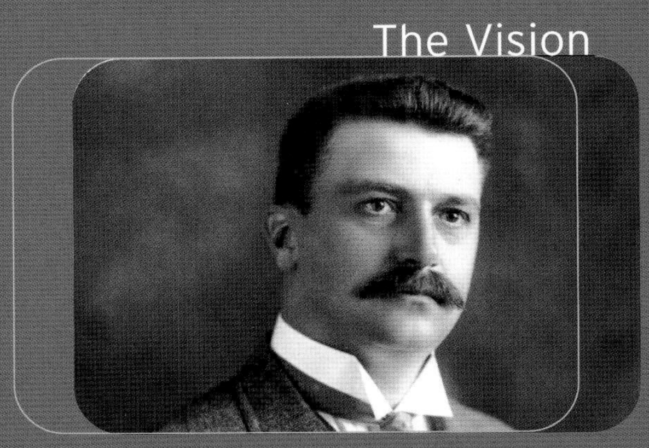

The Partnership

VISA The Power of an Idea

The Technology

The Image

The Global Revolution

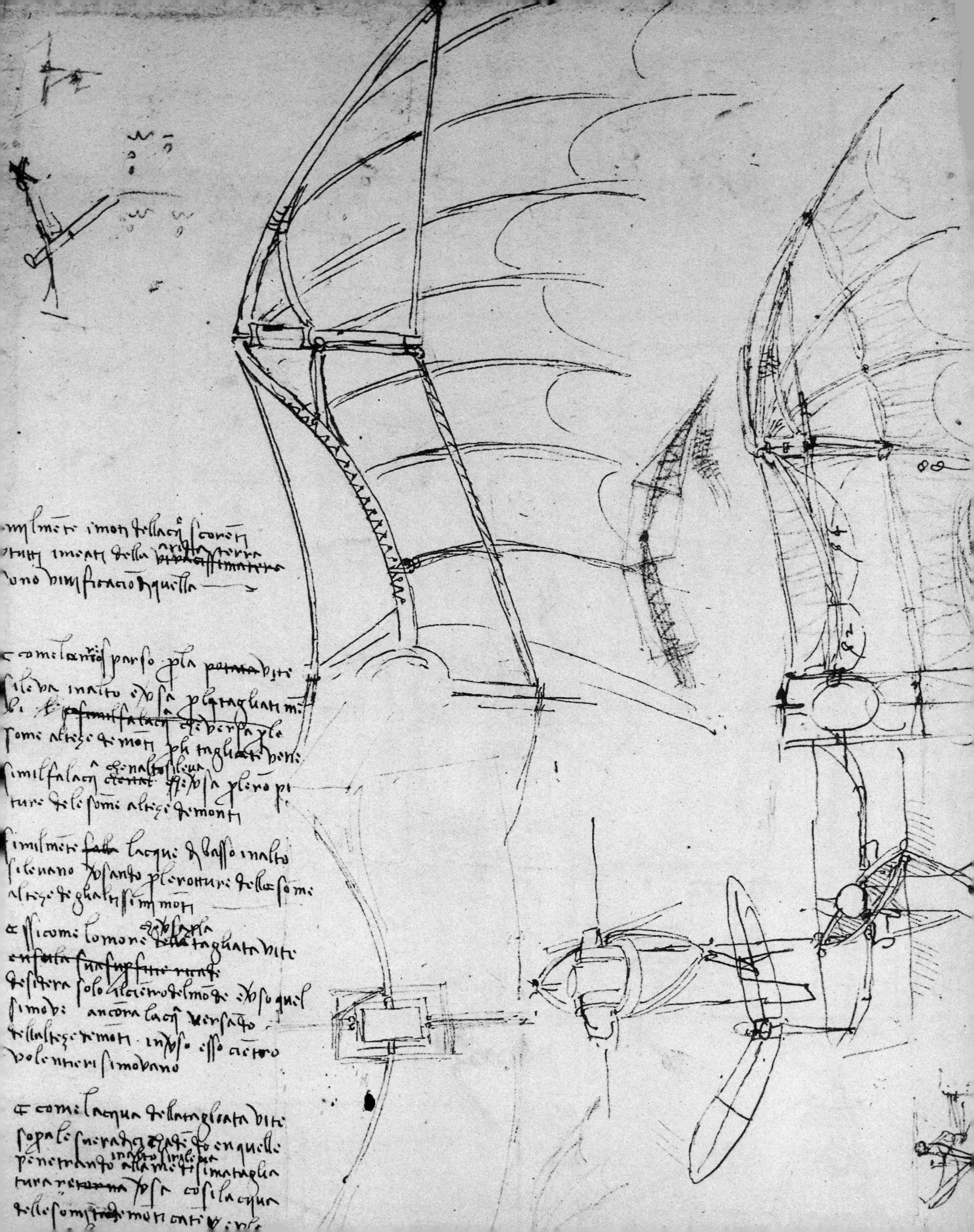

The Genius Inside

In the course of the Twentieth Century, our world was transformed by an array of pioneers and visionaries, men and women who took powerful ideas and turned them into exciting new tools. The automobile. The airplane. Vaccines. Computers. Lasers. Satellites. Television. The Internet. And more.

These innovations, each with a touch of genius inside, transformed our lives. They eased our work and enriched our play. They reshaped our schools and communities, expanded our knowledge and our consciousness, and they catapulted us into an era of amazing technological advancement and economic growth.

As this book will make clear, the Visa card merits a place among the great innovations of the Twentieth Century. This little strip of plastic, and the unique global partnership that supports it, has transformed the way we shop. The way we pay our bills. The way we bank. The way we travel. The way we *live.* The Visa card has also transformed the way countless banks, merchants, and companies do business at home and around the world.

At its most visible level, the Visa card is a tool of personal empowerment. It gives us financial power and flexibility, and that, in turn, gives us greater freedom and capacity to provide for our families, pursue our dreams, and shape our own destinies. Visa does the same for millions of people around the world, whether they live in St. Louis or Sydney, or in Paris, Bogotá, or Beijing.

As you are about to discover, Visa is also a tool of national empowerment. In countries as diverse as Venezuela, Poland, and Taiwan, Visa has helped change the way businesses function, and it has helped stimulate economic growth and social change. Also, thanks to its unique organizational structure, Visa is a universally recognized brand, but in each country Visa has local roots, local management, and local brand identity.

The formula works. In the space of just 30 years, Visa has grown from an idea into a worldwide enterprise, bridging barriers of language, culture, and ideology and drawing the peoples of the world together in a single, efficient system of electronic payments and exchange. How big is Visa? Larger than all of its competitors *combined.* In 1999 alone, Visa processed $1.7 *trillion* in global transactions. Seen in this light, the little Visa card is not just a handy way to pay; it's a global revolution, right in our pocket.

We are now at the dawn of a new millennium, and even greater changes are on the way. The ancient walls and barriers dividing nations are crumbling or gone, and we are entering an era already being shaped by global communications, global travel and business, and global trends in art, culture, and entertainment. No one can see the shape of things to come, but we do know this: just over the horizon there are new pioneers and visionaries, and they will bring us ideas and innovations we can't even imagine.

This book is written for them – tomorrow's pioneers. May the story of Visa and its creators stand as an inspiration and a guiding beacon along their way.

– Paul Chutkow

Part One The Vision

2-385-19

THE CITY OF S

BIRDS EYE VIEW FROM THE

AN FRANCISCO.

BAY LOOKING SOUTH-WEST.

Chapter 1

A.P. Giannini,
An American Pioneer

The tool is amazing.

We use it at the restaurant, the supermarket, the gas station, the doctor, the dentist, the airport, and the ATM. We can use it to rent cars, send flowers, buy computers, pay bills, even do business on the Internet. Many of us use it every day, for big jobs and small, and that little tool works so well – card in, card out, job done – that we rarely give a thought to the magic it holds.

The story of Visa, though, is about far more than a wondrous strip of plastic. It is the story of creating an industry. It is the story of building a unique global partnership. It is the story of marrying money and technology. It is the story of developing one of the most powerful brands in the world. It is even a story about cops and robbers and the worldwide fight against counterfeiting and fraud.

Above all, the story of Visa is the story of an idea – an idea founded on a bedrock belief in liberty, equality, and the integrity and resourcefulness of the common man. In the beginning, a few pioneering men and women, from all over the world, embraced that idea, committed their lives to pursuing it, and with vision, ingenuity, and an unshakeable sense of mission, they turned that idea into a global revolution, a revolution that gathers strength to this very day. Visa, in sum, is quite a story, and it all begins in the heart and mind of just one man:

A.P. Giannini.

A.P. Giannini was a true American pioneer. With vision, innovation, and a business philosophy that was unique in its day, Giannini built a financial empire and stirred a revolution, changing forever the way Americans bank, pay their bills, and manage their money. Giannini also changed the focus of American banking.

Before Giannini, most banks built their business by catering to big business and the monied classes. Giannini focused instead on "the little fellow," and he gave working men and women financial power and flexibility they had never had before. In doing all this, Giannini left a deep and lasting imprint on America. Today you can look at the great city of San Francisco, you can look at the majesty of the Golden Gate Bridge, you can look at the wealth and vibrance of the state of California, and you can look inside banks in every town and village across America, and in each of these places you will find the hand or the guiding spirit of A.P. Giannini.

So who was A.P. Giannini? What were the well-springs of all he accomplished? Above all, how did he pave the way for the creation of Visa, the little card that we all carry today?

The story of A.P. Giannini opens in 1870, in the little town of San Jose, California. Today, San Jose is a big, booming city, located on the periphery of the Silicon Valley. Back then, though, San Jose was a rustic little farm community, with a warm climate, friendly people, and beautiful surroundings. The city of San Francisco, some 50 miles to the north, had elegant shops, fine restaurants, and European manners and charm. San Jose had none of that. This was the American frontier, young and raw, a place where newly arrived immigrants could quickly settle in, get started, and build themselves new lives – provided they had the necessary character, ingenuity, and willingness to work.

In the late 1860s, a young immigrant couple from Italy, Luigi and Virginia Giannini, came and settled in San Jose. They had grown up in the countryside outside of Genoa, and they both came from humble, hard-working farm families. They had married when they were very young – Virginia was barely 15 – and soon thereafter they had emigrated to America and come to San Jose. With a small nest egg they had brought with them from Italy, the young couple leased and began running the Swiss Hotel, a modest establishment catering, in part, to other Italian immigrants and their families. It was there in the hotel, on May 6, 1870, that Virginia, not yet 16, gave birth to the young couple's first child, Amadeo Peter Giannini, later to be known simply as "A.P."

In Italian, there is a beautiful word: *carattere*. Literally, it means a person's "character," but in Italian the word has a much deeper resonance. If you could find a single word to describe a person's heart, soul, backbone, guts, ingenuity, and spirit, that word would be *carattere*. If an Italian describes someone as a person with *carattere*, that is a high compliment. It means he or she is exceptional, strong, and to be admired. Luigi and Virginia had *carattere*. After Amadeo was born, Virginia gave birth to two more sons, Attilio and George, but that didn't slow Luigi and Virginia. In a new homeland, and speaking only limited English, they worked hard, cared for their children, and managed to build the Swiss Hotel into a thriving little business. That's *carattere*.

Once they had firmly established themselves in San Jose, Luigi saw what he thought was a golden opportunity. Merchants in San Francisco were paying high prices for top-quality meats, eggs, and produce. So why not return to farming? The price of land was reasonable, farming was in their veins, and they could earn a good living in the countryside. Besides, it would be a healthier place to raise their sons and build their future.

A less industrious man might have been content to stay put with the hotel. He had a good business going; why rock the boat? But Luigi sold the hotel business and bought 40 acres of farmland in the fertile Santa Clara Valley, not far from San Jose. Luigi was intent on following his dream: he would grow fruits and vegetables and sink permanent roots deep in the California soil, for himself, his family, and for generations of Gianninis to come.

For six years, Luigi worked his land and built his farm. Then, one day, he and a workman got into an argument over a debt. The argument turned violent and the workman wound up killing Luigi Giannini. In one ugly, murderous moment, Virginia became a widow at the age of 22, and her three young sons lost their father. It was a tragedy, made even worse by the size of the debt in question: one dollar. Amadeo was only seven years old at the time, and we can only imagine the pain and anger he must have felt.

Virginia managed the farm for a while, carrying on alone with her three sons, but it was a terrible strain. And then she met Lorenzo Scatena, another Italian immigrant working in the Santa Clara Valley. Like Luigi, he was an industrious man, with a nose for business, but Lorenzo was not a farmer. With his wagon and team of horses, he hauled his neighbors' produce to the docks and to the railroad station for shipment on to the big markets in San Francisco. This was an adequate living – for a single man.

Lorenzo and Virginia courted, married, and had three more children of their own. Now Lorenzo needed to find a way to make more money to support his family, and San Francisco seemed the most promising place to look. So in 1882 he and Virginia sold the farm, packed up their children, and moved to the city.

In San Francisco, Lorenzo and Virginia naturally gravitated to North Beach. Then, as now, North Beach was San Francisco's "Little Italy," a warm, convivial neighborhood that looked, felt, smelled, and functioned just like a small village or

A.P. Giannini's birthplace in San Jose, California.

town in Italy, even though it was located in the heart of the most sophisticated city in the American West. In North Beach, most of the Italian families knew each other, either through their work, the schools, or the local churches, just as they would in a small Italian town.

In North Beach, Lorenzo quickly found his way. Within a year he opened his own business, L. Scatena & Company, buyers and wholesalers of top-quality fruits and vegetables. He set up shop on Washington Street, the heart of the city's thriving market district, and he outfitted himself with a wagon, a team of horses, and a warehouse to store his produce. With these basic elements at hand, Lorenzo went into business. And soon he had at his side a bright and eager assistant: his 12-year-old stepson Amadeo Giannini.

Though Amadeo had always been a good student at school, he was never brilliant like his younger brother Attilio. But once he started to work for his stepfather, after school and on Saturdays, young A.P. began to catch fire. He loved the markets of Washington Street, with their hum of activity and commerce. He also loved to help out in his stepfather's office, in the warehouse, or with the horses and wagon.

On Saturdays, free of school, Amadeo would make the rounds with his stepfather. Starting around midnight, they would go over to Washington Street and hitch up the horses and wagon. Then they would ride down to the wharves and buy loads of fresh fruit and vegetables coming right off the boats. The wharves were the hub of northern California's booming agricultural industry. Most of the produce grown and harvested in the region was shipped to market by boat, via the Sacramento and San Joaquin rivers, arriving at the wharves long before the sun came up.

On the docks, Lorenzo and his young assistant would meet the boats, inspect the produce, conclude their transactions, and then fill their wagon with big crates of fruit and vegetables. From there, Lorenzo and Amadeo would go to the central market or make the rounds of their network of customers, most of them small retailers with shops in different parts of San Francisco.

Amadeo learned quickly; each day brought new lessons in the rudiments of business and the ways of the marketplace. Each day was also an education in how to deal with people from across the spectrum of ethnic, working class San Francisco: Italians, Irish, Chinese, Portugese, Poles,

San Francisco's wharf,
where A.P. worked as a youth.

Russians, and more. There was no need for Amadeo to read a textbook about America's unique "melting pot" society; he lived it every single day.

When he finished grammar school, instead of going on to high school, Amadeo decided to work full-time at L. Scatena & Company. By the age of 15, A.P. was already making his own mark in the fruit and vegetable trade. He was a tall, handsome, rugged young man, standing six feet tall (en route to 6-foot-2) and he weighed 170 pounds. He was ebullient, blunt-spoken, and high-spirited, but he was also mature and responsible, and Amadeo clearly had a fine mind for business and an engaging way with people. These qualities earned him respect. In the eyes of everyone in North Beach there was no doubt about it: Amadeo Giannini was someone to watch. Even young he had *carattere*.

Lorenzo Scatena understood that his stepson was an important addition to his business, and he gave Amadeo as much responsibility as he could handle, in San Francisco and beyond. Soon Amadeo was out on the road, meeting with produce growers from the Santa Clara Valley and as far away as Sacramento and the Napa Valley. This was a business apprenticeship at its most effective, learning quite literally from the ground up.

As Amadeo's responsibilities and travels grew, so did his understanding of how a good business works. In particular, his work week was an in-depth tutelage in the value and power of money. Amadeo learned which grower had, say, the best tomatoes, and he saw what his network of retailers would pay for a crate of those same tomatoes. He also learned what kind of mark-ups his stepfather needed to charge to cover his overhead and payroll. Money, Amadeo learned, was both power and lubricant; it drove business and made the wheels of commerce turn and turn.

Money also did more. Money bought those big crates of fruit and vegetables. It paid the staff, fed the horses, and kept the wagons rolling. For families, it put bread and milk on the table, clothed the children, paid for doctors, medicines, and ice in the summer and wood to burn in the winter. Yes, as Amadeo came to understand, money was an amazingly powerful tool. If used wisely, it could do wondrous, positive things for individuals, families, and whole communities like North Beach.

But there was another side to money, the side Amadeo had first seen in the killing of his father. Murder, over a $1 debt. How pointless, how tragic. On the wharves and in the markets, Amadeo again saw the dark side of money. He saw thievery and greed, he saw how debt and financial distress could breed pain and despair. He also saw how money can push even good men into terrible mistakes. These were lessons that A.P. Giannini would never forget, and they would help shape his life and work to come.

As he matured, A.P. Giannini began to forge

Early on, A.P. developed a deep respect for California's farmers.

his own personal business philosophy, a set of core beliefs and principles that just a few years later would rock the entire American banking establishment, from Wall Street to Main Street. What made a company successful? As Giannini came to understand, the true measure of a company's success was not to be found in any statement of profit or loss, and it was surely not to be found in the size of its storefront or its president's desk. What really mattered, over the long haul, was the quality of the relationships a company forged with its suppliers, customers, and its employees.

In Giannini's view, a good businessman was, first and foremost, a true and caring friend. He always looked his suppliers and customers squarely in the eye. He cared about their families and their businesses, and he always did what he could to help. The real keys to business success were never sales and profits. They were character and honesty. Loyalty and trust. Cooperation and partnership. Generosity and a spirit of community.

How did the strongest business relationships function? As true partnerships. Giannini saw this every day. If the fruit and vegetable growers he worked with were successful and came in with good harvests, that was good for them – and it was good for him. It was also good for Giannini's customers, the San Francisco retailers he sold to and serviced. Ultimately, the joint success of the growers, the brokers and the retailers was also good for the retailers' customers. In the best business relationships, Giannini saw that there weren't winners and losers. Everyone won: the suppliers, the brokers, the retailers, his customers, and, finally, the community at large.

In his years at L. Scatena & Company, Giannini worked hard to put this belief into practice. As he made the rounds of his growers, he counseled them about the best ways to run their businesses and manage their finances. He kept

In his stepfather's produce company, A.P. forged his unique business philosophy.

them advised about changing market prices, and he traded information about the best methods of growing, irrigation, and protecting crops against the elements. Giannini became a one-man storehouse of vital information and know-how, and he was always happy to share his knowledge, because he understood that the better his growers and retailers did, the better he did. Through cooperation and partnership, everyone prospered.

Giannini went further. If a farmer needed funds to see him through a season of spoiled crops or to buy farm equipment, the farmer never turned to a bank for help; banks were for the rich, not for the working man. Instead, the farmer turned to Giannini. And Giannini saw to it that L. Scatena would advance him the money. "Seed money," they called it in the farming community, and to Giannini it made perfect sense: if you prosper, I prosper. If you need a loan to help you prosper, then I have good reason to loan you the money. This was good business and something more. It was money being used for the best possible ends: to empower individuals and to work for a larger common good.

Anytime you loan money, there is risk involved; Giannini had seen that with his own father. But Giannini believed in the power of trust. Call it Giannini's law: Believe in a man, trust him, even loan him money, and it's a safe bet that he will rise to your expectations, prove his integrity, and meet his obligations. On the other hand, if you distrust a man and assume the worst, you deflate him, you demoralize him, and then all bets are off. At L. Scatena, Giannini operated on this principle, and it became a permanent cornerstone of his emerging business creed.

Another cornerstone was his abiding faith in "the little fellow," his affectionate name for the working man, the average Joes and Annies, the people he worked with, joked with, and joined with for a beer or a glass of wine. Giannini himself was a "little fellow" and he was proud of it. In his view, the working men and women were the real backbone of America – not the rich or the well-to-do or the captains of industry. Giannini believed in the little fellow, trusted him, helped him, loaned him money, and saw him as the best business partner anyone could have.

Giannini was also convinced that if the young frontier state of California was going to prosper, and if the colossal experiment known as America was going to succeed, it would be thanks to millions of common men and women working hard and pulling together. They had the guts, intelligence, and wherewithal to do great things; Giannini was sure of that. What they often lacked was know-how, the right tools, and a little extra money for their businesses and families. Out of his impulse to help, A.P. Giannini would soon find his true calling and build an empire.

By 1892, at the age of only 22, Giannini had become a major force at L. Scatena, and he was helping it become one of the largest produce wholesalers in San Francisco. To reward his stepson and demonstrate his trust, Lorenzo made Amadeo a partner in the business, giving him a full 50 percent share of the equity of the company.

On the strength of this foundation, A.P. Giannini now decided to take a bride. In 1892 he married a lovely North Beach woman named Clorinda Agnes Cuneo. She, too, was 22 and came from humble Italian roots. Her father, Joseph Cuneo, had come to California in the heat of the Gold Rush. He had tried mining but had found no gold. Then he moved to North Beach and did well, through a series of timely real estate investments.

His family was well respected in North Beach, and Clorinda, by all accounts, was a young woman of character and grace. Amadeo and Clorinda soon started a family and for the next nine years, A.P.

worked at building the family business. His efforts paid off handsomely. By the turn of the century, L. Scatena & Company was one of the largest produce dealers on the West Coast, and A.P. Giannini was financially secure. Still, he and Clorinda maintained their modest ways; they shunned any hint of extravagance or the trappings of wealth.

By 1900 though, A.P. Giannini was growing restless. He was now 30 years old and had spent his entire adult life in his stepfather's business. He was successful and financially secure, but like his immigrant parents he had a pioneering spirit. He wanted to be out on his own, with a new challenge and a new frontier to explore. But what new frontier? He wasn't yet sure.

Nonetheless, in 1901 Giannini decided it was time to leave the produce business. He talked with his stepfather and they worked out a way to sell his share of the company to a group of L. Scatena employees. That done, Giannini said his good-byes, to his co-workers, growers, and customers. In a larger sense, he also said good-bye to his long years of apprenticeship, learning the art of business and forging his own unique business philosophy.

From this point on, A.P. Giannini was under no financial pressure to work. He had the means to live comfortably with Clorinda for the rest of their lives. With such security, a different man might have chosen to travel the world or take up golf. But not Giannini. He was a proud, resourceful working man, a doer, and he felt that what he had done so far was not an end, only a prelude, a foundation on which to build. And he was right.

As the new century dawned, the great adventure of A.P. Giannini's life was about to begin. And the seeds of Visa were about to be sown.

A.P. and Clorinda Agnes Cuneo, on their wedding day in 1892.

BANK OF ITALY
EL CAMINO REAL
SAN FRANCISCO DE ASIS
MISSION DE LOS DOLORES
3 MILES
SAN RAFAEL ARCANGEL
15 MILES
SITE OF OLD LANDING
"when the water came up to Montgomery"
552
BANK OF ITALY

The Idea

After he left the fruit and vegetable business, A.P. Giannini was eager to find a new frontier to explore. He had youth, energy, resources, and clear ideas about how to run a business. But he found nothing that ignited his passion, nothing that awakened in him a strong sense of mission.

In 1902, however, fate stepped in to give him a hand. Clorinda's father, Joseph Cuneo, died, and the family turned to A.P. for help. He had a sharp mind for business, the sharpest in the family; would A.P. agree to manage Cuneo's real estate and other business holdings? Giannini agreed, but with no evident enthusiasm; he would do it for the good of the family. He refused to accept a salary. Instead, he agreed to work on an incentive system: he would take 25 percent of whatever increase there might be in the capital value of the estate during his stewardship.

Among Cuneo's holdings were shares and a seat on the board of directors of a small, somewhat lethargic bank in North Beach, the Columbus Savings & Loan Society. Giannini attended a few meetings of the board and he bristled at what he saw. In his view, the bank had great potential, but it was poorly managed and its directors showed no signs of ingenuity or vision. Worse, the directors showed almost no interest in serving the little fellow or working for the greater good of the community of North Beach.

For a time, Giannini worked with the board and tried to generate change from the inside, with no results. He'd go to the meetings and come away in disgust. These bankers! They're rigid, narrow, greedy, archaic in their business practices, and totally unable – or unwilling – to see anything beyond their profit and loss sheet. They refuse to think long-term. They refuse to see that in the best business relationships everyone prospers. Finally, during one critical board meeting Giannini's frustration peaked and he stood up and bellowed, "I quit! I'll start my own bank!"

Then he set out to do just that. A.P. Giannini, of course, knew next to nothing about banking. At L. Scatena & Company, he had often loaned money to his growers and clients, with good results for all concerned. But that was a far cry from starting his own bank and making it successful. Some of Giannini's friends no doubt feared he had lost his mind, but Giannini was undaunted. He went to bankers he knew for advice and counsel, and he set out to learn everything there was to know about running a bank.

This much was sure from the outset: this would not be a traditional bank. Giannini had no desire to cater to the rich or to big business. His bank would serve the needs of his people, the little fellow, the average Joes and Annies, the growers, shippers, dock workers, and shopkeepers that had made L. Scatena & Co. one of the biggest wholesale produce businesses on the West Coast. He and his stepfather had built that business from scratch; doubters be hanged, he would do it again! Yes, Giannini had *carattere*, and he also had an all-American can-do spirit.

During this exact same period, some other Americans were also launching ambitious ventures, and many people said they were a little crazy too. In Dayton, Ohio, for instance, two brothers who ran a little bicycle shop were hard at work building machines that they hoped would fulfill one of man's oldest dreams: being able to fly. Inventors dating back to Leonardo da Vinci and beyond had designed various sorts of wings and flying machines, but none had ever worked. But

Orville and Wilbur Wright were just crazy enough to think they could do the impossible.

In 1899, they had built a large kite, with two fixed wings, a rudder, and a place for the pilot to position himself on the lower wing. With Wilbur at the controls, they launched the kite into the wind and it took to the sky – for only 100 feet. In ensuing days, they adjusted the glider until they could keep it under control for longer runs. History salutes these as man's first controlled flights.

In 1903, the brothers built a stronger craft, one they hoped could fly under its own power. It had an aluminum engine and propellers carved out of spruce. On the morning of December 17, 1903, on the crest of a windswept sand dune in Kitty Hawk, North Carolina, on America's Atlantic Coast, they went through their final checks. Then they flipped a coin to see who would be the pilot. Orville won. They started the engine and Orville climbed aboard and settled in at the controls. Finally, he released a lever that put the propeller in gear – and the Wright Brothers' flying machine took to the air.

The first test flight lasted only 12 seconds. The next lasted only 59 seconds. But that was enough. These two humble bicycle makers from Dayton had done it: they had achieved the world's first powered, sustained, and controlled flight. And right there at Kitty Hawk a new industry and whole new era were born.

In this same period, a restless young man named Henry Ford was pursuing another crazy dream. Ford, like A.P. Giannini, was the son of immigrants, Irish in Ford's case, and he grew up in Detroit, Michigan. At the age of 15 he left school to go to work as a machinist's apprentice. In 1899, the year the Wright Brothers first went aloft, Ford left his job and set out to build automobiles.

With a group of partners, he formed the Detroit Automobile Company and set to work. Ford was not starting from scratch. As with flying machines, men for centuries had dreamed of riding in self-propelled vehicles, and engineers in Germany, Britain, and France had been constructing cars for many years, most of them powered by engines running on steam or electricity. Most of these first automobiles were slow, inefficient, and very costly. In fact, they were widely scorned as noisy little playtoys for the rich and spoiled. Henry Ford wanted to change all that.

The Detroit Automobile Company was not a success, and in 1903 Ford broke away and created the Ford Motor Company. He did so with one clearly stated purpose: to build cars for the working men and women of America. The little fellows. Later that same year, Ford rolled out his company's first car, what he called the "Model A." This was a sturdy, capable vehicle, though in price it was still well beyond the reach of ordinary people.

In 1908, Ford unveiled something dramatically new: the fabled Model T. It came equipped with a 20-horsepower engine that could do 45 miles an hour on a smooth road, and it got between 13 and 21 miles on a gallon of gas. Ford introduced the car with a price tag of $850, still out of reach for the average Joe. But five years later, Ford unveiled an amazing new tool: an assembly line system for mass production. With this innovation, Ford was able to manufacture his new model much more efficiently, and he could drop the price tag to as little as $260 on some versions of the Model T.

Now everyone could afford to buy a car – and they did. Over the coming years, Ford would sell 15 million Model T's, and this profoundly changed America. Now the little fellow had wheels and that gave him power. Freedom. Mobility. And vast new opportunities to earn a living and shape his own destiny. Also, the Model T led to the creation of new industries, new companies, and better-paying jobs for millions of people. Soon, spurred on by

Giannini's Bank of Italy opened its doors on October 17th, 1904.

Henry Ford and his innovations, America would be in the throes of a full-scale industrial revolution – and a social and economic revolution as well.

In 1904, the year after Kitty Hawk and the year after Ford started his company, A.P. Giannini was getting ready for a little launch of his own. With modest start-up capital of $150,000, Giannini had formed a corporation, recruited staff, and had taken a lease on an old saloon on the edge of North Beach. While a team of carpenters went to work on the building, Giannini trained staff, prepared marketing materials, and went to see old friends and associates to line up their business. Finally, at 9 a.m. on October 17, 1904, A.P. Giannini turned to Vic Caglieri, one of his young employees, and gave the command: "Vic, you may now open the front door." The "Bank of Italy" was open for business.

From day one, the Bank of Italy embodied the spirit and letter of Giannini's personal business philosophy. "This bank prides itself on expressing the true spirit of democracy. The so-called *'common people'* have made this institution and therefore it will ever remain the servitor of those same people," declared one of the bank's early advertisements. Another trumpeted the simple economic premise on which Giannini's bank was founded: "Small accounts welcomed! The small depositor of today often becomes the rich man of tomorrow."

By today's norms, Giannini's banking philosophy may not sound radical or revolutionary. But it did back in 1904. At that time, banks were still considered the exclusive domain of the rich and privileged. Working men and immigrant families rarely went near a bank. In their minds, the banks were the handmaidens of Big Business and the "robber barons" of the late 19th Century who amassed huge personal fortunes by courting government officials and exploiting workers.

In the eyes of many Americans at the turn of the century, the banking establishment was symbolized by one man: J.P. Morgan. John Pierpont Morgan was the son of a prominent East Coast banker and financier, and he was educated in the finest schools in Boston and Europe. After a stint as an accountant, he joined his father's banking firm in New York. He built his own banking empire, J.P. Morgan and Company, by serving the needs of the captains of American industry: the major railroads, U.S. Steel, General Electric, and the like.

What a stark contrast J.P. was to A.P. While J.P. was Wall Street and East Coast, A.P. was Main Street and the California frontier. The two men also had starkly different ideas about the power and pitfalls of money. In North Beach, A.P. Giannini paid himself only a small salary and he even put a formal cap on what he would earn from his fledgling bank. In Manhattan, J.P. Morgan used his bank to amass a colossal personal fortune. A.P. Giannini openly rejected that path: "I don't want to be rich," he was quoted as saying. "No man actually owns a fortune; it owns him."

Noble though that was, did A.P.'s ideas and philosophy add up to a formula for banking success? There were still many doubters, even among his friends and neighbors. At the outset, Giannini

The great San Francisco earthquake
of 1906 devastated A.P.'s bank.

insistently proclaimed that his was a new kind of bank, out to serve, not exploit, the little fellow. But the people of North Beach did not instantly rally to his cause. In fact, the opening of the Bank of Italy generated little stir in the public or the press.

Giannini was not dismayed. The stock he had floated to launch the bank had sold well, and he was proud of the variety of people who had put their hard-earned wages into his idea: a fish dealer, a grocer, a druggist, a baker, a plumber, a barber, a house painter, and more. Little fellows, not titans. He was also focusing on the long-term. He knew that most of his target customers had never set foot in a bank – and if they had, most banks would have ushered them right out again. He also knew that many of the immigrants in North Beach had trouble with English and would be reluctant to tackle the task of filling out the necessary banking forms. Winning them over would take time and patience.

The bank's first 18 months in operation produced little to crow about. The bank's customer base grew, and so did its assets, but not dramatically. And no one in the banking community was toasting the genius of A.P. Giannini. And then it happened.

In the early morning hours of April 18, 1906, a huge earthquake rocked the city of San Francisco, followed by a series of destructive aftershocks. In the initial tremors, streets buckled, buildings cracked, and gas and water mains were burst. Later, several large fires began sweeping through different portions of the city – and there were not enough men, water, or fire equipment to put them all out.

As destiny would have it, this set the stage for what was to be one of A.P. Giannini's finest hours. The headquarters of his bank suffered little damage at first, and it opened as usual at 9 a.m. that morning. But as the day wore on and the fires spread, panicked residents began packing up whatever they could carry and fleeing the city. From his home in San Mateo, Giannini had trouble getting to his bank; the roads were ruptured or blocked and he had to go much of the way by foot.

When he finally arrived, the fires were spreading rapidly through the city. So Giannini swung into action. He closed the bank to the public and loaded all the bank's cash, gold, and records into a horse-drawn wagon that he had commandeered from L. Scatena & Company. Then he concealed his precious cargo under a load of oranges and drove off through burning streets and scenes of panic and looting. Giannini managed to spirit all his bank's assets to safety – and just in the nick of time: the raging fires soon reached his bank and reduced it to a pile of smoldering ruins.

By the time all the fires were out, San Francisco was devastated – and it would remain so

But Giannini turned the disaster into a decisive triumph.

for almost a year. The day after the quake, state authorities declared a bank holiday, and soon a group of bankers got together to discuss the situation. Most of the city's bankers wanted to declare all the banks shut until at least November. To Giannini, the idea was outrageous. North Beach was in shambles, and many of his friends and neighbors were in dire straits. So Giannini stood up and declared his position:

"Gentlemen, to follow the course you are suggesting will be a vital mistake.... If you keep our banks closed until November you may as well keep them closed. In November there will be no city or people left to serve. Today is the time they need you. The time for doing business is right now. Tomorrow morning I am putting a desk on Washington Street wharf with a Bank of Italy sign over it. Any man who wants to rebuild San Francisco can come there and get as much as he needs to do it. I advise all of you bankers to beg, borrow or steal a desk and follow my example!"

Giannini did as promised. In a move that is still legend in San Francisco, he opened up an emergency branch of his bank out on the wharf. His "loan desk" was made from two barrels with a plank spread across them. On it Giannini placed a big bag of cash – for quake victims and anyone else in need. Given the needs of the moment, Giannini didn't demand collateral or paperwork; he demanded a handshake and worked on trust.

"It's a great town, boys!" Giannini told the dispirited crowds gathered around him. "We've been burned out before and come up fighting. How about getting together and building again?"

Soon Giannini was also spearheading the recovery effort in North Beach. Among his regular customers were plumbers, carpenters, electricians, metal workers, and fisherman with boats that could haul lumber, pipe, and desperately needed supplies. These men volunteered and Giannini pressed cash into their hands and gave them specific jobs to do.

Thanks in large measure to Giannini's leadership, North Beach was able to get back on its feet long before the swankier neighborhoods of San Francisco. His efforts earned Giannini lavish public praise, and they earned him something far more valuable: the trust and loyalty of legions of little fellows, not just from North Beach but from across the city. From that point on, A.P. Giannini's little bank began to boom.

The great San Francisco earthquake of 1906 did not bring forth a singular historic achievement like Kitty Hawk. But it did lead A.P. Giannini to an important decision. During the quake and its aftermath, he saw the awesome power a bank could have: it could help save lives and rebuild a city. It could give hope and material assistance to people in need. He had known this before, but now Giannini understood it in a deeper way. Later he often said that it was during the earthquake that he decided to devote his life to banking and to using the bank for public good. Giannini himself defined his idea of what a good bank should be:

"Our conception of a bank is that of a great public servant – an institution run in the interest and for the welfare of the people it serves."

This idea would soon have a profound impact on American banking and the American public. For A.P. Giannini would now go forth and build his little bank into an institution of towering strength, vision, and commitment to the common man:

The Bank of America.

In a legendary move, Giannini
re-opened his bank out on the dock.

Chapter 3

Innovation, Revolution

In the years following the San Francisco earthquake, A.P. Giannini and his little bank began to transform American banking in ways that would lay the foundation for the creation of Visa.

Some of Giannini's most important innovations were set into motion in 1907, with an international financial crisis that rocked banks from London to Tokyo, and from New York to San Francisco. The crisis hit both the big banks and the tiny, and, ironically, it would become a shining moment for both J.P. Morgan, the king of Wall Street, and A.P. Giannini, the novice of North Beach.

At that time, Britain stood at the pinnacle of a vast colonial empire, and the Bank of England was the most powerful bank in the world. It had huge assets and reserves, and its long tentacles extended through the British Empire and deep into Asia, Africa, and the Americas. The Bank of England also routinely loaned large sums of money to other major banks in Europe and beyond. In periods of peace and stability, this relationship worked well for all the banks concerned. But if, for any reason, the Bank of England caught a cold, many other banks could easily catch pneumonia.

In essence, that is what happened in 1907. Europe was in the midst of a relatively prosperous period, and to fund all sorts of ambitious and worthwhile projects, the Bank of England and some other large European banks had gone on a lending spree. For a time they loaned money lavishly – way too lavishly. Then, with its reserves suddenly at a low ebb and falling, the Bank of England decided it had to tighten credit and hike its interest rates. And this sent waves of anxiety through all the world's financial markets.

The banks had several worries. Was this the beginning of a global cash and credit crunch? Would there be a run on gold? Would there be instability in the currency markets and frenzies of speculation? And how would national and international banking structures handle the stress?

Anxiety led to fear, and fear led to panic. And in a global financial crisis that became known as "The Panic of 1907," waves of alarmed customers ran to their banks and abruptly pulled out their money. Banks in Egypt were the first to be hit, and then the waves of panic rocked Japan, Germany, and Chile. Many banks failed. Others shut their doors in self-protection. When the panic reached Wall Street, it took a heavy toll. Six banks and four trust companies went under. J.P. Morgan appealed to U.S. President Theodore Roosevelt, and he forcefully intervened. Roosevelt had the U.S. Treasury rush $30 million in cash to New York, and J.P. Morgan urgently raised another $25 million. With these cash reserves, J.P. Morgan and others were able to calm consumer demands and bring the crisis under control. In the eyes of many people, this was one of J.P. Morgan's finest hours.

In North Beach, within the tiny confines of his Bank of Italy, A.P. Giannini also did an admirable job of managing the crisis. On a trip to the East Coast he had seen the crisis developing, and when he returned to San Francisco Giannini began accumulating the one precious commodity that he knew would calm and reassure his customers: gold. With an inspired touch of showmanship, he put huge stacks of gold on display, behind his tellers' cages, for all his customers to see. Confidence and trust are the essential bedrock of any bank, and Giannini wanted his customers to see that gold and proclaim, "In This Bank We Trust." The strategy worked; his customers did not panic. As in the earthquake, A.P. Giannini had turned a crisis into an opportunity and emerged triumphant.

Nonetheless, on a much larger scale, the Panic of 1907 laid bare serious problems in the American banking system, some of them dating all the way back to the founding of the country. In fact, the U.S. Constitution gave both the federal government and state governments the power to regulate banks – not a formula for cohesion and order. From the earliest periods of its history, the United States was served by a rapidly changing patchwork of banks and lending institutions, ranging from big banks in the cities to tiny local banks that sprang up wherever settlers and immigrants put down new roots. Laws and regulations varied widely from state to state, creating widespread confusion.

By the early 1900s, there was more chaos than order in the American banking system. There was also chaos in the money system. In terms of coins, the dollar had been the official U.S. currency since 1792, but the California Gold Rush had prompted many private bankers and assayers to mint their own coins, from gold, silver, nickel, and copper. As late as 1901, a private coin designer in Colorado was minting octagonal silver dollars and putting them into circulation.

America's leading bankers gathered in 1908, a key moment for A.P. Giannini.

In terms of paper money, there was confusion as well. The U.S. government did not begin issuing bills until 1862. Its first bills were called "greenbacks" and "shinplasters," and they were not an immediate hit with the general public. The following year, the government authorized certain federally chartered banks to issue national bank notes. If customers so desired, they could redeem each of these banknotes for a specified quantity of gold or silver. In 1907, however, the public remained leery of paper currency, as they remained confused by all the different coins in circulation. This helped undermine public confidence in the whole banking system, and the Panic of 1907 only brought the cold truth rushing to the surface:

The American banking industry was ailing. It was an elitist, archaic, poorly organized patchwork, with no central authority, no cohesion, no effective operating guidelines, and no unifying form of governance.

The following year, in Denver, Colorado, the American Bankers Association convened a meeting of the nation's leading bankers. One of the aims was to examine the ills plaguing the industry and to hear new ideas and possible solutions. A.P. Giannini was in attendance, representing the Bank of Italy.

Among the featured speakers was Woodrow Wilson, a scholar and statesman who would soon become President of the United States. Wilson was a brilliant, high-minded man, the son of a Presbyterian minister, and at this time he was president of the prestigious Princeton University. The bankers were eager to hear his diagnosis of the nation's banking ills and how he proposed to solve them. Wilson stepped to the podium in Denver and all of the nation's leading bankers surely leaned forward to listen. But they were not prepared for the shock of his message.

"The bank is the most jealously regarded and the least-liked instrument of business in this country," Wilson began. "The banks of this country are remote from the people, and the people regard them as not belonging to them but as belonging to some power hostile to them. Now that is the fact, gentlemen."

Wilson then cut deeper. In language that was refined but to the point, he criticized America's bankers for being short-sighted and narrow-minded. Their practices, he said, were not governed by any noble guiding vision; they were governed by personal greed. He even accused some banks of "usury," loaning money at unconscionably high rates of interest. Above all, Wilson said, bankers sought investments that were good only for themselves, never for the common man or the larger good of the country.

"You sit only where [big] things are spoken of and big returns coveted," he scolded the bankers. "There would be plenty of investments if you carried your money to the people of the country at large."

Today we can only imagine the waves of discomfort and indignation that must have swelled and crested around that room. Many of them bristled at Wilson's accusations, while others no doubt wrote him off as an ivory-tower academic with no first-hand knowledge of banking or finance. A.P. Giannini, of course, had a different reaction. Wilson was describing exactly what Giannini had witnessed back at the Columbus Savings and Loan. Wilson was also explaining the reasons why Giannini had felt compelled to go out and start his own bank. Giannini wanted to hear more.

Woodrow Wilson was, of course, an idealist. A decade later, in the wake of all the destruction and death wrought by World War I, he would help pioneer the creation of a new world body whose aim was to end all war: the League of Nations, the forerunner to today's United Nations. But while he was

Woodrow Wilson, then at Princeton, nudged A.P. – and America – into branch banking.

an idealist, Wilson was no fool. Having shocked the bankers with his harsh critique of their outlook and practices, Wilson then offered them a prescription he believed would cure all the ills of their industry: branch banking.

Branch banking was already proving successful in Canada and many European countries. Under this system, the large, profitable banks in big cities like London or Toronto established networks of outpost banks in small towns and rural communities. This was good for those communities because it brought them infusions of capital and desperately needed banking services. At the same time, it served the banks' self-interest: they were able to build their customer base, their influence, and their profits.

As Wilson described it, branch banking was a cooperative venture, a true partnership, and an ideal remedy for banking's ills.

In what stands today as a historic prophecy, the future President of the United States then painted a clear and compelling picture of how this partnership might work in America, for the good of the banks, the common man, and the nation as a whole.

First, Wilson explained, branch banking would help repair the bankers' terrible image and restore public confidence in the whole banking system: "If a system of branch banks, very simply and inexpensively managed, could be established, which would put the resources of the rich banks of the country at the disposal of whole countrysides, to whose merchants and farmers only a restricted and local credit is now open, the attitude of plain men everywhere towards the banks and banking would be changed utterly, within less than a generation."

Second, Wilson told the bankers, once you overcome the hostility of the common man and earn his trust and loyalty, your business will grow — and so will your profits. With a system of branches,

In war and peace, Giannini built his bank by serving the needs of the common man.

he explained, banks would have "agents in hundreds of villages who knew the men in their neighborhoods who could be trusted with loans and who would make profitable use of them."

Third, Wilson explained, the establishment of a national branch banking system would have a strong and stabilizing effect on the entire banking industry. Specifically, branch banking would promote cooperation and partnership among the banks and with state and federal banking authorities. To make a national branch system work, state and federal banking regulations would have to be clarified and harmonized. All the confusing coins and paper monies in circulation would have to be replaced by one common currency. Together these steps would strengthen and unify the banking system, build public trust, and help stave off future crises of confidence like the Panic of 1907.

Above all, Wilson said, the creation of a branch banking system would bring fresh capital and new economic opportunities to millions of common people across the country. "Your money," Wilson assured the bankers, "would quicken and fertilize the country." As a result, everyone would prosper, thanks to the wisdom, foresight, and community spirit of America's bankers.

In 1848, a half-century before, Karl Marx issued his legendary Communist Manifesto, setting forth his blueprint for world revolution and issuing his rallying cry, "Workers of the world, *unite!*" In Denver, Wilson was issuing a kind of capitalist manifesto, setting forth a different blueprint for revolution and a different rallying call: Bankers of America, *unite!* He urged the bankers to evolve a new philosophy and a new banking system, founded on the principles of cooperation, partnership, trust, and a spirit of community. In more specific terms, Wilson felt that two principles should guide American banking: *inter-bank cooperation* and *the democratization of credit.*

Woodrow Wilson was a visionary. The blueprint he set forth in Denver drew a cool reception from America's bankers at the time, but we still need to hold that blueprint firmly in mind. For 60 years later, America's bankers would join hands in the kind of cooperative venture he envisioned, a unique banking partnership designed to promote the democratization of credit, in America and around the globe. That unique partnership would be called Visa.

Wilson, though, was way ahead of his time. At the Denver gathering, or in the days that followed, every prominent banker in America surely heard Woodrow Wilson's appeal, either in person, in the newspapers, or in conversations with startled colleagues in the banking community. But only one banker jumped into action: A.P. Giannini.

Giannini shared Wilson's view of the ills plaguing the industry; they were a mirror image of his own. Giannini also saw merit in Wilson's belief in branch banking. In fact, he had already tested the idea by opening a branch of the Bank of Italy in San Francisco's Mission District. Now Wilson's address encouraged Giannini to go out and create a whole network of branches.

The following year, Giannini bought out an ailing bank in San Jose and turned it into his bank's first branch outside of San Francisco. His aim was to serve the working man and the area's many newly arrived immigrants. "The new institution," reported the *San Jose Mercury and Herald*, "is to pay special attention to the affairs of people who speak English with difficulty and will have employees who speak the French, Italian, Spanish and Portugese languages."

The San Jose location appealed to Giannini's business sense and to his sentiments. San Jose was where his father and mother, Luigi and Virginia, had first settled when they emigrated from Italy. It was also home to many of the people Giannini had

Giannini's first branch outside San Francisco, on one of the main streets of San Jose.

befriended and helped back in his days in the fruit and vegetable business. Now Giannini had the tools and resources to serve those farmers and tradesmen in more comprehensive ways.

The intent of the branch, furthermore, was not to siphon profits away from San Jose; it was to bring vital new capital in, to spur economic growth and opportunity for everyone. Giannini's younger brother Attilio was going to help manage the new branch, and he made this element of the bank's mission crystal clear: "The transformation of the local bank into a branch of the San Francisco institution does not mean that San Jose coin will be taken away to San Francisco, but that San Francisco coin will be brought into San Jose," the *Mercury* quoted him as saying. "The officers are in no sense intruders in the local field, as many of them are well known in the community, having lived here."

Woodrow Wilson would have been delighted by those words and by one of Giannini's first moves in San Jose. At that time, local farmers had to pay eight percent or more for mortgages on their land. Giannini offered them mortgages at seven percent. This was good business and good citizenship: it helped the farmers and it undercut the competition and helped build business. As Wilson and Giannini had both envisioned, everyone won. The branch's activities helped, in Wilson's words, to "quicken and fertilize" the economic growth of the entire region.

Emboldened by his success in San Jose, Giannini soon opened many more branches in farming communities in northern and central California. Within a few years, Giannini was operating a robust network of branches up and down the state, bringing new vigor to rural communities and, at the same time, leading his bank into an era of growth and prosperity that was unprecedented in American banking history. Giannini's push into branch banking was so successful that other banks would soon follow his lead.

As he built his network of branches, Giannini also plunged into troubled industries where old-line bankers of the J.P. Morgan ilk would never deign to tread. For instance, Giannini helped the California wine industry get onto its feet at a very difficult time — 70 years before wine became popular across the United States. Robert Mondavi, the famous winemaker and Napa Valley pioneer, still has warm memories of A.P. Giannini and all that he did, and it is little wonder that today Mondavi and many other California vintners remain fiercely loyal to the Bank of America.

By 1923, Giannini was reaching out to another struggling industry that most traditional bankers shunned: the motion picture business. At his bank, Giannini created a special loan initiative to support movie ventures, and that enabled Charlie Chaplin, Mary Pickford, Douglas Fairbanks, and D.W. Griffith to build their now-legendary studio, United Artists. In the process, Giannini earned the allegiance of important Hollywood cre-

Early on, A.P. Giannini supported the fledgling wine industry in California as well as several other industries that would become the pillars of California's booming economy.

ators and producers, and his bank soon became a leader in the financing of feature films and other Hollywood ventures. With this influence, Giannini was able to expand his network of branches across Los Angeles and in other growing markets across Southern California.

To build his business in Hollywood, Giannini made some very shrewd moves. For instance, he put Cecil B. DeMille, the famous producer-director, in charge of his loans to the movie industry, and that gave Giannini credibility and a high profile in Hollywood. Some years later, when Walt Disney ran over budget with his animated feature *Snow White and the Seven Dwarfs*, Giannini gave him an emergency loan. The film, of course, became a classic. This was good business in the short- and long-term, as it helped him solidify a friendship with one of Hollywood's leading creators. Giannini would later finance Disney's *Fantasia*, *Pinocchio*, *Bambi*, and other animated films. Giannini played a similar role in the making of *Gone With The Wind*.

There was no great mystery in A.P. Giannini's approach to building his bank. To the contrary, his strategy and his actions were clear and direct. When California's farmers were in need, Giannini was there. When the infant wine industry was struggling, Giannini stepped forward, wallet in hand. When Hollywood's most important creators were in dire straits, it was Giannini who came to the rescue, as banker and friend. This was good business, good citizenship, and wonderful public relations. Naturally, in the early 1930s, when the city and county of San Francisco wanted to build a majestic bridge to the north, across the mouth of the San Francisco Bay, who stepped in to bankroll the construction of The Golden Gate Bridge? A.P. Giannini, of course, once again demonstrating the power of an idea, his simple idea of what a good bank should be.

Agriculture, Hollywood, the wine industry, and tourist attractions like Disneyland, the Napa Valley, and The Golden Gate Bridge – in the course of the Twentieth Century these would become the most powerful engines driving the California economy, and by the 1930s A.P. Giannini was already helping them get onto their feet. The strategy worked brilliantly, for the young state of California and for A.P. Giannini. Consider this:

Back in 1904 Giannini had launched the Bank of Italy with start-up capital of just $150,000. By 1924, he had bought out several banks in the state, including the Bank of America of Los Angeles. By 1928, with capital that had swelled to $250 million, Giannini was able to create a vast holding company called the Transamerica Corporation. By 1930, Giannini was in command of an immense and diversified financial empire, encompassing his bank and its network of branches, large overseas holdings, and affiliate banks in New York and Milan, Italy. To consolidate his bank holdings under a single banner, in 1930 Giannini changed the name of his flagship, dropping the name Bank of Italy in favor of a name that reflected the full breadth of what was now his guiding ambition: the Bank of America.

Woodrow Wilson's vision was that the banks of America would come together and build a national banking network; A.P. Giannini's vision was to build his own national network, under the banner of Bank of America. He envisioned a great institution that would serve the entire nation, with branches that would dot the map from the Atlantic to the Pacific, with every branch serving the needs of common people and their communities.

Throughout his career, Giannini pursued his dream of building a truly national bank, but at every turn he was opposed by rival banks and state and federal bank regulators. In 1927, the U.S. Congress passed the McFadden Act, banning interstate banking, and many people thought it was aimed directly at A.P. Giannini. It would not be until the 1990s that the U.S. Congress would finally see the light and lift the last barriers to national banking networks. To put it mildly, Giannini's vision was ahead of its time.

In the early 1930s, however, Giannini was faced with more immediate problems to solve. The stock market crash of 1929 had been a terrible blow for Wall Street and the monied classes. But the years of depression that followed, with high unemployment, bread lines, and terrible money crunches, were even worse ordeals for working people. Often they had no jobs, no means of transportation, and little food to put on the table for their wives and children. In the best of times, workers had trouble getting credit. Most banks built their loan portfolios by catering to businesses and making large commercial loans. That was profitable for them, but it left the average worker out in the cold, and often at the mercy of unscrupulous loan sharks charging outrageous rates of interest.

Giannini's bank, typically, took the opposite approach. Right from the start, he built his bank's loan portfolio by catering to the needs, large or small, of working people. In the crisis years of the 1930s, Giannini went much further. Millions of workers needed cash to buy essentials like food or appliances. Others needed tools for their work. Many just needed a quick $25 to tide them over. A.P. Giannini and his team were determined to help.

To that end, Giannini helped pioneer the practice known as "installment credit." For those who needed a heater, an icebox, or a new set of tools, but could not afford to pay for them, Giannini's bank gave them an installment credit plan. Under this plan, they could put a little money down on the purchase and pay off the remaining debt in small monthly increments, whatever they could afford. This new credit device was an absolute godsend for struggling families.

Giannini's concept of installment credit paved the way for the eventual creation of the Visa credit card. Today, installment credit is directly embedded in the workings of the card. If you need a new set of tools, but are strapped for cash, you buy the tools with your Visa card and pay off the remainder, with interest, in increments that you

By 1930, Giannini's Bank of Italy had become a growing empire, the Bank of America.

can tailor to fit your needs. Visa and other credit cards, in fact, have allowed banks to do away with small loans altogether. This saves time and money for the bank, and it's more flexible for the consumer. Everyone wins. In the 1930s, though, installment credit was seen as a major innovation.

During the Depression, Giannini also pioneered other new forms of consumer credit. He created a line of auto loans with flexible terms – and at rates far below the 15 to 30 percent the money lenders were charging. He created home improvement loans, student loans, and low-cost mortgages with flexible terms. Whatever the needs of the average man, the Bank of America was determined to develop carefully tailored ways to meet them.

Giannini's innovations attracted more and more customers to the Bank of America; his business boomed. Not everyone was happy, though. Giannini's new credit devices and his liberal lending policies infuriated his competitors in the banking world. So did another Giannini practice that most traditional bankers were loathe to stoop to: using advertising and public solicitations to attract new customers. Infuriated or not, though, once Giannini blazed these trails, other bankers had little choice but to follow suit. Soon Giannini's innovations and philosophy began to take hold in other parts of the country. Under the fierce pressure of the competitive marketplace, bank after bank was forced to expand its focus beyond business and commercial banking – and serve the needs of working people as well. The big urban banks opened branches in small towns and the ill-served countryside, and this, in turn, stimulated economic growth and development across the nation, just as Woodrow Wilson had envisioned back in 1908.

Innovation. Revolution.

Looking back now, we can see what A.P. Giannini set into motion and we can see the deep and lasting imprint he left on the state of California and on American banking as a whole. Today, in almost every town and village across the country, people do their banking in a convenient local branch of some large banking institution. And once inside their branch, millions of people have at their fingertips a wide variety of auto loans, home loans, flexible mortgages, and installment credit tools, many of which owe their very existence to A.P. Giannini.

A.P. Giannini did not fly at Kitty Hawk, and he didn't invent the Model T, but his innovations did transform American banking, and so did his simple idea of what a good bank should be. And if anyone doubts the power of Giannini's idea, one singular event of 1945 should make the record undeniably clear.

That year, with Giannini at the helm beside his son Mario, the total assets of the Bank of America climbed to what was then a dizzying pinnacle, more than $5 billion. This surpassed the total assets of the Chase Manhattan Bank in New York, up to then the largest bank in America, and it surpassed the total assets of any bank in Britain, Germany, France, Italy, Switzerland, or Japan. By 1945, the Bank of America had grown, from its humble roots in North Beach, into the largest bank in the world.

This achievement helped turn A.P. Giannini into a legend, and it crowned one of the most amazing success stories in American business history. Little wonder that in its Year 2000 issue, *Time* magazine placed A.P. Giannini among the 100 most important people of the Twentieth Century.

❀ ❀ ❀

In 1949, as the first half of the century drew to a close, so did the life of A.P. Giannini. He died at the age of 79, and it was a sign of the man and the strength of his character that the estate he left behind totaled only $489,278.

Never mind that he was the chief architect of what had become the largest bank in the world; right to the end Giannini refused to amass wealth or the trappings of power. And right to the end, he kept in place the formal cap he had long ago placed on his earnings. The aim of that cap was clear: Giannini never wanted to stray too far from his humble roots in the fruit and vegetable business or from the needs and concerns of the little fellow, whose strength and character were the wellsprings of his vision and all he accomplished.

Death, however, did not bring an end to the influence of A.P. Giannini. Inside the Bank of America, his spirit and guiding vision lived on, and so did his commitment to innovation. Indeed, when Giannini died, a team inside the Bank of America was already developing a brand new idea, an idea that would lead to the creation of another new tool of consumer credit, a little plastic tool with wondrous powers and a touch of genius inside.

FIFTEEN CENTS
APRIL 15, 1946
TIME
THE WEEKLY NEWSMAGAZINE
EUREKA
Artzybasheff
CALIFORNIA'S GIANNINI
Along the West Coast, hearts are high.
VOLUME XLVII
(REG. U. S. PAT. OFF.)
NUMBER 15

FLIGHT
734
BOEING
Stratocruiser
UNITED AIR LINES
Mainliner Stratocruiser

BankAmericard, "Think of it as Money"

CHAPTER 4

The 1950s in America bore little resemblance to the depression years of the 1930s. The automobile, the airplane, and the assembly line had proven to be tools of revolution, bringing America profound economic and social change. The average Joe now had much more money in his pocket, and his financial and banking needs were growing far more diverse and complex.

The automobile industry was a good indicator of the depth of change. By the 1950s, the automobile, just as Henry Ford had envisioned, had become a centerpiece of American life, both for the rich man and the average worker. The Model T had become a collector's item, and Ford cars and trucks now featured rugged steel frames, automatic transmissions, and engines with as much as 400 horsepower. For the rich and the growing middle class alike, the automobile was no longer just a convenient mode of transportation; it was a ticket to freedom, economic opportunity, social status, and pure enjoyment out on the road.

The automobile had also become a colossal industry – and a colossal engine of national and international economic growth. Britain, France, West Germany, and Italy each had several major automakers; Japan would soon join their ranks. America had "the big three" in Detroit: General Motors, Ford, and Chrysler. By now, Ford was an industrial giant, with arms reaching around the globe, via affiliates in Canada, Brazil, Venezuela, Argentina, and throughout Western Europe. In 1958 alone, Ford cars and trucks generated total sales of more than $4 billion – more than the individual output of dozens of small nations.

Automobiles were also changing the American landscape. In the 1950s, owning a car encouraged many families to move out of cities to larger, more affordable houses in the suburbs. This generated a boom in the construction of new roads and houses, and new shops and businesses. Automobiles also stimulated increased travel for business and pleasure. "See the U.S.A. in your Chevrolet," was one of Detroit's most effective ad campaigns of the time, and many families took the urging to heart and set off in long car trips around the country. Like mushrooms, motels and gas stations sprang up to handle the traffic. A savvy Midwestern businessman named Ray Kroc saw the trend and began building a chain of appealing, low-priced hamburger shops to cater to young families on the go. Kroc's chain was named McDonald's, of course, and it spawned countless imitators and opened the era of fast food.

Americans were also falling in love with air travel. Before World War II, commercial air travel in the U.S. was not a popular endeavor; it was a luxury reserved mostly for business men and the rich. In 1939, U.S. commercial carriers operated 340 planes, and during that year they carried only two million passengers. By 1949, however, 1,080 commercial planes were in service and they carried almost 17 million passengers.

By the mid-1950s, the boom in air travel was on in force. The airlines expanded their fleets, fares came down accordingly, and Americans took to the air in massive numbers. To keep up with escalating demand, the Boeing Airplane Company of Seattle developed the Boeing 707, America's first commercial jet carrier.

The British and the French were already operating commercial jetliners, but the Boeing 707, launched in 1958, accelerated the growth of both domestic and international travel. Air travel has been growing ever since, and now reaches almost every corner of the globe. Orville and Wilbur Wright would surely be amazed.

By the 1950s, the economic and social status of the average Joe and Annie had also changed dramatically. The high unemployment and bread lines of the Depression were now a distant memory, and by 1958 the median income of the American family had climbed to $23,000 a year. With his greater spending power, the little fellow was now the darling of American business. The automakers built cars for him, the big oil companies battled over him, the airlines courted him, suburban developers lured him, and the masters of advertising and television did everything in their power to seduce him. With good reason: in the march of economic growth and progress, the little fellow was now king. His dollars were both power and lubricant; they drove big businesses and small, and they made all the wheels of commerce spin.

Now, however, the average Joe faced a new dilemma. With the dazzling array of goods being spread before him, and the whole world of travel opening at his feet, how was he to pay for all his escalating needs and wants? How was he to buy that home in the suburbs, plus the big refrigerator, the lawn mower, and the TV that went with it? How to finance that shiny new car and, at the same time, pay for those long family car trips and all the motels, burgers, and shakes along the way? And what about those costly airline tickets? How to pay for those, along with everything else?

For many families, the answer was credit. Installment credit, small loans, and the rest. Retailers offered credit, but at very high rates of interest. So the Bank of America and other banks worked hard to keep up with the exploding demand for loans. But there was a downside. The Bank of America and its vast network of branches in California were being buried under mountains of paperwork. Each year the bank was spending millions of dollars and countless man-hours initiating, processing, and servicing the growing volume of loans.

The bank was eager to find an innovative solution. As early as 1944, the bank's planners had searched for some new form of all-purpose credit device, a wonder tool which could accomplish three objectives at once:

1. Help the bank consolidate its diverse loan and credit plans into a simplified, streamlined, cost-effective system.

2. Help the bank's customers better manage their money, their purchases, and their various loans at the bank.

3. Build business. The new device had to be convenient, easy to use, and very attractive to consumers.

At the end of World War II, Bank of America planners examined the idea of issuing a charge card. The idea was by no means new. Back in 1914, Western Union, the nation's leading telegraph company, issued what is believed to be the first charge card. It was a small metal plate that looked like a military dog tag, and it was often referred to as "metal money." The card bore the name of the customer and it allowed him or her the convenience of sending large quantities of cables and then paying for them all at once, at the end of the month, from an itemized bill. In 1924, General Petroleum Corporation of California issued the first gasoline credit card to its employees and select customers. The company slowly expanded the service to include the general public. Mobil and Shell soon followed suit.

The Depression of 1929 halted further development of credit cards. In the late 1930s, however, AT&T introduced the "Bell System Credit Card," a convenient tool designed to build customer loyalty. The railroads and airlines followed AT&T's lead, issuing what became known as "fidelity cards."

In the 1920s, following the lead of Western Union, the big oil companies were among the first to issue charge cards.

Many hotels and department stores then began issuing cards.

These charge cards served a dual purpose. First, they were a valuable tool for "the issuer" – meaning the department store, hotel, or airline. The cards identified the customer by name, usually accompanied by their charge account number. Once-a-month billing cut paperwork, processing time, and postage costs. The issuing merchant could also track and analyze the spending patterns of its customers. At the same time, the cards were also a convenient tool for the customer. They simplified payment, reduced the need to carry cash, and the monthly bill was helpful in doing expense accounts and the annual paperwork demanded by the Internal Revenue Service.

Nonetheless, the Bank of America was not seduced by the idea of launching a card. In the immediate aftermath of the war, money was tight, the financial future remained uncertain, and the bank chose to place its emphasis on launching another round of branch expansion. So the card idea went onto the shelf.

In 1950, however, the charge card concept got a big boost in usage and prestige. One night a business executive named Frank McNamara was wining and dining clients at a fancy Manhattan restaurant. When the bill came, he got a potentially humiliating shock: he did not have enough cash in his wallet to cover the bill. In a panic, McNamara phoned his wife, and she rushed to the restaurant with sufficient cash in hand to cover the bill.

His pride saved, McNamara made a vow: never again. So in 1950 he created Diners Club, a card that allowed its holder to dine at a wide range of restaurants, located nationwide, and pay for the meals at the end of the month. Later, some hotels and rental car companies agreed to accept the card. This was the birth of the multi-purpose "travel and entertainment card." In 1958, American Express, Diners' arch-rival, began issuing cards, in America and abroad, and it rapidly grew into the leader in the lucrative travel and entertainment niche. Later, the Hilton Hotel chain launched its own card, Carte Blanche.

At the start of the 1950s, however, America's banks were still not enthralled by the charge card concept. To many bankers, there was something a bit unseemly about these cards; they were not what a proper bank should be doing with its name and staff. Nor was there an evident formula to make charge cards profitable for the banks: they were, after all, devices for *payment,* not *credit.*

There were a few exceptions, however. Back in 1947, an independent-minded banker named John C. Biggins, a consumer credit specialist at Flatbush National Bank in Brooklyn, New York, launched a neighborhood credit plan called "Charg-It." His plan covered all of two-square blocks in Brooklyn, but it worked pretty well, and in 1950 a small bank in Paterson, New Jersey, issued a similar card. These programs offered charge cards, but without a revolving credit option.

In 1951, the Franklin National Bank of Long

Island, New York, went a few steps further. It issued cards that displayed the cardholder's account number and the amount of funds available for use. Card applicants submitted credit applications and went through typical screening procedures. Merchants participating in the program would copy information from the card onto sales slips. There was an effort to control credit limits and bad cards: if the purchase exceeded a certain bank-determined "floor limit," the merchant had to call the bank for approval. The merchant would then have his Franklin account credited, minus a "discount fee" that Franklin took to handle the transaction. Franklin charged no annual fee or interest and required payment within 30, 60, or 90 days. Franklin thus became the first bank to issue a card with some form of revolving credit. In 1953 the First National Bank of San Jose, California, also began issuing credit cards.

The idea caught on. By 1955, about 100 banks were operating card programs. Some offered revolving credit, but only on a 30-day basis. Others offered simple charge cards, without charging the customer an annual fee. Most of these bank cards were usable only in a small local area, and few generated enough transaction volume to be profitable. For both types of cards, the main source of revenue was the "merchant discount," the small fee that participating merchants paid the bank to guarantee and process cardholder purchases. Alas, the merchant fees were not enough to cover the banks' operating costs, and most of these banks, too, wound up shutting down their credit card programs.

Could the Bank of America find a better formula? In 1954, the bank sent a research team out to study how these other banks operated their charge card programs and they also looked at Mobil Oil's experience. They visited 55 banks and spent literally weeks at each one, talking to bank officers and employees, to local merchants, and to bank customers. At the end of their nine-month study, the researchers came back with two main conclusions as to why so many of the charge card programs had failed. First, the banks had chosen too small an area of operation, with too few merchants participating. Second, the banks had failed to properly educate merchants and consumers about how to use credit cards properly.

So in 1955, the Bank of America, the BofA, stood at a crossroads – and so did the history of bank cards in America. The BofA's comprehensive nine-month study had documented a history of failure. No sound business case could be made for moving forward with a charge card. Accordingly, several top Bank of America executives urged the bank to drop the whole idea.

Now, however, the enduring spirit of A.P. Giannini rose to the fore. A.P.'s son Mario had guided the bank after his father's death in 1949, but Mario himself had died in 1952. The new president, S. Clark Beise, had been one of A.P.'s most trusted lieutenants, and he provided the crucial continuity of spirit and policy. Beise wanted the card project to go forward.

Two other Giannini admirers would also play key roles in the bank's move into credit cards: Joseph Williams and Ken Larkin. Williams had worked in a staid, old-guard Philadelphia bank prior to World War II. After serving in the U.S. military in Germany, Williams went out to California and knocked on the door of the Bank of America, expressly to work for the great A.P. Giannini. Now Williams was in charge of the six-member team that was evaluating the bank's credit card options.

Ken Larkin's was a similar story. Larkin had grown up in Brooklyn, in the shadow of Ebbets Field, the home of baseball's Brooklyn Dodgers. After serving in the war with the Navy's Seabees, he too came out to California and signed on with the bank that Giannini built, eager to become a part of its noble vision and pioneering spirit. In his early years with the bank, Larkin had traveled up and down California looking for promising places to open new branch offices. By the mid-1950s, he was managing a branch in Bakersfield, California, and becoming a specialist in the field of installment credit. That would soon lead him to Joseph Williams and the charge card project.

Larkin was a tall, droll gentleman, a man of impeccable integrity, and by this time he was becoming a respected and influential decision-maker at the bank. And Larkin thought a credit card was an idea with enormous potential. "The concept of a bank card always made sense to me," Larkin explained, in one of the scores of interviews on which this book is based. "We were always a leader in installment credit. Anything you could buy on time, we financed: student loans, cars, boats, trailers, home loans, personal loans, you name it. The credit card was just a natural extension of that."

As Larkin explained, customers met with their loan officers three or four times a year, making the loan program very costly to administer. Larkin believed that a card offering an all-purpose line of credit could serve the needs of the bank and its customers. It could be, in the best A.P. Giannini tradition, win-win. "The card would be cheaper for us to manage, much cheaper. And it would be more convenient for our customers," Larkin explained. "And that was really the basis for our getting into the credit card business. President Beise was totally on our side."

Like Larkin, Williams was inclined to move forward with a credit card program, but he knew he first had to solve several complex problems. One was the chicken-and-egg problem of "critical mass." "The cardholder wanted to know that the card would be widely accepted, so we needed to sign up a large number of merchants to participate. And the merchants wanted to know that a lot of customers would have the card," Larkin said. "So we had to develop a large cardholder base."

Another major problem was profitability. Nearly 100 banks across the country had already lost money with what amounted to a glorified charge card with a 30-day credit period attached to it. The merchant discount fees had barely covered their operating costs. So Williams and his team decided to make their card a *true* credit card, with revolving, flexible credit. The idea was simple enough: at the end of each month, the customer could choose to pay off his entire balance or pay only a portion of the balance and pay interest on the remainder. How much interest? After much reflection, the bank's policy makers decided to follow the policy of one of America's leading department stores, Sears Roebuck.

"Sears was a pioneer in the field of installment credit," Larkin explained, "and they were charging 18 percent interest a year. If it was good enough for them, it was good enough for us."

By making their card a credit device, and charging what amounted to 1.5 percent per month on outstanding balances, Williams knew that the card would open for the bank a potentially important stream of revenue, on top of the merchant discount fees. At the same time, a card that would be a true consumer credit device would be appealing to both the customer and the merchant. With a credit card in hand, the customer would have enormous financial flexibility. If, at Christmas, he or she went on a bit of a spending spree, those purchases could be paid off over the first several months of the following year. The cardholder would gain greater control of his or her money management.

A credit card would also facilitate travel. We tend to take financial mobility for granted today, but in the mid-1950s traveling away from home, by car or air, was a daunting proposition. Many out-of-town merchants, gas stations, restaurants, and hotels would not take checks. Booking an airline ticket was not easy without a corporate account, nor was renting a car. A credit card, providing full identification and bank authorization, could help solve all these problems. At the same time, with their card in hand, parents could take their kids on a big family vacation, spread out the payments, and still have enough left over to pay the mortgage.

For merchants, a true credit card offered more advantages than a charge card. First, a credit card would stimulate sales; with credit in hand, shoppers would be more inclined to buy – and to buy more. Second, the bank would ensure swift payment, and that would help merchants manage their cash flow, inventory, and financial planning. With traditional charge account systems and monthly billing, a merchant who did a great business at Christmas might have to wait a month or more to get paid – and a large portion of his operating capital would be tied up in "receivables" pending payment. Swift payment would allow merchants to put their resources to more profitable use. Again, though, "critical mass" was key. Merchants would not be willing to pay a 6 percent fee to the bank unless they were guaranteed that a large number of their potential customers were carrying that card.

As attractive as the credit card promised to be, Williams and the bank faced very complex problems of implementation. Which customers were worthy of this form of instant credit? How much credit should be built into the card? Who in the bank should make credit decisions? The credit card people? Or the traditional loan officers? If the credit policies were too tight, how would the bank attain the "critical mass" of cardholders necessary to make the program work? And what if people failed to pay their balances? How would the bank manage that risk? These were very difficult questions, and in the initial stages of the project, the answers were not yet clear. At this stage, Williams and his team were waist-deep in roiling, uncharted waters; they were inventing and making decisions as they waded forward.

There was another vexing problem, and this might have stopped many bankers cold and sent them wading to shore: how do you process all the expected transactions? The concept of charging a purchase sounds easy enough – until you consider each step in the process. The customer's account had to be debited – quickly and reliably. The merchant's account had to be credited – quickly and reliably. These steps were far from simple to handle, and with its existing credit tools, the Bank of America was already drowning in paperwork. What to do?

Embrace technology.

In keeping with A.P. Giannini's commitment to innovation, the Bank of America had been among the first banks to embrace the emerging technology of computers. In the early 1950s, the bank had hired the Stanford Research Institute to develop a method for handling checks by machine. Together, they built a large computer and developed a magnetic check encoding process that remains the industry standard today. The prototype was completed in 1955. Also in 1955, the BofA became the first American bank to install the IBM 702, a large-scale, general-purpose computer that would become central to the bank's operations. By 1956, the bank had also designed, built, and begun experimenting with an automatic teller machine. This model could only receive deposits, but it was a forerunner to today's ATM machines.

In late 1956, Williams and other bank executives began examining the feasibility of using their state-of-the-art computer technology to process credit card transactions. The problems here were enormous. The issue was not only how to handle

Giannini's Bank of America was
a pioneer of bank innovation.

credit card transactions inside the bank, but also how to link that system to the merchants accepting the bank's credit card. Williams and his team decided, finally, that computerization of the transaction process would have to wait. In the interim, they hired IBM to work out the best way to automate the system without computers.

With these cornerstones in place, Williams and his team moved to the next logical step: creating a pilot project. Now they designed prototype cards and evaluated production costs. They looked into various imprint machines that merchants could use to record their transactions. They also began developing operating manuals, marketing materials, and ad campaigns to support the card. And, crucially, they chose what they hoped was the right locale to launch their pilot program: Fresno, California.

Fresno is located in the middle of the state, in the fertile San Joaquin Valley, and at the time it was a sleepy farming community of 250,000 people. In most towns of comparable size in California, the Bank of America enjoyed the loyalty of between 25 and 30 percent of local families. In Fresno, the bank really ruled the roost, with 45 percent of all families doing business with the bank. So Williams and his team felt that if they couldn't make a credit card program fly in Fresno, it wouldn't fly anywhere. That was a depressing possibility, but if the pilot did flop in Fresno, the damage to the bank would be limited. Also, news of the failure would stir few ripples in the important urban markets of San Francisco and Los Angeles.

In early 1958, Williams began sending some of his team, now 37 people, into the Fresno area to put the pilot program into operation. They explained the credit card concept to branch managers and began enlisting the support of local merchants. They ran training programs for bank employees and merchants, and they met with local business groups and credit associations to make sure their intentions were clear and well understood.

They were presenting a totally new concept to the people of Fresno and it demanded six months of very hard work.

By the summer of 1958, Williams and his team had worked out their credit policy, using mostly their own intuition. The bank would have two tiers of cards. Simple cards would carry a credit limit of $300. Cards with a special star, for preferred customers, would carry a credit limit of $500. For the protection of the merchant and the bank, both tiers would have "floor limits" on customer purchases. With the simple card, a customer could purchase any item up to $50 without problem; over that floor limit, the merchant would have to call the bank for authorization. On the starred cards, the floor limit was $100. Neither card would carry an annual fee – a marketing advantage over American Express and Diners Club. Merchant discount fees would be lower as well.

On the key question of "critical mass," Williams made a leap of faith. Instead of having loan officers sift through the credit worthiness of every bank customer, Williams decided that the bank should issue credit cards to *all* of its customers in Fresno. He believed that the vast majority of the bank's customers would be honest and would understand the nature and mechanics of this new credit tool, which amounted to an instant personal loan of $300 or $500. Delinquencies, he esti-

mated, would run no more than three or four percent of total sales – a manageable figure. As for potential fraud or theft of cards, Williams did not foresee this as a major problem.

Williams also decided to boost revenue by charging participating merchants a fee of $25 to rent the little counter-top machines, later known informally as "zip-zaps," that would imprint the account number from the customer's card and the amount of the purchase. In addition, participating merchants would pay the bank six percent of each purchase, as the "merchant discount fee." The bank would provide sales drafts, a procedure manual, and deposit envelopes, all free of charge.

Amazingly, while the numbers and the technology have evolved, the guiding principles that Williams and his team established remain in place to this day in bank card programs throughout the world. At the time, though, no one was certain they would work, including Williams and his team. There were just too many unknowns to be sure of the outcome.

On June 30, 1958, Williams sent an internal memo to President Beise reporting on the progress of their pilot project. "The results to date are very encouraging," Williams wrote. Local merchants were enthusiastically signing up for the program, and in the space of only nine days, 719 customers had inquired about the card. If Beise and the board gave the green light, Williams planned the launch for September 18, 1958.

On August 25, Williams again wrote to President Beise: the program was gaining momentum. Some 900 merchants in Fresno had signed on and the branches had received 3,400 calls from customers wanting the card. By the date of the launch, Williams estimated that 65,000 residents of Fresno would have in their hand a brand new credit card. And what an appealing card it was going to be: a small, rectangular strip of plastic, adorned with distinctive blue, white and gold bands, and emblazoned with a name that did the bank proud:

BankAmericard.

How A.P. Giannini would have loved this new plastic tool. The card was simple, attractive, and convenient to use, an ideal fit for the little fellow's wallet or purse. This was not a tool for the rich man; leave that terrain to the high-rollers using Diners Club or American Express. BankAmericard was for the masses, and it was designed to give them financial power, control, flexibility, mobility, and, ultimately, greater freedom to shape their own destinies and follow their dreams.

If it worked as planned, the BankAmericard would be a new set of financial wheels for the little fellow – and it would reaffirm the bank's reputation as the Henry Ford of consumer credit. Also, if this little plastic tool could help its customers prosper and grow, then the bank, too, would continue to prosper and grow. Yes, if it worked as planned, this little plastic tool would be hailed as the perfect embodiment of A.P. Giannini's entire business philosophy.

In 1958, the BofA launched a revolutionary credit device, the BankAmericard.

In aviation and the space race, too, 1958 was "The Year of the Launch."

"If."

Thus it was that on September 18, 1958, in the same year that Boeing launched its fabled 707 and NASA began launching satellites, the Bank of America launched the BankAmericard. And it did so with all the appropriate fanfare. "Announcing a new, revolutionary charge account plan," trumpeted one BofA ad that ran in Fresno's Sunday papers. The bank also began running a series of ads that were designed to resonate with America's most basic yearnings and change its most basic notions of the nature of money. One ad urged consumers to forsake their hotel or oil company cards in favor of one convenient, all-purpose solution: "BankAmericard, the only credit card you really need."

Other ads appealed to the common man's longings for the material comforts of the American Dream: "BankAmericard, an easy way to make dreams come true." Another ad conjured up appealing images of happy families nestled in their suburban homes: "BankAmericard, the family credit card." One later ad campaign suggested the ultimate aim of the BankAmericard, namely the replacement of coins, bills and checks:

"BankAmericard. Think of it as money."

The launch of the card provoked reactions that ran from the quietly positive to the wildly negative. Many press articles assailed this new tool of consumer credit. And many politicians denounced it. One U.S. congressman even expressed fear for the future of the Republic: "A rapidly expanding credit-oriented economy is morally and financially ruinous to the public welfare."

Most merchants and consumers, however, responded positively to the new BankAmericard. Merchants reported that card usage was strong, and people tended to spend a little more freely than they did with cash. Many merchants also felt they gained prestige through association with the Bank of America, a view that BofA officials eagerly reported in an internal memo: "The entry of banks into the consumer credit field has tremendously upgraded credit selling. Now, with bank identification, credit buying has reached a new height of respectability."

For consumers, the little card needed some getting used to, and a few people didn't quite grasp the idea that at the end of the month, or later, they would actually have to pay for what they bought. Others did not grasp how fast card interest could build up and they found themselves heavily in debt – a problem that plagues some consumers even today. Still, a vast majority of consumers said the card was a wonderful addition to their wallets or purse. It was convenient and easy to use. It meant you could leave your checkbook at home and not worry about running to the bank for cash. In sum, it gave people greater financial power and flexibility, just as its creators intended.

The system supporting the card, however, was riddled with problems. Merchants complained that the little zip-zap machines churned out too much paper, in the form of flimsy sales drafts and carbons. Far worse were the problems with "floor limits." If a cardholder wanted to make a purchase that exceeded the floor limit specified by his card, a shopkeeper might have to spend several minutes calling the bank and then waiting for a bank staffer to hand-check the cardholder's account. The process was slow, cumbersome, and annoying – and it hurt business.

Joe Williams and his staff faced problems that were far more serious. Williams' leap of faith regarding mass issuance of cards proved to be disastrous. The percentage of delinquent accounts was not 4 percent as he had hoped – it was 22 percent. In most cases, the problem was not fraud. Many customers just did not grasp the credit card basics. The learning curve was steeper than Williams and his team had imagined, and their efforts to educate the consumer had not been up to the challenge.

As a result, the bank's initial losses were steep. Nonetheless, Beise and his board decided to press ahead with their larger ambitions for the little BankAmericard. In March 1959, the bank began issuing credit cards in its home region of San Francisco – mostly because of a rumor that a rival bank was planning to beat them to it. By June, they had extended the BankAmericard program to Sacramento and Los Angeles, and by October it was in operation throughout the state of California.

Soon, however, a sinister problem emerged: card theft and fraud. In the Los Angeles area, well-organized gangs were stealing cards and bribing merchants to help them use the stolen cards to maximum advantage. The gangs quickly figured out how to decipher some of the coding on the cards, including the card's "floor limits." With that knowledge, they could use the cards for scores of small purchases, with little fear of getting caught. The original cardholder was not obliged to pay for the fraudulent use; the bank was. So now the bank's losses really began to escalate. Soon they were a tide of red ink.

By the close of 1959, 15 months after its launch, the verdict on the BankAmericard program was in. Merchants and consumers liked the card, but in financial terms the BankAmericard was a disaster. A $20 million disaster. In December of 1959, the Bank of America was forced to write off total card losses of that whopping sum. It was a stunning blow for the bank, in terms of dollars and prestige. That same month, Joseph Williams left the bank. And there was no avoiding the hard truth: the entire BankAmericard program was in shambles. Now what?

In the face of a humiliating $20 million loss, almost every bank president in America would have elected to cut his bank's losses and close down the credit card program. But Clark Beise, in a move that would have delighted A.P. Giannini, took the opposite course. Ken Larkin vividly recalled the defining moment:

"President Beise told us, 'There's nothing wrong with the idea, only our execution of it. Let's get busy!'"

With Beise's endorsement and energy behind it, the little BankAmericard would soon rise from the ashes of its initial disasters. A new program director was brought in to pick up the pieces and chart a fresh course. Ken Larkin and other specialists in the field of installment credit were brought in to revamp credit policies. Larkin would soon emerge as the bank's most respected standard-bearer in the credit card field. To stem the flow of red ink, the new team sifted through the customer and merchant bases, dropping delinquent accounts and targeting higher-profile merchants, to help improve the public image of the card. The ad campaigns were also given a creative boost, and soon they would include a marvelous new touch.

This was a cheerful little animated orchestra conductor, dressed in tails and with a baton in hand. The conductor was a master stroke. With him, the BankAmericard was no longer an

A stroke of marketing genius: the BofA's "little conductor."

impersonal little piece of plastic; it was a lively little figure with wit and charm and an endearing face and spirit. Along with the arrival of the little conductor, the bank made a key shift of advertising medium. Up to then, the bank had used newspapers as the main focus of its ads and announcements. Now the main focus was television, a medium that was rapidly establishing itself as the powerhouse of American advertising. Thanks to the little conductor, TV and the BankAmericard became a wonderful fit.

All this retooling brought swift dividends. One year later, in the bank's annual report reviewing the results of 1960, President Beise remained bullish on the future of the little BankAmericard, even though it had been awfully cranky in its infant days: "The advantages to both consumer and merchant promise expanded BankAmericard usage in the year ahead. This greater volume will increase profitability, and BankAmericard should become a significant source of earnings in the period ahead."

Many people, inside the bank and out, probably thought the president of Bank of America had lost his marbles – along with that initial $20 million. But Clark Beise's bullish prediction was

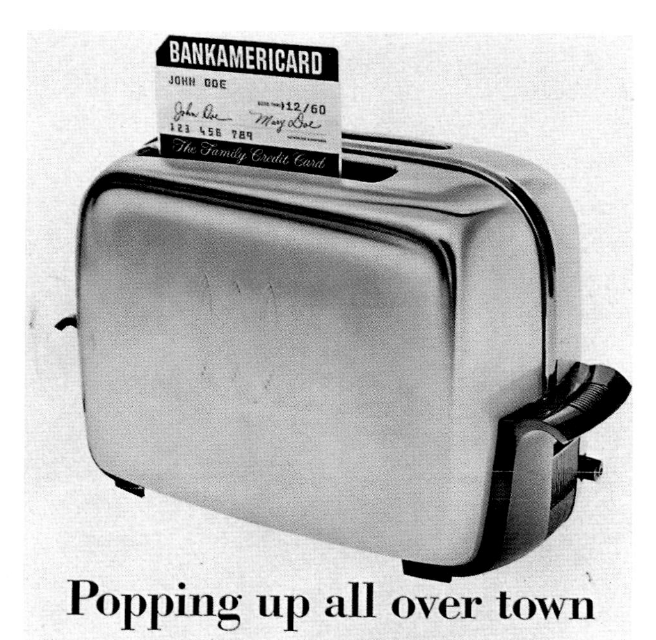

soon proved to be correct. In April, 1961, with many of the start-up problems now sorted out, the bank reached a milestone: the BankAmericard program was now turning a profit. From this point on, the little plastic tool began to fly. By 1963, Californians were using their card for purchases and cash advances that totaled $111,100,000 for the year. The Bank of America pocketed only a small percentage of that, but it was enough to put plenty of salve on those painful initial losses.

As the BankAmericard program continued to grow in sales and popularity, other banks in California and around the country watched with a mixture of envy and admiration. During this period of the early 1960s, some 200 other banks were running card programs, few with success. Saddled with vexing problems of management, operation, and profitability, many banks were ready to throw in the towel. In 1962, in a dispiriting sign of the times, Chase Manhattan closed down its bank card program. Others followed suit, and by the mid-1960s only 80 banks were still issuing cards. Was this the death knell for bank cards in America?

It could have been. Except for the Bank of America. By 1966, the bank remained the shining example that many banks were eager to follow. How had the bank Giannini built succeeded where so many other banks had failed? Bank executives from across America would have loved to travel to San Francisco to meet with BankAmericard specialists and find out their secrets. And this set the stage for a remarkable business decision by the Bank of America.

Imagine what would happen today if, say, a tiny computer software company in Cambridge, Massachusetts, sent a team out to visit Microsoft in Seattle and the team said, "Hey, fellas, tell us how you managed to engineer Windows 2000. Let us in on your secrets!" The folks at Microsoft would probably laugh and show them the door. And they would be in line with conventional business wisdom. Cut-throat competition, yes. Cooperation, no. Not among rivals in the same industry.

In fact, to build the necessary base of consumers and merchants, Larkin knew the BofA needed help. So why not invite a select group of banks from around the country to join forces in the BankAmericard program?

In a memo of March 25, 1966, Larkin suggested that the bank do essentially that. He proposed that the bank negotiate licensing agreements with a number of reputable banks across the country, so that they could issue BankAmericards to their customers. The BofA would charge the licensee banks an initial fee of $25,000, and then take a small percentage of all card transactions. In this way, the BofA could utilize the brand and build a very profitable revenue stream.

Larkin argued that licensing made good strategic sense as well. At that time, the bank card industry was in chaos. Many individual banks, seeing their own card programs falter, believed they could do better by forming regional card consortiums. The year before, four big Chicago banks had formed the Midwest Bank Card Association and had begun issuing cards. There were rumors that a group of rival banks in California was planning to form a consortium to compete with the BankAmericard and that a group of East Coast banks were going to do the same. There was also talk that First National City Bank of New York, now Citibank, was going to move aggressively into the credit card market. In Larkin's view, the BofA could preempt the competition by building a broad network of licensees, on the West Coast and beyond.

Larkin's plan also fit a much longer-range objective of the Bank of America: pursuing A.P. Giannini's ambition of creating a truly national bank. The little BankAmericard could prove to be a valuable step in that direction, as Larkin intimated in his memo: "The ultimate objective of this program is to make the name BankAmericard a household word throughout the nation."

Larkin made a persuasive case, and in 1966 the Bank of America decided to move forward and develop a franchise system. It invited several banks to join its BankAmericard program, thus becoming the first bank in the nation to license its card. In the process, the Bank of America preempted its rivals and became the first bank to build a nationwide credit card network. By the end of 1966, Larkin had signed up eight licensees, most of them on the West Coast: Puget Sound National Bank of Tacoma, Washington; National Bank of Commerce in Seattle; U.S. National Bank of Oregon in Portland; First National Bank of Oregon in Portland; Bank of Hawaii in Honolulu; City National Bank and Trust in Columbus, Ohio; Philadelphia National Bank in Philadelphia; and State Street Bank and Trust in Boston.

The idea caught on quickly and by the end of 1967, only a year later, 17 banks in 17 states were issuing BankAmericards. By the end of 1968, 41 banks were issuing BankAmericards, and another 1,823 banks were signing up merchants or acting as agents for the issuing banks. By the end of the second year of licensing, the little plastic tool had burst out of the confines of California and was now serving banks and their customers in 42 states. And, just as Ken Larkin had hoped, BankAmericard was rapidly becoming a household word throughout the nation.

BankAmericard's rapid growth sent other banks scrambling into the credit card business. In 1966, 14 East Coast banks created Interbank, an "interchange" association which enabled banks to issue cards with a common symbol: "i." Their customers could then use their card throughout a wide network of merchants in the program, each displaying the "i" symbol. In 1967, as rumored, four big California banks – Wells Fargo, Crocker Bank, the Bank of California and United California Bank – introduced the Master Charge program and formed the Western States Bankcard Association. WSBA then joined Interbank and later sold it the name Master Charge, now known as MasterCard. By the end of 1969, 1,207 banks were issuing cards, and these new credit cards had already produced outstanding loans totaling $2,639,000,000.

Those numbers represented quite a triumph for the Bank of America. The little BankAmericard had set a new industry into motion, and it was rapidly transforming American banking. For Clark Beise, Ken Larkin, and other BofA policymakers, the success was especially sweet. For 10 years they

The BankAmericard was a true partnership among banks, merchants, and consumers.

had patiently nurtured their ornery little wonder tool, and in the early years they had persevered while most banks abandoned their card programs. Now all the risks – and hard work – were paying off, and the Bank of America could rightly claim another huge pioneering success, in the best tradition of A.P. Giannini.

"We had more damn fun," Larkin recalled. "It was exciting. Everything was positive. We started from zero and then the totals started climbing. And this was just the beginning...."

Looking back now, we can see what a wild and gutsy ride those first 10 years were, its creators inventing on the run and then watching their little tool spread wings and begin to soar. In the space of just 10 years, the little BankAmericard had changed the way millions of Americans shopped and managed their money. From its home in California, the little tool had marched across the entire nation, carrying financial power and flexibility to legions of "little fellows" and drawing hundreds of banks together in a unique partnership that served their own needs and the needs of their customers and communities.

Imagine how all this would have delighted A.P. Giannini, the grandfather of the little BankAmericard. He had dreamed of creating a great national banking institution, operating in the spirit of a "public servant," a pioneering institution whose ideas and influence would spread all across the nation – and now the little BankAmericard was helping turn Giannini's dream into a reality.

Imagine, too, how all this would have delighted Woodrow Wilson. Back in 1908, Wilson had dreamed of an economic and social revolution, a noble revolution set in motion by enlightened bankers working for the public good. And, as we saw, Wilson had set forth a comprehensive blueprint for achieving his revolution, a blueprint based on two guiding principles: inter-bank cooperation and the democratization of credit.

Now, 60 years later, the little BankAmericard was hard at work, putting credit in the hands of millions of people across 42 states – "democratization" on a grand scale. And while Wilson's fervent message, Bankers of America, *unite!*, had moved only one banker to action, here was the little BankAmericard opening bankers' minds to new ideas and leading them into a bold new era of inter-bank cooperation. Quite a feat for a little piece of plastic.

And this was just the beginning of the story; the best was yet to come.

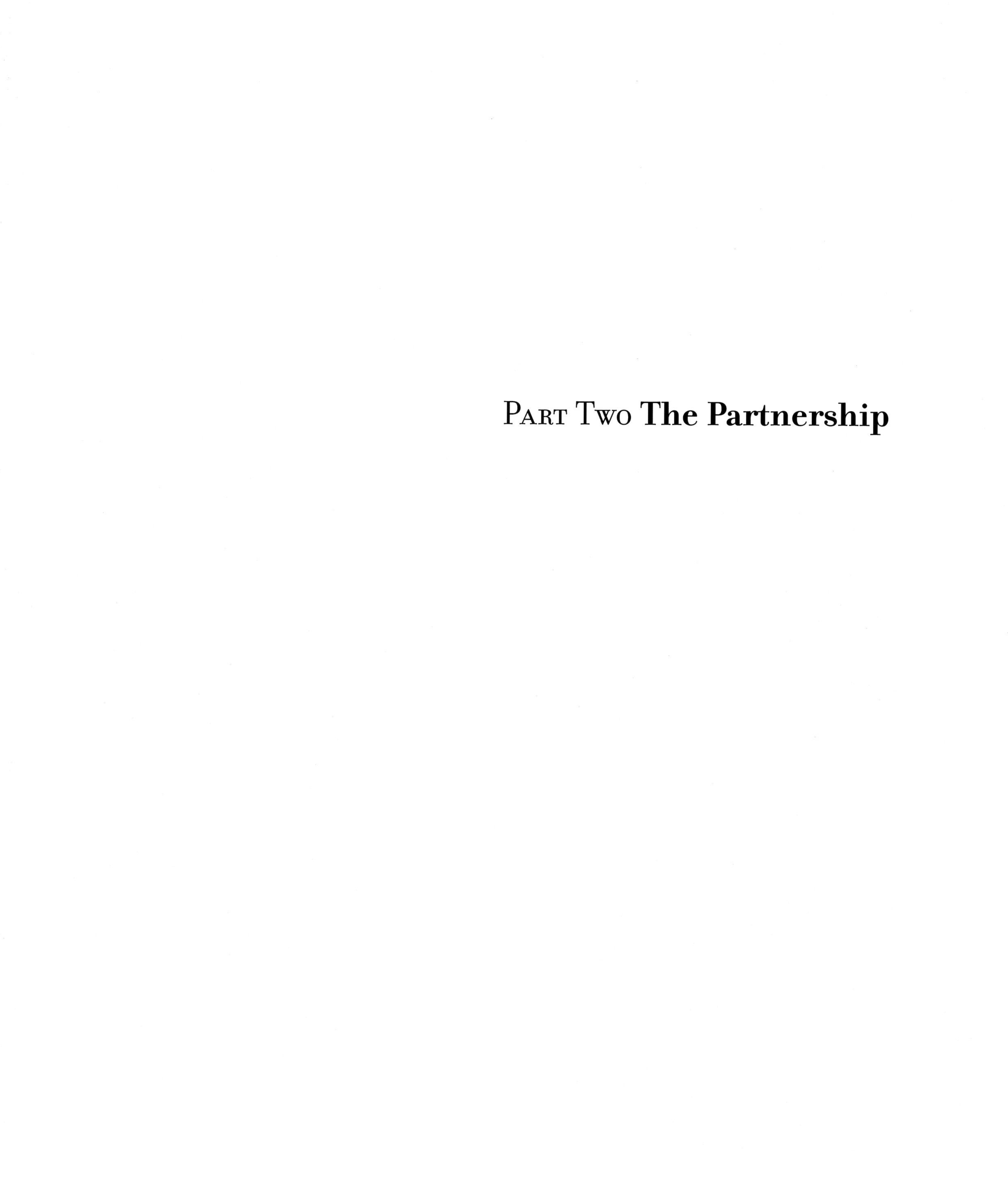

Part Two The Partnership

CHAPTER 5

Dee Hock,
Visionary, Founder, Enigma

A.P. Giannini, as we've seen, stirred a revolution in American banking. His philosophy, his spirit of innovation, and his commitment to the common man led directly to the birth of the little wonder tool, the BankAmericard. This was only the foundation, though, for what was to come.

In Giannini's footsteps, another pioneer came to the fore, with an equally grand vision, and he would be the architect of the vast worldwide partnership that Visa is today. Who was this man? What was his vision? And how did he build on Giannini's legacy and create a financial giant that in the year 2000 would generate and process more than $1.7 *trillion* in global transactions?

This part of the Visa story begins in 1968, a year of terrible turmoil in many corners of the world. In Saigon, with the Vietnam War raging, February of 1968 brought the Tet Offensive, a deadly campaign launched by North Vietnam and its allies in the south. The offensive rocked Saigon – and the confidence of U.S. military leaders guiding the war. It also emboldened the anti-war forces in America and helped push President Lyndon Johnson to announce he would not seek another term.

In May of 1968, angry students and workers took to the streets of Paris, demanding institutional reforms and greater equality in French education and society. Paris universities were closed, barricades went up around campuses, and student rebels squared off in bloody confrontations with police. The revolt shook public confidence in France's ruling war hero, General Charles de Gaulle, and the following year he would relinquish his presidency.

In the United States, 1968 brought assassinations, inner city riots, and student rebellions. In April, Martin Luther King was gunned down, and terrible rioting ensued in several cities. In June, Robert F. Kennedy was shot and killed while campaigning for the presidency. Then in August, student activists gathered at the Democratic Party's national convention in Chicago, to protest the Vietnam War. During their demonstrations, the Chicago police moved in, there were bloody confrontations, all televised live, and the result was shock and a national furor.

In San Francisco, the rebellion took on psychedelic hues. "Make love, not war" was the rallying cry, and young people flocked to San Francisco to join the ranks of the "flower children." Folk singers like Bob Dylan and Joan Baez were suddenly folk heroes and leaders of the counter culture. And as President Johnson called for more troops to be sent to Vietnam, choruses of college students rose up and chanted, "Hell, no! We won't go!"

In October of 1968, though it was pale by comparison, a whiff of rebellion even reached into the usually staid proceedings of the Bank of America. The place was a hotel in Columbus, Ohio, and the occasion was a meeting of all the banks that were now licensees in the BankAmericard program.

The licensees were not a happy lot. Many of them were suffering from the same painful start-up problems and heavy financial losses that the Bank of America had experienced in Fresno and across California. The BankAmerica Service Corporation, a division created to work with the licensees, had called together the card program managers of the licensee banks in the hope of assessing the situation and working through the many technical problems at hand. But the licensees had deeper concerns they were eager to raise.

On the first morning of the two-day meeting, some 120 card managers from around the country gathered in a conference room and sat down to business. On their agenda were such passion-inflaming topics as operating rules and inter-bank clearance procedures – the means by which a bank in Ohio, say, would handle the BankAmericard purchases of someone visiting from California. To an outside eye, these issues would hardly seem to be the kindling of insurrection, but almost as soon as it began, the meeting erupted into an angry gripe session. And almost all of the gripes were aimed at the Bank of America.

One after another, card managers rose to complain that their programs were losing money. Worse, nobody knew what to do about it. The licensees had no proper operating guidelines, no effective way to share information, and no organized mechanism for sorting out their problems. Card fraud was rampant, there were huge problems with the authorization system, and the licensees were facing growing mountains of paperwork – and so were their merchant partners. The system, in sum, was a mess. Worst of all, there were now deep suspicions surrounding the real intentions of the Bank of America. The bank that A.P. Giannini had built had promised its licensees a wonder tool; now many of them felt they had been sold a lemon.

The disputes and acrimony grew worse in the afternoon. There were no police barricades and no tear gas, of course, but by banking standards of decorum the meeting was veering out of control. There were shouting matches, there were rival factions in the room, and the middle managers running the meeting for the Bank of America were clearly at a loss about how to calm the bankers down. Some of the participants, sensing there would be no progress, considered leaving the meeting a day early and going back home. Others grimly wound up the first day's session and headed for the bar – and lots more griping.

By the end of that first day, many people felt that the future of the entire BankAmericard program was now in doubt. Sure, the Bank of America, with its power and reach in the booming state of California, had been able to make the card profitable, but no one else. The licensees had made a huge investment in that card, in time, money, and resources, and that investment was not paying off – and some of the card managers doubted it ever would. Was the whole licensing idea a dud? Was there any way to fix all the problems and make the BankAmericard program profitable? And who would step forward to lead the way? Nobody knew the answers or could see any hope on the horizon.

The next morning was even worse. Anger against the Bank of America was peaking, and the meeting was lurching toward disaster. Desperate to calm their licensees, the BofA managers running the meeting turned to a time-honored bureaucratic fig leaf: they appointed a seven-member licensee committee to examine the problems and suggest possible solutions. The licensees endorsed the idea. But as the bankers broke for lunch, one crucial question remained: who would chair the committee?

During the lunch break, there was some frantic, behind-the-scenes wrangling, but there was no easy solution. All the bankers had their own jobs to do. Who had the time or energy to deal with this can of worms? Besides, this promised to be a difficult and tedious job – a job with no rewards in sight, only severe headaches.

Nonetheless, some serious arm-twisting ensued, and when the 120 card managers reconvened for their final session, a Bank of America spokesman nervously took the floor. Standing at his side was a modest-looking, brown-haired man in his mid-30s. He was the director of the BankAmericard program at the National Bank of Commerce, a small, well-respected bank in

Seattle, and he was now introduced as the chosen head of the new committee:

"Gentlemen, meet Dee Hock."

Who?

As Hock stepped forward, there must have been a good deal of puzzlement and skepticism in the room. Hock had been vocal during the meeting, but he was by no means a formidable figure in the credit card world, and he did not represent one of the more prominent banks. So who was Dee Hock? Was he the type of fellow who could stand up to the Bank of America and be an effective advocate for its struggling licensees? Or was he just some poor sucker the BofA boys had corralled in a last-ditch effort to gain a little time and save a little face?

When Hock took the floor, he immediately set forth a clear, well-articulated course of action. His committee, he told the bankers, would not plunge into the various technical problems plaguing the BankAmericard program. Instead, Hock said his committee would first grapple with a much larger question: how to organize the licensees into a cohesive, effective, working body. A self-governing body.

Once they had created a new self-governing body, Hock explained, the licensees could then work together to solve their own problems and maximize the enormous potential of their common tool, the BankAmericard. Hock put no answers on the table, and he promised no easy solutions. But his presentation was calm and persuasive, and after all the earlier acrimony, the exhausted bankers quickly endorsed his chairmanship and the direction he set. Everyone heaved a collective sigh of relief; at least for now, Hock had helped them avert a major disaster.

Viewed from our vantage point today, this whole episode may sound like nothing more than a minor bureaucratic tiff. But it was far more than that. In fact, this was the first tentative step in what would soon become a gentlemanly insurrection against the ruling hand of the Bank of America. And this was also the moment when Dee Hock first stepped to the fore. In the weeks and months ahead, Hock would lead his fellow licensees on an extraordinary journey, a journey that would convince them to join hands and create the Visa partnership. And here there is a supreme irony.

If the bankers gathered in Columbus had examined his background and resumé, if they had talked with some of his early employers in the world of banking and finance, they would have concluded that Dee Hock was definitely not the answer to their problems. And if you had told them that Dee Hock would soon become the founding father and guiding light of a financial giant spanning the globe, many of those bankers in Columbus might have laughed right in your face. With good reason:

Dee Hock's track record was an enigmatic blend of success and failure. For 16 years, he had hopscotched around America's West Coast, going from job to job in banking and consumer finance. Hock had not built a career; he had built a puzzling history, often producing fabulous results – but just as often disappointing himself and others. No one doubted Hock had amazing potential, but as employer after employer had learned, Hock's temperament was not that of a traditional banker; it was that of an iconoclast. Hock was bright, at times even brilliant, but he was also a mercurial, starry-eyed idealist, a dreamer with his head so far in the clouds that many people wondered how he had ever wandered into banking and finance.

Yes, many of those bankers might have laughed right in your face. And yet, when the entire BankAmericard program was in crisis, and no one else would step up to help, destiny reached down and placed her hand on Dee Hock's shoulder. And how he rose to her touch is the real story of the creation of Visa, a story not just of a little plastic wonder tool but of a man with a calling, an unusual man borne on the wings of an extraordinary vision.

❀ ❀ ❀

Today, whenever you sit down and talk with old Visa hands, sooner or later the conversation settles down around just one subject: Dee. The first time I met Dee. The first time I incurred his wrath. That time, in the meeting, when he got so angry he made so-and-so go stand in the corner. Dee. Charismatic. Mesmerizing. Intimidating. Infuriating. A man with grand, visionary ideas – but a managerial style that even his admirers often found exasperating. Still, despite his quirks and enigmatic ways, everyone today agrees: Dee, at his best, was pure inspiration.

"He was an intense, intuitive, charismatic leader of the first order, and most of us would have stormed Pork Chop Hill into a stream of machine-gun fire if Dee had given the orders."

That is the view of Tom Cleveland, a Visa veteran, and today you hear similar assessments from nearly everyone Dee enlisted to his cause. By all accounts, he was a fierce iconoclast, a brilliant strategist and debater, a severe task-master, a fanatic about preparation and detail, and a man with an amazing power to organize and persuade. Everyone also agrees, that in the realm of credit cards and global payments systems, Dee Hock was a true visionary. And even his greatest detractors agree on this: without Dee Hock, there would simply be no Visa as we know it today.

In the year 2000, Dee Hock was living happily amidst the magnificent wilderness and greenery of the Pacific Northwest. Hock agreed to be interviewed for this book, and he added marvelous color, detail, and perspective to many parts of the narrative that follows. But to understand this complicated man, and to understand the spirit he brought to the creation of Visa, the place to begin is with Dee's own words and recollections, as he set them down in a memoir and treatise entitled *Birth of the Chaordic Age*, published in 1999 by Berrett-Koehler Publications. The book is brilliant, chaotic, impassioned, at times exasperating – and always fascinating and provocative. The book, in sum, is Dee distilled.

"A Lamb and the Lion of Life" is the title of Chapter Two, and this is exactly how Hock viewed himself in his early years: a naive, young lamb thrown into the jaws of life. He was born in Utah, the sixth of six children in a poor, rural, laboring family of austere Mormon heritage. "Riches are not in the number of possessions, but the fewness of wants," was one of the homilies his parents used to raise him. "Wish not, want not," was another. And there was another that A.P. Giannini would have surely adored: "Money's manure, no good unless you spread it."

Money, indeed, was scarce in the Hock household, but a spirit of community was not. Hock opens his personal story when he is just five years old and he is witnessing an unusual event: a group of neighboring farmers have gotten together to help Hock's family move their cottage a quarter-mile down the road. They've hoisted the cottage onto old telephone poles and they're rolling the poles and the cottage to its new location. The operation takes hours of back-breaking jacking, heaving, pushing and pulling, and when it's all over, and the family cottage is settled onto its new foundation, there's no celebratory meal or exchange of money, only the joy of a good deed done. As Hock writes:

"One by one, the neighbors shoulder tools and trudge into the night to shouts of 'Thanks!' and 'Welcome!'"

Even as a boy, Hock was a loner. Books were his closest friends and even as a boy he was a voracious reader. Later, at Visa board meetings, Dee would

FOSTER and KLEISER
BANKAMERICARD.
AUTHORIZED SIGNATURES
C J SCHLOSSER
GOOD THRU 00/00 BAC
019 123 456 789
Spend Christmas with us.

Now–10 major airlines honor BANKAMERICARD!
NATIONAL
UNITED
TWA
TRANS WORLD AIRLINES
BONANZA
AA
AMERICAN AIRLINES
WESTERN
AIRLINES
CONTINENTAL
PACIFIC
AIR LINES
DELTA
PSA

spice his speeches with dazzling arrays of quotes from the classics and the great philosophers – usually to the bafflement and annoyance of the bankers present.

But the bankers' reaction would be nothing new to Hock. As he wrote in his memoir, even when he was a little boy people found him to be a bit strange and remote – even his family. "Love me as they will," he wrote, "there is a growing feeling of estrangement from family; a feeling of not belonging."

In the fifth grade, however, Hock found a soulmate, a kindred spirit, a partner who would believe in him and stand by him for the rest of his life. Her name was Ferol, and Dee wrote lovingly about the moment their hands first touched: "In the way of all young boys craving attention from girls, I slyly slipped my hand onto the desk behind, to tip her books to the floor. Without so much as acknowledging my presence or the slightest change of expression in her magnificent brown eyes, with her fingernails she put four bloody, crescent moons in the back of my hand. We have been together every step of the way since."

Their early years together were no picnic. Dee and Ferol grew up in a little country town, and to help his parents Dee worked at all sorts of rigorous farming jobs, from picking beans to mucking out dairy barns. He adored hunting and fishing and he adored the wilderness; the mountains and trees gave him comfort and solace. Thanks to his triumph in a high school debating contest, Dee was awarded a $50-a-year scholarship to attend Weber Junior College, now Weber State University. Ferol had been a straight-A student in grammar school and high school, and she wanted to go on to college, but when her father died of cancer she set her dream aside and went to work as a seamstress to help her mother and younger sister. Two years later, after Dee graduated from Weber Junior College at the age of 20, she and Dee married. Dee at the time was working as a laborer, carrying bricks and mortar, but then the brick contractor shut down and the workshop where Ferol worked burned down. So Dee had no choice: he had to go out and find a job. Any job.

Dee fell into a job at a small branch office of a consumer finance company. The work itself was no problem; Dee could handle that. But Dee was a dreamer with a history of clashing with those in power – and right away he chafed at the rules and rigidities that come with most corporate structures and hierarchies. "Command and control" hierarchies, Dee would later call such organizations, and in his mind they squelched individual creativity and initiative – two traits he felt were essential for his individual happiness and for true success in any business. Dee Hock, it was clear even then, was simply not a man to be commanded or controlled.

Still, Dee worked hard at the finance company, and he produced results; nine months later he was promoted to manager of a small branch. As Dee relates in his memoir, he and three other junior colleagues set to work in their own way, by ignoring the rules and regulations. We "trashed the company manual, ignored commandments, and did things as common sense, conditions, and ingenuity combined to suggest. Within two years, business tripled and the office was leading the company in growth, profit and quality of business."

Management was impressed – and threatened, at least according to Dee. As punishment for his success, and to cure him of his maverick ways, the finance company sent Dee out to open a new office, in a remote Oregon town. The branch was an immediate success, and he and Ferol, with one small child and a baby, settled down to make a new life there – until Dee's principles got in the way. One day, feeling he had been cheated out of a raise, he picked an absurd, self-destructive fight with his

In the 5th grade, Dee met his match and lifelong companion, his wife, Ferol.

regional manager, and soon Dee was sent packing again, this time down to Los Angeles. There, a more skilled and cunning misfit named Dick Simons took him in hand.

"What you don't understand," he told Dee, "is that in organizations like this, procedure is more important than purpose, and method more important than results." The key, Simons told him, was to learn the art of gentlemanly guerrilla warfare, to learn how to use corporate rigidities and shortsightedness to your own advantage. Simons, in his own little corner of consumer finance, was the kind of wily strategist Machiavelli would have admired, and Dee now learned at the knee of the master.

"I have never forgotten Simons," Hock wrote in his memoir. "Countless times over the years I have asked diverse groups of people to reflect very carefully on their work within organizations and to make a simple balance sheet. How much time, energy and ingenuity did they spend obeying senseless rules and procedures that had little to do with the results they were expected to achieve; how much time did they devote to circumventing those rules and procedures in order to do something productive?"

Dee learned valuable lessons from Simons, but they did not bring him either success or career stability. For the next 15 years, Dee bounced around the world of banking and consumer finance, and every place he went he was a corporate misfit and rebel. As a result of this inconstancy, Dee wound up deeply in debt, and by his own admission he felt like a miserable failure. He also felt like he had let down Ferol and their three children. At one stage, out of work and deeply depressed in a city he detested, Dee and Ferol agreed he had to go to the unemployment office and apply for financial assistance. Dee drove to the office but then he just sat in the car paralyzed – he just could not bring himself to go in and ask for help. To do so would be to admit defeat – and that he could not do.

At this juncture, as he wrote in his memoir, Dee's life was in shambles and he knew he had no one to blame but himself. With brutal self-scrutiny, he even had to admit that the criticisms he had so often heard from his employers held kernels of

truth: "stubborn, opinionated, unpredictable, unorthodox, rebellious. The power of those words to wound came from elements of truth each contained; their weakness from the fact that none contained the whole of it."

By his own admission, Dee Hock was a man torn by his own internal conflicts. In his memoir, Dee stands back and considers himself in the third person: "He was filled with desire for acceptance in the world as he found it, for his piece of the American dream. He wanted to believe and belong; to rise to a place among the powerful, rich and famous. But he was also filled with many things he would not do to get there. Side-by-side with a compelling desire to excel in the world as he found it was an equal desire to behave in accordance with the world as he wished it to be."

Yes, Dee was not happy with the work-a-day world as it was; he was always preoccupied by how he wished it to be – and he felt frustrated by the huge gap between the real and the ideal. No wonder he was torn in two. What's a conflicted, dreamy idealist – with a wife and three children – to do? Especially in the world of banking?

In 1965, heavily in debt and in desperate need of a job, Dee went for interviews at several banks. At Seattle's National Bank of Commerce, later known as Rainier, he immediately liked what he saw: these were "decent people." Maxwell Carlson, president of the bank, saw something intriguing in Dee, and despite Dee's discouraging track record, Carlson offered him a job without title, promises, or set responsibilities. And the pay was half what Dee had previously made. But at the age of 36, at least he had a job.

"I would be a trainee, a nobody," Hock wrote, but it was a paycheck. An opportunity. And Dee grabbed it. For a full year, he was shunted from department to department inside the bank, and then he landed in something new: the bank's embryonic credit card program. The National Bank of Commerce was one of the Bank of America's first licensees, and in 1966 Dee was asked to help a man named Bob Cummings launch their BankAmericard program throughout the Seattle area.

Dee was not a fan of credit cards; indeed he had torn his own to bits many years before. But now Dee found what he had long been searching for: freedom. Freedom to break the rules, to skirt the hierarchy, and to use his own wits and ingenuity to attack what seemed to be an impossible mission: to launch the bank's entire credit card program in the space of just 90 days.

Dee and Bob Cummings got the job done, on schedule. The following year, when their BankAmericard program was up and running, Cummings moved to another job in the bank and he urged Maxwell Carlson to let Dee take over the program. Dee, he said, understood credit cards, he had good, creative ideas about how they could work for the bank, and Dee brought enormous passion and enthusiasm to this new tool of consumer credit. Carlson agreed with Cummings' assessment, and he gave Dee full responsibility for the card program at his bank.

For Dee, this was a wonderful endorsement, and his promotion no doubt came as a relief to Ferol, and to Dee as well. At last, Dee had found a proper avenue for his energy and talents. At last, Dee the idealist could put his own ideas into motion. And at last, in his own specialized little realm of the bank, yesterday's frustrated rebel was now the commander-in-chief.

This, in sum, was the man who stepped reluctantly to the fore in Columbus, Ohio. But though he saved that meeting from disaster, there were still plenty of questions hanging around the neck of Dee Hock. Was he really the right man to lead the new committee of the licensees? Could he find a way out of the crisis threatening the whole BankAmericard system? Was he a man who had put all his failures behind him? Or would his stubborn, rebellious temperament rise up and do him in once again?

At this stage, nobody knew. Least of all Dee.

Charismatic, inspiring, and determined, Dee knew how to get his way.

Chapter 6

Ideals and Principles

Dee Hock was a perpetual ruminator. He loved to tackle big ideas, tear them apart, look at them from many perspectives, and then ruminate on what he found. Perhaps this love of ideas came from his being a loner, or from all his reading, or maybe it just came from a natural inclination toward theory, philosophy, and intellectual stimulus. In any event, in his memoir Dee refers to his psyche as "Monkey Mind" for the way it bounds and scampers around the cages of his mind, picking through his thoughts and ideas, foraging for the ripest bananas and the sweetest plums.

On the plane from Columbus back home to Seattle, Hock and his Monkey Mind began to ruminate. What was the best way to draw together the BankAmericard licensees? What formula would have the most appeal for the licensees and for the Bank of America? On the plane, Dee also talked with Jim Cronkhite, a colleague from the National Bank of Commerce, and soon the two of them were busy conceptualizing a framework under which the licensees could join together in an effective, self-governing body.

Their first idea was to divide the card-issuing banks into manageable groupings based on their regions. Each region would establish committees to coordinate BankAmericard activities in such as operations, marketing, credit policies, card fraud, and the like. An executive committee composed of the chairman of each functional committee would unify and coordinate the information. Comparable national committees would be composed of the chairman of each regional committee. A national executive committee would coordinate the whole BankAmericard program across the United States. Fine; to Dee that seemed like a workable framework.

In the following days, Dee put his Monkey Mind to work on a more complicated issue: what principles should govern this new self-governing body? Here Dee the idealist came into play: the new body, he decided, should be pure democracy in action. Each card-issuing bank should be represented on the various regional committees. And all the licensee banks should be treated equally; the big urban banks would have the exact same rights and responsibilities as the little fellows. Consensus would be the goal; no bank would rule by fiat or by its size or influence. "Everyone would be heard, but no one would dominate" – that was Dee Hock's formula for success.

That said, Dee was not envisioning a full-scale revolution. He realized that special consideration would have to be given to Big Daddy, the Bank of America. The BofA, after all, was the sole owner of the distinctive blue, white, and gold BankAmericard logo and of the franchising company that controlled the card and how it was used around the country. So the BofA management had to be comfortable with any new arrangement, or it would never work. Accordingly, the BofA should have representatives on all committees, with no greater or lesser rights than any other bank. In addition, the BankAmerica Service Corporation, which ran the card program, would have ex officio members on each national committee. In political terms, we could say that Hock was seeking autonomy and self-rule for the licensees, but not full independence.

Not yet.

For their first meeting, Dee and the new working committee convened a few weeks later in Atlanta, Georgia. There, Dee presented his idea for regional committees and the principles he felt should guide them. The committee approved Dee's direction, and over the next six months the licensees organized themselves into eight regional committees and a set of national committees. Hock was asked to chair the executive committee for the Pacific Northwest region and to be chairman of the national executive committee. He agreed. But his workload suddenly escalated.

"It was thankless, unpaid, often unpleasant work," Hock wrote. It was also a huge burden on top of his existing duties as director of the card program at the National Bank of Commerce. But his role was now clear: he was the leader of the disgruntled licensees – and they were counting on his leadership and the committees to find effective ways to fix their BankAmericard programs and make them profitable.

During those same six months, Hock and his colleagues also got a clearer idea of just how serious the BankAmericard's troubles really were. Initially, they had thought the licensee banks were losing tens of millions of dollars in their card programs. Working together, however, they discovered that their total losses were in the *hundreds* of millions of dollars – and climbing rapidly.

Those numbers were chilling. Something had to be done. Something radical. And it had to be soon.

At this juncture, Dee Hock faced a serious conflict, and he turned for advice to Maxwell Carlson, the president of his bank. "Mr. Carlson," Hock said, "I'm in trouble. When I shot my mouth off at the meeting in Columbus, I had no intention of getting so involved."

Hock told Carlson that, on the one hand, he felt an obligation to throw himself into solving the crisis now threatening the whole BankAmericard program. On the other hand, that would take enormous time away from his duties at the bank. It was a painful dilemma; what should he do? Maxwell Carlson then began to gently probe.

"Well, young man, how much of your time do you think this might take?"

"I honestly don't know. In the beginning, perhaps a quarter or more, but if something comes of the effort, it might be more than full time. There's simply no way of knowing."

"I see," Carlson said. "If something is not done, what will happen?"

"Again, there's no way to predict. If the BankAmericard system fails, we'll either have to convert to a private card program or make an affiliation with another system." Either would be costly. If the industry fails, Dee said, all their collective efforts to date would have been for naught.

The picture Dee painted was dark, and it presented Maxwell Carlson with a dilemma of his own. He wanted to see the BankAmericard succeed. His bank had strong historical ties to the BofA; for many happy years they had been the Bank of America's correspondent bank in the Pacific Northwest. There were also close family bonds between the two banks, dating back to A.P. Giannini. But if Hock took on this new responsibility, who would pay his salary? And, Carlson asked, would there be any long-term advantage for the National Bank of Commerce?

Salary questions would have to be worked out, Hock told him, but up to that point, all the banks had been paying their own way. Hock valued that principle. He also made clear that the bank should not expect special treatment. If the BankAmericard partnership was going to work, all the banks would have to be on an equal footing. This, too, was a matter of principle.

"Whoever does this job must be above reproach with respect to openness and fairness," Hock said. "It simply can't be done without a great deal of trust and confidence, and that will be hard to develop. I don't want to attempt the work if this bank receives preferred information or treatment."

To an outsider reading Dee's account, an amazing transformation appears to be taking place. Three years before, Hock had gone to Carlson seemingly on bended knee; he was deeply in debt and desperate for a job. Yet here was Hock now, sounding self-righteous and unbending, and asserting his principles and independence to the president of the bank. A different bank president might have cut short Hock's involvement with the new initiative and told him to get back to his main duties for the bank. But not the kindly Mr. Carlson. Hock had proved his worth before, and Carlson figured he would again. So he now gave Dee a wonderful gift, the kind of gift every ambitious manager dreams of one day receiving from his boss: Carlson gave him his blessing and he gave him wings.

"Well, young man, sometimes we just have to be good citizens," Carlson told him. "Go where you have to go and do what you have to do. Treat us as you would the others. We will ask no more. The resources of the bank are at your disposal." Hock was stunned; this was the liberty and trust he craved. He was never going to let this man down.

So now, in early 1969, Dee Hock had the challenge of his life and he had the mandate and freedom to undertake it. His bank would keep him on as a vice president and as head of the credit card program – and yet the bank would free him to think and plan. And, above all, to dream. At the same time, Dee knew he had to move quickly, in concrete, practical ways, to mold the licensees into a self-governing body.

At this juncture, Dee knew he needed help. His national executive committee had several good people, top-flight bankers with hands-on experience with credit card programs. But Dee wanted something more – a chosen few with strong characters and independent minds, not yes-men. Dee was also looking for kindred spirits, people eager to share in what could turn into a great business adventure – with some very high risks.

After much consideration, Dee asked three men to join him for a week-long brainstorming session. One was Sam Johnson, an Irishman from Boston with generous capacities for enthusiasm and friendship. Another was Fred James, a drawlin', down-home banker from Memphis, Tennessee. The third was Jack Dillon, a 30-year veteran of the Bank of America and a wonderful raconteur and a connoisseur of fine wine and food. He'd be great company but, more importantly, Dillon was now in charge of the credit card program at the Bank of America, reporting to Ken Larkin and to the president of the bank, Rudolph Peterson. Dee had been working closely with Dillon for more than a year, and Dee knew that Dillon's support would smooth the way forward. In Dee's view, these three men were able, articulate, and good-humored. Dee also felt they were open-minded and would be responsive to new ideas.

The four men gathered at the Alta Mira Hotel in Sausalito, California, just north of the Golden Gate Bridge. The Alta Mira was small and quiet with a view that swept the San Francisco Bay. On the rippling waters, you could see sailboats meandering around the bay or heading out to sea for greater adventures. It was an ideal setting for expansive conversations and for contemplating great issues and dreams – just what Dee had in mind.

For a long time, Dee had been ruminating about the true natures of banking, money, and credit cards, and about the impact computer technology would have on the world of finance. He was convinced that digital technology, which was just beginning to emerge, would radically change banking, credit cards, and our most basic concepts of money. While he could not predict the future, or envision anything even remotely resembling the

Internet, to Dee this much was already clear: a full-scale financial revolution was on the horizon. So he had been pondering several fundamental questions:

What was a bank, really? What was money, really?

"The nature of a bank, its essential function, was the custody, exchange and loan of money," Dee later wrote. "But what was money? Money was not coin, currency or credit card. That was form, not function. Money was *anything* customarily used as a measure of equivalent values and medium of exchange."

Currency and coin, furthermore, no longer derived their value from gold and other precious metals, as in the old days. Now money was just symbols imprinted on worthless paper or metal. What would that mean in the future, as computers made their way into the core functions of banking? Money would become nothing more than numbers transmitted by electronic impulse, what Hock called "alphanumeric value data." When money became nothing more than digitalized data, where did that leave banks? Endangered. They would have to either change how they thought of and managed money – or face extinction.

Digitalized money, Dee foresaw, would transform the way consumers and businesses purchase goods and services and manage their money. Digitalized money would also transform the way companies did their business across both corporate and national boundaries. With computers, exchange rates would be calculated in the blink of an eye; a transaction made in London, say, could be cleared by a bank in New York or Tokyo in a matter of seconds. Digital money, Dee was convinced, would transcend national currencies and national borders. In essence, sooner or later, *digital money would be a universally accepted global currency.*

And what, at its core, was a credit card?

In 1969, it was a convenient payment and credit device. But Dee could foresee a day when a credit card would be far more: it would be a person's private passkey into the world of digital money. With his card, a consumer could buy goods, pay for services, and take out a personal loan – and all the transactions would be handled digitally. No coin, paper currency or checks would change hands in these transactions, only what Hock called digital "exchanges of value." All this led Dee to ponder another question:

Who would handle the world's digital transactions?

Again, Dee could imagine the future: consumers around the globe would use their credit cards as digital money. But there was no existing organization that could handle such an immense, complex, and diverse volume of transactions. As Dee pondered that fact, he came to a startling idea. Yes, the BankAmericard program was in a terrible crisis. But was there buried in that crisis a huge, even historic, opportunity? Could he, the Bank of America, and the licensees create an organization that could handle the digital transactions of tomorrow? Now Dee began to get excited.

"Exhilarating realizations followed one after the other," he wrote in his memoir. Any organization that could guarantee, transport, and settle alphanumeric monetary data 24 hours a day, seven days a week, around the globe, would have a market that beggared the imagination. But there was a problem. "No bank could do it. No hierarchal stock corporation could do it. No nation-state could do it. In fact, no existing form of organization we could think of could do it....

"I made an estimate of the financial resources of all the banks in the world. It dwarfed the resources of most nations. Jointly, they could do it, but how? It would require a transcendental organization linking in wholly new ways an

Dee envisioned a vast global network, computer-based, to handle card transactions.

unimaginable complex of diverse institutions and individuals. At that time, did I think it could be done? No! It was impossible!"

Still, Dee could not calm his Monkey Mind, and thus it was that even before they reached Sausalito, Dee asked his group of fellow thinkers to begin contemplating one transcendent question:

"If anything imaginable was possible, if there were no constraints whatever, what would be the nature of an ideal organization to create the world's premier system for the exchange of value?"

What a treat it would have been to see the faces of those bankers when Dee first popped that little question. In his memoir, Dee admits the first response was "head-shaking and rolled eyes," and we can imagine it elicited even more than that. Back in 1969, this entire line of thinking might have sounded to the average man on the street like the stuff of science fiction, or just plain old gobbledygook. Dee had visions dancing in his head that no one else could see. And he spoke of those visions using a lexicon that was entirely his own. "Exchange of value." "Alphanumeric data value." Those sounded pretty fancy, but what in tarnation did they really mean? Was this Dee Hock a brilliant visionary or was he off wandering with Alice in Wonderland?

Jack Dillon was convinced that Dee was no nut case; he was a man of brilliance and purpose. In the year they had worked together, Dee and Dillon had always emphasized the long-term and how banking would work in the future. "In Sausalito we were in a final preparatory phase of what we wanted to do," Dillon said in an interview. "Dee and I had an idea that went way beyond the needs of the day. We were already thinking in global terms."

The way Dillon recalls the meeting, Fred James and Sam Johnson were not enamored with Dee's line of thinking. After all, what Dee was contemplating required a huge leap of imagination and faith. On the one hand, the BankAmericard program was in crisis and the licensees were losing a fortune with it. On the other hand, here was Dee imagining that these same licensees might be

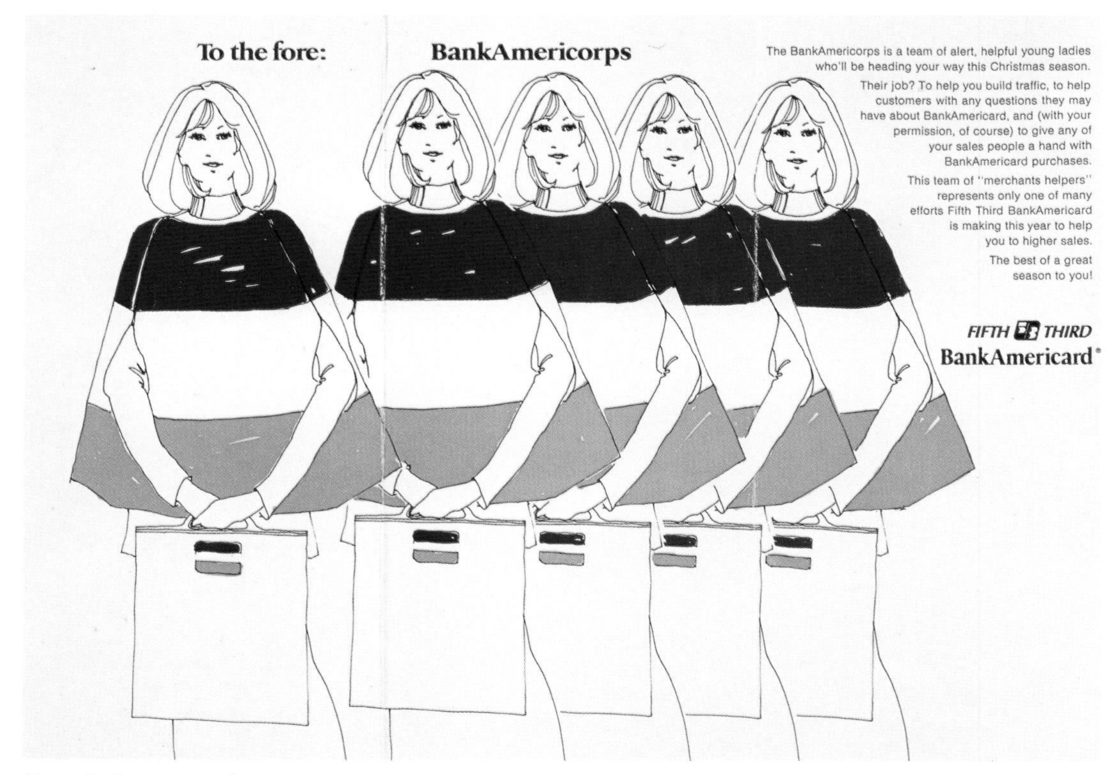

From the beginning, the BankAmericard had distinctive blue, white, and gold bands.

ready, willing, and able to join hands and create a global venture of colossal size and ambition. It was fine to dream, but where was Dee's bridge to the realities of the present?

For four days, Dee and his fellow thinkers holed up in a cottage on the grounds of the Alta Mira – and got nowhere. They tried to envision ways to create an organization that would link all the world's banks and settle all the world's digital transactions. They also tried to figure out a formula by which banks might be convinced to put aside their own immediate concerns and enter into some new form of cooperative venture. But no one came up with any viable answers. Dee became frustrated and upset. The whole meeting appeared to be an exercise in futility. And Dee began to worry that all his arduous ruminating, all the ideas and visions that he had been playing with, amounted to nothing more than fantasy. Intellectualized drivel.

On the fourth night, however, as Dee wrestled alone with his ideas and frustrations, his Monkey Mind sprang forth. Up to then, the four men had been looking for concrete answers and final results. What if, instead, they started focusing on the ideal and thinking about process? Nature follows a process. Trees, flowers, animals, and people all grow according to a process, a process dictated by innate genetic coding. Why not organizations? And now Dee had an inspiration: "What if we quit arguing about the structure of a new institution," he wrote in his memoir, "and tried to think of it as having some sort of genetic code?" What, then, would be the genetic coding of an *ideal* organization?

Now Dee's mind began to churn. He knew, all too well, what most companies were: the rigid "command and control" hierarchies that he despised. So now he and his Monkey Mind stripped all that away and cut to the bone: what, at its core, is a company? "The truth is that a commercial company or, for that matter, any organization, is nothing but an idea," Dee wrote. "All institutions are no more than a mental construct to which people are drawn in pursuit of common purpose; a conceptual embodiment of a very old, very powerful idea called *community*."

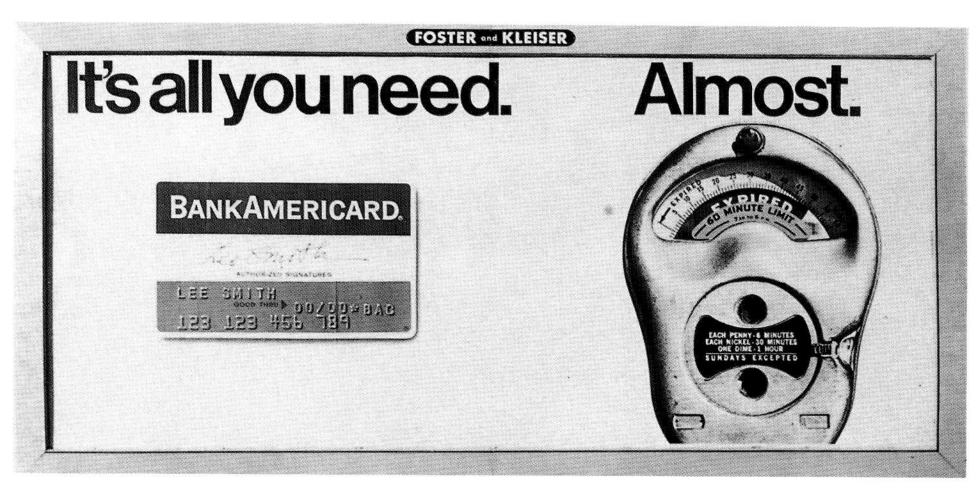

Community. Hmmm. Community implies common purpose.

It also implies common beliefs. Common values. Common ideals and principles. Were these the makings of an ideal genetic code?

Could these be the DNA building blocks that we could use to grow a new financial institution? Now Dee saw a way forward: what if we began examining our common purpose and our common ideals and principles? Where would that path lead us?

A few hours later, Dee greeted his colleagues with a full head of steam. Today, he said, let's not discuss banking, money, and credit cards; let's discuss ideals. Let's discuss principles and our common purpose. Jack, Sam, and Fred liked that approach and were willing to give it a try. So they began talking and quickly found there was room for agreement. In fact, they all got excited and thought they had found common elements that might convince the licensees to draw together in a self-governing body, one that could later grow into the digital clearinghouse that Dee envisioned. The way Dee describes the scene, in talking about ideals and principles, he and his colleagues did not sound like four bankers discussing money and joint ventures. They sounded more like Thomas Jefferson, James Madison, James Monroe, and Alexander Hamilton discussing the principles that should be enshrined in the Declaration of Independence and the U.S. Constitution. Indeed, Dee would later go so far as to refer to his inner circle as the "Founding Fathers of Visa."

What ideals and principles did he and his colleagues finally agree upon? As Dee wrote in his memoir, the four men came up with an extensive list:

- The organization should be equitably owned by all participants. No one would be subordinate, no one superior.
- Participants should have equitable rights and obligations.
- It should be open to all qualified participants.
- Power, function, and resources should be properly divided and shared.
- Authority should be equitably shared within each governing entity.
- To the maximum degree possible, everything should be voluntary.
- The organization should induce change, not compel it.
- The governing structure should be infinitely malleable and elastic and yet extremely durable.

If you distill out their essence, their guiding ideals and principles were these: Cooperation. Partnership. Democratic procedures. Equitable power-sharing. Openness. Trust. And a spirit of community. A.P. Giannini would have been flattered.

Now Dee was pleased. He and his colleagues had evolved a vision and a set of guiding principles with which to pursue it: the creation of a democratic, self-governing *partnership* of banks that would work together to manage and settle credit card financial transactions from any place in the world. In the short term, the partnership could handle BankAmericard transactions. In the longer term, it could grow into the vision Dee had articulated: the world's premier system for handling digital transactions.

Dee was convinced that this new partnership should not be under the control of the Bank of America or any other single bank. Instead, it should be a partnership in the truest sense, people and their banks coming together for their own mutual benefit and profit – and the larger good of their customers and communities. The others basically agreed. So one more tenet, though not boldly declared, was ingrained in their ideals and principles:

Independence.

Theirs was a grand idea, but Dee and his colleagues had little confidence that they could ever turn it into a working reality. Dee's own doubts ran very deep. "We had no money with which to purchase the system from the Bank of America," Dee wrote, "no money to hire consultants, advisors or other experts, no money to engage in research or hire employees. We had no power to influence regulators, legislators, or others in political power."

So Dee left Sausalito in his usual state: conflicted. On the one hand, he had persuaded three very hard-headed bankers that his ideas and vision had merit, and together they had worked out a sturdy set of guiding ideals and principles. On the other hand, he knew he faced monumental hurdles ahead, from one corner in particular:

The Bank of America.

Sausalito, Ca., where Dee held a
critical brainstorming session

142924

BANKAMERICARD®

John Doe

AUTHORIZED SIGNATURES

JOHN DOE

GOOD THRU

131 000 000 000

6/67 BAC

Chapter 7

Independence

In June of 1969, just a few short weeks after their brainstorming session in Sausalito, Dee and his confidants went to the headquarters of the Bank of America for three days of important meetings. During the first two days, Dee and the others set forth their ideas about self-governance and reported on their progress in setting up regional and national committees.

These initial meetings went without problem. On the third day, however, Dee and his colleagues walked into a meeting with Ken Larkin, the chief architect of the troubled licensee program. And Larkin gave them a greeting they would never forget.

"Well, well, well," Larkin said. "Here they are – the leaders of the revolution!"

Larkin's greeting unsettled Dee, and understandably so. At this stage, everything that Dee and his team were doing was exploratory. Their only mandate flowed from the creation of the fact-finding committee that had been created in Columbus, Ohio. Whether the licensees liked it or not, the BofA held the reins to the BankAmericard program. If the BofA chieftains didn't like the direction Dee and his colleagues were going, they could stop them at any time. So Dee and his team were doing a high wire act: trying to secure self-rule for the licensees, but trying to do so without overly antagonizing the Bank of America. And now Larkin had made the precariousness of this high wire act brutally clear.

The meeting went downhill from there. As Hock relates in his memoir, they sat down with Larkin, and the group presented their plans for molding the licensees into a self-governing body. A body that would include the Bank of America at every level, but not be dominated by it. This, Dee explained, was a matter of principle.

As Dee continued in this vein, Ken Larkin went into a slow burn. Larkin had fathered the licensing idea. He had designed the program. He had hand-picked the first licensees and negotiated their licensing agreements. He had run the marketing campaign for the card and designed incentive programs to stimulate card sign-ups and usage. In one year, he had flown over 300,000 miles for that card – and he had a horrible fear of flying! In sum, Ken Larkin had worked like a dog to make the BankAmericard a success – and his effort had paid off, handsomely. So for Larkin, the little BankAmericard was more than a job. It was his baby, his pride and joy, and it was a huge personal success.

And now here was this man Dee Hock talking about all the failures of the BankAmericard program – and talking about the licensees' right to self-governance. Self-governance! The nerve! In Larkin's eyes, Hock was a small-bore upstart come to banking from the bottom of the financial world: a finance company. And yet here he was, full of high-flown rhetoric and pious principles, and talking about taking control of Ken Larkin's baby. Dee droned on, and finally the usually quiet, dignified Larkin had heard all he could stomach.

"Ken rose bolt upright in his chair," Hock wrote. "His face grew red. His neck swelled. Veins in his forehead stood out. His anger fed on itself as he bellowed, *'We own the *#~*'d system! We invented the system! We produce 40 percent of the system volume! *##d if we will be pushed around!'"*

For a long moment, everyone in the room sat in stunned silence. Then Larkin composed himself and with great dignity returned to business. He promised the group that the BofA would give careful consideration to their recommendations – and then Larkin ushered them out the door. The meeting was over.

Hock and his colleagues left in shock. They worried that their entire effort was now doomed. And they suspected that the BofA had been acting in bad faith all along. "It seemed as though the bank had little understanding, appreciation, or sympathy for what was being attempted," Hock wrote. "Were they merely creating a facade of cooperation, waiting to see what benefit might accrue while looking for an opportunity to put the upstarts in their place?"

So at this point, in mid-1969, the future of the entire BankAmericard program was ensnared in a fascinating – and potentially fatal – clash of egos and perspectives. The group viewed Larkin and the BofA as the failed stewards of the BankAmericard venture. The bank may have meant well, and it had pioneered the bank card industry in America, but then Larkin and the bank had run into a wall and the whole program was awash in red ink. In their minds, Larkin and his colleagues were victims of their own shortsighted, hierarchical, tradition-bound ways. Larkin, on the other hand, viewed Hock as a pompous, presumptuous rabble-rouser, hell-bent on storming the gates of the largest bank in the world and heisting one its most precious assets.

A deep cultural divide also separated the two men. Dee was small-town Utah, and he never seemed comfortable around big city bankers. Too often, Hock felt, they were the sons and daughters of privilege, coming from the best schools and eased into the upper echelons of banking almost as a birthright, not as a testament to any talent or fondness for hard work. Dee preferred scrappers with real world experience and proven fire in the belly.

Ken Larkin, on the other hand, typified the BofA man: he was a gentleman banker, well-educated, self-confident, urbane. In the mold of A.P. Giannini, he saw banking as a business, yes, but also as a social good and a higher calling. Larkin thought Dee had a monster chip on his shoulder and he suspected that what really drove Hock was his own personal ambition – and that spelled trouble for the Bank of America. "Dee Hock came to the fore as the head of the credit card section of a small bank in Seattle," Larkin said. "He was making about $16,000 a year. He left Visa at $400,000 a year. Naturally, he saw the Bank of America as a rival power base."

Personal feelings aside, Ken Larkin now faced a difficult dilemma. Clearly, the licensees were angry. And, just as clearly, the BankAmericard program was in crisis. But that did not mean that Hock's plan for self-governance was the right solution. Larkin suspected that if Hock had his way, *he* would take over as the chief architect of the BankAmericard program. Was that what was best for the card? Or for the interests of the Bank of America?

With so much at stake, Larkin and the top management of the Bank of America took their time weighing their options. In fact, for a full month they left Hock and his cronies to twist in the wind.

Finally, in a frosty letter to Hock, Larkin delivered their verdict. While the Bank of America had "sympathy" for the avowed aims of Hock and his committee, the bank would agree to the creation of a new partnership only on several conditions.

First, in light of the huge investment the bank had made to create and sustain the BankAmericard, and in light of the fact that the BofA represented 40 percent of the card's total sales volume, the bank insisted it have 40 percent of the seats on any new board of directors. Second, the bank insisted that it remain as the managing

Ken Larkin was one of the chief architects of the BankAmericard program.

partner of the new association for the next five years. Third, for those five years the BofA would retain ownership and complete control of all trademarks and would remain the exclusive licensing agent for the BankAmericard. The tone of the letter was this: These are our terms, Mr. Hock. Take them or leave them.

Dee was disgusted. He saw the BofA's position for what it was: a complete rejection of his committee's demand for an equitable sharing of power, resources, and revenues. The BofA's position was, in fact, a direct threat to everything he and his team had envisioned and set into motion. If the bank's position stood, Hock might as well fold up his tent and go home. That, in fact, was his first inclination. According to Jack Dillon, he and Dee got the news while they were in transit at Chicago's O'Hare Airport; Larkin's letter was read to them over the phone.

"He was going to quit, on the spot," Dillon recalled. "I understood how he felt. I was all for the idea of the bank trying to protect itself," Dillon said. "But not the way Larkin's letter was written. It was unreasonable."

Dillon himself was now caught in a bind. He had worked at the BofA for 30 years, and he was now running the credit card division under Ken Larkin. On the other hand, Dillon had been working closely with Dee for more than a year and he supported his plans for self-governance. That gave him divided loyalties.

"I was on the hot seat," Dillon explained. "I had taken a firm stand against the bank, in favor of keeping the momentum going on Hock's project. Because I thought that would be ultimately the best course for the Bank of America. The big East Coast and Midwest banks, like Citibank in New York and First Chicago, didn't want to issue a card with the name BankAmericard on it. The way I saw it, if the BofA threw out Hock's idea, Dee would have start-

ed it without them. Then there would be no protection at all for the bank."

From this unique position, Dillon now moved into action on two fronts. First, he tried to buck up Dee, by threatening him. "If you and the others quit now, I'll write a minority report criticizing you. I know the bank is wrong in this, but that's no reason to quit," Dillon told Dee. Dillon then lobbied inside the bank. He and Ken Larkin were good friends, and they had a long chat about the situation. Dillon also met with Sam Stewart, the highly respected head of the BofA's legal department and vice chairman of the board. Dillon and Stewart found common ground on one crucial point: the BankAmericard program was in a terrible mess and they needed a strong central organization to fix it. Dillon urged Stewart not to totally shut the door on Dee Hock and his initiative.

Dee had other reasons to be dispirited. Since Sausalito, he and his staff had been immersed in the monumental effort of trying to create a corporate structure capable of carrying forward their ideas and vision. They had been working with lawyers, trying to find a strong legal framework for the unique partnership they envisioned. They had been working with accountants, trying to find a workable financial formula that would allow all the licensee banks, large or small, to join the partnership on an equitable footing. Dee and his team had also been busy drafting operating guidelines and regulations that would apply to present and future banks joining their partnership.

These tasks were enormous – and frustrating. To cover the network of some 2,700 BankAmericard licensees and affiliate banks, Hock's lawyers had to examine federal interstate banking laws and the relevant laws in every state in the union. They also had to write a charter, bylaws, and a constitution.

The legal formalities cut to the core of one of

Dee's most difficult challenges: creating a framework in which competition and cooperation could coexist. Several of the BankAmericard licensees were proud and fierce competitors. If they joined the new partnership, these competitors would be issuing similar products and competing with each other on price and additional features and functions on their cards. At the same time, they would sit at the same board meetings and share information about the card industry. In sum, Dee would be asking competing banks to work together and cooperate for a larger common good. This was a tough notion to sell. Would Ford cooperate with General Motors? Even many of Dee's closest supporters had their doubts.

Time, moreover, was critical. There was now increasing competition and turmoil in the U.S. credit card market. Through consolidation, MasterCard now encompassed a large number of banks in California and on the East Coast. In fact, MasterCard was now leading the bank card market, and the market itself was growing. In 1969 more than 1,200 banks were offering credit cards, and those cards had generated more than $2.5 billion in outstanding loans. American Express, meanwhile, was consolidating its hold on the lucrative "travel and entertainment" charge card market. So Dee and his team had to move quickly or else all their dreaming and planning would go for naught.

Dee refused to see that happen. He also refused to accept Ken Larkin's letter as the end of the story with the BofA. In order to mobilize support, Dee convened an emergency session of his executive committee. In Dee's mind, this was it: his committee had to stand up to the BofA and press for independence. If he failed to earn enough support for that stand, Dee would have no choice but to quit and go back to Seattle. End of story.

The committee gathered, and at the appointed moment, Dee stood before his troops and framed the situation to them in a very shrewd way. This was not a business problem, he said, this was a matter of *fundamental principle.* Would they sacrifice their principles and bow to the will of the Bank of America? Dee gave an impassioned speech, even quoting a letter Thomas Paine had written in the throes of the American Revolution: "As to you, sir, history will be hard put to decide whether you abandoned principle, or ever had any."

Dee also unfurled another gambit. In the middle of the meeting, he stepped away and placed a call to Ken Larkin. Ken, our committee is in session, Dee said. Before making a decision, could we go over the bank's position point by point, just to make sure there's no misunderstanding? He and Larkin then went over Larkin's letter, line by line. Finally, Hock told Larkin he wanted to go back to his committee and accurately report back the upshot of their conversation.

"Ken, let me repeat the position of the Bank of America so that I can get it down precisely." Then Dee proceeded aloud, while taking notes: "Ken Larkin, Senior Vice President of the Bank of America, said, 'The Bank of America will not agree to an organization equitably owned by all banks – unless – it – can – unilaterally – control – management – for...'"

Larkin abruptly interrupted: "What are you doing?"

Dee continued this theatrical ploy until Larkin was reduced to a long, deafening silence. "All right," Larkin said. "Maybe you should come to San Francisco and meet with Sam Stewart."

A reprieve! A glimmer of hope! Dee was pleased. With his artful gambit, he had managed to gain a little room for maneuver. The door was not definitively closed. Now he could go over Larkin's head at the bank and renew the battle. Dee had given quite a performance and it had paid off – for a time. Machiavelli would have been impressed, not to mention P.T. Barnum.

Ken Larkin certainly was impressed. As much as Dee annoyed him, Larkin had to admit that Dee had moxie. Larkin was further impressed by what Hock pulled off next. Dee came to San Francisco and made his case directly to Sam Stewart. Again, he was clever and persuasive. At the end of their tête-à-tête, Stewart asked Dee to put into writing his specific ideas for creating a new association of licensees.

Dee came away with a deep respect for Sam Stewart. "I think Sam finally understood how successful this thing could be if the Bank of America took the lead and became a dues-paying member," Dee said in an interview. "He was a real statesman and became a dear friend."

As promised, Dee outlined his plan in a letter to Stewart, emphasizing why he felt it would serve the long-term interests of the Bank of America. Dee's argument went like this: if the BofA controlled the management of the new partnership, it would be doomed to fail. The new organization would have no heart, no spirit, because the new member-owners would not have the same motivation to make the new venture a success. Dee felt that no single bank should control the new partnership; that would violate the basic ideals and principles that made the venture so unique in the first place. In harder business terms, Dee argued that the new BankAmericard organization, with many more banks participating as member-owners, would expand the card market way beyond anything the Bank of America could imagine. The bank would thus earn far more from its share of the expanded market than it ever could from royalties in the present market. In other words, Dee argued, under his plan, everyone would win, everyone would prosper, first and foremost the Bank of America.

Dee's letter was an impassioned, tightly argued plea, and it generated serious reflection at the BofA. Two weeks later, Sam Stewart called Dee in for another meeting at BofA headquarters. This was the moment, and Dee knew it: the final verdict was at hand. Stewart sat him down and came right to the point. "We've thought very carefully about what you said and have come to the conclusion that, in the main, it is right," Stewart told him. "There are many things to be better understood and some to be negotiated, but you'll have our full support in the attempt to form a new organization and our good faith in negotiating terms and conditions for transfer of ownership."

Transfer of ownership.

It took a moment for those words to sink in. Transfer of ownership. Independence. *Victory.* Dee had done it. He and his little band of rebels had stormed the gates of the mighty Bank of America and liberated the BankAmericard. *Vive La Révolution!*

For the Bank of America and for the credit card industry, this was a historic decision. And the reasons behind it remain the subject of disagreement right to this day. Ken Larkin insists that the BofA made this huge decision willingly. The BofA's network of licensing agreements, Larkin explained, had been a crazy patchwork of individualized deals. Many of the deals were unprofitable, and most were a nightmare to manage. By turning over the reins to a new organization Dee would soon create, National BankAmericard Inc. (NBI), the Bank of America was able, in effect, to unload many of its problems while still maintaining a healthy and growing revenue stream for itself.

"The Bank of America prospered in two ways," Larkin explained. "First, from the royalties we received for ceding the brand. And then we paid lower fees to NBI than the other banks. Over the years, I'd say that what NBI, and then Visa, paid us amounted to millions and millions of dollars."

Dee Hock disagrees. In his view, the rising financial losses – and the rising anger – of the licensees were just too steep to maintain the status quo. The licensees wanted independence and there was just no way to stop them, provided there was a viable alternative plan that everyone could embrace. When Dee put that plan on the table, the Bank of America was pinned into a corner. "They didn't give it up voluntarily," Dee said in an interview. "Later they even tried to gerrymander the management of the organization."

Whatever the reasons behind it, the BofA decision cleared the way for Dee Hock – and a new ally he had at his side: Sam Stewart. In February of 1970, he and Stewart invited a dozen top American bankers to a meeting in New York. These were CEOs and other key decision-makers from licensee banks, many of whom served together on elite committees of the American Bankers Association. Dee and Stewart wanted to enlist their support for the creation of a new self-governing partnership for the BankAmericard program, an alliance that they both felt could transform the credit card system.

In front of this august group, Dee outlined his case and gave each CEO a large packet of information with the specifics of his proposal. His hope was that they would not only endorse the idea, but also enlist the support of other banks in their regions. Ultimately, to make the venture work, they wanted to bring 200 card-issuing banks and nearly 2,500 sub-licensees into the fold. If they could get two-thirds of those banks to join, the venture would become operational. If not, they were prepared to abandon the effort. The meeting went well, and the CEOs took their packets back home for careful evaluation.

A month later, the group met in Chicago and there was intense questioning about the details of the venture. There was also a wrinkle: many of the banks said they would join the new organization – provided Dee would agree to lead it. Dee, as usual,

was conflicted. A part of him wanted to return to his settled life in the Pacific Northwest. On the other hand, he was eager to bring his grand dream into being. Finally, he agreed to take the job – but only for three years. In any case, the truth was clear: Dee was now the anointed leader of the revolution.

Dee and a small team now set out to do the impossible: win the support of 2,700 banks. They had to meet with each bank, convince them to surrender their BankAmericard licenses, and sign them on as charter members of the new organization. If they got the necessary numbers, Dee would immediately convene a meeting of the new member-owners and have them elect a board of directors. In terms of logistics alone, meeting with 2,700 banks was a dizzying task, never mind convincing them all to sign on. A reasonable time frame for the whole operation would have been nine months. Dee being Dee, he set his deadline at just 90 days.

Dee knew there was only one way to make this phase work: set hard and fast rules from the outset, and insist that the rules apply equally to everyone. For instance, every bank electing to join the new organization as a member-owner would sign an identical agreement. All member-owners would have voting rights, but voting would be weighted. Each charter member would have one vote for every $1,000 of BankAmericard sales volume that bank recorded the preceding year. Service fees would also be weighted. Those would be one-quarter of one percent of that same sales volume. As Dee put it, "taxation and representation would be linked."

Under Dee's formula, the big banks would have more say, but they would also pay more of the freight. However, there would be strong measures of protection for smaller banks, such as a rule that no bank could have more than one director on the board. Also, there were to be different types of directors. There would be board members elected by their own regions, plus five members elected at large. To protect the interests of the banks with the smallest BankAmericard programs, they would always be allowed to have one of their own serve on the board.

For three months, Dee and his team worked feverishly, talking with every bank, addressing every concern. By mid-1970, it was done. All the franchisees, without exception, had decided to join the new venture. The revolution was on. The speed of it was dazzling. Just two years before, Dee had taken the reins back at that tumultuous meeting in Columbus, Ohio, and now he was leading the BankAmericard licensees into an exciting new era in the evolution of consumer credit and plastic money.

From here, the process moved smoothly. Dee announced the formal creation of National BankAmericard Inc., NBI. This was a non-stock, member-owned company, incorporated in Delaware and operating on a not-for-profit basis. The ideals and principles that Dee and his colleagues had adopted in Sausalito were enshrined in the constitution. The new organization would be run as a true partnership, with equitable power-sharing, democratic procedures, and full financial transparency. There were 243 charter members, most of them BofA licensees. But NBI would now be open to all qualifying banks who wanted to join.

NBI was to have several missions. One, of course, was to maximize profits for its member banks and affiliated merchants. Another was to expand credit and services to millions of bank card customers. But Dee also had a larger mission for NBI: from the outset, he wanted it to be a model of what an enlightened organization should be. A model of leadership and vision. A model of efficiency and innovation. A model of how competition and cooperation can work together, for everyone's mutual gain.

In this spirit, Dee was eager to properly compensate the Bank of America and soothe its wounded pride. In exchange for relinquishing exclusive rights to the BankAmericard trademark, the Bank of America demanded $5 million. Dee counter-offered $7 million – provided NBI could spread out the payments. Done and done. Dee also worked out a formula by which the BofA would have five seats on the board for the first years, a number that would then steadily decrease to one. That, too, the BofA found acceptable. The BofA did, however, retain control of all BankAmericard operations abroad – for a time.

On July 9, 1970, Dee Hock convened the first meeting of the new board of directors. Sam Stewart was elected chairman of the board. Dee was named president and given a three-year contract, at $44,000 a year. And Ken Larkin? The battle over, Larkin was gracious in defeat. He had earned himself a seat on the new board and he had forged a certain grudging respect for the wily Mr. Hock. The two men would work together for the next decade and more, and though the term "friends" might not always apply, both men would play key roles as NBI grew into Visa, the global giant we know today.

"In the beginning, Dee and I were rivals," Larkin recalled during a chat in 1999. "Philosophically, we were miles apart, but I admired him and his Machiavellian ways.... People often say that Dee Hock was a visionary, and in his domain he certainly was. He saw a potential for bank cards that many others failed to grasp early on. And he certainly was fascinating to watch in meetings!"

What Dee accomplished, and how fast he did so, are both remarkable. In the early days of the BankAmericard crisis, he had perceived a unique opportunity. An opportunity to create a new organization that he believed could grow into the world's premier system for handling digital money. To pursue that opportunity, Dee had forged a grand vision and a set of ideals and guiding principles. His challenges were immense, but with a brilliant mix of persuasion and raw determination, Dee somehow managed to wrest control of the BankAmericard from the BofA – and he even managed to make them allies in his new venture. All this in the space of just two years.

Dee looks back on this phase of the story with pride and a sense of amazement. "I had absolutely no credentials to do any of this," he said, relaxing in his office. "You have to remember, I was 38 when I got into all this and only 40 when I became president of NBI. We came up with a radical idea, a whole new concept of ownership, and we convinced people to join us and make it work. I sit here today and say, 'How the hell did I do all this?'"

Yes, it was a radical idea, and at this stage no one, not even Dee, could fully imagine the power of that idea or what it would immediately set into motion.

LIFE
A political fringe turns to terrorism
THE BOMB RADICALS
BANKAMERICARD
master charge
The U.S. Takes Off on Credit Cards
MARCH 27 • 1970 • 50¢

Taking Off

Charter members. A board of directors. And that name: National BankAmericard Incorporated. These sound strong and impressive, but at this juncture Dee Hock's venture was still only a fragile start-up, a grand idea inside an almost hollow shell. He had no staff, no office, and no experience in creating a company from scratch. But Dee had something more important: zeal.

To start his new venture, Dee convinced the Bank of America to rent NBI some office space in their former, old brick headquarters on Montgomery Street in San Francisco's financial district. The BofA gave him what they felt his fledgling operation deserved: two rooms that were so tiny and cramped you practically needed a shoehorn to get in the door. In banking terms, this was the garage. And the layout was anything but pleasant: to go to the bathroom down the hall you had to walk right past Dee's personal office, and that was not an inviting prospect. As one old Visa hand, Bennett Katz, recalled, "We were working in very tight quarters."

There were other constrictions as well. After chafing for so many years in other people's companies, from day one Dee appeared determined to do everything his way. He immediately did away with traditional office hierarchy and rigidities. Job descriptions he left purposefully vague; he expected everyone on his team to do whatever needed to be done, days, nights, or weekends. He also refused to recruit by the book. Dee, for instance, distrusted MBAs – he judged people on character and performance, not on academic credentials – and he subjected every prospective employee to a hiring interview that was grueling and often intimidating.

Bob Miller was one of Dee's first recruits. In August of 1970, when Dee was just getting started, Bob was working at the National Bank of Commerce in Seattle, where he had earlier worked with Dee in card operations. "One day I got a call. It was Dee in San Francisco," Miller recalled. "'Bob, how would you like to come down here? I can't pay you much. And no benefits.' Most people wouldn't take an offer like that. But I thought it would be fun. And a challenge."

According to Bob, he knew the basics of banking and he knew all the elements of putting out a publication: writing, editing, layout, proofreading, and typesetting, even distribution. But he was by no means a specialist in credit cards. But that didn't stop Dee. Bob had exactly what Dee wanted: he was a hard worker, a self-starter, and an able jack-of-all-trades.

Miller arrived in San Francisco with few preconceived ideas, but Dee's operation and management style still came as a bit of a shock. "There was no form, no structure. Our facilities were poor and money was tight," Miller recalled. He was hired to work in marketing, but right away he was doing everything from designing business cards and letterheads to organizing a filing system and learning the complexities of BIN, the Bank Identification Number that appears on every card. "Every day was something different," Miller recalled. "Something interesting. Challenging. And that was part of the excitement. I put 150 percent of myself into the work and so did everyone else."

And then there was Dee.

"This was a moving train and Dee wanted only one thing: results," Miller said. "Right away he had problems with some of the staff. His style was so idiosyncratic. He didn't value social things. What he valued was *purpose.*"

Ron Schmidt came aboard a few months later, in January of 1971. Ron was a quiet, industrious, self-effacing man, and he came to NBI with excellent credentials. He had studied aeronautical engineering and business in college, and he had gone on to earn an MBA. After graduate school, Ron looked for a career that would combine high technology and finance. For a time he worked for the aerospace giant McDonnell Douglas, and then he did a stint in corporate planning at Kaiser Industries, a leading holding company and conglomerate in California. Ron was recruited to Visa by Chuck Hamel, Dee's chief financial officer and himself a Harvard MBA.

Ron started out doing statistical research on the member banks, but he soon was handling chores in marketing and looking into the problems of interchange fees. It was an apprenticeship on the fly. Each day was exciting, and you never knew what you'd do next. But this was always clear: you'd better not fail – or there would be hell to pay. "Everything was results-oriented," Ron recalled. "Dee made us take ownership of whatever we did and be accountable."

But that was only one side of the story. Yes, Dee did away with traditional corporate rigidities, but he replaced them with his own rigidities. Dee, for instance, insisted that memos be no more than one page. Likewise, he would not tolerate a messy desk. If you left papers out overnight, you'd hear about it the next day. Even during the day, he wouldn't tolerate a mess. As Dee liked to put it, "Cluttered desk, cluttered mind." Once Ron was doing a report, on an urgent basis, and as he typed away he had papers strewn around his desk. Dee did not approve and scolded him on the spot. Other times it was worse.

"You're stupid, Ron," Dee once started in, Ron recalled. "It's not enough to work hard. Donkeys work hard. You gotta work smart."

Dee also loved to preach. For every occasion, he had his little maxim, and in spirit they recalled the homilies his Mormon parents had used at home when Dee was just a boy. These were the rules of business according to Chairman Dee. "Dee used to tell us there were four elements of management," Ron recalled. "Manage yourself. Manage your boss. Manage your peers. And manage your subordinates." Dee had another favorite maxim: "Managers aren't leaders." And Dee made it clear which he preferred: leaders. Provided they did everything his way.

The more Dee preached, the more confused – and sometimes amused – his flock became. The man was a walking contradiction. An enigma. In his memoir, for instance, Dee more than once expressed contempt for the military, the ultimate "command and control" hierarchy. Yet, in the minds of many of his staffers, Dee treated them exactly the way a drill sergeant would: first he set out to break them and then to remold them into a competent, hard-driving team, executing his orders to the letter. Likewise, Dee loved to urge his flock to seize the initiative and use their own ingenuity; in practice, though, he was often an obsessive micro-manager. In the early days, no important letter left the office without Dee's stamp of approval, no detail escaped his scrutiny.

"It was an emotional roller coaster," Ron Schmidt recalled. "You never knew where you stood with Dee. And you could never win an argument with him. He was outspoken, and so aggressive, and yet he was someone you could totally respect. I've never had my adrenaline flowing as I did with Dee."

Adrenaline wasn't the only thing that flowed around Dee; there was plenty of discontent as well. In fact, late in the first year of NBI's existence, Dee was faced with a covert palace revolt. Several of his

When Dee created NBI, he
started out with a two-room office
in the old BofA building in
San Francisco's financial district.

senior officers, all in their fifties, and none with banking experience, resented Dee and his irksome managerial style and decided they could run the company better than he could. They began to whisper and plot, determined to see Dee ousted, and no doubt hoping one of them would be anointed in his place.

One day, in the midst of this Shakespearean-style intrigue, a new recruit came waltzing in the door. His name was Charles Russell, but he preferred to be called plain old Chuck. Russell was a down-home, plain-talking, easy-going guy with his feet planted firmly on the ground. And he came to NBI with a wealth of practical experience in managing credit card programs.

Chuck was by no means a traditional banker. He had been born into a musical family, and by the age of 13 he was working as a professional trombone player. At 18, he was tooting his horn in a popular burlesque house in Pittsburgh. After studying business at the University of Pittsburgh, Chuck did a stint in the U.S. Army. Then, more by happenstance than design, Chuck landed in banking. His first job was with People's First National Bank, which later became the Pittsburgh National Bank.

Chuck got involved with bank cards in their earliest days. His bank was a founding member of the Interbank card system, and Chuck quickly became a specialist in the new plastic money. In 1969 he moved to Winston-Salem, North Carolina, to start a MasterCard program for the Wachovia National Bank & Trust. Soon, though, Chuck found himself caught in the middle of an unpleasant power struggle at the bank, and Chuck's side lost. He was referred to Dee by an NBI director, and Dee offered Chuck a job as a vice president for operations. Chuck leapt at the chance, hoping that a start-up company would have less politics and intrigue.

Fat chance. During one of his first days on the job at NBI, one of the old-guard bankers took Chuck aside. "See that crazy little man over there?" he said, pointing to Dee. "We are all in agreement that he has to go. And we're about to pull the trigger."

They invited Chuck to join their little plot, but Chuck said, "No thanks." Been there, done that, got burned in the process. But Chuck assured the conspirator he'd keep his lips sealed. The political intrigue turned Chuck's stomach, and in his first days on the job he wanted to turn right around and walk out. "I walked into a buzz saw," he recalled in an interview. "A coup d'état in the making. And I wanted no part of it."

Russell contacted his recruiting agent to see what other jobs might be available. The agent put the word out and, as fate would have it, a member of NBI's board of directors heard Chuck was back in the job market. The director called Dee: "What's going on over there? Why's Chuck unhappy?"

Dee had a pretty good idea. Several weeks before, a close friend had tipped him off about the covert palace revolt. "Dee," he told him, "I just want to warn you that you have a knife in your back and you might not feel it yet." Dee already had his own suspicions and was digging into the situation. When he learned Chuck was looking for a job, and knowing about Chuck's earlier experience with internal politics, he put two and two together.

Dee then moved in typical Dee fashion. According to Dee, he called Chuck into his office and told him he had heard he was looking for another job. He asked for no explanation, but he suggested that Chuck be patient for a few months, for he was not as uninformed as Chuck might think. "Within the week, the leader of the coup was given an opportunity to resign," Dee recalled. "A few months later, the second member of the plotters was given the same opportunity and within a year, the last of the bunch. All were allowed to leave with their reputations intact."

The political crisis over, Chuck Russell decided to stay at NBI and he forged a good working relationship with Dee. There was no great warmth between them, but there was mutual respect. As a result, Chuck was one of the few chieftains at Visa who never faced Dee's public wrath. "He didn't dare," Chuck recalled. "He knew how I'd respond."

If ever Dee Hock had his mirror opposite, Chuck Russell was it. Dee was the grand thinker, the visionary, the fiery preacher given to temper tantrums and unfathomable flights of rhetorical fancy. Chuck was unflappable and self-effacing, and the flights he liked to take were in his own private plane. Chuck was a skilled pilot and he was a man who not only loved to ride his Harley; he could take it apart, clean every piece, and then reassemble it, bolt by bolt – and get it right. As opposite as they were, Dee and Chuck were also complementary. If you had a Dee at the helm, you needed a Chuck behind him, to make the grand dreams into a working reality – and to pick up any broken pieces along the way. Dee intimidated; Chuck calmed. Dee Hock inspired achievement and innovation; Chuck Russell inspired confidence.

"When I want vision, I go to Dee," Ken Larkin often said. "When I want something done, I go to Chuck."

Yes, they were an odd couple, but together Dee and Chuck got results. For the next 15 years, they worked in tandem, building Visa and turning it into the largest payments system in the world. Later, when Dee left Visa, Chuck would be the natural choice to take over the reins.

There was another early recruit who enjoyed a comparable stature. His name was Bennett Katz, and the role he played was vital to the creation and growth of Visa as we know it today. Bennett was pure New York: street-smart, articulate, charming, and able to tiptoe through any political crisis without getting so much as a smudge on his loafers or mussing a single hair on his elegantly coiffed head. Bennett was smoooooooth. Bennett was classy. He might have made a first-rate U.S. ambassador – but Bennett would never work for an ambassador's pay. By temperament and ambition, there was only one

Chuck Russell was one of Dee's earliest recruits and a pillar of NBI's growth into Visa.

career for Bennett: the law. And we're not talking public defender; we're talking corporate counsel.

Bennett went to Hobart College and then to the prestigious law school of the University of Chicago. As a youth, he dreamed of becoming a criminal lawyer. In law school, though, he got married, and after graduation, when many of his colleagues were headed for America's courtrooms, Bennett headed for the boardroom, taking a job with a financial services company. Bennett served three years as general counsel to the Home Credit Company in Worcester, Massachusetts, and then he moved to where his heart was: California. For five years he served as chief counsel for Avco Financial Services in Newport Beach. Bennett was recruited to NBI by the then general counsel James Ravelin, and he joined the company on December 1, 1970, as general counsel. He had a daunting task in front of him.

Bennett Katz, chief counsel, helped craft NBI's unique partnership framework.

"The Bank of America had turned over all the existing licensees to us, and we had to develop an interchange system for them," Bennett recalled in an interview. "We also had to develop a system for merchant servicing. And we faced dangers in the marketplace: MasterCard at the time was a much bigger operation than we were. So we had all sorts of problems to solve. Urgently. Frankly, it was a real mess."

For help, Bennett brought in a brilliant right hand: Dave Wagman. Bennett had recruited Wagman to Avco, and the two men had worked well together. Bennett conceptualized; Dave executed. Dave would study Bennett's plans, flesh out the legal issues, draft the necessary contracts, agreements, and other legal papers, and handle all the details. Bennett and Wagman took this working relationship and made it work at Visa – for 30 years.

"We were a team," Wagman recalled in an interview. "And we had a huge job to do. Remember, back in the beginning, we had no computers in the credit card business. It was a manual system. Fortunately, our directors had infinite patience. Their card programs were hemorrhaging dollars at a frightening rate."

In the early days, like everyone else, Wagman did all sorts of odd jobs at NBI. He wrote the legal language for the early sales drafts. He wrote the regulations for clearing transactions. He set down the general rules for operating standards and fees, and for resolving disputes. "Everything had to be done from scratch," Wagman recalled. "There were no statutory mechanisms for this industry. To make everything work, we had to go state-by-state and examine each state's regulations on consumer lending."

What made it all work?

In Bennett Katz's view, two elements were absolutely key: the brilliance of the original conception for NBI and the brilliance of Dee Hock. "Visa as a corporation is a joint venture of 22,000 banks. Visa is the hub; the spokes are the banks. Also, Visa was formed as a for-profit, non-assessable corporation, meaning that if there are problems, you can't call on your partners for more money. Visa doesn't have a life of its own. In fact, it's the largest joint venture in the world today."

In 1970, MasterCard was present in 49 states and the BankAmericard was present in only 42. But Bennett believed that MasterCard had some structural disadvantages that worked in NBI's favor. For one thing, MasterCard at that time was run by top managers who were not businessmen; they were retired bankers. Dee's management team, by contrast, was lean, aggressive, and entrpreneurial. "Our management team made decisions much faster than MasterCard's," Bennett explained. "Dee was driving the industry. They followed."

This was where Dee Hock's brilliance and personality really paid off, quirks and all. "Dee had a vision, which I agreed with," Bennett said. "He was tough, which you needed in a start-up. Dee aggravated me, and I'm not easy to aggravate. But I'll tell you this. He pushed you to the nth degree, and he had zero tolerance for mistakes. But Dee never put politics above getting the job done. And he always got results. We had excellent execution, with very few failures. You simply couldn't have bad execution under Dee Hock. He wouldn't allow it."

Bennett Katz's assessment is echoed by almost all the old Visa hands. "Visa was never a place where mediocre people could survive," explained Fran Schall, who joined Visa in 1975. "From the beginning, Visa was run like a small entrepreneurial venture. There was less structure, less hierarchy, and fewer confinements than most companies. For many of us, this was liberating. You could do your own thing. You could almost design your own job description. And if you were flexible enough mentally, you could be whatever you wanted to be."

In Fran's view, all the preaching, all the barking, and all the relentless demands for excellence – and nothing but – were understandable: Dee Hock was a man with a mission and he wanted every member of his team fully enlisted in his cause. And she and Bennett Katz, Dave Wagman, Ron Schmidt, and Bob Miller were among the many who did enlist, heart and soul.

"The pay was adequate, not abundant. The working conditions were acceptable but not comfortable," Fran said of the early years. "But when Dee hired you, he convinced you that here was an adventure that you couldn't get anywhere else."

For Dee, the dimensions of his mission were enormous – and he was passionate about instilling that mission in his staff. "We were going to change the way people conducted their lives and their businesses," Fran explained. "Dee was seeking to build a new system of commerce. Visa was to be a form of identification and a guaranteed form of payment that everyone would trust, buyer and seller. He wanted to change life itself. And he believed in the greater good of what he created."

Dee the preacher. Dee the zealot. Dee the missionary, believing he could change the world with a little strip of plastic. Grandiose as it sounded, Dee made progress much faster than anyone expected, Dee included. In 1970, the year Dee took over the BankAmericard operation, there were 23.7 million cardholders in America, and they charged a total of some $2.7 billion on their BankAmericards. By the following year, Dee and his team had helped their member banks weed out some four million bad risk cardholders from the system, but total charge volume jumped to $3.7 billion for the year. Over the next three years, total charge volume more than doubled and reached more than $7.7 billion.

Dee was also making huge gains in fulfilling his dreams of gaining universal acceptance for the card. In 1970, there were some 680,000 American merchants accepting the BankAmericard. By 1974, the number had jumped to 1,049,000. And those trends would soon begin to accelerate.

By the mid-1970s, the little card was really starting to fly, and how fast it climbed, and how high it flew still amaze old Visa hands like Dave Wagman. "Sometimes I can hardly believe it," Wagman said in 1999. "This year our sales volume will reach something like $1.7 trillion dollars. *Trillion.* Incredible. We started with a blank page and built a company. A giant company."

While this book focuses on the decision-makers inside Visa, the unsung heroes of the Visa story are the men and women of Visa's member banks and financial institutions. They invested enormous time, energy, and money in the Visa concept and tools, and their success in their own markets paved the way for the larger success of Visa. Visa members number in the thousands, and each of them has his or her own portion of the Visa story to tell. If they are not mentioned here by name, this book is nonetheless dedicated to their vision and entrepreneurial spirit.

Even Dee was amazed at how quickly NBI took off. Later, as was his bent, he stepped back and took time to ruminate. The cause of NBI's initial success, he decided, did not reside in his own powers of persuasion or any brilliance of leadership. Rather, it was that in his own early travails in the workplace he had come to understand a fundamental truth:

Great leaders don't rule; they inspire.

"Ordinary people can consistently do extraordinary things – if they have the freedom and motivation to do so," Dee explained. "Healthy organizations induce behavior. Unhealthy organizations compel it. I believe that induced behavior has infinite constructive power. My approach is to free people, let them do what they want to do. And they love it."

Along with that freedom, though, Dee believes that people need a clear sense of direction – and an equally clear sense of purpose. Dee wanted his people to feel they were part of an important and uplifting mission, a grand design they could dedicate themselves to heart and soul. Naturally, Dee encapsuled his thinking in a guiding maxim:

"Without question, the most abundant, least expensive, most underutilized, and most constantly abused resources in the world are human ingenuity and the human spirit."

Your
BANKAMERICARD
welcome here

Chapter 9

Global Vision, Local Roots

In the first years of NBI's existence, Dee Hock had his hands full. He had to build his staff. He had to computerize the transaction system. He had to develop marketing and advertising campaigns for the BankAmericard, and he had to compete head-on with MasterCard and American Express. The last thing he had time to contemplate was international expansion, but this was the next inevitable step of what Dee had set into motion.

This part of the story really begins back in the days of A.P. Giannini. In 1921, as he was building his system of branches in California, Giannini decided he wanted to give his burgeoning financial empire a foothold in Italy. So he purchased a bank in Naples, Banca dell'Italia Meridionale, and turned it into the Banca d'America e d'Italia, the "Bank of America and Italy," known as BAI for short. Giannini had several aims for BAI. He wanted it to help Italian immigrants in the United States move money back and forth between the two countries. He also wanted to stimulate business and goodwill between America and Italy as both nations emerged from the traumas of World War I.

Giannini's timing was propitious. Italian banks were in turmoil at the time and handling remittances from America was a profitable, though complicated, business. BAI, headquartered first in Rome and then in Milan, stepped into that niche and became an important bridge between the two countries, helping immigrant families and facilitating international business. BAI also did something far more important: it brought Giannini's banking philosophy to Italy. That, in turn, set into motion profound changes in Italian banking.

Ugo Scarpetta, whose father was the first general manager of BAI, saw first-hand the impact of Giannini's philosophy. "At that time, banks in America were certainly not eager to help an immigrant who had just arrived from Sicily and wanted a loan to buy a boat," Ugo explained. "The situation in Italy was not much different. The banks were inclined to loan money to rich people, not the average man. A.P. Giannini, though, believed that it was not only rich people who deserved credit, and BAI operated on the same philosophy." BAI operated like a traditional Italian bank, but it emphasized helping small businesses and Italian families from all levels of Italian society. This strategy worked well for BAI, and for the first 40 years of its existence it maintained a steady, comfortable niche in Italian banking.

Ugo's own life was strongly influenced by A.P. Giannini, starting when he was a boy and his father was managing BAI. "I was born in 1921, the same year BAI was founded," Ugo recalled. "So the names Giannini, Bank of America, and BAI were part of my life from the beginning. I think I was destined to be a banker." Ugo studied economics at Luigi Bocconi University in Milan. After graduation he was intent on going into banking, but there was no question of him joining BAI. "My father was purer than pure. He didn't want his son to join the bank if he was there as general manager," he explained. "So I waited." Ugo finally joined BAI after his father retired in 1949 – the same year Giannini died. "The giant was gone," Ugo recalled. "But his philosophy remained."

Ugo worked in the bank for the next dozen years, learning the business and developing contacts throughout European banking. In 1963, he went to San Francisco to see Giannini's Bank of America in action. The trip was an eye-opener. At one of the main BofA branches in the city, for instance, Ugo was astonished to see the lending

we becoming second-class citizens?'"

Undaunted, Ugo and BAI unveiled another tool that was new to Italy: installment credit. Now Italian consumers could buy furniture, housewares, tools, appliances, and more and pay them off in convenient monthly installments. "This, too, was a revolution in Italy," Ugo recalled, "and for BAI it was an enormous success."

The next obvious step was to issue credit cards, and here BAI became part of a much larger program spearheaded by the Bank of America. Ken Larkin was the linchpin. In the same way he had signed up licensee banks across America, Larkin had signed similar accords with banks in Europe, Canada, Japan, and Latin America. These banks were free to customize the BankAmericard for their home markets, issue it to their customers, and sign up merchants. The processing procedures and handling fees were similar to the U.S. operation, and they all operated under the same umbrella, the BankAmerica Service Corporation.

Larkin chose only top banks in their regions, in order to safeguard and promote the BankAmericard and the image of the Bank of America abroad. His original international licensees were Barclays Bank in the United Kingdom, BAI in Italy, the Canadian Imperial Bank of Commerce in Toronto, the Sumitomo Bank in Japan, Banco de Bilbao in Spain, Banco Pinto Sottomayor in Portugal, Banco Comercial in Mexico, Credit Libanais in Lebanon, BancUnion in Venezuela, Credibanco Colombia, and Banco Credito in Puerto Rico.

Barclays led the parade, launching its "Barclaycard" in 1966. According to several people involved with Barclaycard, the business case at the outset was far from convincing, because the concept had not yet been tested in Europe. Nonetheless, the bank went forward on the conviction that credit cards were the tool of the future. Barclays launched the card with great marketing and operational skill, and its success soon transformed British banking. It also encouraged other European banks to follow their lead, and that helped build the credit card market in Europe. At the time, American Express and Diners Club had a presence in Europe, but few banks were issuing cards.

There were several reasons for Barclays' success. Thanks to its name, Barclaycard right away was perceived as a British product, with local roots and local brand identity. At the same time, it also carried BankAmericard's distinctive blue, white and gold bands, which gave it wide recognition and acceptability in the United States and, later, in the emerging European market. The card also had a strong, media-savvy personality behind it: Richard Dale, the founder and director of the Barclaycard.

"Dickie Dale was a tremendous personality," Ugo Scarpetta explained, and he generated constant publicity for his bank's new credit tool. "His photograph and stories about Barclaycard were in the *Financial Times* on an almost weekly basis. Thanks to Dickie, Barclaycard's success was such that over the years the name became synonymous with credit cards in the United Kingdom, like Hoover was to vacuum cleaners."

Barclays also learned a thing or two from their "American cousins" at the Bank of America. For instance, to overcome the problem of reaching "critical mass," Barclays aggressively signed up cardholders and merchants before the launch date. When they were finally ready to go, Barclays hit the ground running, with one million cardholders and 100,000 merchants accepting the card. To handle the flood of transactions, Dale commandeered an old shoe factory in Northampton and established his technical team there. Such were the dimensions of Barclaycard's success that it soon had a staff of more than 1,000.

Barclays spread the bank card gospel far beyond the United Kingdom. Through its overseas division, Barclays opened card programs in the Caribbean and many other countries that had Barclays subsidiaries. Again, the cards were tailored to fit the needs of the local market. Barclays National Bank of South Africa, for instance, issued two different cards. One was designed to compete with American Express and Diners Club and called for full balances to be paid in 30 days. The other was a "budget account," allowing cardholders to pay off their balances in 6, 12, or even 18 months. This proved to be a particularly attractive feature when Barclays began affiliating itself with major airlines flying in and out of South Africa.

On October 1, 1969, Ugo Scarpetta and BAI entered the fray. They began on a more cautious scale than Barclays, with only 50,000 cardholders and 1,000 merchants. Still, BAI's move once again raised eyebrows in the Italian banking community. "'What's this? Another credit device?' other bankers sniffed," Ugo recalled. "We also started commercial advertising, which was totally alien to Italian banking."

BAI had a catchy slogan for its new card: "La Banca in Tasca," the Bank in Your Pocket. BAI also followed the BofA model and set up various types of licensing agreements with local and regional banks across Italy. "We were giving these banks the tool of a big bank, a product that they could not have developed on their own," Ugo explained. The card program quickly proved to be a resounding success.

"Within two years, we had a network covering Italy, and we had a large number of cardholders and affiliated merchants," Ugo said. "The cooperative venture grew the credit card market and increased the size of the pie for all the banks. Everybody won."

While Ugo was delighted with this success, he was not about to cry it from the rooftops. When other bankers inquired about the card, Ugo played down its success. "My philosophy was to act and not tell," he explained. "Banks would say, 'Wow, your card program must cost a lot. Is it profitable?'"

"'No.'"

"'Oh, it's mostly p.r.?'"

"'Yes,' I'd say. I didn't want to wake the sleeping dog."

From the outset, the new licensees in Europe worked in close cooperation with the Bank of America – and with each other. For instance, when BAI was nearing its launch date for the program, it ran into a nightmarish problem: its supplier was late in delivering the machine necessary to emboss the cards with the individual cardholder's name and account number. BAI urgently contacted Barclays' card staff in Northampton, and they agreed to emboss 50,000 blank cards for BAI on an emergency basis. The finished cards arrived in time for the launch.

This spirit of cooperation also helped grow the European market. In early 1970, Ugo Scarpetta contacted Paolo Cornaro, whose family owned and operated the Corner Banca S.A., based in Lugano, Switzerland. Paolo was so impressed with the benefits of the BankAmericard system that he convinced his father, Vittorio, the founder and chairman of the bank, to launch a card program. Soon it became the bank's most important profit center. Cornaro's bank wound up with 40 percent of the card market in Switzerland, and the extension of the European network meant that customers of Ugo and Dickie Dale could use their cards when they traveled to Switzerland. Again, everybody won.

The Banco de Bilbao, one of Spain's largest, was another important link in the growing system. The bank brought a special flair to marketing the card in Spain, where it was renowned for its innovations. For instance, the bank had opened special

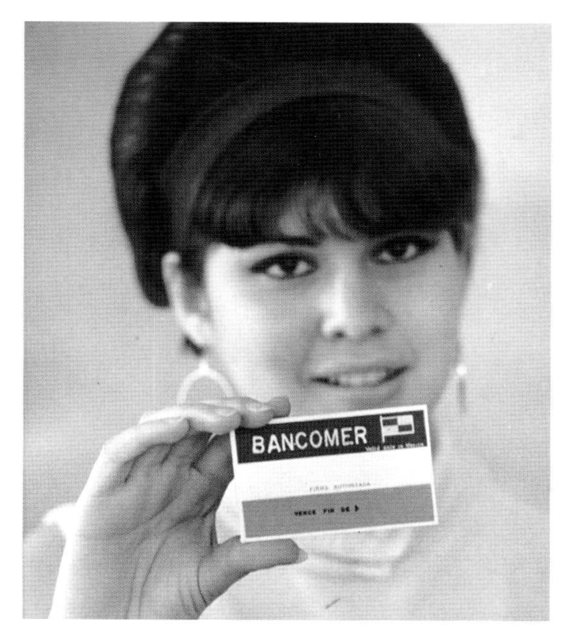

branches that catered only to women. "El banco de la mujer," the venture was called, "The woman's bank." The bank was managed by female officers and all the employees were women, in an effort to give Spanish women a feeling of power and independence when it came to money. As a special touch, the day it opened these branches, the Banco de Bilbao sent 25,000 women customers cellophane-wrapped boxes containing a single long-stemmed red rose. Using this same sort of marketing flair, the bank built a strong credit card network throughout Spain, and it soon became the second largest card program in Europe.

Santiago Zaldumbide, who ran Banco de Bilbao's card program, played a prominent role in the European expansion of the BankAmericard network. He was a witty, courtly, Old World gentleman, with impeccable manners and diplomatic skills, and at meetings of the international licensees, Santiago was often called upon to mediate difficult issues. His diplomacy often smoothed the way for other countries to join the credit card movement.

The Banco Pinto e Sottomayor of Lisbon ran a much smaller card program, but it had a major asset: João Ribeira da Fonseca, a dynamic, entrepreneurial card manager who spoke five languages and had tremendous enthusiasm for credit cards. João came to banking after serving in the military and with Alitalia airlines, and he brought a valuable outsider's perspective to the world of consumer credit. His linguistic ability also made him a natural liaison for the European licensees.

To further their cooperation and coordination, the BofA's international licensees formed regional committees and began meeting quarterly to share their growing expertise and discuss technical and operational problems. Their first meeting was held in London in 1970, the next was in Osaka, Japan. "We were a small club in the beginning," Ugo said, "and over the years we became like a family."

Still, there were serious problems, especially between the BofA card people and the European bankers. The Americans were just not accustomed to doing business the European way. None spoke a foreign language, and most had no experience abroad, beyond overseas stints during World War II. They also had little understanding of European banking practices or culture. "They're regular cowboys," Dickie Dale used to say, his voice dripping with disdain.

This cultural and business divide surfaced in amusing ways during the annual meetings. At the daytime meetings of the bankers, the Americans wore dark suits and ties, like the Europeans, but the nighttime cocktail and dinner parties were a very different story. "In the early days, it must be said that the Europeans, especially the Latin countries, were very formal in their manner, behavior and garments," recalled Paolo Cornaro. "Sometimes at the annual meetings, the chairman would feel compelled to announce the attire for a given event. But the word 'casual' meant little to the Europeans. And when they learned, they had to make an effort to go further than just a jacket and tie, especially the Italians and Spanish. By contrast, out of business hours, Anglo-Saxons in general wore the most fanciful attire, probably as a reaction to having spent eight hours in a business suit. I remember Americans at cocktail parties wearing green pants, fancy striped blazers, yellow polo shirts, and white shoes, while we wore dark blue suits."

Many of the old European hands still tell a revealing story about Ken Larkin, who came to the annual meetings as president of the BankAmerica Service Corporation. Larkin missed the first meeting in London, and a BofA colleague announced that Larkin had "other engagements" – an explanation that left many of the licensees puzzled, because Larkin had been scheduled to deliver a major address to their gathering.

The next year in Osaka, the truth came out, from Larkin's own lips. It turns out that when he checked in at the airport, to go to London, Larkin discovered that he did not have his passport with him. He had asked his secretary to pack his briefcase and there had been a mix-up about the passport. So instead of going on to London, Larkin was forced to turn around and go home. Veteran travelers do not make those kind of mistakes, but as Larkin confessed, apart from his tour with the Navy Seabees, he had never before traveled abroad! The Europeans appreciated Larkin's candor and self-deprecating humor, and he was teased about his passport mishap for years to come.

There were, however, more substantive problems plaguing the international side of the BankAmericard system. The system for transaction clearance and settlement was antiquated, labor-intensive, and very expensive. Everything then was still done with paper. Banks around Europe had to sort sales drafts by hand and send them to the Bank of America for processing. The BofA sent transactions to the merchant's bank for crediting and to the cardholder's bank for debiting. The process, with any necessary currency conversions, could take weeks or even months.

Nor was there a coordinated approach to building the business within Europe. In one revealing episode, Barclays convinced the National Bank of Greece, by far the largest bank in Greece, to become a BankAmericard licensee. At the same time, the Bank of America itself had recruited the Commercial Bank of Greece, the nation's second largest bank. Dick Dale was furious. There was also a problem recruiting banks in Scandinavia, and the problem was political. One Norwegian banker wanted to join the system, but his hands were tied. As he explained it, "How can you expect a socialist

Ugo Scarpetta at a BofA licensee meeting with Mrs. Claire Giannini Hoffman, A.P.'s daughter.

bank to sign a licensing agreement with an American bank, especially one named Bank of America?"

By early 1972, the founding European licensees had come to an informal agreement: something had to be done. The BofA had been an admirable partner in the start-up years, but now the Europeans had to fend for themselves. Their plan was to follow the example of the U.S. licensees and form an independent group similar to NBI. "We made a decision: the time had come to form a European company and we must speak in the name of Europe and not in the name of the Bank of America," said Ugo Scarpetta. But who would take the lead to form a new organization?

The logical choice was Barclays. They were the first licensee and they controlled a full 40 percent of the card business in Europe. Also, Dick Dale was chairman of the European group and was the leading figure in European credit cards. But Dale declined the responsibility. He knew that Barclays would not allow him to devote the time and resources necessary to start a new European organization; to them the present situation was fine.

Ugo Scarpetta and Tony Ellis from Barclays then went to Paris to consult with a French lawyer about the best way to form a European company. Their initial idea was that the BofA would retain control of the trademark; the blue, white and gold logo; and the operating company and procedures. But the licensees would be free to develop the brand in Europe as they saw fit. The lawyer told them the exercise would yield only a meaningless fig leaf; ultimate control would still remain with the Bank of America and everybody would know it. Ugo and his colleagues had to agree. So now the Europeans saw only one solution to their problems: Dee Hock.

"He was the expert," Ugo explained. "We wanted a European corporation; Dee had set up an American corporation. We figured it would not be too difficult for him to translate that into a European scheme." The Europeans had met Dee – he and Ferol had attended the Osaka meeting the year before – and the Europeans had liked what they had seen of him. Now Ugo and his colleagues decided to broach the subject with Dee at their next annual meeting, set for August of 1972 in Stresa, Italy, on the eve of the Olympic Games in Munich, Germany. By tradition, the meetings were hosted by one of the licensees, usually in attractive places. This one was to be organized by Ugo Scarpetta.

Stresa is one of the most charming resort towns in all of Europe. It's located in northwestern Italy, an hour's drive from Milan, and it sits peacefully at the edge of idyllic Lake Maggiore. As a conference venue, Ugo chose the Grand Hotel des Iles

The Grand Hotel des Iles Borromées in Stresa, Italy, was the birthplace of today's Visa International.

Borromées, a dignified, palatial hotel with Belle Epoque grandeur and an enchanting view out to the four Borromean Islands that dot Lake Maggiore. The islands, gardens, and palaces on them belong to the Borromeo family, Italian aristocrats who have owned them since the twelfth century. The Grand Hotel also had a literary pedigree. Ernest Hemingway wrote parts of *A Farewell to Arms* while staying in the hotel. In every respect, the Grand Hotel was an ideal setting for an historic occasion – and that was precisely what Ugo and the Europeans had in mind.

Dee arrived in Stresa with Ferol, and again the couple deeply impressed the Europeans. Dee's demeanor was quiet and dignified, on a par with any bank president in Europe, and Ferol seemed to remember all the European bankers by name. At such functions, Dee maintained an austere presence. He rarely drank alcohol, and while others might occasionally party late into the night, Dee and Ferol always retired early, usually no later than 10 p.m. For themselves, the Europeans cheerfully endorsed wine, women and song. For a leader, they wanted Dee.

"Dee gave off a definite feeling of trustworthiness," Ugo explained. "I didn't expect any trick out of him. He represented what I considered to be the typical moral American guy. The man who gets married while at university and stays married. He was a straight arrow. There was nothing of the libertine about him. We were the kids who could drink, dance, and make friends. He was the sober visionary, always slightly apart."

João Ribeira da Fonseca had a similar reaction. "Dee was not a man of the city. He was not a man of the establishment. He was a man from the mountains of Utah," João recalled. "He did not live easily in society. He was a man on his own. And when you spoke with him, you knew he was a true visionary."

On the first night, the Europeans hosted a gala dinner in the Grand Hotel. It was Old World Europe at its finest: crystal chandeliers, fine china, and freshly polished silver, dark suits for the men, evening gowns for the women. After dinner, Dick Dale, Ugo, João, and Santiago Zaldumbide took Dee aside. They wanted to create a European organization, in the model of NBI. Would he help them do it?

Dee said he sympathized with their many operational problems and with their desire to free themselves from the yoke of the Bank of America; of course he would agree to help. Dee asked the NBI board for its permission, and they readily gave it. The Europeans were ecstatic; this was exactly what they had wanted to hear. The Europeans were not sure how to move forward, but they were sure they had found the man who did. The event called for champagne, and by evening's end, Ugo, João, Santiago, and Dickie Dale were certain that Stresa would prove to be a historic turning point in the evolution of both NBI and European banking and consumer finance. They weren't wrong.

Dee went back to San Francisco to study the problems inherent in creating a European organization – and he was not enchanted by what he found. "The effort would be immensely more complex than NBI," he wrote. "A global organization would need to transcend diverse languages, cultures, currencies, customs, legal systems, political traditions, and technologies. It would involve thousands of banks scattered around the world, as well as national consortiums of banks in France, Canada, Scandinavia, Japan, the United States, and other countries. It must anticipate that tens of thousands of diverse financial institutions in more than 200 countries and territories might wish to participate. It could easily take two years of effort with no assurance of success."

At the same time, Dee saw in the European suggestion a larger opportunity. From the beginning, his guiding dream had been to create the world's premier system for handling digital transactions. Dee wasn't really prepared to move so fast toward that goal, but he also realized this was not an opportunity he should miss. Why not replicate the NBI model on a larger scale?

A month or two later, Dee flew to Milan and set before the Europeans a huge dossier, listing the relevant issues – and their solutions. On every point, Dee's analysis offered options, with supporting pros and cons. The study was comprehensive, thoughtful, and in vision it was beyond anything the Europeans had been contemplating. It also struck several themes that responded directly to European concerns. For instance, the new venture should definitely *not* be American in its organization, its name, or its brand identity. For it to work across Europe, there needed to be a coherent, unifying vision, but the organization needed strong local roots in every country. Management should be entirely local, and in close touch with the needs of its specific credit card and business markets.

Dee also addressed the complex issue of the name that would appear on European cards. In light of Europe's political sensitivities and the success of the name Barclaycard, Dee foresaw the need to adopt a new common name, something truly international, to identify the blue, white, and gold system throughout the world. Here Dee's concerns were not confined to Europe; they were global. The BankAmericard was marketed as Barclaycard in the United Kingdom, South Africa and the Caribbean; as Chargex in Canada; as Bancomer in Mexico; and as the Sumitomo Card in Japan.

Dee's analysis of all these issues drew raves from the Europeans. Here was a man who understood the future of credit cards and retail banking. Here was a man who also understood their particular needs and sensitivities. In their view, Dee's analysis was nothing short of brilliant. His conclusion, though, as paraphrased below, dropped their collective jaws:

"Now you know what has to be done, and the decisions which have to be made to form a European corporation. But my personal conclusion is that the company should be worldwide. A European corporation can always be constituted whenever you want, in a second phase, and would be a member of the worldwide corporation, just as NBI is now."

A worldwide company? The Europeans had been thinking in terms of establishing a regional organization, and they had no idea how to do that. Yet here was Dee thinking global. "We were shocked," Ugo recalled. "He was telling us: Think bigger." After careful consideration, the European licensees concluded that Dee was absolutely right. So they dropped their plan and eagerly agreed to follow Dee's lead. Global it would be, and that decision led directly to the creation of what is today Visa International.

What happened in Stresa and afterwards shows Dee the visionary at his diplomatic best. He knew the Europeans were absolutely key to his dream of creating a global payments system. But he also knew that the Europeans were proud, contentious, and never inclined to follow an American lead. He also knew he couldn't reject their own plan out of hand; that would be insulting. Instead, Dee took their initiative seriously and used it as an opportunity to win their trust and to bring them into the inner workings of his own guiding vision. Dee did not show them the error of their ways; he showed them the wisdom of his.

"Many a brilliant idea," A.P. Giannini once said, "has been lost because the man who dreamt it lacked the spunk or the spine to put it across." But as he showed in handling the European initiative, Dee Hock had brilliant ideas and a grand vision –

and he also had what it took to put them across.

Dee being Dee, he embarked on the international phase of his venture excited but still wracked by nagging doubts. He had NBI up and running, and he had earned the allegiance of a few influential bankers in Europe. But so what? What about Asia, Latin America, and the rest of the world? How was he going to tackle Europe's problems when he was still trying desperately to get NBI safely off the ground?

"Could we afford to divert time and energy from the many difficult problems in the United States?" Dee wrote. "On the other hand, could we afford not to, since our success was irrevocably intertwined with the success of the program overseas? How could our ultimate dream of a global device for the exchange of value be realized without an effective global organization?"

Back in San Francisco, Dee put those doubts aside and plunged into the monumental task of creating a worldwide partnership of banks, merchants, and cardholders. The problems he had faced with launching NBI paled by comparison. Now Dee and his team weren't worrying how to settle a card transaction between New York and Denver; they were trying to establish the means to handle inter-bank transactions between, say, Tokyo and Stockholm, and Boston and Bologna. To get this done, Dee knew he had to build a staff that had technical competence, on the one hand, but also an ability to bridge barriers of language, culture, business practices, and technological development. He would have to train his top-level managers to be statesmen and sensitive emissaries of what was becoming a global message.

All start-up companies face huge problems, of course, but Dee was not just starting a company. He was building an industry and trying to create a unique global partnership from scratch. To do this, he himself had to be a skillful statesman. He had to go abroad and open foreign bankers' minds to the concept, win their confidence and trust, and then educate them about the strengths and intricacies of forming the partnership he envisioned. At the same time, he had to inculcate in their banks a true sense of ownership in the new system; the success of this cooperative venture would depend on the success of each link in the network.

Saddled with these burdens, Dee's spirits often slumped and he feared that this whole initiative was nothing more than an idealist's dream, a wonderful idea but impossible to achieve. In the months and years ahead, his frustrations would often peak and he would have an almost overwhelming desire to give up and quit. But he never did. At these critical junctures, countless people would say to him, "Damnit, Dee, what you're asking is just impossible!" At times like those, Dee could pause and take heart from another reflection of A.P. Giannini:

"The best fun I've had in life has been doing things that other people declared impossible."

The Art of Persuasion

Over the next two years, Dee and his team tackled the problems of creating an international credit card association. In keeping with their usual approach, they set up regional committees to work on the effort. Initially, there were to be four regions: North America; Latin America; Asia-Pacific; and one covering Europe, the Mideast and Africa. In some areas of the world, this was not a job for bankers; it was a job for diplomats.

"Each regional committee contained representatives from countries with long histories of bitter commercial, ethnic and cultural conflict," Dee explained in his memoir, "including open warfare and periodic subjugation of one another." Dee was often called upon to act as mediator in this crucial start-up phase.

Dee had his own problems as well. In the summer of 1973, the international organizing committee gathered in Mexico City to continue work on the concept of a new global organization in anticipation of the next annual meeting of licensees, to be held a few weeks later in Spain. In Mexico, Dee became convinced that a small faction of international licensees was out to sabotage his entire effort. He could not pinpoint the source of the trouble, but he felt that some unknown group was hard at work, perhaps with the participation of some members of his own committee. So Dee decided to take a dramatic stand. Up to this point, he and other officers of NBI had been acting as an independent organizing agent. Now he formally withdrew from that role. He would continue to participate in the international organizing effort, he explained, but not as its leader. Someone had breached the openness and trust necessary to make the venture work; principle demanded that he step aside.

The move was classic Dee. In effect, he was saying to the international licensees: "Wake up! This is a huge venture we're undertaking. There are huge profits in it for all of us. Be smart. Put aside your individual interests and work for the common good and hold everyone to the same standards. And if you don't, I'll walk away and the whole effort will collapse. And if you don't, we cannot continue to lead the effort." The underlying message was clear: Explain that to your boards of directors!

The Mexico City meeting ended in a tense stalemate. Dee returned to San Francisco and notified the board of NBI and other bankers around the world of his decision to step aside. The news touched off a flurry of inquiries to NBI headquarters, but Dee remained tight-lipped about his decision. The tactic heightened the crisis atmosphere and set the stage for high drama in Spain.

At the annual meeting, there was again tension, but no one openly wanted the international effort to fail – and no one wanted to take the blame if it did. So Dee's brinksmanship paid off. In a spirit of consensus, the licensees agreed to reshuffle the bankers on Dee's organizing committee. The new group then reaffirmed its commitment to working in an open and constructive manner. Dee resumed his role of organizing agent with his leadership and vision reaffirmed – for the moment. But serious problems remained, problems that threatened the entire international organizing effort.

How much autonomy would the regions have? And what about the many names being used to market the BankAmericard? How would the new organization be governed? After a great many meetings and two years of intense work, there remained a half-dozen issues on which the licensees could not agree. A final meeting was scheduled in San Francisco in one last effort to break the deadlock. If not, Dee was prepared to abandon the whole international effort. It was proving to be a grueling responsibility anyway, and he had plenty to do at NBI.

In fact, a serious crisis was developing on the U.S. front. The crisis was over the issue known as "duality." Could one bank be a member of both the BankAmericard and the MasterCard systems? Could that same bank issue both cards and sign up merchants for both systems? This question of dual membership was fundamental to the future of NBI and the future of bank cards in America. Among the licensee banks and Dee's own ranks there was deep disagreement about duality. As Dee liked to say, "Where you stand depends on where you sit."

From where Dee was sitting, the answer was clear: banks had to choose one card or the other; they could not be dual owner-members in both charge card organizations. He was firmly committed to keeping the two systems separate, for several good reasons. He feared that duality could choke off NBI. If the banks could issue both cards, Dee feared that the BankAmericard and MasterCard systems would wind up in lockstep, each a carbon copy of the other, and sooner or later the banks would say, "What's the point of running identical programs? Let's fold the two systems into one." The idea of limiting Visa in this manner was anathema to Dee. It was the exact opposite of the sort of distribution of power he believed in and advocated.

Dee had other concerns about duality. The structure and work of NBI depended on maintaining several delicate balances: between big banks and small, between inter-bank cooperation and inter-bank competition, and between banks that had "Class A" licenses to issue cards and sign up merchants and "Class B" banks that could act only as agents of the Class A banks. Dee feared that duality would upset all those balances and thus strike a blow at the spirit of consensus and cooperation on which NBI was built. That blow, too, could put an end to Dee's whole dream.

The Worthen Bank and Trust, in Little Rock, Arkansas, brought the duality issue to a crisis point. Worthen, a small Class A member of the BankAmericard system, decided in 1971 that it wanted to become a member of MasterCard and issue both cards. If NBI tried to stop it, Worthen warned that it would sue. Dee rushed to Little Rock for urgent talks. As usual, Dee stood on principle and urged Worthen to act for the greater good of the whole NBI system. This time, though, Dee's powers of persuasion failed, and his intervention produced no accord. The NBI board then voted to amend its bylaws, barring its Class A members from holding dual memberships in the competing systems, although it did agree to allow Class B banks to continue to accept sales drafts from MasterCard merchants.

Worthen, as promised, sued NBI, claiming that NBI's new bylaw was a violation of the Sherman Antitrust Act, an act of the U.S. Congress designed to curb concentrations of power that restrain competition and interfere with free trade. Worthen argued that NBI's prohibition was an unfair restriction on its freedom to issue both cards and to sign up merchants for both products. The issue of duality thus went into the U.S. court system – where it would stay for the next several years, keeping Bennett Katz, Dave Wagman, and other lawyers extremely busy and frustrated.

By mid-1974, Dee's frustrations on the international side were running pretty high as well. He and his team were preparing for the critical meeting of the international organizing committee in San Francisco. Dee had hoped that this meeting would see the culmination of all his work. But the prospects were not looking good. In preparatory meetings and conversations with the licensees,

Dee and his team saw that positions had hardened.

Canadian banks were a major source of the contention. They had their own card association and it was very successful. So they were not inclined to join Dee's venture, which was still largely untested. In addition, they shared one of the concerns of the Europeans: that Dee's new organization would be American-dominated. That would not fly in Canada. In fact, Canada's success stemmed largely from its own national roots.

The Canadian card program had an interesting history, one with important lessons for other countries getting into the card market. In 1968, Roger Woodward, a veteran banker with the Canadian Imperial Bank of Commerce, went to San Francisco and met with Ken Larkin. After two solid weeks of negotiating, Woodward came away with the rights to license BankAmericard in Canada. As with the other licensees, Canada would be free to customize the card to suit its local market, and Woodward knew that several changes were imperative.

One significant problem was how to reach "critical mass." Geographically, Canada was a vast country, spanning the top of North America from the Atlantic to the Pacific; starting a credit card program from scratch was going to be a difficult and very costly venture. Worse, in 1968 no one in North America was doing it profitably, except for the Bank of America. So the Canadian Imperial Bank of Commerce decided to form a cooperative venture with three other banks: Royal Bank of Canada, Toronto Dominion Bank, and Banque Canadienne Nationale of Montreal. They, too, had individual licensing agreements with the BofA, but they decided they could more effectively build the market in Canada by working together. They named their new venture the Canadian Bank Card Association.

The partnership made perfect sense. Together, the four banks represented more than 70 percent of Canadian banking; joining forces gave them strength in numbers. Since there was no duality in Canada, the four banks would assure themselves of a dominant hold on the whole bank card market. Joining forces would reduce the costs and the risks for each individual bank, while guaranteeing them maximum exposure and profit potential. "We wanted to spread the risks," Roger Woodward explained in an interview. "We had no cardholders and no merchants. Collectively, the four banks could solve those problems better than we could alone."

The new association faced another problem: the name. "The name BankAmericard wouldn't fly in Canada," Woodward explained. The four banks had to find a name that Canadians could feel was their own. With the help of an outside marketing firm, the banks found a solution that was not only creative but helped stimulate public interest in this new tool of consumer credit: they ran a public contest. More than 1,000 suggestions poured in, and they produced the winning name: "Chargex."

From the outset, the association's formula was cooperation *and* competition. The banks would run competing card programs and merchants were free to sign up with any of the four member banks. At the same time, the four harmonized their marketing, ad campaigns, and operating procedures. This meld of cooperation and competition was, of course, highly unusual, and its success was by no means assured.

The Canadian approach worked. Despite some initial frictions among the banks, the association was able to blanket the nation and sign up large numbers of cardholders and merchants. On August 10, 1968, they launched the card nationwide, with the slogan "Will that be cash or Chargex?" Right away the new credit tool was a hit with consumers and merchants, and the card business soon began to soar. So did bank profits. "We rapidly became the No. 1 country in terms of cards per capita," Woodward recalled. "We still are, apart from Iceland."

The Canadians' success, however, translated into headaches for Dee and NBI. Put simply, the Canadians had found effective ways to make the most of their licensing agreement with BofA; why tamper with a winning formula? "We were happy with Chargex. It was working well," recalled Malcolm McLeod, a lawyer who has represented the card association since its formation. "We were used to running things pretty much on our own."

National pride was also a factor. Dee was envisioning an international organization where voting would be determined by a given country's annual sales volume. For the Canadian banks, that would create an uncomfortable paradox. They would find themselves dominating their home market, but their voice in the larger organization would be small. "By sales volume, Canada represented only 10 percent of the total, while the United

Dee and his staff spent enormous time and energy orchestrating board meetings to achieve their objectives.

States represented 80 percent," McLeod said. "So our main concern was protecting our regional autonomy." On the eve of the meeting in San Francisco, the issue of regional autonomy loomed as a potential deal-breaker.

So did the issue of a new name for the card. Dee and his team had already made it clear that, sooner or later, the name BankAmericard would have to go. In its place, they would have to find something that was thoroughly international, politically neutral, and understandable and translatable in nearly every corner of the globe. That was fine with the Canadians, and they had a ready replacement. They had spent a fortune launching and establishing the name "Chargex." The name was on millions of cards, merchant doors, zipzap machines, sales drafts, outdoor billboards, and TV and newspaper ads. If they joined Dee's venture, NBI would probably take them back to ground zero.

"We had ideas that Chargex should be the worldwide name," McLeod explained. Failing that, McLeod at least wanted assurances that individual regions could veto important decisions such as a name change. McLeod was all for the principles of cooperation, consensus, partnership, and trust – provided the most powerful regions could not impose their will on the smaller. It was with these concerns that McLeod and an officer of the Chargex banks left for San Francisco.

On the eve of the meeting, Dee feared that no agreement would be possible. His entire effort could end right there where it started, in the "City by the Bay." But Dee was not about to give up. In fact, he had a simple, powerful strategy to break the deadlocked issues between the banks and neutralize the opposition he expected from the Canadians. One part of his preparation was a Dee trademark: rehearsals. Dee and his team would tightly script important meetings, send out the proposed agenda to member banks, discuss with them in advance every agenda item, feel out their positions, and make modifications along the way. In diplomatic circles, there is an old adage: "Revolutions don't just happen; they're carefully stage-managed." Dee applied that principle to the credit card business.

In the weeks and days leading up to important meetings, Dee would convene his key players for formal rehearsals. People presenting agenda items would make their addresses and face rigorous questioning. Substance at these rehearsals was critical, but so was style. Dee would critique people's ability to present material, field questions, use their voice, and bond with the audience. He even brought in professional speech coaches to work with the staff and show them the tricks of public speaking. Videotape was one of their tools.

"The first time I saw myself on videotape I was shocked," recalled Tom Cleveland, a former chief financial officer at Visa. "But the coaching really helped my presentations. It helped everyone's."

These rehearsals served Dee in several ways. Of course they helped prepare and fine-tune what would happen at the meeting. But they also educated his own staff and instilled in them both a sense of excitement and of the importance of what Dee was trying to accomplish. They were even a reward. "It was considered a high honor to be invited to a rehearsal," Cleveland said. It was an even higher honor, of course, to be invited to present an item on the NBI agenda and defend it to the licensees.

Dee, for his part, loved the rehearsals. "I'd take the role of every nasty board member," Dee laughed. "If my people could survive these sessions, they'd be ready for the real thing. They used to think the board was a bunch of pussycats next to those rehearsals."

Dee paid comparable attention to the setting and side events of NBI's annual meetings and board meetings. His staff would spend months finding the best site for the meeting. Then they spent months tailoring the conference rooms, planning meals and wines, and organizing day trips for the wives and evening entertainment, always with appropriate local flavor. On the eve of the meeting, Dee would conduct a final inspection of the premises and a dress rehearsal, for final polishing.

This level of planning and attention to detail paid huge dividends. Meyer Rubin, a banker from Israel who played a key role in the international development of Dee's vision, felt they were vital to Dee's success. "I remember arriving for my first board meeting in Paris and phoning David Wagman and saying, 'David, let's go out and have dinner together.' David's reply was: 'I'm terribly sorry, Mike, but we're having a dress rehearsal in a few minutes.' I said: 'David, a dress rehearsal? What are you talking about?' He said: 'Well, for tomorrow's meeting.' I said: 'What happens?' And David said: 'Well, they ask me any possible question that we think you might ask tomorrow, and I must be ready with the answer.'" Meyer was deeply impressed. "I think that tells an awful lot about the organization and why it was successful. You had a dedicated staff who were willing at 9:00 or 10:00 o'clock at night to do dress rehearsals."

For the San Francisco meeting, Dee typically left nothing to chance. Dee and his team had tried to defuse the Canadian problem beforehand, but they had no success. At one stage, Dee raised questions about Malcolm McLeod's participation in the meeting. No other banks brought their lawyers, after all; why should the Canadians? The Canadians insisted, however, and Dee backed off. In Malcolm McLeod's view, Dee had been trying to isolate anyone he thought might disrupt the spirit of consensus. "Dee tried to get me thrown out of the meeting," Malcolm recalled with a laugh. "It didn't work."

The special day-and-a-half meeting was held at the headquarters of the Bank of America, and it began just as Dee and his staff had feared. "It was polarized and cantankerous," Dee wrote in his memoir. "The four large banks which composed Chargex in Canada were adamant. Unless others around the world came to their position, they would not participate."

Dee was ready, though. "I looked around the group and asked, 'Well, it is obvious Canada cannot accept the position of others on this issue. Is it the sense of the group that you wish to proceed to form the new organization without our friends from Canada?' Nods all around. 'Well, then, it appears Chargex representatives will no longer be part of the process. Would it be appropriate to have them remain as observers with the understanding they will not disrupt remaining discussions?' Again, nods all around. The Canadians were shocked, but did not leave."

"Going into the meeting, the Canadian banks gave me my mandate: don't join unless you gain certain guarantees," McLeod recalled. "But the banks also said I could agree to join the new organization, at the last moment, if I wanted to."

The stalemate continued throughout the day, and there was seemingly no way to bridge the areas of disagreement. "As the day ended, gloom deepened," Dee wrote. "I suggested we adjourn the meeting, since agreement appeared impossible. We could meet in the morning to discuss how to disband the effort."

This was just the sort of brinksmanship Dee had used so successfully in Mexico. This time, though, Dee had one final maneuver up his sleeve. To conclude the long day's effort, Dee and the members of his international organizing committee, more than two dozen in all, boarded a private boat at Fisherman's Wharf, rode past Alcatraz, and headed across the bay to Sausalito. A lovely dinner awaited them at Le Vivoire, a French restaurant just a few minutes walk from where Dee and his inner circle had gathered for their initial brainstorming session, a full six years before.

Le Vivoire was a warm, convivial setting for the dinner, and its name held an ironic note that Dee and his organizers were probably unaware of: "vivoire" was not French at all. It was French-Canadian, and it meant "living room," a place of comfort. Le Vivoire was anything but comfortable for Malcolm McLeod and the other Canadians. At that moment, they felt they were standing in the way of Dee's dream; they felt they were the skunks at the garden party. Nonetheless, Dee and his guests had a sumptuous dinner, with several courses and several

Cuff links with Dee's motto for Visa: "The will to succeed, the grace to compromise."

bottles of fine wine. By the end, the mood was mellow, though a bit subdued due to the apparent failure of their grand adventure.

Finally, after dessert, Dee rose to say a few concluding words. He thanked them all for their incredible effort, for the long journey they had made together, and briefly reminded them about all the obstacles they had overcome along the way. "It is no failure to fall short of realizing such a dream," Dee said. "From the beginning, it was apparent that forming such a complex, global organization was unlikely. We now know it was impossible."

As he spoke, a small token of his appreciation, presented in a beautifully wrapped box, was placed in front of each licensee. The assembled bankers opened their boxes and each found inside a pair of magnificent gold cuff links. Each link was in the form of a delicately crafted half-globe, the continents etched into the gold in elegant relief. Put together, the two links formed a whole, interlocking globe – representing the ultimate aim of Dee's guiding dream.

Each link also held half of a Latin inscription: *Studium ad prosperandum, voluntas in conveniendum.* The will to succeed, the grace to compromise. The message was that it took both those qualities to create a new global financial system. Alas, he now told the group, the former had been present in their labors, but not the latter. Without the grace to compromise, the entire effort was lost. Finished. Failed.

"But if, by some miracle, our differences dissolve before morning," Dee said, "this gift will remind us to the day we die that the world was united because we had 'the will to succeed and the grace to compromise.'"

There was a long silence, and then one of the Canadians blurted out, "You miserable bastard!" And the room collapsed in laughter. The master showman and persuader had done it again.

Those cuff links did work a miracle. At the next morning's session, the Canadians had an announcement to make: "We're in! We're in!" Dee's clever maneuver had once again turned imminent failure into a success.

The Canadians did win some important concessions. Dee and the board agreed to make them a fifth regional grouping unto themselves, thus ensuring their regional autonomy. The board also agreed to set up special voting rights, with protections for less powerful regions. No single region could veto an initiative; it took two. The issue of a new name was also put off to a later time, a skillful diplomatic fudge. "It all worked out in the end," Malcolm McLeod recalled. "The Canadian delegation did not want to be the odd man out."

The agreements in San Francisco, covering Canada's stance and a host of other problems, cleared the way for a new worldwide organization of BankAmericard licensees. A few months later, in September of 1974, at a festive inaugural meeting in Vancouver, British Columbia, the licensees created IBANCO, a multinational, non-stock membership corporation. This was the forerunner of today's Visa International. The licensees chose a board of directors, headed by a banker from Puerto Rico named James Partridge. Dee was named president, and he continued to head up the NBI operation in the United States. For its corporate motto, the board adopted, of course, "The will to succeed, the grace to compromise."

IBANCO had a strong beginning. There were

18 charter member banks, from 14 different countries, and their collective assets totaled over $400 billion. Furthermore, in their existing card programs, those charter banks had 37 million cardholders and 1.5 million participating merchants in 111 countries. For 1974, the projected gross volume on those cards was in the range of $10 billion. And now those 18 banks were going to work together to build the market, extend their network, and create the global payments system Dee had long envisioned.

Dee's success in creating IBANCO showed how well he understood the inner workings and the pressures inherent in the process of consensus, and like a skilled general he used them to maximum advantage. But Dee also used more subtle forms of persuasion. At the outset of the industry, credit card managers were outsiders, with very little status within their own banks. Dee changed all that. The people who served on his boards and committees were made to feel like a privileged club, a family of visionaries who were going to change the world of banking and consumer finance. They would meet in magnificent locales and luxurious hotels, dine in splendor, and enjoy the cultural and artistic delights of their host country. These were delightful perks – and anyone tempted to opt out would thus think good and hard before leaving the club and the life it offered.

Ugo Scarpetta recalled one gala dinner at the Hapsburg Palace in Vienna. There was a magnificent orchestra playing all through the cocktail hour. "Then trumpets announced that dinner was served, and every three steps there stood a manservant in white wig and full livery."

This was lavish, even pretentious, but Dee was instilling a mindset and esprit de corps. "Dee was trying to get people to believe they were part of a historic venture," Ugo explained. "NBI was moving retail banking to the highest level of banking. For the first time, retail bankers felt they could look at corporate bankers and feel they were on an even plane. Local bankers were always invited to our functions. From then on, they always wanted to be a part of what we were doing, so they, too, joined the Visa family. The luxury was a marketing tool."

Dee was also trying to build a new kind of banker: open-minded, worldly, and sensitive to other cultures and their special concerns. "Dee would tell people: be statesmen," Ugo recalled. "By that he meant 'don't be mean. Don't consider that your own little garden is all you have to husband. You must think of the larger garden as well.'"

Dee also believed in the power of spouses. At the time, banking was still a male-dominated world (and many women say it still is) and Dee convinced his boards to invite wives to the annual meetings and even to some sessions of the board. Dee was trying to turn his group into a closely knit family, and he felt that wives were essential to the process. "I was always asking myself, 'How could I break down that barrier?'" Dee explained. "How am I going to get people off their typical corporate identities so we could get to know each other as people? The wives always got to know each other. And when their husbands started griping about what so-and-so said in a meeting, the wives would say, 'Wait a minute! I know these people and they're very nice!' The wives brought us back to the essence: creating the feeling of family."

This feeling of family was essential to building IBANCO into a multinational, multicultural partnership, able to transcend differences of language, culture, and race. "This was family, and that was a powerful, powerful tool," Jim Partridge explained. "Time and time again, the family feeling prevented this thing from falling apart. In a business sense, we were a family of interests. In a business sense, we were a family of interests. In a personal sense, we were also a family, and that acted like lubricant on the whole machine."

Dee wanted his staff to feel like they were part of an elite family as well. He could not recruit people by offering big salaries or stock options, but he could offer vision, adventure, a sense of higher purpose – and a few good perks. When his top managers traveled to distant board meetings, for instance, Dee insisted they fly first class. He wanted them to work on the plane, arrive rested, and if the CEO of a big member bank happened to be on the same plane, Dee wanted to show that NBI decision-makers had an equal status – and thus deserved equal respect.

Was there a thread common to all of Dee's weapons of persuasion? Yes. "Logic doesn't drive the world, emotions do," Dee explained. "If I could understand where someone was coming from, emotionally, then I could touch him. But then I had to have something clear and logical to present. My aim was to create the conditions by which agreement could happen, and to do that I had to be impeccable in my logic and arguments. This gave people the 'clothes' – the rationale and logic – to do what they felt, emotionally, they wanted to do."

As a leader, therefore, Dee was constantly operating on two levels: as the passionate participant and the dispassionate observer, looking for the emotional underpinnings of every situation he faced. "There were two mes," Dee said. "One listened intently and participated intensely in the discussion. But there was always another me, sitting in the back of the room, dispassionately watching and trying to understand the nuances of the relationships among all the participants in the room."

This was agonizing work; the hours were never-ending and his life was often terribly lonely,

Dee always wanted Visa to feel like a great international family, at work and at play.

mission. He wasn't building a company; in his mind, he was building something much larger.

"We were building a community," Dee explained, "a global community, and we were building it piece by piece, bit by bit. We called it the Visa family."

With this spirit, Dee was able to recruit a gifted staff, and many of his best people came from member banks. To head up his operations in Europe, Dee enlisted the services of João Ribeira da Fonseca of Portugal. Ugo Scarpetta came aboard to help João. To open up Latin America and Asia, Dee recruited Jim Partridge, who would be instrumental in the creation and building of Visa International. During this same period, Carl Pascarella came aboard, and he would play a pivotal role in opening Japan and other key markets across Asia. Later, Carl would take the reins of Visa U.S.A.

Each of them was eager to join Dee's international venture. Each of them also became a true believer in Dee's vision and philosophy, and each went out into the world as his missionaries, evangelists preaching the gospel according to Dee. None was more passionate than Jim Partridge.

"Dee just fascinated me," Partridge recalled in an interview. "I thought he was brilliant. Not a good manager, really, but a true visionary." Partridge was also dazzled by Dee's ability to persuade people and build a consensus for what he hoped to achieve. "He knew how to paint the picture people wanted to see. He knew what people wanted. And he managed to make people believe that what they wanted, he wanted. His policy of ruling by consensus is part of the genius that exists to this very day."

Above all, Jim believed in Dee's guiding vision and in the power embedded in that little plastic tool. "The democratization of credit – that's what the credit card did for banking and consumer credit," Partridge said. "We were leading a social revolution. We were fully aware of that, but we didn't say it very often. We were too careful for that. But I always felt proud that we were making credit available to the masses."

Imagine the smile on the face of A.P. Giannini – and on Dee Hock's as well.

Part Three **The Technology**

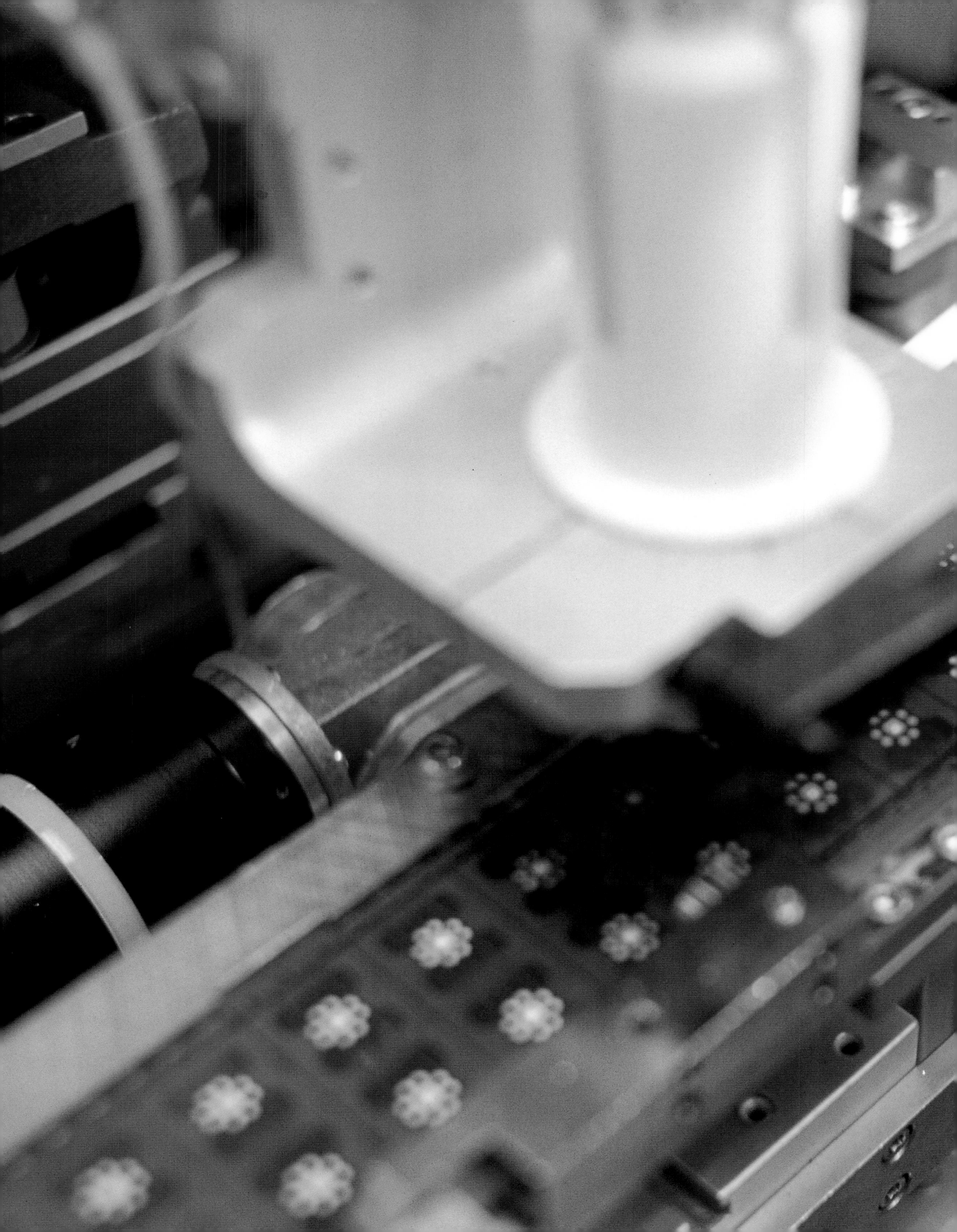

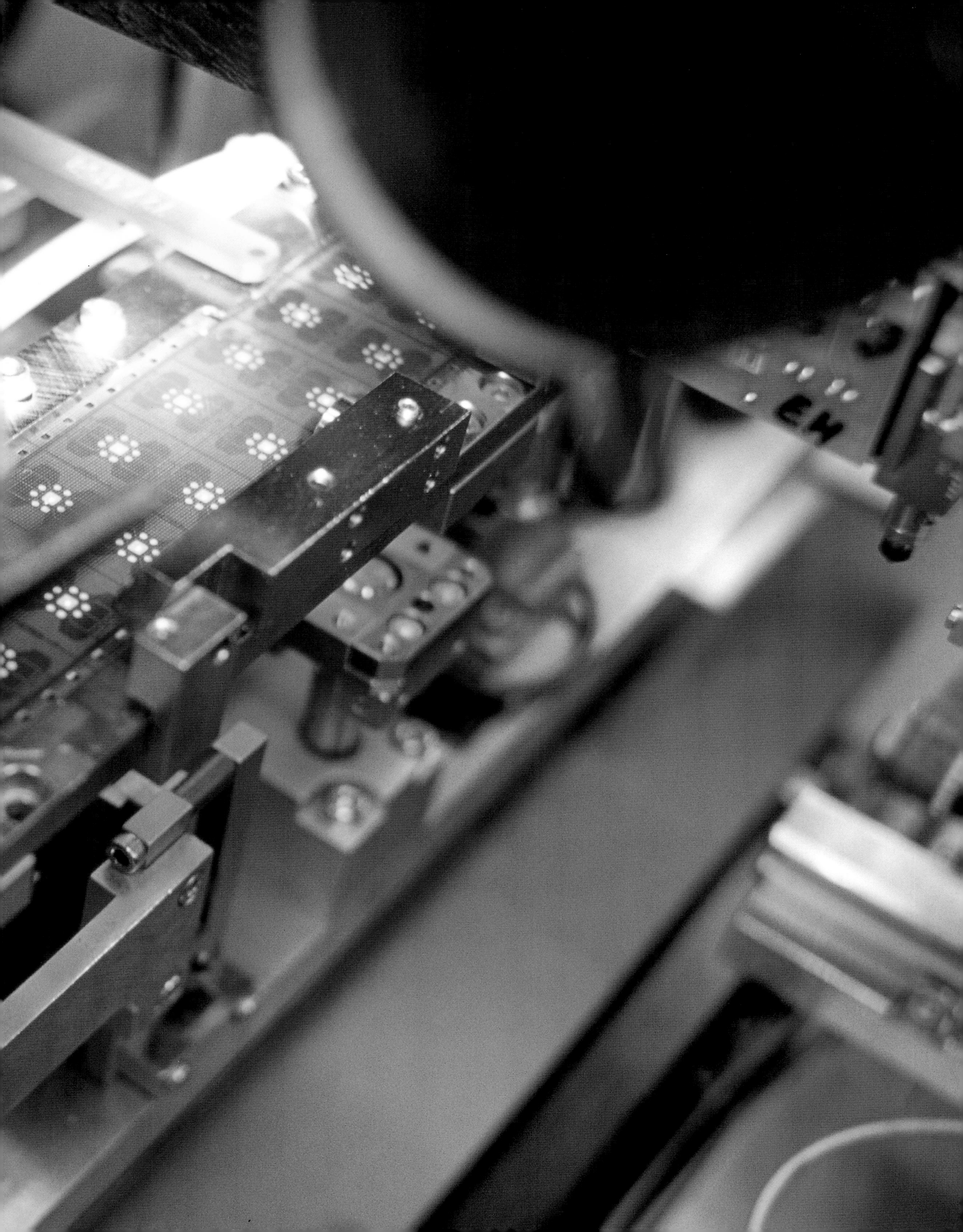

691786
691739
READY U
READY U

Chapter 11

Marrying Money and Technology

It all began with a daring gamble.

At the start of the 1970s, when Dee Hock was in the first days of creating NBI in the United States, American Express was secretly developing a major new initiative. AmEx was now one of the largest issuers of charge cards in the world. The use of plastic money was rapidly accelerating, and the U.S. card industry was in desperate need of a nationwide computer system able to handle the exploding volume of plastic card transactions. American Express was hatching plans to build such a system – to serve its own growing needs and to secure much bigger game: control of the emerging card-processing market. AmEx planned to invite BankAmericard and MasterCard to join the processing venture and use this new network – at a substantial up-front fee to cover the start-up costs and with later usage fees as well.

The AmEx plan was seductive. The card system was still in the dark ages of dial-in authorizations and paper sales drafts. Merchants across the country were grousing about how long it took to approve purchases that exceeded the floor limits specified on a customer's card. In regular business hours, the process took an average of five minutes. On Sundays, holidays, and after bank hours, it took even longer. That was hurting merchants' business.

The banks were having even worse problems. For them, the authorization and clearance processes were both costly and cumbersome to manage. Those tissue-paper sales drafts were a nightmare to sort, verify, and settle. The system of "interchange" – settling card transactions with banks from other regions – was also fraught with operational hassles. NBI's Chuck Russell ran a bank card program in those days, and he saw the resultant mess first-hand. "One weekend we took over a whole gymnasium to try to sort out our credit card paperwork," Russell recalled. "The whole room was filled with piles and piles of sales drafts that we couldn't reconcile. Those drafts were worth millions of dollars – and we didn't know whose accounts to debit. Our customers thought we were Santa Claus. It was an absolute disaster."

The banks also faced a much more sinister problem: rising bank card theft and fraud. In these early days, many banks issued cards indiscriminately, and not only to their own customers. Some banks bought mailing lists and issued cards to everyone on them, without any credit analysis or screening. Mass mailings led to massive thefts, often directly from mailboxes, and that led to massive fraud. Each year, fraudulent transactions were costing the banks millions of dollars. On top of that, the banks had to expend large sums to track down and remove "hot" cards from circulation. All these problems had galvanized a broad consensus in the industry: something had to be done.

Computer technology was the obvious answer, and most banks knew it. Like the Bank of America, many U.S. banks were now using computers for check processing and other basic banking functions or they were about to do so. The American Bankers Association was also convinced that computers were the way of the future and it was studying ways to computerize the nation's existing, overburdened system for processing paper checks. AmEx's planned system for plastic money transactions looked like a natural companion to that, a network that would cut costs, speed authorizations, and curtail fraud and its attendant losses. The start-up cost might be high, but in the end it would save America's banks millions of dollars. To many bankers, the AmEx plan made perfect sense. But not to Dee Hock.

Dee learned of the American Express initiative in a most upsetting way. On the night before he was to open his first annual meeting of NBI members in 1971, lawyers from the Bank of America asked to meet him in the strictest confidence. "I was speechless at what they had to say," Dee recalled in his memoir. "The bank had been in secret discussions with American Express for months, developing a plan for the two companies to jointly create, own, and control a credit card authorization system. The plan would be announced within days."

Dee was livid. He, too, was convinced of the need to build a nationwide computer system to handle card authorizations and payments. That was part of his grand vision from the outset – and he was not about to cede it to anyone. Moreover, Dee was vehemently opposed to the idea that American Express should build and run any overarching system. In the infancy of the card industry, many bankers did not see American Express as a direct competitor, but Dee did. That the BofA was secretly in on the plan, but hadn't deigned to inform him sooner, made him all the angrier. "The joint venture, from my perspective, was nothing but an attempt by the two credit card giants to make tenant farmers of the remainder of the industry," he wrote. It would also make a tenant farmer of Dee Hock and his vision. As Dee admitted, "I felt completely betrayed."

Nonetheless, he respected the confidentiality of his discussions with BofA attorneys and kept silent about them during the annual NBI meeting – even if he was steaming mad. In due course, AmEx and the BofA publicly announced their joint venture and canvassed the nation for support. When they received little, the two companies formed a committee composed of card issuers and major merchants, with the aim of creating a broader-based joint venture. NBI was asked to join and Dee agreed, the better to keep tabs on his rivals. Given the crying need in the industry, American Express and the BofA were now able to generate some fresh support for their joint venture. But Dee remained convinced that the AmEx concept was seriously flawed.

"Neither the institutional nor technical thinking made sense," he wrote. "It was another attempt to centralize power and control. It was contrary to all my beliefs about the nature of organizations and the possibilities inherent in electronic communications. Exchanging authorization information and monetary value in the form of electronic particles not only might become, but *ought to be* a highly decentralized, competitive business. Trying to design and impose a single, monolithic system on such an essential flow of information seemed absurd."

On the strength of this conviction, Dee moved into action. He began assessing what it would take for NBI to build its own proprietary system for handling electronic transactions, run by NBI in partnership with its member banks. American Express and MasterCard would be NBI's competitors, not its allies. Building such a system was a monumental task, one he had no experience in or credentials to do, but Dee was not about to be stopped. If AmEx got the jump here, he knew that would be the end of his dream of building a global payments system.

By mid-1972, Dee had done all his homework and had his plans ready for the next meeting of his board of directors. There he laid out a strong case against the American Express initiative. Yes, he agreed that something needed to be done to speed authorizations and clearances, but building one monolithic system was not the answer. If American Express controlled the tools of electronic transactions, NBI and its member banks would lose the freedom they needed to react and adapt quickly in the coming Information Age. It was essential, Dee argued, for NBI and its member banks to be masters of their own fate. They needed their own computer system, under their own control, to serve their own needs in a complex and rapidly changing marketplace. Dee then urged the board to invest in the future. By building its own system for handling electronic transactions, NBI would *lead* the card industry, not follow American Express or anyone else.

Several bankers on his board remained openly skeptical. Dee was just getting the infant NBI operation up and running. He was still operating out of a tiny "garage" at BofA headquarters. He had only a skeletal staff, a small budget, no computer expertise, no computer staff, and no experience in applying computer technology to the demands of banking and finance. Was he, therefore, really the man to entrust with this awesome task?

Dee, however, rose to this challenge, mustering the full force of his persuasive powers and demolishing all the opposing points with his relentless filibustering style. Finally, one member of the board hoisted the white flag. "I move that we approve the effort," he said. "How many of you want to join me and vote for this shot in the dark?" It was a shot in the dark, indeed, but Dee carried the day, with unanimous support. The following day, NBI withdrew from the AmEx initiative and announced it would build its own electronic payments system, from scratch.

This was no small gamble. Dee was betting NBI's future – and his own – on his grand blueprint for the future. If he could build a successful electronic payments system, and do so before American Express or MasterCard beat him to it, he would transform the credit card industry and save NBI member banks millions of dollars. Also, Dee would be firmly on course to pursue his ultimate dream of building a global payments system. But if he failed, Dee knew he would have to crawl back to Seattle with his tail between his legs. "We had little experience building such systems. We had few employees with the requisite skills," Dee admitted. "We were off the high dive. There was no way back."

With so much at stake, Dee poured himself into this new challenge with more than his usual energy and zeal. He hired a computer team, met with potential suppliers like IBM and Digital Equipment Corporation (DEC), and examined every aspect of building and running an electronic payments system. He became architect, contractor, electrician, plumber, and interior designer. He fussed over every detail, right down to the placement of the sockets in the wall. "Think big, manage micro" seemed to be Dee's mantra.

Dee envisioned a nationwide system that would operate 24 hours a day, seven days a week. The plan was to use dedicated phone lines to link the processing centers, and local and 800 phone numbers to link merchants to their banks. Through that telephone network, a merchant would communicate electronically with a cardholder's issuing bank to get authorization to approve the transaction. If the card had been lost or stolen, or if the purchase exceeded the cardholder's available credit, the transaction would be declined. Otherwise it would be approved. If the merchant's call went to the bank after its business hours, the call would be automatically diverted to an NBI center, which would have the numbers of bad cards and other relevant information on file.

Soon Dee had a handsome plan on his desk, with an equally handsome price tag of $10 million – more than double what his board had authorized. Worse, his new advisors said it would take twice as long as expected to build. Dee reacted in typical

Dee fashion: he fired his computer team and started over.

Soon Dee and his own staff, with the help of a new team of outside specialists, came up with a new formulation. Like the earlier plan, this was to be a nationwide system with a central processing center in California linked to all of the BankAmericard processing centers around the country, including Hawaii and Alaska. Each processing center would be equipped with computer terminals to send authorization requests, and NBI would set up these centers and train the staff. Dee fixed the budget for building the whole system at $3 million. The target launch date was set as April 1, 1973, less than a year away. And the new authorization system would be called Bank Authorization System Experimental, or simply Base I. Later the name was changed to BankAmericard Service Exchange.

Dee then hired TRW, a contractor with vast experience in the fields of defense, space, and the auto industry, to come in and build the new system. Dee and his team, however, would keep tight control of the reins and the budget. IBM had promised to provide $250,000 worth of software and support in the phase of connecting member banks to the central system. According to Dee, IBM waffled and he promptly threw them out of the project. Dee then chose to build the system with a powerful DEC 11-45 mainframe as its central processor.

To house his new computer system, Dee leased 8,500 square feet of space in an office complex in San Mateo, just south of San Francisco. He only needed half that room, but Dee was confident the system would work and he wanted to have plenty of room to grow. He also took a first option on a much larger chunk of office space in the complex. Dee thought this a prudent move; his detractors saw empire-building and delusions of grandeur.

George Glaser, a specialist with McKinsey Consulting, was hired to supervise the project, and Aram Tootelian, a TRW systems whiz, came to San Mateo to run the BASE I project. Tootelian, in turn, brought aboard a young man named Win Derman, fresh out of Stanford with an MBA and a stint with the Stanford Research Institute. Win had gotten into computer programming during a tour in the U.S. Army and he was very excited about getting in on the ground floor of a brand new concept: the marriage of money and high technology.

"It was just the thing I was looking for," Win recalled in an interview. "We were going to do something unique."

The work began in the fall of 1972, and Win had never seen anything like it. "When we started out, we had no technical design, no equipment, no staff, no building, nothing but our own raw energy and ingenuity," he recalled. And the result was pure excitement. "The feeling was almost palpable: we were all on a mission. Something extraordinary was going on. We were betting the existence of the company that we could get it right."

At the new office complex, there was a central control room and Tootelian convened a staff meeting there every morning at 9 a.m. Each day when Win arrived one entire wall was covered with a bulletin board listing every day remaining on the project. Each task that remained to be done was listed on a scrap of paper, and the scraps were stuffed into a dirty coffee cup, hung by a string pinned to the current date. "Every task that needed to be done was in that cup, and every morning people just reached in and grabbed a new assignment," Win said. "We called it The Dirty Coffee Cup System and it became both a legend and symbol of how we built Base I."

As always with Dee, there was no hierarchy in the project and no constraints on anyone's ingenuity. "In the early days, everybody knew everything, and if you didn't know everything, you had to learn," Win explained. "There were no specialists

and there was no pigeon-holing. I got coffee. I wrote manuals. I did anything to help and so did everyone else."

By March 30, 1973, the big DEC computer was up and running, and the regional processing centers were wired in and ready to go. Now the system was ready for its first two-hour test. On the first go, the system failed. Tootelian's technicians tracked down and fixed the problem, and the next day the whole system was up and running. By April 4, the banks were using the system four hours a day, and by May 1 it was fully operational. Dee and his team had brought the project in on time and on budget.

For Dee and NBI, the success of BASE I was an important victory. It was the first step in transforming plastic money into electronic money. The American Express venture had meanwhile withered on the vine, and a similar MasterCard venture was running somewhat behind. With BASE I, NBI established itself as the industry leader in applying new technology to consumer payments. "It brought us credibility," Win said. "We took a concept and turned it into a reality that is still functioning in the year 2000, and we did it with quality, style and elegance. That might sound self-inflating, but there's no other way to describe it."

Two measuring sticks bear out Derman's assessment. As soon as BASE I was fully operational, the average authorization time dropped from five minutes to 56 seconds – a godsend for merchants, banks, and busy consumers. Also, in the fight against card fraud, BASE I is estimated to have saved NBI banks $30 million or more in its very first year of operation. BASE I spotted bad cards very efficiently, and so right away Dee's gamble paid off for the banks and NBI – handsomely.

The following year, Dee and his tech team did it again: they completed and launched another system, BASE II, the computerization of the entire interchange paper processing system. Now, in the blink of an eye, NBI's computers could take a transaction in hand, credit the merchant's bank – deducting the merchant discount fee – and, at the same time, send the transaction overnight to the cardholder's bank for debiting and billing anywhere in the United States. Dee brought BASE II in on time as well, and on budget at $7 million. In that first year in operation, BASE II cleared 200 million transactions, efficiently and cheaply.

With BASE I and BASE II in operation, Dee and his team brought forth another jewel. In February of 1975, they distilled their growing expertise into a comprehensive, clearly written guidebook. The title sounded gray and uninspiring: "Orientation and Training Guide." But for anyone in the bank card industry, this was the bible. It traced the history of credit cards in the United States, and it explained the creation and intent of NBI and IBANCO. Then it got to the core issue: how a bank could set up a card program and turn it into a profit stream.

The guidebook laid down a detailed blueprint for success, complete with recommended staff levels, marketing plans, credit policies, training procedures, card design specifications, floor limits, and even the placement of desks, carpeting, and electrical outlets in a bank's card processing center. One section explained the inner workings of BASE I and BASE II. Another explained how to collect bad debts and guard against fraud. "Managing for profitability" was the title of another key section, and it could have been entitled "The Gospel According to Dee." One typical entry:

"Accurate and candid two-way communication must be established with subordinates by:

a. Being available and approachable
b. Listening with understanding
c. Openly exchanging relevant facts
d. Taking appropriate action on feedback
e. Promoting cooperation within the [card]

center." The entry noted that "effective motivational approaches must be tailored to the individual needs of the employee."

Together, the new technology and Dee's operations bible worked wonders. Merchants were thrilled: BASE I cut fraud and ended the days of slow, cumbersome authorizations. BASE II was the beginning of the end of paper sales drafts. Cardholders were thrilled: using the card was now easier than ever before. And the banks were thrilled, as the costs of processing, sorting, clearing, and protecting against fraud were greatly cut.

"Those costs were killing the banks," explained Win Derman. "The process was labor- and cost-intensive, and as card usage grew, the costs had become exponentially harder to bear. BASE II slashed those costs." Now, with the new system, huge flows of money, digitally encoded, moved quickly and efficiently through the interchange process and into bank coffers.

All this helped spur NBI into a period of extraordinary growth. The number of cards in circulation soared. Usage per card soared. Bank card revenues increased. And more and more banks rushed to join the NBI, eager to follow Dee Hock and his team into the dawn of electronic money.

A few numbers tell the story. In 1975, the first full year BASE II was in operation, Dee's network of U.S. banks had 30 million cards in circulation, generating a total sales volume of $9 billion. Over one million U.S. merchants were in the network, and NBI's share of the U.S. bank card market, as measured in sales volume, was 44.3 percent. By 1980, the number of member cards in circulation had more than doubled to 64 million. U.S. sales volume had tripled to $28 billion. The number of merchant outlets had jumped 50 percent. By 1980 Dee's venture had catapulted over MasterCard and was now the market leader, with 53.5 percent of all U.S. bank card transactions. In September of 1980, 108 financial institutions joined NBI, the largest one-month jump in its history, illustrating once again how success breeds success.

Two developments during this period were absolutely key to NBI's success. The first involved duality. As readers will recall, Dee was vehemently opposed to duality and NBI had passed a bylaw forbidding issuing banks to hold dual memberships in the BankAmericard system and MasterCard. That triggered the lawsuit by the Worthen bank in Arkansas, which demanded the right to issue both cards. In 1975, after four years of complicated and fruitless legal back and forth, NBI asked the U.S. Justice Department for a "Business Review" letter, asking for approval of NBI's ban on duality. In support of this request, Dee and his legal team went to Washington and pressed their case against duality. "If we withdraw or fail to enforce a prohibition against duality, within two years you will find it difficult to discover a half-dozen banks which are not dual members of both systems," Dee argued, as he later related in his memoir.

The Justice Department denied NBI's request, a decision which cleared the way for duality to proceed. Now banks were free to join both sides. And they did. Once the floodgates were opened to duality, streams of new banks joined Dee's NBI and MasterCard lost its primary position in the industry.

In 1976, Dee and his team added a true masterstroke to their venture. To facilitate marketing the card and to consolidate the association's growing strength, Dee and his team came up with a brilliant new name for the old BankAmericard and its supporting network: Visa. In 1976, NBI became Visa U.S.A., and IBANCO became Visa International. This was a key step in the evolution of Visa and in the campaign to establish it as a globally recognized and accepted brand. The name change and its ramifications will be examined in detail in a later section called "The Image."

As his success expanded, Dee's sense of mission also expanded. As his operations bible suggested, Dee no longer saw himself as just the chief architect of a new payments system. Dee the iconoclast, Dee the rebel, Dee the corporate misfit was now trying to reach deep into every bank he could and open the minds and thinking of bankers around the globe. He was trying to foment a revolution – quietly. "Our institutions tend to stifle human ingenuity and growth," Dee explained in an interview. "So I was concerned with one fundamental problem: How do you organize human relationships into structures that develop and foster autonomy, creativity, and a sense of community?"

Dee saw NBI, IBANCO, and later Visa as a laboratory for testing and refining his views about leadership, motivation, and communicating ideas and core values. In the past, banks were rarely catalysts for social and economic change. Dee felt that through his growing influence in the world of banking and finance he had a chance – perhaps a small chance, but a chance – to promote positive change on a global scale. "Leadership is to go before and show the way," was one of Dee's favorite maxims, and he tried to live up to what it meant.

Dee, like many master creators, was a frustrated idealist, unhappy with the world as it was, and he was determined, by wit and sheer force of will, to remold the world into the way he felt it ought to be. This helps explain some of the episodes that Dee's staff and banking colleagues found to be so outlandish and irritating. His fanaticism about detail. His revulsion at the sight of a messy desk. His refusal to tolerate an inferior work product or a slacker on the job. His virulent critiques of staffers and their work. His insistence on full-scale dress rehearsals for major meetings.

Every day Dee had to work and he had to teach, for each day was a new opportunity to inspire and enlighten. This was what made Dee Hock seem to most everyone like a driven man: he wouldn't rest until every person saw the light, until every single detail was perfectly shaped and nestled in its rightful place.

There is a wonderful story that illustrates Dee's unbending sense of purpose and his passion for perfection. In January of 1974, a young computer ace named Tom Schramm joined Dee's tech team, which was then busy building BASE II. In the computer center, there were seven work stations, with people taking authorization calls and feeding them into the BASE I system. One day Dee came by, and to his eye something was woefully wrong with the set-up.

"Dee said to me, 'Schramm, why are those people facing inward, towards the entrance? They should be facing outside, onto the hillside and that beautiful view,'" Tom recalled.

By the time he was done, Dee saw to it that his staffers not only faced outside, they faced out onto a lovely sylvan setting, complete with an attractive bird feeder and even a salt lick to entice deer to what amounted to the company's backyard. Dee personally approved each phase of these adornments. Reminded of the incident today, Dee laughed and said that at times he loved to pull the legs of his staffers, by insisting on this tiny detail or that. But Tom Schramm saw in the episode something much larger: here was a man who had in his imagination a crystallized vision of how things ought to be. He could see, in his mind's eye, how every corner of his realm should look – and he was going to work and work and work until every detail was in its rightful place, even down to the bird-feeders and the now-infamous salt lick. Young Tom Schramm was deeply impressed.

"Dee was very aesthetics-conscious," Tom recalled. "He wanted everything to look just so. We called him The Grand Architect."

Dee took endless pains to make sure his tech team worked in an agreeable setting.

PUSH
OR
PULL
HERE

Wiring The World

Landmark innovations such as the Model T, the Boeing 707, and the personal computer were not only products, they were catalysts of awesome power. They transformed industries. They transformed people's tastes, habits, and daily lives. And, inevitably, they spawned new markets, new industries, and whole new waves of innovation.

BASE I and BASE II were catalysts of comparable power. They began the transformation of plastic money into electronic money. They catapulted Visa to the top of the bank card market and began transforming Dee Hock's association into a powerful high-tech operation. BASE I and BASE II also set Dee and his tech team into motion on another ambitious task: extending their expertise and the technology of electronic money to their member banks and merchants in the United States and around the globe. The ultimate goal here was already clear: to wire the world for electronic transactions and commerce.

This promised to be a monumental undertaking, but Dee knew what it could mean for the future of Visa and the bank card industry. MasterCard had shown little taste for the costs or risks of technological innovation. American Express did not have the network of international relationships it would take to wire the world. But the partnership Dee had knitted together with IBANCO, now Visa International, gave Dee the platform on which to build. The member banks around the world would join forces with Visa's tech teams and share the costs of developing the necessary national and regional infrastructures. The resulting network, if it could be built, would become the brain and central nervous system of a vast computer and telecommunications network – capable of becoming the world's premier system for processing electronic transactions. It would also make Visa the undisputed leader and driving force of the electronic money revolution.

If it could be built.

Some leaders, if they had such grand designs in mind, might draw up a master plan, go to their boards of directors, lay out the concept, and ask them to approve and fund the plan at one go. Not Dee. He knew that no board of directors, no matter how kindly disposed, would ever agree to the whole. So Dee the Machiavellian moved step by step, presenting his boards only with small, appetizing pieces they could easily swallow in one bite. First it was BASE I, then BASE II, then a small research project here, then another small venture there.

In 1980, Dee began forging two key pieces of his grand design. With the volume of card transactions now exploding around the world, Dee asked his U.S. and international boards to fund the construction of a European computer operations center, to be located in Basingstoke, England. The processing center would work in tandem with Visa's computer hub in San Mateo and with a sister Visa facility operating in McLean, Virginia.

Again, some board members balked, but Dee now had considerable credibility and leverage. His success with BASE I and BASE II had transformed a money-losing sector of banking into a rapidly expanding profit center. He also had a growing reputation in the industry and the press as the leading pioneer of electronic money. Against that, no one on his boards wanted to say "Stop" or "Go slow" to Dee and later be accused of timidity or lack of vision.

So Dee got his way, and Basingstoke would eventually become a vital element in Dee's grand design, together with another regional computer hub for Asia located in Yokohama, Japan. These new centers, together with San Mateo and McLean, would form just what Dee had envisioned: a powerful global transactions network called VisaNet.

In 1980, Dee and his tech team solved another piece of their puzzle: how to wire merchants into their electronic network. Visa planners and technicians had begun working on the problem several years before. The original zipzap machines were now antiquated and had to be replaced. Visa planners needed a new tool, one that ideally was small, inexpensive to make, easy to use, and attractive enough that merchants would be happy to have it sit next to their cash registers. Ideally, the new tool would be activated by a customer's Visa card and immediately plug the merchant, the cardholder, and the details of the transaction into Visa's electronic network. But that tool did not yet exist.

So with a Visa senior systems manager named Frank Fojtik, Visa came up with a workable concept – a small dial-in terminal using existing phone lines. Visa asked four companies to develop prototypes, GTE, Northern Telecom, Sweda, and TalTek, and each produced 200 models. Visa then put them into a pilot program that also used Visa-developed dial-up software for transaction processing.

Dee's team then moved on several fronts. Each of these initial dial terminals would cost merchants about $600, and many merchants, especially small shops, were reluctant to make the investment. It would take several years to convince merchants to make the changeover. In the interim, Visa set up a separate unit to help merchants tailor the new terminal hardware, software, and services to their individual business needs. Following the pilot, Visa set up a supply agreement with the manufacturers that cut the price to merchants in half.

At the same time, Visa opened discussions with its main competitors: MasterCard, American Express, Diners Club, and others. They had a common problem: no merchant would agree to lease and install three or four dial-in terminals, one for Visa, another for MasterCard, another for American Express, etc. The solution was evident – even to bitter rivals: a single dial terminal that could handle all the cards. Visa offered to carry its competitors' transactions through the Visa system for a small fee. Visa and its competitors hammered out the agreement and established a set of industry-wide standards and protocols for dial terminals. In this limited realm at least, cooperation and partnership were the order of the day – the technology and the marketplace demanded it.

Soon merchants across America were equipped with terminals, making payment quick and easy for merchants and consumers alike. Other manufacturers rushed into the exploding market for terminals, including a small California start-up venture called VeriFone. Small, nimble, and customer-oriented, VeriFone soon began building a commanding position in the dial terminal market, and two decades later its name was on 70 percent of the millions of easy-swipe terminals in the U.S. By 1997, VeriFone was also the leader in point-of-sale

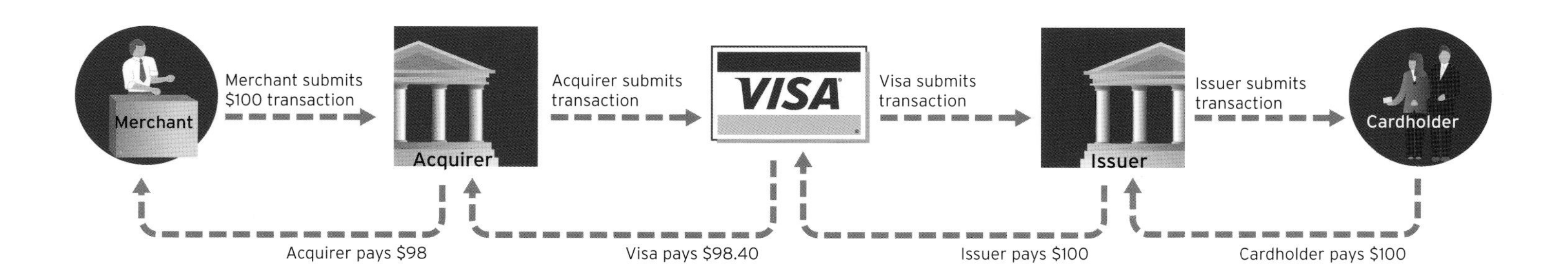

terminal technology, and with those credentials Hewlett-Packard bought the company for $1.29 billion.

To keep up with the escalating volume of electronic transactions, Visa had to constantly expand and upgrade its computer systems. Chuck Russell, chief of operations, oversaw this effort and much of the technical responsibility fell to an able, experienced former IBM ace named Roger Peirce. Roger had grown up in Fort Bragg, a lumbering and fishing town in the far northern reaches of California. Eager to leave, he went south to San Jose State University and found his calling in computers. After stints with Lockheed Aircraft and United Technologies, Roger joined IBM as a systems engineer. Later he moved into sales and canvassed what is now Silicon Valley selling and helping install IBM 360s, the company's mainframe workhorse of the time.

In the fall of 1973, Roger met Dee Hock. At this stage, Dee was ready to start building BASE II, and despite his earlier spat – and a potential lawsuit – with IBM, he went to Big Blue looking for help and a fresh start. "Dee was looking for respect," Roger recalled. "He had a vision of what he wanted to do at NBI and he wanted to be recognized as the leader of the bank card industry."

After several meetings, Dee became convinced that IBM was the partner he wanted for the next phase of his quest. Soon thereafter, Roger paid a visit to NBI's computer operations center in San Mateo. "What I found was an empty computer room, an ocean of raised floor space," Roger recalled. "It was a salesman's dream."

By November 1973, Dee had placed a major order for IBM equipment. DEC would continue to handle authorizations, and IBM would handle BASE II. Roger and other IBM specialists then worked hand-in-hand with Visa's tech team to build the system and get it up and running. Leading Visa's side of the operation was a big, bulky Texan named B. Ray Traweek.

"Building BASE II was a monumental task and I was too young and dumb to know what a challenge it was," B. Ray recalled. "We worked 80-hour weeks for the first six months. We brought in cots so we could catch a little sleep."

Their effort paid off, in several ways. "We brought BASE II in on time and on budget," Roger said. "That gave IBM credibility with Dee, and for a long period thereafter, IBM was his privileged partner in building the system."

For Roger, working with Dee was always a wild ride. Dee was challenging, stimulating, at times infuriating, and often he was refreshingly unpredictable. After BASE II was up and running, Dee asked IBM to help with the next step in his master plan: EVE. This was an Electronic Value Exchange system that Dee believed could provide the processing brain and central nervous system of a futuristic global payments system. Roger and his team designed a conceptual framework for the new system, with specifications and projected costs. In the end, Dee, Chuck Russell, and B. Ray nixed the idea. "It was too ambitious for its time," Roger said.

But Dee was committed to innovation and rapid growth, and he next invited IBM and DEC to propose plans to revamp the BASE I authorization system. The existing system was handling 5,000 authorizations an hour. Dee, thinking big as always, wanted a system that could handle 50,000 authorizations an hour. DEC and IBM developed competitive projects and bids, and after the two computer giants made their formal presentations, Dee's entire management team recommended giving the project to DEC. But then Roger and Bob Erwin, who were managing the IBM bid, had a private meeting with Dee.

"Dee told us he was going with DEC," Roger recalled, and that appeared to be the end of the story. "But then Bob threw a tantrum. He ranted and raved and told Dee that he was making a big mistake. And, to my shock, Dee changed his mind. He said that anybody who believes that passionately in their solution must be okay!"

Dee gave IBM one year to revamp BASE I, and Roger was given overall authority for the project. "We didn't have the best solution," Roger recalled. "What we had was based on the big airlines' system, ACP, the Airline Control Program. We had one year to take a staff from IBM, only one or two of whom had ACP experience, and develop software and hardware that could meet Dee's demands."

Done and done, and in January of 1981, Roger made the leap: he left IBM to help run Visa's computer systems and global network. Later, after Chuck Russell took over from Dee, Roger would be his chief lieutenant. For Roger, Visa was not just a job or a smart career move. When he joined on, like so many others before him, Roger Peirce was a true believer: "Dee was good at inspiring people and getting them to believe in what he was doing," Roger explained. "We were evangelists. We were changing the world."

B. Ray Traweek felt the exact same way. B. Ray had grown up in Ingram, Texas, a booming metropolis of 300 people. His father was a butcher, his mother a civil servant. Before B. Ray, no one in his family had attended high school, much less college. B. Ray broke the mold. He attended the University of Texas, earned a B.A. degree, and then went on and earned a master's degree in mathematics.

After university, B. Ray went to work for General Dynamics, which at the time made B-52 bombers. That brought him into the dawn of computer technology. B. Ray learned the innards of the big mainframes and how to use computers in aircraft design. He then joined TRW as a systems manager. TRW at the time was developing a financial system for Morgan Guaranty Trust, and through that project B. Ray Traweek found his calling: figuring out how to marry money and the new technology.

"I was fortunate to be in right at the beginning of the computer industry," B. Ray recalled, "and right at the beginning of the card business."

By the early 1970s, B. Ray was looking for a change, and he went to see Dee Hock. It was an experience he would never forget. By this time, Dee had a new office on an elite floor of the Bank of America building, looking out over San Francisco, and to a small-town guy from Texas that office was something out of a dream or a Hollywood picture. The way B. Ray's wife later put it, "It was the kind of office where you'd expect Cary Grant to woo Katherine Hepburn."

Dee was just as dazzling. "Dee personally interviewed everyone," B. Ray recalled with a laugh, "right down to the crew that cleaned the men's room. He sat me down and said, 'So, what do you want to accomplish with your life?' I was overcome by the whole experience." Overcome and

The cooling system for Visa's computers in San Mateo, California.

seduced: B. Ray joined Visa and spent the rest of his career as one of Dee's top managers and globe-trotting evangelists.

In that capacity, B. Ray played a key role in the next step of Dee's grand design: taking Visa expertise and technology out to Europe, Asia, and Latin America. Visa's regional processing centers in Basingstoke and Yokohama would serve as anchoring hubs, but individual banks and merchants still had to be wired into the system. This meant going around the world, meeting member banks, convincing them to come aboard, training their staffs, and installing computer and telecommunications equipment.

This also meant bridging several different languages, cultures, and levels of technological development. Wiring the world was not just an awesome technological challenge; it was a diplomatic, political, and cultural challenge as well. B. Ray and his teams had to get the French to work with the English, the Italians to cooperate with the Swedes, the Israelis to join hands with the Germans, and that was just the beginning. This was a daunting assignment, especially for a small-town, straight-shooting, Coke-sipping, down-home, get-it-done Texan like B. Ray Traweek.

"I'm a pragmatist," B. Ray explained. "The single most important thing for me was to find ways to implement our guiding vision. We were a member-driven association. We really believed that we'd be rewarded most by helping our members."

Here Dee's guiding vision of partnership and cooperation, even among fierce competitors, provided B. Ray and his teams with a valuable framework and roadmap. Like Dee, B. Ray relied on an intricate web of advisory boards, working committees, and ongoing consultations, with an orderly calendar of meetings to make sure the process was on track. "Our system of advisors' meetings was a key ingredient of our success," B. Ray explained. "We'd get together with 20 of our larger members in any given geographic area, and we'd socialize, lobby, and talk shop. It helped us detect problems early and deal with them right away. The formula worked well nearly all the time, and it got embedded in our process."

There were some amusing bumps in the road. Old Visa hands recall one meeting when B. Ray came to Europe to find out why the new system wasn't going up as fast as he had hoped, both in Europe and the Middle East. B. Ray gathered his various country managers together, and he was determined to solve all the problems, then and there. It was a very hot day, B. Ray was drinking Coca-Cola in copious quantities, and he first demanded to know why the Europeans couldn't get their act together and make the system work 24 hours a day, seven days a week. "We Americans did it," B. Ray barked. "Why can't you?"

The Europeans tried to explain their problems. In Italy, for instance, the Visa processing system just couldn't operate 24 hours a day. Italian unions insisted that the system be shut down for two hours in the middle of the day – so that Italian workers could have a proper lunch break. That explanation cut no mustard with B. Ray. And as he went around the table, he was getting more and more exasperated. Finally, he turned to a fellow named Moshe, who worked for the Bank Leumi in Israel.

"Now look, Moshe, you're going to have to do something," B. Ray scolded him. "You're closed on Saturday. That's the peak day for airlines, the peak day for hotel checkouts, and you're closed! Why the goddamn are you closed?"

Moshe, who was known for his understated wit, shrugged his shoulders and replied, "It's the religion, my boy."

That didn't stop B. Ray. He stuck a thick Texas finger out to Moshe and said, "Well, then, you're just gonna have to change your religion!" And everyone collapsed in laughter.

Wiring Latin America posed a different set of problems – and the task of solving them fell to a little dynamo named Sonia Vicente. Sonia was born

Sonia Vicente played a key role in wiring Latin American banks into the Visa network.

and raised in Cuba, but she left in 1961 to accept a full scholarship at the University of Dubuque in Iowa. There she studied math, physics, and economics and became interested in computer technology. After college, Sonia worked for IBM for five years, and then she joined the Banco de Ponce in Puerto Rico, to help computerize bank operations and install a network of ATM machines. In 1980, Sonia was recruited to Visa by Jim Partridge, who was then setting up a regional office in Miami to coordinate business and technology for Latin America.

"I was the sixth employee to join Jim in the Latin America office," Sonia recalled. "My job was operations and systems."

At that stage, no banks in Latin America were on-line to the Visa computer network. Mexico, Puerto Rico and Venezuela were considered advanced; their banks used dedicated telex lines to handle merchant authorizations. Other countries used ordinary telex lines. The average authorization time was six minutes. The bulk of merchant transactions were recorded on tape, which were then mailed to Visa for processing. "The average time for clearing a transaction was 45 days!" Sonia laughed. "The situation was impossible."

So Visa and Jim Partridge gave Sonia a mission: "Build us a system!" Sonia studied the Latin American situation first-hand, traveling country-by-country and bank-by-bank. Then she devised a master plan. It called for wiring the region with point-of-sale dial terminals and a small computer for every member bank, to speed authorizations and clearances. For these small computers, called Member Interface Processors (MIPs), Sonia wanted to use IBM Series 1 computers. But there was a problem. In the U.S. market, those computers sold for $500,000 apiece. However, importing them into Latin America, with duty and taxes, doubled the price.

"There was just no way we could afford to install those in each bank," Sonia said. "So I came up with an idea: one MIP per country, connected to all the banks."

The regional banks approved Sonia's solution. In 1983, the system's first shared MIP went into operation, in Puerto Rico. It immediately slashed the time and costs of authorizations and clearances. By 1984, MIPs were up and running in Venezuela, Mexico, and Colombia. This brought to an end the days of paper sales drafts and mailed transaction records. The electronic money revolution had come to Latin America.

"We wired the main countries," Sonia explained. "They were linked to a shared MIP in Miami. The system worked."

As always with Visa, the main thrust of the global vision was carefully tailored to local needs and capacities. For instance, many of the merchants in Latin America set down a pragmatic and understandable demand: that their transactions be handled in Spanish. Visa turned to VeriFone for help. If VeriFone would invest the time and resources necessary to develop a Spanish-language terminal, Visa would guarantee a first order of 5,000 dial terminals, with many more to come. Done and done. Visa was delighted. Merchants and banks throughout Latin America were delighted. And VeriFone secured a strong position in another rapidly expanding market. Everyone won.

This story, with differing local flavors and problems, was repeated in country after country, region after region – and the Visa network went up at an almost unbelievable pace. And Visa business went up right along with it. The year 1984 brought forth a few milestones that illustrated Visa's success – and the speed, power, and extent of the electronic money revolution:

- The BASE II system processed one billion transactions that year, an average of 3.9 million transactions per business day.

- The value of those transactions was nearly $53 billion, a jump of 25 percent in just four years.
- Visa member banks were now operating in 160 countries, meaning Visa was now spanning the globe.
- Dial terminals accounted for 69 percent of all transactions – the changeover to electronic money was galloping forward.
- Every month Visa was processing about 925,000 MasterCard transactions, about 805,000 from American Express, and 12,900 from Diners Club – meaning that cooperation, even among fierce competitors, was serving everyone's interest.

Since then, VisaNet has, of course, continued to grow. Today this network links your Visa card to 22,000 banks and to millions of merchants, businesses, and ATM machines around the world – usually in the blink of an eye. Contemplate this fact for a moment: on any given day, the Visa system is processing about 2,000 transactions *per second.* During the Christmas shopping rush, it handles about 3,000 transactions per second, no matter what time of day, no matter what diverse currencies are involved. The average Visa transaction runs about $80, meaning that at Christmastime Visa is smoothly and accurately processing about $240,000 every single second. That's more than $43 million every three minutes. And those figures continue to climb.

Looking back now, it is clear that building this vast global network represents one of the most important achievements in Visa's history. The network transformed Visa. It transformed the credit card industry. It transformed the way millions of merchants and cardholders go about their daily business. And it transformed money itself. Chuck Russell, B. Ray Traweek, Roger Peirce, Win Derman, Sonia Vicente, VeriFone, and thousands of other experts and managers around the world helped build the Visa system and advance the course of the electronic money revolution. They were pioneers all, and history will surely see them as such. And so were the member banks.

Dee, of course, was delighted by what his technical teams had achieved – and by the resultant profits for his member banks. But he held fast to a loftier perspective. His managers and their technical teams had reached around the world and built strong bridges of trust and cooperation. As a result, Visa now had a first-class computer and telecommunications network – and a first-class network of business and personal relationships. It also had a staff that was learning how to run a truly global operation. Dee knew that over time this meld of relationships and expertise would be far more important to his ultimate mission – building the Visa community – than any hardware or software, or any measure of transaction volume or member profit.

"Only fools worship their tools," Dee later wrote. The true and enduring success of Visa would reside in two things that no one could measure: the quality of relationships it developed with its different partners and how successfully it served and enriched the higher interests of the community as a whole.

"Community is not about profit," Dee cautioned. "It is about benefit. We confuse them at our peril."

VISA INTERNATIONAL
VISA

CHAPTER 13

The Passkey

How far we've come.

In the early days of plastic money, the BankAmericard, Chargex, Barclaycard, and the Sumitomo Card were rather simple tools. They bore the name of the issuing bank or institution, and they carried the easily recognizable blue, white, and gold bands. Each card identified its holder by name and account number – in raised letters so a merchant could easily imprint them on a sales draft with a zipzap machine. Essentially, though, the cards were inactive, not very different from a driver's license or a library card.

No longer. The development of BASE I, BASE II, point-of-sale terminals, and Visa's global support network set in motion a radical transformation of the little card itself. Today, Visa cards only look simple. In reality, they are powerful, interactive, high-tech tools – electronic passkeys with sophisticated codes and secret security devices embedded in their plastic. In some parts of Europe and Asia, the new coins of the realm are "smart cards," equipped with microchips that multiply their power and versatility. With chips or without, these new generations of cards are major leaps from the past. They serve as our passport, and our visa, into the new and rapidly expanding world of electronic money.

Think, for a moment, about what we can do with these new cards that we could never do before. We can get cash at the ATM. Buy food or gas. Pay the doctor, the dentist, or the hospital and leave our money at home. We can buy computers, car insurance, or concert tickets over the phone or over the Internet. With the click of a mouse, we can buy airline tickets or trade stocks on-line. We can even travel to remote places – including parts of the Amazon rain forest – without cash or checks or even a travelers cheque. Once there, we just pay with our card and get whatever local currency we need at a nearby ATM. Presto! No muss, no fuss, no panic. The revolution's in our pocket.

How can a slender piece of plastic accomplish all this? How are Visa cards made? What security devices are built into them? And what about that elegant bird in flight that is set into the face of the card? Is it decorative or functional? What magic is embedded in the little card we carry that allows us to do all this?

The man with the answers to these questions is Murdoch Henretty. Murdoch is a jovial, unflappable Scotsman with a twinkle in his eye and some very unusual expertise. For two decades, he played a major role in the evolution of the Visa card's design, manufacture, and security devices. In a larger sense, too, his own background and career mirror the transformation of traditional money and the emergence of the new electronic currency.

Murdoch grew up in Edinburgh, about a half-mile down the road from Sean Connery. As a boy, in addition to going to school, he delivered newspapers and had a milk route. At the age of 16 he went to work for a local printer. There, and later at art school, Murdoch made a discovery. "I had an eye for matching color," Murdoch recalled. "So I became an 'ink formulator.' My job was to blend inks to match whatever color we wanted to print."

When Murdoch was 24, this talent led him to a job with Thomas De La Rue & Co., an English firm that specialized in printing paper currency and other documents with built-in security features, like travelers cheques, postage stamps, and passports. "I came in as an ink manager, and later I worked as a print and project manager," Murdoch said. "After a time, De La Rue sent me out to

Murdoch Henretty, one of
Visa's multi-talented specialists.

Colombia, Malta, Germany, Ireland and the Philippines, to train staff and build sophisticated, secure facilities for printing their currencies." After a dozen years with De La Rue, Murdoch had developed an unusual array of skills: plant management, ink formulation, currency and document design, printing, specialty papers, and printing plant construction and security. He also knew how to develop innovative security devices for printed products.

In 1978, Murdoch was ready for a change. He had a sister and brother who had moved to California and were very happy, and the weather on the West Coast was certainly more appealing than the cold and damp of Scotland or England. So Murdoch immigrated to California. There, with his unusual skills, he quickly landed a job at Jeffries Bank Note Company, a respected security printer in southern California. As part of the sales team, Murdoch was given several high-profile assignments, among them one to design a new travelers cheque for Visa International and another to enhance the security of travelers cheques for Citicorp and the Bank of America.

Murdoch's knowledge of security printing impressed Visa, and in 1984 he got a call from Dave Huemer in the travelers cheque group. "I understand you know something about printing and ink," Huemer said. Indeed he did. Huemer told him Visa was in desperate need of someone with his unusual skills. Dee, it turned out, was on the rampage. Visa had announced the launch of three new Visa card designs, and all were having problems in production. Dee was not happy with the prototypes developed by his design team. In fact, Dee had just chastized the lot of them. "The job's yours, if you want it," Huemer told him. "But you have to hurry. Dee's getting antsy."

Murdoch took the Dee Hock challenge and moved from paper money to plastic. "I had to go out and understand the card business," Murdoch recalled. "I knew paper and printing, but not plastic." Right away he plunged into the gold card project. He met with various manufacturers of Visa cards, and the results were dismaying. Dee's design team had unwittingly created card designs that could not be printed by the conventional silk screen process, only by a lithographic process. But gold inks, which use metallic filings, could not be printed by lithography, and various experiments with simulated gold pigments were giving uneven results. So Murdoch had a serious problem to solve. Millions of Visa cards were scheduled to be printed in different production sites around the world. Murdoch had to find a consistent color and a process for printing and laminating that could be used by all the manufacturers.

Murdoch was able to resolve the problem, and he has been with Visa ever since. Now he works on card design, new technologies and production techniques, and the implementation of tight security measures at Visa's affiliated card manufacturers. Murdoch is, therefore, the perfect fellow to take us on an insider's tour of the whole production process.

Oberthur Card Systems, located in an industrial park on the outskirts of Los Angeles, is a good place to see how far credit card technology has come since the days of BankAmericard. The Oberthur plant, first of all, is a model of tight security. It's a single-story facility, protected by barbed wire fencing on the roof and by security cameras placed at key positions along the property. Inside, access to different parts of the facility is controlled by a system of electronic badges and state-of-the-art "manholder" doors – if anyone unauthorized gets caught inside, those doors will clamp shut. Supervising the security at the plant is Tony Panzica, a former member of the Los Angeles police. This might not be Fort Knox, but the prin-

CAUTION
DANGER

VISA
X.com

ciple is the same: protect the currency housed inside.

Oberthur is a large card manufacturer headquartered in France, and it bought out this operation at the close of the 1990s. It also owns and runs five other card production plants in the United States. Before Oberthur took over the Los Angeles facility, it was Kirk Plastics, a family business with a history dating back to 1919. Even in its early days, Kirk's specialty was printing on, and then laminating, plastic. During World War II, it made security badges for the U.S. military. In 1955 it entered the realm of plastic charge cards, making two million cards for Union Oil. Kirk Hyde grew up in the family business and, until the Oberthur takeover, he was president and CEO. "We made the original BankAmericards," Kirk recalled. "When I was in high school, I delivered a half-million cards to a Bank of America card center in Pasadena."

In the early days, Kirk Plastics made cards directly for a large number of banks, printing them on two-color presses. The company had only 30 employees. But the changing technology and the explosion of plastic money transformed Kirk and its business. It grew into a company with 300 employees and it used sophisticated six-color presses. In peak periods, the company churned out 14 *million cards a month* – credit cards, gold cards, debit cards, and smart cards. By the time it sold out to Oberthur, Kirk's major clients were no longer banks. They were third-party card processing companies like First Data Resources and Equifax, which run card programs, from issuance to billing, for hundreds of client banks and lending institutions. Kirk saw the impact of this consolidation every single day. "Our business has changed dramatically over the years," he explained. "Now First Data is our biggest client, and 98 percent of our business is with ten people."

The Oberthur facility reveals, at a glance, the size and importance of the credit card industry today: the plant is 106,000 square feet. It's a high-tech facility, with state-of-the-art graphics and printing facilities. Business is booming: the plant often runs around the clock to keep up with demand.

Everything here happens under one roof: card design, the printing of the cards, the laminating, the embedding of signature panels, the addition of electronic coding and security devices, the embossing of client names and account numbers, even the sorting, envelope stuffing, and the final mailing. Many of the early steps are labor intensive, but one state-of-the-art machine, using robot technology, can do 10 of the last steps by itself.

Banks have the freedom to design their own cards or they can work with Oberthur designers, though card designs must conform with Visa and industry-wide specifications. The border of the card, for instance, has to be white. And the Visa logo, with its distinctive blue, white and gold markings, must be of exact colors and a certain size and position on the card. In one of the card's many hidden security features, the Visa logo is surrounded by micro-printing. Each manufacturer has its own micro-signature and the difficulty of reproducing it helps curb counterfeiting.

To print cards, Oberthur uses big German-made printing presses that were originally designed to print on paper but have been adapted to print on plastic. Cards are printed on large sheets of polyvinyl chloride, with 54 cards to the sheet. The fronts and backs of the cards are done separately and later laminated together. There are actually four layers of plastic to be laminated: a clear front sheet, the front of the card, the back of the card, and a rear lamination strip that includes the "mag stripe" – the magnetic tape that will later be encoded with data specific to the cardholder. "The tape you could buy at Radio Shack," Murdoch explained. "But what's on the tape is difficult to replicate."

The new lamination presses can turn out 250 plastic sheets an hour. In one automated process, they gather together the four plastic sheets and spot weld them, to make sure they are properly stacked together before heat-lamination. "In the old days," Murdoch explained, "lamination was done by a dinosaur of a press. Operators gathered the four layers together by hand, and lamination took 45 minutes to do one plate. With today's equipment, it takes just 8 minutes."

Once the individual cards are die-cut from the big sheets, Oberthur staff verify the quality of every card. They inspect the cards for any defects of color, ink, or foreign particles. Any card that is rejected is carefully logged and destroyed – lest it find its way into the illegal marketplace for hot cards. Naturally, too, all Oberthur employees come aboard only after they have passed a strict security screening – a process Visa helped devise and still monitors through regular on-site inspections and reviews.

Cards that pass inspection then make their way, via an assembly line, to a special "personalization area," where they are embossed and encoded with names, Personal Identification Numbers (PINs), and other data the issuing bank has sent to Oberthur – electronically, of course. "Smart cards" equipped with microchips have a different step here. A hole is precision-drilled in the card and then the chip is nestled in and glued tight. Then the chip is "loaded" with the necessary data. This same "smart card" production train is also used for fixed-value charge cards and telephone cards, both of which use chip technology.

And what about that bird? Now therein hangs a story.

In 1978, when Murdoch was still working at Jeffries Bank Note, Dee decided to develop a travelers cheque for Visa. Then he hired Jeffries and Thomas De La Rue & Company to develop ideas and designs. Both companies put their design teams on the project, developing distinctive looks and logos. In November of 1978, both teams went to Visa headquarters to finalize the new cheque design. In the course of the meeting, a Jeffries' designer named Kurt Roald came up with a design idea. He took a pencil and began sketching a bird in flight. "It was a dove," Murdoch recalled, "and Dee liked the idea of a dove in flight, as the dove was the international bird of peace."

To turn the concept into a polished image, Dee's design team found a real dove and a photographer and they set to work. They wanted to photograph the bird in flight, so they tied its legs together so it couldn't land. "The photographer took over 100 pictures, and if you looked carefully, you could see the legs tied together," Murdoch said. "The artist who engraved the original steel printing die for the travelers cheque didn't see that the bird's legs were tied together, so the travelers cheque wound up with an engraving of a dove that appeared to have only one leg."

In 1983, Dee decided he wanted to redesign the Visa card, and he was looking for some new and unique security device to put on it. By this time, Murdoch had joined Visa's travelers cheque group, and he was part of the search for fresh ideas and a fresh look. They examined various "lenticular devices" that could create interesting visual effects on the face of the card, but none had the necessary "Eureka!" quality.

At this same time, a currency printer named American Bank Note was experimenting with something new: hologram technology, specifically holograms mounted on foil. Visa's design team was intrigued by the hologram technology – but they weren't the only ones. "MasterCard at the time was redesigning its cards and decided to go with a hologram, before us," Murdoch said. "Quickly, Dee made a decision to go with a hologram and he used the dove from the travelers cheque as the image."

Visa's design team then sent photos of their dove to a sculptor, so he could make a three-dimensional sandstone model of the bird. But the first prototype holograms were not successful. There were engineering problems. There were chemistry problems. The costs of applying holograms were too high, and about 28 percent of the cards were coming out flawed. "It took a long time to eliminate all the problems," Murdoch recalled. "Six or eight months."

But the effort was worth it; the result was a jewel. Over the years, the dove's size and look have evolved, but the dove has remained Visa's most artful and distinctive symbol. Turn the card a bit and the bird's wings actually move – a three dimensional effect achieved by splitting a laser beam and projecting the resultant image onto polyester film. But Visa's dove is more than artful; it is a subtle yet attractive security feature. Produced from a sculptured model, it is very difficult to reproduce accurately, and examining the dove is an easy way for merchants to spot a counterfeit card. "The dove is one security feature that has given Visa a long run for its money," Murdoch said. "It went onto the card in 1984 and it's still effective. We still see counterfeits, but the ones we see aren't very good." Visa sends out posters and brochures to show merchants the tell-tale differences between the real thing and the poor imitations.

The holograms are produced under license by only a few specialized manufacturers, and they come to Oberthur and other cardmakers on large reels of foil, which arrive by armored car. Each reel is numbered. Each hologram is numbered. Security is tight through every step of the application process. Finally, the reels roll and six manually driven, specially designed machines burn the holograms into the plastic cards. Each machine can apply 100,000 holograms a day – and often they do. At the end of every day, there is a complete audit of cards and holograms. "We have to account for every hologram," explained Tony Panzica, director of security.

Since Oberthur took over, there has been something of a sea change at the plant in southern California. Kirk Hyde is gone, chip card production is on the rise, and the only certainty in this corner of the credit card business is that the pace of change will surely accelerate. "What's the future bank?" Kirk wondered aloud. "Is it brick and mortar? Or is it electronic? No one knows."

Visa planners echo this sentiment. As we will see, the new technology is evolving rapidly. In the future, the payment device we use might not even be a card at all; it might be a computer chip embedded in a key ring, a cell phone, or a hand-held computer. Right now Visa researchers are working with such high-tech companies as Nokia, Microsoft, and Schlumberger to develop the wonder tools of the future.

Whatever direction the new technology leads, Murdoch Henretty and his Visa colleagues know one thing for sure: gangs of card thieves, counterfeiters, and computer hackers won't be far behind. And that leads us to a whole new part of the Visa story.

The origins of Visa's distinctive hologram dove.

The Secret Handshake

CHAPTER 14

You don't mess with Dick Held.

Held is a tall, calm, methodical man, precise in his words, and impeccably gracious in his demeanor. But make no mistake. Beneath his velvet exterior, Dick Held is one tough cookie. Held's father devoted his life to the FBI; Held himself served 26 years in the corps that J. Edgar Hoover built. In his final post with the bureau, Held was in charge of the northern California office, and part of his mandate was to investigate criminal activity in the Silicon Valley – and its foreign tentacles. This would prove to be ideal training for where Held chose to go in 1993: Visa International.

Held took on a very challenging assignment: coordinate Visa's worldwide fight against credit card fraud and counterfeiting. This is a highly specialized corner of the crime world and it's big business: fraud costs Visa's member banks about $1 billion a year. The issue is not just money lost. Card crime strikes at an essential component of what makes plastic, electronic, or any other currency work: trust. "This industry is built on trust," Held explained. "People have to believe they can trust this way of doing business."

So Held had twin goals: keeping Visa transactions secure, and holding down fraud. Those are not simple tasks, especially today. In the early days of plastic money, the methods of credit card crime were relatively crude. Thieves would pick pockets, snatch purses, and rifle mailboxes for envelopes containing credit cards or monthly statements. They would also bribe hotel or restaurant cashiers for card numbers or receipts to copy. In those days, a valid account number was almost as valuable as a card itself. Counterfeiters would take valid numbers, put them on bogus cards, and then put them into circulation. At the very bottom of this malevolent crime chain were the "dumpster divers," penny-ante thugs who would sift through a merchant's garbage, looking for discarded sales drafts or carbons containing those precious credit card numbers.

As the industry evolved, however, so did the criminals. Today card thieves don't snatch purses; they snatch electronic data. They use computers and powerful software to try to hack their way into bank files, company data bases, and Internet sites. In search of card numbers to steal, criminals no longer sift through garbage cans; now they run telemarketing scams and Internet porno sites. Counterfeiting, too, has gone high-tech. Criminal gangs now use laptops, complex graphics programs, and sophisticated embossing machines to turn out high-quality counterfeit cards that are very difficult to spot.

One of Held's biggest headaches was a high-tech practice called "skimming." Here's how it works: an unsuspecting cardholder dines at a Chinese restaurant in Toronto, for example, and pays with his credit card. The waiter disappears with the card and gives it to a cashier, who swipes it through the usual point-of-sale card reader and processes the transaction. In a second motion, however, the corrupt cashier swipes the card through a second electronic reader, which "skims" the relevant data off the card's magnetic stripe.

The unwitting customer retrieves his card, but before he's out the door, data from his card is on its way, via e-mail, to a counterfeit card operation based in Hong Kong, or Malaysia, or the Bahamas, or elsewhere. There the valid data is downloaded onto a bogus or stolen card, and the card is sent to an accomplice somewhere around the world – Bangkok, Amsterdam, or New York.

The accomplice uses the card to buy fancy watches, designer clothing, cameras, or expensive electronic gear. These are resold on the black market and the profits are used to fund other criminal activities such as drug trafficking and prostitution. All the resultant charges, of course, are billed to the original cardholder, but he or she does not have to pay them. The issuing bank is stuck with the tab.

Skimming takes other forms as well. Some gas stations on America's West Coast have seen another layer to the scam. Their pumps will take an ATM card, but as you punch in your PIN number, hidden cameras record the number. A corrupt employee ends up skimming all the key data off your card – including your confidential PIN number. "Skimming is our biggest problem today," explained Ben Patty, one of Held's right hands and himself a former FBI man. "From a single swipe, they can duplicate an entire mag stripe."

How to fight skimming and other types of card fraud? How to protect Visa's banks, merchants, and cardholders? How, above all, to ensure trust in the Visa logo and brand?

These questions have been paramount to Visa since its inception. In the start-up years, Dee Hock relied on a small, makeshift unit to deal with card fraud and security issues. In the late 1970s, though, Dee turned to a real pro: Bill Neumann, head of the FBI's San Francisco office. Neumann joined Visa to create a top-flight, well-funded unit to combat credit card fraud. He had several priorities: the security of the Visa card itself, the security of card manufacturers and the processing centers of member banks, coordination with law enforcement agencies, and investigating actual fraud cases. To help in the effort, Neumann recruited several former FBI investigators and a group of specialists with backgrounds in bank security; currency, card and computer security; cryptography; and computer analysis.

Neumann's team developed security devices for the card itself and for the safeguard of the payment process. As we saw at Oberthur, they also developed strict procedures to govern the card manufacturing process. At the same time, they forged close working relationships and shared their knowledge and methods with Visa member banks and police agencies around the world. In the process, they earned Visa the reputation as the pre-eminent clearinghouse for credit card fraud information and expertise – a position it proudly maintains today. "Bill Neumann built the team and set the direction," Held said. "He's the architect of the whole thing."

Even with the right team and the right tools, however, Neumann and his team faced serious obstacles. Many police agencies, for instance, did not understand the complexities of card fraud and were reluctant to make it a high priority. Fighting organized crime, murder, drug dealing, rape, and armed robbery was seen as a better allocation of police attention and resources. Also, investigating and prosecuting fraud cases was a long, expensive process with little payoff: convicted card thieves and counterfeiters often faced very little jail time. So Neumann's priority was not stomping out card

Credit card fraud is high-tech and big business.

crime; it was holding it to absorbable levels for the banks. The goal was called "risk management," and his dream target was to hold fraud down to about five cents per $100. "Some fraud is just the cost of doing business," Held explained. "There are just not enough investigators, prosecutors or financial resources to go after every fraud case. Sometimes the costs of prosecution are more than the cost of the fraud itself, and no one winds up in jail anyway."

When Neumann was ready to retire, he recruited Dick Held from the FBI. By this time, the realm of card fraud was rapidly changing. The penny-ante local thug was being replaced by highly mobile international gangs that were well-organized and technologically savvy. Many of them were based in Asia but operated on several continents, making them all the more difficult to combat. Held had to make several changes and improve coordination at the international level. "Plastic money acknowledges no borders," Held explained. "Also, plastic money is not controlled by national treasuries. That reduces government control."

To combat the international gangs, Held tightened Visa's cooperation with police agencies like Scotland Yard, Interpol, the international police consortium headquartered in Lyons, France, and the U.S. Secret Service, which has responsibility for the security of U.S. currency and "access devices" like credit cards.

At the same time, Visa beefed up its training courses around the world to help fight card counterfeiting and trafficking. For many years, Visa itself aggressively investigated major fraud cases, using its staff and technology to help law enforcement agencies build their cases. Held chose to put a higher priority on planning, coordination, product security, and improved communications with member banks and merchants. Now Visa also sends out monthly bulletins to banks, merchants,

Experts can spot the fakes:
The top card has been re-embossed.
The middle card has a fake hologram.
The bottom card is a total counterfeit.

and police agencies, informing them of the latest trends and methodology being seen on the criminal front. It also alerts merchants about the latest tell-tale signs to look for on suspect cards.

This effort has saved Visa's banks hundreds of millions of dollars over the years. Yes, card fraud today is running at about $1 billion a year but, Held explained, that's not so much when you consider Visa's total international sales volume of more than $1.7 trillion a year. "The cost of fraud is about 7 cents on the $100," he said. "We think that's quite phenomenal."

In their fight against fraud, Held's team and Visa member banks have two powerful weapons to use: the cards themselves, and Visa's global computer network. As we've seen, the hologram on every Visa card is not only decorative; it's a distinctive security device that is very difficult to counterfeit. Each Visa card also has other built-in security devices to help check fraud. (See card opposite.)

Your Visa card, for instance, repeats the first four digits of your account number underneath the embossed numbers. This prevents "ironing." In this process, a stolen card – whose number has been hot-listed and thus rendered useless – is ironed out flat and then embossed with a new, workable number. The flying "V" on the Visa logo is also difficult to reproduce, as is the micro-writing that surrounds the logo. These devices help merchants spot phony cards.

The visible markings, though, are just the beginning. Far more complex security devices are embedded in the back of the card, on the magnetic stripe located above or below the signature panel. Bill Neumann and Roger Peirce devised for the "mag stripe" a secret algorithm called the Card Verification Value, or CVV. When you or a merchant swipes your card through a card reader, your specific CVV code is sent back to your issuing bank for verification. If the code on the card fits the bank's, the bank will authorize the card transaction. If the code does not fit, the bank alerts the merchant to seize the card and notify the police. With today's "skimmers" eager to crack the CVV, Visa developed an added measure of protection: another important line of coding called the CVV-2. These codes represent a "secret handshake" between every card and Visa's computer network; if the handshake fails, the transaction is stopped dead.

In Dick Held's mind, the most effective anti-fraud device now in existence is the "smart card," equipped with a microchip. The chip can be loaded with more devices to ensure the security of "the handshake" and the transaction. France was the first country to go full-bore into chip cards – and the changeover cut counterfeit card fraud in France down dramatically. Britain, Japan, and Singapore, among others, have also moved to smart cards and the early indications were promising. But the conversion to "chip" is an expensive proposition, as bank and merchant hardware, ATM machines, and all the related software have to be converted at the same time. As an interim step, Visa and its members are examining the potential of high-density mag stripes, capable of carrying significantly more data and more security protections.

"The potential of chip technology is absolutely astounding. There is just no end to what it can ultimately do for us," Held said before he retired in 2000. "But we have 20 years experience understanding the technology and risks of the mag stripe. We don't have that expertise yet with chips." Also, the chip technology is changing so rapidly that Held and other Visa planners cannot be sure where it will lead.

Visa has another secret weapon in the fight against fraud: VisaNet, its own vast computer network. Visa's computers not only process transactions; they monitor them. Using advanced "neural network technology" – a form of artificial intelligence – VisaNet examines each transaction and assesses the probability that it might be fraudulent. The assessment is based on finely tuned models that have been developed for specific card markets. The Visa team has turned this neural network capability into a tool called CRIS, meaning Cardholder Risk Identification Service.

This sounds complicated, but you may have already seen the results. For instance, if you buy shoes in Chicago in the morning and then have dinner in Los Angeles that same day, and pay for both with your Visa card, your bank might call you and ask if both charges are legitimate. That call means the CRIS system spotted the geographically distant transactions and sent up an alert that triggered the protective call from your bank. The aim, of course, is to protect the consumer and to spot fraudulent card use before it escalates into substantial losses for the issuing bank.

Using this and other technology, Visa experts can also track the course of a fraudulent card. In Singapore in 1998, for instance, three male Indonesian Chinese were nailed by police with seven counterfeit cards in their possession. In fact, the arrests were the fruit of an intense investigation involving four member banks, close cooperation with Visa, and substantial input from Visa's computer network. It turned out the group was using cards with Indonesian faces but with French account numbers. Once the anomaly was discovered, Visa and its banks were able to pinpoint the fact that the culprits used the bogus cards mostly on Fridays and in one particular shopping area of Singapore. That facilitated their arrest and prosecution.

Visa analysts use similar methods to track down the skimmers. Once they have detected a skimmed card, they can use their neural network tools to track the movement of its transactions. In several cases, Visa analysts back-tracked the movements of several skimmed cards and succeeded in pinpointing the single corrupt shop or restaurant responsible for initiating the skim operation on all the different cards.

This illustrates another risk that Visa combats: corrupt merchants. Through its Risk Identification

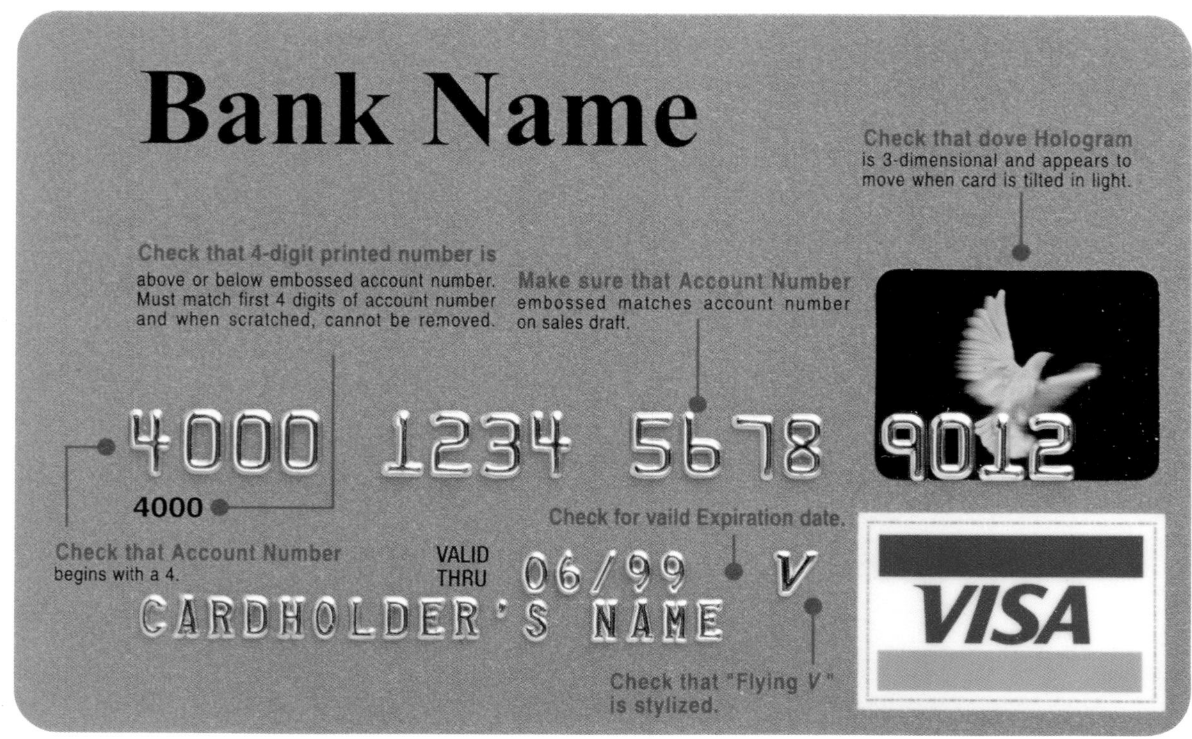

VISANET
Making Quality Count
VISA

Service, Visa monitors the transactions of its member merchants, hoping to get an early fix on fraudulent activity or weaknesses in security. If Visa does spot a problem at a particular merchant, it alerts the "acquiring bank" – the bank that handles the accounts of the merchant in question – so the bank can take steps to protect against fraud at that location. To close the cardholder-merchant-bank circle, Visa also scrutinizes, on a continuing basis, the financial health of its member banks. A bank failure can cause huge losses for Visa cardholders and merchants and for Visa itself – the risk management team is determined to be alert to that possibility.

None of this is enough. Just as Ian Fleming's fictional Goldfinger dreamed of cracking Fort Knox, today's skimmers and computer hackers no doubt dream of cracking the electronic security of Visa and its member banks and merchants. Vigilance, therefore, is the mantra of the risk management team. And part of that vigilance is a constant search for more advanced technology and more secure protective devices and codes.

Visa specialists like Richard Hite work in this domain. He and others at Visa work in tandem with Philip Yen, who is playing a lead role at Visa in the development of e-business. Hite is eager to find ways for chips to tighten the security of individual cards and the transaction process. Visa also supervises outside testing of chip technology and security to help in product development and ensure that any new technology Visa puts into place will meet the strictest security requirements. Visa's risk management team also keeps close tabs on advances in the field of cryptography – a crucial tool in Visa's effort to safeguard its electronic data from computer hackers.

Hite, like many Visa specialists, came to the organization with unusual expertise. In his native Ohio, Hite earned a Ph.D. in Russian history and mathematical analysis, which brought him to computers. After teaching at the university level for 10 years, Hite shifted careers at an exciting moment: the dawn of electronic banking. He joined Bank Ohio and ran a Visa Gold and a Visa Debit Card program. Then in 1993 he joined Visa and helped run its network of point-of-sale terminals, a system called Interlink. In that capacity, Hite became a specialist in the field of data security and cryptography, expertise that made him Visa's unofficial "Mr. PINs and Codes."

As sophisticated as the new technology is, for Rick Hite and other Visa specialists, it is a never-ending struggle to stay a few steps ahead of the criminals. How to guarantee the security of Internet transactions? How to develop a more sophisticated PIN system for chip technology? How to work with MasterCard, American Express, Discover, and other card issuers to develop industry-wide standards for electronic money? These are the sorts of questions that daily preoccupy Visa's risk management team, both in California and at the various regional headquarters around the world. And all these questions bear directly on how Dick Held defined their mission: "Protecting the chain of trust."

What we have seen up to now, though, is only part of the risk management effort, the objectives as defined and seen from Visa headquarters outside San Francisco. But what is the view out in the field, where Visa's anti-crime measures and specialists are really put to the test? What, in fact, is the situation in Asia, ground zero in the war against card counterfeiting and fraud? And how does it look through the eyes of Visa investigators, hot on the trail of the card gangs and skimmers?

It's time to find out.

Bus ads never get tossed

Chapter 15

The Shadow Warriors

Downtown Singapore, 9 a.m.

Jack Miller is at his desk, answering a flood of e-mails. A stack of papers sits on the side of his desk, awaiting his attention. At first glance, Miller's job looks mundane. Paperwork. Administration. Running his staff. Managing budgets. Setting priorities. But there is far more to it than that. For the past 15 years, Miller has run Visa's risk management operation in Asia and the Pacific, a job that puts him at the forefront of the worldwide battle against credit card fraud and counterfeiting.

"We have the best and brightest thieves in the world here. They understand technology and they understand finance," Jack explained. "It's a great challenge to work against them. It's why I still enjoy it after 15 years."

Miller has impressive credentials for the job. He was born and raised outside Chicago, went to Marquette University in Milwaukee, Wisconsin, and then earned a law degree at Georgetown in Washington, D.C. In 1966, Jack joined the ranks of the FBI, then under the direction of J. Edgar Hoover, and he was soon sent to the American South where he chased fugitives and investigated auto theft, white collar crimes, and civil rights abuses. Then Jack shifted into FBI counter-intelligence, and he learned two dialects of Chinese, to prepare him for work with Asian connections.

In 1974, Jack was sent to Hong Kong as legal attaché in the U.S. Consulate. For Jack and his family, this was the beginning of a long love affair with Asia. After six years in Hong Kong, Jack left the FBI and went back to Chicago as a prosecutor in the state's attorney's office. But he and his family yearned to go back to Asia, and in 1985 he got his chance. Carl Pascarella asked Jack to join Visa and set up a risk management team for Asia and the Pacific basin. It was exciting work.

"In those days, we all did everything – emptied ashtrays, washed windows, whatever had to be done," Jack recalled. "You also had tremendous freedom. When you came into the company, you weren't a bag carrier. You could go wherever your talents took you."

Jack's job took him right to the heart of high-technology card fraud and counterfeiting. In 1986, a Chinese counterfeiter based in Taiwan managed to put a workable magnetic stripe onto a bogus card. This meant the counterfeiter could use the bogus card in a regular merchant terminal and have the transaction routinely authorized. It was a license to travel, spend, and buy fraudulently – with little immediate risk of getting caught. When Visa analysts, however, spotted his heavy spending, they began tracking his movements. "He used his card in Tokyo, Hong Kong, Bangkok, Singapore, and Australia," Jack recalled. "Then he just disappeared. We lost him."

But the larger meaning of his exploit was painfully clear: card counterfeiting had entered the age of electronic money. Jack knew what was going to happen next. The ingenious counterfeiter was going to share his new mag stripe duplication methods with associates in the Chinese crime syndicates, and others in Asia and around the world would learn how to do it. Visa's risk management team had to find effective countermeasures. Fast.

The problem mushroomed. By 1989 it was costing Asian banks about $40 million a year. Worse, it was clear that tracking and prosecuting the perpetrators would not be the most effective solution. In fact, it would be slow and very difficult. Still, it would have to be done while a technological remedy was being developed. To that end, Jack and Visa's risk management team focused on finding a new piece of technology that would protect the mag stripe, thus stopping the losses and safeguarding cardholder confidence. The challenge was to find a technology that would protect the card but not, so to speak, break the bank. MasterCard was contemplating making a global shift to smart cards, but chip cards at that time were very expensive to produce, several times the cost of magnetic stripe cards. Moreover, the changeover would mean that point-of-sale terminals and all the related software would have to be changed as well. The projected price tag for going to chip on a global basis was a hefty $40 billion. MasterCard decided not to jump into chip at that time – and neither did Visa.

Enter CVV, Card Verification Value. As we saw, this technology uses secret algorithms to produce a code that is unique to each card, thus making the mag stripe much more difficult to fabricate. CVV was also far cheaper to implement than chip cards. Jack was a great believer in the CVV technology, and in 1988 he went to Visa's Asia-Pacific board of directors and urged them to make the change. The board approved the move, though it would take time to implement. Given the size of their problem, the Asian banks had little choice; fraud was costing them a fortune.

The shift to CVV technology was immensely successful. "CVV cut fraud here by $25 million the first year," Jack said. "And it gave us more than a decade of protection. CVV was probably the most significant risk management tool implemented so far in the credit card industry. We were two years ahead of every other Visa region," Jack recalled. This was understandable enough: other regions were not hit as hard, and so their banks were reluctant to spend money and effort on preventative measures.

"There has to be blood on the floor," Jack explained. "Banks have to feel the pain before they'll implement change. Then, however, it takes time to implement technology changes, and losses continue to grow during that period." To meet that challenge, Visa in Asia had to simultaneously build a competent investigation and prosecution unit to help staunch the losses until the new technology became effective.

Enter Philippe Bertrand.

Philippe is a veteran of Belgium's Judicial Police, and he is a tough, disciplined, and very shrewd investigator. He is also a walking encyclopedia of knowledge and important detail about card fraud and counterfeiting – and the Asian gangs that make it a staple of their criminal activity.

Philippe came to his specialty in a rather unusual fashion. He was born in Brussels in 1955. He studied the classics in high school, and after doing his military service Philippe entered a teacher's college in Belgium. Academia, however, failed to hold his interest and he dropped out at 19. What now? Philippe had no clue. He wanted to find something real, something with immediacy and excitement, some mission he could call his own. But he wasn't even sure where or how to look. In the interim, he did odd jobs and tended bar.

One day his father told him that the Ministry of Justice was looking for a clerk. Philippe got the job and was sent to work in the evidence unit in the office of the King's Prosecutor. There he catalogued guns, drugs, bricks, body parts, and more, everything and anything that police investigators entered into evidence for their criminal cases. The work itself was routine, but it did have an extra kick: it put Philippe into constant contact with policemen and detectives. That opened a window onto a whole new world. "I suddenly realized these people were doing what I wanted to do: instant history, the archaeology of the present," Philippe recalled, adding with a sly grin: "They also looked good, made more money

tions fallout."

Asia promised to be the worst of the problem. BCCI had a huge presence in Pakistan, with offices in Karachi, Islamabad, and Lahore, but it also had offices in the Philippines, Bangladesh, and several other Asian countries. All of them would have on hand stocks of unissued travelers cheques. If they got into the wrong hands and were cashed, Visa could suffer a huge financial loss. "Asia was 50 percent of the problem," Jack recalled. "We had to get those cheques off the streets and out of the vaults."

Jack, like Visa's other regional risk management chiefs, set up a crisis center, and he and his staff fired off faxes and telexes to banks in Asia to alert them to the situation. They also warned airlines, hotels, and major merchants not to accept BCCI travelers cheques. At the same time, Visa promptly honored, with little vetting, the travelers cheques of anyone in genuine travel status who was relying on those cheques for their travel expenses. As part of this coordinated effort, Jack urgently put together several teams to descend on BCCI offices across Asia. "We took marketing people, accountants, anyone we could recruit," Jack said. "We needed bodies." Then Jack, Philippe, and their colleagues rushed to Pakistan.

Within hours, Jack and his troops, along with a team of chartered accountants, were walking into BCCI headquarters in Karachi, where the bank was still open for business. They asked the bank managers to kindly hand over all their outstanding travelers cheques and the accompanying inventory records. "It was a rather interesting situation," Philippe recalled. "Under the circumstances, I must say everyone was extremely nice."

The local BCCI managers understood the situation and agreed to turn over the travelers cheques. But there was a rather large and complicated problem: there were tens of thousands of cheques. After each was properly catalogued by the accountants, what to do with them all? "We were looking at millions of dollars, and they came in wrapped packets of three, five, or ten cheques, many in small denominations, as little as $10 a check," Philippe said. "That is a lot of paper. And it was very, very good paper."

At first, Jack and his team tried tearing up the packets with their hands. That was laughable; they'd be there for weeks. Next they called for a shredder. Someone in the bank produced a small desktop shredder. That did the job – for about 12 minutes. The BCCI people then were hospitable enough to take a Visa staffer out to look for an industrial-strength shredder, one capable of quickly destroying tens of millions of dollars. Finally, they found a wholesaler who had just the ticket. The shredder, he said, cost $6,000. Would that be a problem? No, the Visa team said, no problem. "Fine," the chap said, "I'll order the machine for you. It should be here in about six weeks." Six weeks! They had to get the job done now.

Back at the bank, they found two big oil drums, lugged them onto the roof of the bank, filled them with gasoline, and set them ablaze. Jack's team then began feeding the cheques into the fire. In a matter of minutes, the equivalent of millions of dollars was going up in smoke. "We counted the cheques inside the bank and then brought them up onto the roof," Philippe recalled. "We couldn't just toss whole packets into the drum; they wouldn't burn well. We had to fan out each packet."

To speed the process, the BCCI staff cheerfully offered to help, and together the group formed quite a scene: people from Pakistan, America, Belgium and beyond, each diligently feeding millions of dollars into the flames. "It took hours and hours," Philippe said. "We had a contest to see who could make the most amusing remarks as we fed in the cheques. 'There goes my Porsche. My holiday in the Bahamas. The education of my son.'"

In the end, Jack's crisis team burned between $40 million and $50 million at this one location. Over the next several days, their colleagues played out similar scenes in several parts of Asia. At night, Jack's teams would phone each other and compare notes. "I burned $12 million today. How did you do?"

At one stage, Bill Neumann, Visa's risk management chief in California, expressed shock that Jack's Asian unit was getting the job done so speedily. "How did you move so fast?" Neumann asked Philippe. Well, Philippe replied, we just walked into the BCCI office in Karachi and demanded the cheques. Neumann was flabbergasted. "On what authority did you do that?"

"Jack wrote them a letter," Philippe replied drily.

The operation ended well. Jack's teams and the others around the world destroyed several hundred million dollars in travelers cheques and pulled BCCI's Visa cards out of circulation. A financial disaster was averted and so was a public relations nightmare. Since then, the world of travelers cheques has changed dramatically. With the spread of ATM machines around the world, the use of travelers cheques has greatly diminished. Also, Visa members now manage their travelers cheques much more carefully, primarily by keeping a much tighter hold on inventory. In Jack's mind, that was one of the key lessons of the entire BCCI episode.

The Case of "Six Fingers"

In May of 1991, Philippe Bertrand made a little trip to France. Interpol, located in Lyons, was hosting an international conference on counterfeiting in Asia, and Philippe was going to attend on behalf of Visa. On the way, though, he stopped in Paris to pay a visit to some old colleagues in France's financial crime unit, people he had known during his time with Belgium's Judicial Police. His arrival was serendipitous. "Oh," they said, "funny you should be here. We have these two cops from Versailles who've arrested three Chinese people. They're coming here in a minute to show us the stolen credit cards that they recovered from the suspects."

The two policemen arrived and showed the cards to their Parisian colleagues – and to Philippe. "Those aren't stolen cards," Philippe said. "They're counterfeits." The two cops were new to card fraud and eager to know more. Philippe said that if there were three suspects arrested, there were probably more in the vicinity. "Really?" they said. "Why is that?" Over his years of observing Chinese card gangs, Philippe explained, he had seen that they usually work in groups of five or six.

"Do you think the others will run away?"

"No, no," Philippe said. "I think they're going to continue. It's not because three of them got nicked that they're going to stop. They're here to make money."

Chinese runners typically use the counterfeit cards to buy merchandise, Philippe continued, which is then either sent back to Asia or fenced locally. Either way, the runner usually gets 10 percent of the total take. The syndicate pays their airline tickets and expenses. When Philippe told them about the meeting at Interpol, the two cops from Versailles quickly asked if they could attend. Philippe arranged it, and while the three of them attended the meeting in Lyons, Philippe's prediction was borne out: three more people were arrested in Versailles trying to use counterfeit cards to buy luxury goods.

A few days later, the first three Chinese being detained received a visit at the jail from a purported "uncle." This seemed routine enough, and the French police paid it little attention. A short time later, however, four more Chinese were arrested with counterfeit cards, this time in Rouen, northwest of Paris. Now the case started to look extremely interesting, and the French police decided to dig.

Moving quickly, they searched a house where some members of the group had been living, and there they found a photo of a Hong Kong Chinese man. French police suspected he was the boss of the entire operation. The French then tracked down and arrested several more Chinese, making a total of 21 in detention. They were charged with fraud and other crimes and sent to Versailles for an eventual group trial. However, the suspected leader – the "uncle" – was nowhere to be found.

In a preliminary phase, as the investigating magistrate in Versailles developed the case, Philippe was called in three different times to explain to him how Chinese syndicates operate, where they're based, how they make counterfeit cards, and what they do with their ill-gotten gains. In effect, Philippe was running a seminar for the French on what he had learned during his years as an investigator in Hong Kong and other parts of Asia. The French authorities, including the judge overseeing the case, became so intrigued – and alarmed – that they went to Hong Kong for two weeks to learn, first-hand, about the nature of Asian credit card fraud and counterfeiting.

The case finally came to trial in 1992, in a large, opulently decorated courtroom in Versailles. "There were 21 detainees, 52 guards, and 16 defense lawyers," Philippe recalled. "The defense had very well-appointed lawyers. We're not talking about Mr. Public Defender there by default. These were people who really wanted to make a job of it. How they got paid was a bit of a mystery."

In Philippe's mind, this smacked of a lucrative, high-level criminal operation. "In other instances, if a runner got caught, their Chinese friends would drop them like flies. It was their fault for getting caught. Also, they were creating an embarrassment and would later have a financial debt to pay their bosses. We're not speaking about friends. We're talking about people who routinely exploit other people."

During the trial, Philippe was called as an expert witness. One of the French defense lawyers asked him to clarify one point that puzzled him: "Why were the accused buying Rolex watches?" Philippe was amused by the question. "The average Frenchman, you see, is not in love with Rolex," Philippe noted. "He may be in love with Piaget or Patek-Philippe, but not Rolex. In Asia, however, Rolex is a status symbol, especially in Hong Kong. You get a higher price there for a second-hand Rolex than anywhere else in the world." Also, as Philippe explained, inside Chinese crime syndicates, the runners are given a specific list of items to buy with their bogus cards. If they say Rolex, it's Rolex.

The defense attorney then took another tack with Philippe. "Don't you think these people are actually victims?"

"Well, they *are* being exploited," Philippe acknowledged. "But they knew exactly what they were doing. They came here for a fee, expenses paid, to do a job. And they got caught."

"And what will happen to them?"

"Well," Philippe said, "they will serve their time and then they will start paying their debt."

"You mean they're going to do it again?"

"Of course they're going to do it again! They have to pay their debt!"

The trial ended with multiple convictions. The 21 detainees were sentenced to a cumulative total of 54 years in jail, meaning most would be out in just over two years. But the story was not over. After the trial, Philippe returned to Hong Kong. Waiting for him was a report from German police about some earlier arrests, months before, of another group of Hong Kong Chinese, picked up at the Swiss-German border. They were found to be carrying, interestingly enough, a large quantity of Rolex watches. The report included i.d. photos of the suspects. And there was more.

In a second envelope in his mail, Philippe found a note from Norway. It informed Philippe of some suspicious, unnamed Hong Kong Chinese spotted in a luxury store in Norway. Attached to the note was a photograph of one of the suspects – taken by the store's security camera. To Philippe's amazement, the photo from Norway matched one of the i.d. photos sent to him by German police. And – *mais oui!* – both photos matched one that Philippe had seen in the Versailles case: the suspected leader of the gang, the mysterious missing "uncle." The German police even had a name: Tam Wai Keung.

Philippe, of course, was ecstatic. Now he was hot on the trail of the leader of a nefarious international counterfeiting ring, whose tentacles reached into several countries in Europe and no doubt beyond. "The matter in France was a big one," Philippe said. "But guess what? It was only a slice of a much bigger case. And now we had a major figure in our sights. The face was the same and now we had a name."

Philippe rushed over to the Hong Kong Police and showed them the photo: "This is the leader of the gang." Then he went home to search through his files. Sure enough, he found Tam Wai Keung. He had been arrested before in Hong Kong for using counterfeit cards. Now the various pieces of the puzzle were coming together, and Philippe's pulse was beginning to race. "I was a man obsessed: Tam Wai Keung. Tam Wai Keung. I was becoming a major pain in the neck for everybody."

From here, the Hong Kong police stepped up their inquiry, and they began cooperating with the U.S. Secret Service on the case. The two law enforcement agencies also began trailing the sus-

pect's wife, Lai Hui Shui, convinced that she was an active member of the ring.

Good detective work then turned up a lead: Tam Wai Keung and his wife were planning to hit the United States. At the time, they were believed to be in Europe, making major buys with bogus cards. From there they would purportedly head to America, for more big scores and perhaps to buy embossing and encoding equipment for their clandestine counterfeiting operation.

Now the noose was tightening. In January of 1993, law enforcement agencies from several countries were planning to conduct raids in Hong Kong, Macao, and Los Angeles, in an effort to close down the counterfeiting ring. It was to be a huge, well-coordinated swoop, hitting some 60 suspected sites.

On the very eve of the raids, however, an alert security guard at a shopping mall in Palm Beach, Florida, noticed four suspicious-looking Chinese men doing some very heavy buying. He made a few quick inquiries and then placed them under arrest. It turned out that during the morning the men had made more than $100,000 worth of purchases. And one of those arrested was none other than Tam Wai Keung. His wife was later picked up in San Francisco.

The episode ended as so many counterfeiting cases do. Tam Wai Keung and his wife were convicted of counterfeiting and other charges and spent five years in U.S. jails. In 1997 they were released and returned to Hong Kong.

There is a footnote to the story. Once Tam Wai Keung was caught, one telltale detail emerged, a detail that had previously eluded Philippe. Tam Wai Keung had six fingers on one of his hands. "Imagine it," Philippe said, leaning back in his chair in Singapore and shaking his head. "If we had known that one tiny detail, it would have made our work so much easier. We probably could have tracked him down years before."

In Philippe Bertrand's mind, the true lesson of the case now widely known as "Six Fingers" was not the arrest and conviction of a major crime figure. Rather it was the overwhelming importance of amassing and cataloguing detailed information and sharing that information among cooperating banks and law enforcement agencies.

To that end, Philippe created a huge data base and telecommunications center to bolster the risk management effort in the Asia-Pacific region. The data base serves as a central archives and collection center for information on credit card crime with Asian links. Any criminal activity that has taken place against the Visa brand winds up as a dossier in the system. Names, photos, operating methods, known contacts, equipment used – it's all here. The center operates around the clock, collecting information and handling inquiries from member banks and law enforcement agencies throughout the region.

"Since 1995, we have run this as a 24-hour operation," Philippe explained. "Everything is here and cross-referenced. Cases, suspects, merchants hit, all the different devices for embossing, encoding, and skimming. All recovered counterfeit cards are catalogued, classified, and instantly available for scrutiny and cross-checking."

The resultant information network is one of the world's most comprehensive data bases devoted to credit card crime. To run it, Philippe has put together a team of 12 eager young packrats. They have a big job on their hands. "We handle 10 or 12 reports of card crime every day," Philippe said. "We support the majority of fraud control programs that we have deployed throughout the Asia-Pacific region."

With credit card crime a continuing menace, Philippe spends much of his time doing what he had dreamed of when he was a youth in Belgium: teach-

dreamed of when he was a youth in Belgium: teaching. "Every case, every counterfeit card we see as an opportunity to teach," Philippe said. "Every time the system works, we have a chance to learn something more. And this data base is vital to our war against card crime. If you don't have a place where information is collected, you haven't got a chance to learn from what you have or to magnify it."

It is now sundown in Singapore. The office buildings in this go-go center of Asian trade disgorge their weary bankers, traders, and computer whizzes. Soon the bright lights will come on, and the cafes and restaurants will fill with evening revelers. For Jack and Philippe, it's been another long day at the forefront of the battle against credit card crime. Tomorrow the struggle will begin anew. The card criminals rarely rest, and neither do they.

Part Four The Image

YOU'LL ALWAYS
at your
friendly
WHITE
FRONT
DISCOUNT
DEPARTMENT
STORES

GREEN LIGHT
Your
ANKAMERICARD
welcome here

Your world is waiting and Visa is there.
• 120 countries
• 2.6 million shops, hotels, restaurants and airlines
• 70,000 banking offices
For traveling, shopping, and cash advances...
Visa is the most widely recognized name in the world.
We're keeping up with you.
VISA

A Touch of Magic

Chapter 16

What's in a name?

Just ask the folks at Rolls-Royce. Mercedes Benz. IBM. Apple. Sony. Nikon. Hermes. Chanel. Yves St. Laurent. Château Margaux. Or Dom Perignon. As they will tell you, a winning name can be pure gold in the marketplace. It can help elevate your product into the pantheon of premium brands – and it can help reduce your rivals to also-rans knocking frantically at the door.

But how do you find or create a great name? How do you generate and maintain a winning image? In today's world, with image being lord of the realm, most big corporations turn to highly specialized professionals, either in-house or out, to promote their name and burnish their image. Those teams use the most modern techniques of advertising, marketing, design, public relations, sponsorship, and overall "brand management."

Here, as usual, Dee Hock went his own way. In the early years of NBI, he did not bring aboard teams of professionals to build and nurture the image of the BankAmericard. Nor did he rely on outside creative houses. In Dee's view, they were rarely worth the princely sums they charged, and few, if any, understood the complexities of the credit card industry, much less the nature and true strengths of NBI. Instead, Dee formed a committee of his most trusted staffers – never mind their area of expertise – and put them in charge of advertising, marketing, design, and the like. Dee, of course, chaired the committee; when it came to the crucial matter of image, he was not about to cede authority.

To most advertising and marketing pros, Dee's reliance on amateurs might seem short-sighted and risky – or worse. What, for instance, did Bennett Katz, fine lawyer though he was, know about advertising, marketing, or design? To Dee, though, this was admirable self-reliance. Besides, he insisted on hiring only self-starters with fine, independent minds. How hard could it be for them to master the arts of image-building and global branding?

Some people around Dee took a different view of his approach. To them, the real issue was control. "Regarding how NBI appeared in the marketplace, from media ads to brochures to corporate business cards, nothing went anywhere without Dee's express approval," recalled former CFO Tom Cleveland. "There was absolutely no delegation of authority in this area. Since Dee felt he could not control an external advertising agency, he decided to create his own set of in-house professionals."

No matter what his motives, Dee the Creative Director did get some good results. In the early 1970s, for instance, he and his team continued the "BankAmericard, Think of it as Money" ad campaign, and they turned it into a long-running success. In 1974 they created a follow-up campaign: "More Than Money," and it, too, worked pretty well. Likewise, most of the early design and logo work done at NBI was crisp and appealing, though few experts would call it brilliant. Another solid success was the orientation and operations bible that Dee's team created for member banks. In addition to being a clear, comprehensive "how-to" guide, the handbook was a good promotional tool, showcasing the expertise of the NBI staff. The handbook declared, quietly but persuasively, that in the realm of bank cards, Dee and NBI simply had no peer. That is image-building at its very best.

Dee and his team also had at their fingertips a marketer's dream: the distinctive blue, white, and gold bands. Those bands, which NBI had purchased from the Bank of America, were classy, easily recognized, and they worked in any country, in any language, and with any name on the face of the card. Since 1958, with the launch of BankAmericard, those bands had adorned millions of cards and countless store windows and sales counters from Peoria to Pretoria. They had been featured in newspaper, magazine, and television ads around the world. On a merchant's door, the bands proclaimed to cardholders, "Here is a place where you can put your trust and confidence, a place where you and your business will be warmly welcomed and properly treated." And the bands proclaimed to merchants, "Here is a cardholder I can trust and an issuing bank that will guarantee payment." As a result, they had become a huge asset to the brand and to NBI's entire image.

For all their importance, the precise origin of those bands has, alas, been obscured by the passage of time. Dee has no recollection of their origin, nor does Jack Dillon, even though for a time he ran the BankAmericard program. Win Derman, who for years served as Visa's resident historian, has unearthed most of the story, though a few details have probably been lost forever.

According to Win, the story traces back to early 1958, when the BofA's design team was struggling to find a winning look and image for the BankAmericard. The design team experimented with hundreds of ideas and developed various logos, markings, and colors. But none elicited that visceral, unqualified "Yes!"

Then one fine morning that spring, one of the BofA's creative people, a fellow living in Pleasanton, California, looked out his back door and saw a hillside dappled with sunlight. On it were magnificent sprays of golden California poppies and delicate lupines of a sumptuous and inspiring blue. The man rushed back to the design table, took in hand his brush and palette, and – voila! – out sprang the distinctive bands. The creator's name, alas, was never properly enshrined in BofA history, and no one among the old Visa hands is sure who deserves the credit. But this much is certain: four decades later, the blue, white, and gold, in evolved form, still symbolize the Visa brand all around the globe.

The process that gave birth to the name "Visa" was far more complex – and far more important in turning Visa into one of the world's most powerful brands. As we saw earlier, the name BankAmericard had worked well for the Bank of America, but not for many NBI member banks on the East Coast and in other parts of the United States. Furthermore, the name BankAmericard didn't fly at all in Canada, Britain, France, Mexico, and Japan, where the card was marketed under different names.

"In 1973 it became apparent that continuing proliferation of names for the card could hinder growth of the system," Dee explained in his memoir, *Birth of the Chaordic Age*. "The product had a different name in every country and in some countries, several names. In Canada, Chargex. In the remainder of the world, it was usually known by the name of the issuer, such as Sumitomo Card in Japan or Barclaycard in the United Kingdom. Once the card had been introduced in the name of one bank, others in that market were reluctant to join." The different names were confusing to merchants, and it also hampered NBI as it tried to develop coherent ways to market cards and build the brand. So Dee and his creative team knew they had to find a new name with universal meaning and appeal.

The usual corporate approach, of course, would be to call on the image-makers of Madison Avenue in New York or their counterparts in London, Paris, Tokyo, or Milan. The right name, after all, was a basic building block of a winning image and a successful brand. And the right name

To do anything, to go anywhere, you must begin where you are right now.

Your choice is not where to begin, but whether to begin.

To complete a journey, you must choose to begin it. To fulfill a dream, you must follow it.

Whatever journey you begin, whatever dream you follow, we hope you will include Visa. In as small or as large a role as is appropriate to your course, your needs, and your style.

Visa is the most widely used name in the world for shopping, travel, and cash.

You can count on us.

You can do it. And you can count on us.

You know who you are. You know where you're going—your plans, your goals, your dreams. And you know what you require to get there.

We'd like to help. With the new premium Visa card.

The new premium Visa card is custom tailored by banks for people who require exceptional financial services. For business. For pleasure. For travel. For shopping. For entertaining. For cash. In the U.S. And in 155 countries outside the U.S.

The new premium Visa card is welcomed at six times more places in the U.S. than the "leading" gold card. Eight times more places in Europe. Literally millions more places around the world.

The new premium Visa card comes in many background designs, each featuring the Visa emblem in Gold, White and Gold—your assurance of worldwide recognition, acceptance, and convenience.

If value is measured by usefulness, the new premium Visa card is without question the most valuable card in the world.

Ask your banker.

You know where you're going. We'd like to help.

could give NBI a strong competitive edge over MasterCard, American Express, Discover, and the others. With so much at stake, wouldn't it be best to turn the task over to the best professionals anyone could find?

"Bah!" said Dee. "Let's do it ourselves!"

But how? How do you go about finding a great name? Some ad and marketing people might have begun looking for a new name by trying to define the business advantages of the NBI card. Universal acceptance, for instance. Convenience of use. Flexibility of payment. Utility for travel and entertainment. That sort of thing. Dee, however, began with a different approach.

"With no thought to what the new name might be, we began to create principles that it must embrace," Dee wrote. "One by one they emerged. The new name must be short, graphic, and capable of instant recognition. It must be easily pronounceable in any language. It must have no adverse connotations in any language or culture. It must be capable of worldwide trademark protection for the exchange of value and all related activities. It must have no restrictive connotations, whether related to geography, institution, service, or form, such as *Ameri, Euro, bank, charge, credit,* or *card.* It must have implications of mobility, acceptance, and travel."

With those criteria defined, Dee initiated the hunt, again in a rather unorthodox way. He invited his entire staff, from his top managers to the newest additions to the staff, to submit ideas and suggestions. Dee felt that if challenged and inspired, some member of his staff would come up with a brilliant solution. Dee even added a little incentive, very little in fact: a check for $50. The reward, of course, was only symbolic, but Dee felt the check would be a fine memento for the winner to frame and hang on the office wall.

Dee's challenge galvanized his staff. "There was an explosion of ingenuity," Dee later wrote. "The effort swiftly self-organized. Those technically inclined wrote software programs to fabricate names from letters of the alphabet. Family and friends were engaged. Dictionaries of roots and meaning were sifted and combed. Meetings and groups evolved and dissolved. I doubt anyone involved read, saw, or experienced anything in their daily lives without wondering if it might contain a clue to the answer."

Over the next several months, hundreds of ideas emerged. The suggestions were catalogued and separated into lists, which were then reviewed by a committee Dee established and slowly whittled down. The name "Visa" was proposed early on – and rejected. People just assumed that it was in widespread use and would be impossible to trademark. Still, the name "Visa" was short, graphic, easily recognized, and it did convey the required traits: mobility, acceptance, and travel. Indeed, with a valid visa in your passport, you could travel to most any country in the world. Why not a financial tool that gave you a similar sort of access and freedom?

On every short list Dee's team compiled, the name "Visa" reappeared. Dee's legal team began a quiet search of trademarks to determine if the name had ever been used in the field of financial services. The search produced some startling results. There was, for instance, a Visa car. And Visa pens, Visa golf clubs, and Visa appliances. But nothing significant surfaced in the field of banking and finance. "If I recall correctly," Bennett Katz later noted, "there was a Chinese bank in Taiwan that was using the name Visa. There was also a company in the Philippines that used the name. Beyond that, the field was clear."

Memories differ slightly about the next step. In Bennett's recollection, the entire search culminated in a climactic meeting. "We were 12 people around the table, and at one end we had a big chart with 40 prospective names on it," Bennett recalled. "We went around the table, talking, debating, and each of us giving our first and second choices." Soon the list was winnowed down again, this time to a short-list of five names. One was "Aurora" – a name Bennett rejected. The three others, too, quickly fell away. "Visa was the unanimous choice," Bennett recalled. "It had everything we wanted. We all agreed it just felt right."

Dee knew that finding the right name was just the first step in the process; now would come the colossal challenge of putting it into effect. "Every card in the world would have to be reissued," he wrote. "Every merchant decal on every window and at every point-of-sale counter would have to be replaced. Every electronic sign would have to come down, 20,000 in Japan alone. Every form, every bit of stationery, and every sign in every bank would require replacement. All advertising would have to be changed. It would involve dozens of languages, cultures, and legal systems. No single center of authority or management group could ever hope to know, let alone understand, the full extent of the diversity and complexity involved."

As Dee expected, changing the name worldwide proved to be a monumental task, among the most complicated trademark conversions ever undertaken. On the legal front, Bennett Katz contacted the bank in Taiwan and the company in the Philippines and negotiated the sale to NBI of all the rights to use the name in the realm of financial services. He, Dave Wagman, and the rest of the legal team then filed worldwide trademark registrations in every necessary venue around the globe.

One of the most difficult parts of the process fell largely to Dee: selling the name change to skeptical directors in Britain, France, Canada, and Japan. At an international member meeting in Hawaii, Dee singled out the key decision-maker from each of these countries, met with them one-on-one, and poured on the charm. He also invoked, of course, the Visa ethos of "The will to succeed, the grace to compromise." In the end, everyone came into Dee's fold – except the French. To this day, the Visa card is known in France as

VISA

"Carte Bleue." Still, by the end of the meeting, the member banks had agreed to change the name of NBI to Visa U.S.A. In 1977, the name IBANCO was changed to Visa International Services Association, the acronym being VISA, and the global venture was henceforth called Visa International. The banks also agreed to change the name of all products to Visa.

Now came the task of implementing the name change. The target was to phase in the conversion over a period of four years, but Visa managed to pull it off in just 18 months. How? There is some disagreement on this point. In Dee's view, the key was an enlightened "self-organization" by the member banks. "There were no commandments, threats, or penalties," Dee wrote in his memoir. "No member was told how to do anything. Instead, dates were agreed upon by which they would be expected to reach certain objectives. Cardholders and merchants responded with enthusiasm, the conversion self-organized, and a year and a half later there were few old cards, decals, or forms to be found.... Within another three years, Visa had surpassed all its rivals by a substantial margin."

Chuck Russell, however, said the speed of implementation was not driven by any enlightened "self-organizing" among the members; it was driven by fierce competition in the marketplace, led by Citibank. According to Chuck, two key events occurred almost simultaneously: the name change to Visa and the U.S. Justice Department's position that cleared the way for duality, letting banks issue both Visa and MasterCard. Citibank felt those two developments were going to shake up the credit card market, and it was determined to take quick and maximum advantage.

The company immediately sent out a mailing to something like 60 million potential new customers, heralding the arrival of the exciting new name, Visa. The message of the mailing was clear: "BankAmericard is changing its name to Visa. If you want a new Visa card, just fill out the enclosed form and we'll send you a Visa card within 30 days." Other banks were planning to cycle in the name change at a more leisurely pace, when their customers' existing cards were up for renewal. So they were caught completely flat-footed. Citibank also launched an aggressive ad campaign to bolster its Visa membership drive, and the response was huge.

"Citibank issued between 20 million and 30 million pre-approved Visa applications in a single month," Chuck recalled. As soon as the other banks saw the popularity of the new name – and the success of the Citibank promotion – they rushed to follow suit. "We had a stampede, literally, by banks that wanted to change to Visa. When the dust settled, we were the biggest card issuer by far and MasterCard fell by the wayside."

The campaign was an important turning point for Citibank's Visa card program. On the one hand, Chuck said, the bank was a bit indiscriminate in the way it signed up new customers and lost a lot of money due to bad credit risks. But Citibank executives did achieve their ultimate goal: they saw an explosion in their list of credit card customers – and their resultant profits. "Almost overnight, Citibank became the king card-issuer," Chuck said, and they remain a major issuer today.

The change of name stands out now as one of the most important milestones in Visa history. The name "Visa" had flair, panache, universal appeal, and what the marketing pros always strive for but only rarely find: that elusive touch of magic. Citibank was just one of scores of banks around the world that proceeded to make Visa one of their main tools for marketing, building their customer base, and cementing the relationship with their existing customers. Visa, for them, became pure gold.

In the view of many long-time Visa hands, the new name also helped galvanize the spirit inside the company. No longer was NBI a fledgling step-child of the Bank of America. Now it was a mature, high-flying global enterprise, with its own name and a unified corporate identity, mission, and product line. Visa veteran Fran Schall explained it well. "The name connoted travel, prestige, and global reach," she said. "It gave who we were and everything we did a common identity."

By 1980, Visa was soaring, and a few facts and figures from that year serve as important markers of just how far NBI had come in its first 10 years of existence. By now, NBI and IBANCO had both changed their name to Visa, and the new name had been launched with great fanfare and aplomb. BASE I and BASE II were digitizing the transaction process and dial terminals such as Verifone's were coming on stream. The world's financial community had adopted the magnetic stripe as the standard for the technology of electronic payments, and Visa was getting ready for aggressive international expansion. The European Operations Center at Basingstoke was approved, and Visa International signed an historic accord with the People's Republic of China, opening China to the Visa card and the dawn of electronic money.

With its new name, Visa's popularity began to soar – and so did card usage and acceptance. In 1980, U.S. sales exceeded $28 billion, more than triple the sales in 1975. International sales climbed to $43 billion, also triple the figure for 1975. There were 89 million Visa cards in circulation, and they were accepted at more than three million merchant outlets around the world. By this time, too, there were 12,614 banks and financial institutions in the rapidly growing Visa family. Visa was not operating as profitably as some of its board members hoped, but most of the vital signs were strong.

Dee was understandably proud of what he and his team had accomplished in their first 10 years, and to commemorate their decade of triumph he gave every employee worldwide a specially minted one-ounce coin of pure silver. On the coin were engraved six watchwords that Dee held dear: integrity, motivation, capacity, wisdom, knowledge, experience. "I have always believed that a corporation has no tangible reality," he wrote in an

accompanying letter to his staff. "It is merely an embodiment of the idea of community, a concept around which people assemble for a common purpose. Visa's success is nothing but the sum of the ideas, energy, and acts of all of us."

The story behind the name "Visa" would not be complete without mentioning two small footnotes. First, by the end of the lengthy name search, no one could recall for certain who had first proposed the name Visa. Many people, of course, claimed the credit for coming up with the winning name, but no one made a convincing enough case. So Dee issued the symbolic $50 check in the name of the entire Visa staff, in recognition of what had been a truly collective effort.

The second footnote belongs entirely to Bennett Katz. As Bennett tells the story, as soon as the final decision on the name was taken, he raced over to the nearest office of California's Department of Motor Vehicles. "I want to order a personalized license plate," he told the clerk.

"What do you want on it?" the clerk asked him.

"One word: VISA."

The clerk laughed. "Oh, that's too common. I'm sure it's already been taken!"

Bennett was not to be put off. "Do me a favor, will you? Just look it up."

The clerk checked and, lo and behold, no one had taken the name, a fact that delights Bennett to this very day.

"So," he beamed, "guess who's got the VISA plate!"

The Changing of The Guard

Chapter 17

Shakespeare would have loved Dee Hock.

Like so many of the bard's protagonists, he was a complex and fascinating figure. Dee loved ideas, he loved words, and he loved to speak his mind with grand rhetorical flourish. His vision and unbending sense of mission produced great initiatives and monumental achievements. Taking A.P. Giannini's legacy as his foundation, Dee and his team built Visa upon it and then turned it into a financial colossus. And yet, like a Hamlet or King Lear, in the eyes of the people around him, Dee appeared as a sullen, hypersensitive man, and even his closest friends and admirers were sometimes chilled by his overbearing manner and self-righteous fits of pique. Finally, at the height of his glory, in a twist of fate that Shakespeare himself might well have conjured, Dee the Visionary seemed to stumble blindly into trouble – trouble that many people around him could plainly see.

At the start of the 1980s, though, Dee's star was still in full ascension. By then, the name Visa had proved a winner in the marketplace, and in its head-to-head duel with MasterCard, Visa now commanded over 53 percent of the U.S. bank card market. To press their advantage, in 1981 Dee and his team were planning an ambitious campaign of international expansion. To pave the way, Dee launched one of his most important and far-sighted contributions to the evolution of Visa: a complete restructuring of how Visa operated around the world.

Up until that time, Visa International had no real identity or staff of its own. Most of Visa's activities abroad were directed by the U.S. team in San Mateo, and their time was billed to the international operation. A few years before, Dee had sent some of his most trusted emissaries out to build the business in Europe, Asia, and Latin America, but their effort was still in its infancy. Furthermore, Dee's team of evangelists had a severe handicap: in the early days of Visa's expansion, the international operation had a limited revenue base and was strapped for cash. So there were scant resources for adding manpower or beefing up marketing and promotion where Visa was eager to grow.

There were also problems of image and perception. "Many people outside the United States saw Visa as an American company doing business in Latin America or Europe," Bennett Katz recalled. "In the late 1970s, when we went out to meet the banks, they complained that Visa International was predominantly thinking about the U.S. market. True, the U.S. market was driving the business, but banks abroad felt no one was sensitive to *their* needs. Italians and others said of the product line, 'What's this got to do with *our* market?'" Many old Visa hands recall the line their European competitors liked to use: "Every time a Visa card is used in Europe, a cash register rings in the United States!"

So Dee and his team were presented with a dilemma: how do you structure and operate a truly international enterprise? How can you promote a global brand while at the same time tailoring your products and marketing to the needs of individual countries and markets? These questions cut to the core of Dee's guiding vision. Dee sincerely wanted to develop an enterprise that bridged national boundaries, languages, cultures, and ideologies. He was insistent that no single nation or financial institution should dominate Visa – that would drive a stake into the very heart of the venture and what made it unique. Cooperation, partnership, consensus, equitable power sharing, a spirit of community were the ideals that Visa was founded upon.

Dee and Ferol at a board meeting in Japan.

If the organization was dominated – or was even *perceived* to be dominated – by U.S. banks and by the demands of the U.S. marketplace, Dee knew that Visa would never mature and flower as a truly international enterprise.

To solve these problems, Dee set out to transform Visa's system of governance and its internal chemistry. The key was decentralization. He wanted to give real, substantive, and *visible* power to the different geographic regions that constituted the Visa family. To do that, Dee proposed that Visa International not be governed by a single transnational board of directors but by five regional boards. One for the United States. One for Canada. One for Europe, the Middle East, and Africa. And one each for Latin America and Asia-Pacific. These regional boards would have wide authority and leeway to admit new member banks, set fees, design their own advertising and marketing campaigns, and develop the necessary computer and telecommunication links into Visa's electronic payments system. To draw the Visa family together, each regional board would elect representatives to a single international board of directors, which would oversee and harmonize the workings of the whole. Dee's guiding philosophy was, put simply, "Think globally, act locally," and he wanted a supple, *elastic* structure that could happily accommodate and serve the vastly different needs of big countries and small – and big banks and small.

Dee also decided it was time for Visa International to have a proper staff in San Mateo and in its regional offices around the world. Visa should have a staff of Europeans to serve European banks and merchants, a staff of Latins for Latin America, and a staff of Asians for Asia Pacific. Like its regional boards, Visa's regional offices would have broad authority and leeway to run their operations as they saw fit, according to the needs of their individual markets.

On paper, Dee's grand design looked wonderful, a model of shared effort, aims, and equality. But would it work in practice? And could Dee sell the concept to his members? The big banks, in particular, like Citibank and Barclays, already felt that their interests were often subordinated to the group's needs. They felt the Visa partnership tended to "level the playing field" by giving small banks the same prestigious credit tools as the big banks – at a fraction of the cost paid by the big banks. On the other hand, the smaller banks in emerging markets feared that the big banks could drown out their voices.

Bennett Katz, who helped craft a revised charter and legal framework for Visa International, said that balancing the interests of all the members was a primary goal from the outset. "Under the new structure, individual countries had a say in what happened," he explained. "Each country in Europe, Latin America, and Asia elected representatives to the regional board. Then the regional boards elected representatives to the international board. It was a federated process. As such, it was a political solution as well as a business solution."

To fine-tune the new governing structure, Dee and Bennett found a formula to weight the composition of the international board. While each region was guaranteed proper representation, some regions got additional board members in proportion to the sales volume they generated. "In the beginning, each region was given a director's seat for every 10 percent of total sales volume," Bennett said. "Now it's 5 percent."

Selling this grand design to the members was no simple matter. In Europe, for instance, Dee ran into some cantankerous opposition from Barclays and the French. On one occasion, at a key meeting in Paris, some 40 European bankers gathered in a hotel ballroom to discuss the plan. According to British banker Seymour Fortescue, who was there representing Barclays, the French perceived Dee's plan as an Anglo-Saxon plot to maximize their clout within the Visa family. Barclays, which at the time held 40 percent of the total sales volume in Europe, feared that the new structure would undercut its dominance in the marketplace. Dee was really on the hot seat. As critics of the plan stepped forward and voiced their concerns, Dee sat and listened, making no comment and taking no notes.

"When everyone had had their say, Dee took the floor and proceeded to systematically demolish all their arguments," Seymour recalled. "I must say that his entire presentation, and the clarity of his argument, constituted one of the most remarkable things I've ever seen in my business career. He forced us to look at the big picture, rather than at our own parochial interests."

In his response, Dee presented a practical way to allay the concerns of Barclays and the French. The international board, he said, could include special 'at-large' directors, to protect the interests of individual countries or financial institutions. With that compromise formula, Dee won European approval for his grand design. Through a similar process, he and his team secured the support of all five regions in the Visa family.

Seymour Fortescue came away from that meeting a fervent admirer of both Dee and his grand design. Later, Seymour served for many years on the international board, and today he remains convinced that its decentralized structure was, in large measure, what propelled Visa to market eminence around the world. "I think the new structure was a real piece of genius," Seymour said. "The conception, with its remarkable global outlook and its system of checks and balances, was very carefully crafted. It was a bit like the American Constitution – it was very finely conceived at the outset."

The new structure, along with the new name, helped ignite a phase of phenomenal international growth for Visa. Outside the United States, it also gave Visa a strong competitive edge over its rivals American Express and MasterCard. American Express was inescapably perceived as a U.S. venture – blame the name – and, in fact, it was a highly centralized U.S. corporation run out of New York. MasterCard, at that time, simply could not match either the approach or the flair with which Visa pursued global expansion. As Chuck Russell bluntly put it, "Internationally, MasterCard was asleep at the switch."

Chuck played a key role in the international expansion. After running the operations side throughout the 1970s, he was named president of Visa U.S.A. in 1981, just as the new structure was put into place. Over the next dozen years, he was one of the chief architects of Visa's rise to market dominance. In Chuck's view, giving power and autonomy to the regions was an historic step in the evolution of Visa. "Dee was a genius at structure and his concept of creating international boards was absolutely brilliant," Chuck said in an interview. "It gave everyone in every country a voice and a sense of ownership in the organization."

To properly spread the Visa gospel worldwide, Dee emphasized three guiding tenets for the regional boards: integrity, openness, and financial transparency. "Our credibility was always our most important currency," Dee explained. "Everything we did had to be open, above board, and beyond reproach." In this spirit, when the regional boards held their regular meetings, Visa would invite other non-Visa bankers from the area to sit in on the proceedings. "We wanted everyone to see how democratic the process was," Bennett Katz explained. "Our aim was to show everyone that this was not a dictatorial organization. And we wanted people to have a proprietary feeling about Visa.

VISA

After all, they owned it."

As Dee had hoped, the restructuring not only spurred growth, it also helped transform the internal chemistry of Visa International. With restructuring, the regions agreed to raise their membership fees. To further increase operating capital, Visa worked out an arrangement to sell bonds to its member banks. The result was a godsend for Dee's evangelists. Now João Ribeira da Fonseca, running the European operation from London, had the leverage and resources he needed to build Visa's presence across Europe and the Middle East. Likewise, Jim Partridge, a native Spanish speaker, could recruit a strong Spanish-speaking staff and build a dynamic Visa operation for Latin America – run by Latins. Carl Pascarella set up a Visa office in Tokyo, recruited local staff, and began building the business throughout Asia. In San Mateo, Bennett Katz and his colleague Bruce Marcus were among the first to join the permanent staff of Visa International, and soon they were traveling the world signing up banks and negotiating contracts.

"Most Americans, including me, have a rather poor understanding of the rest of the world," Bennett said. "Dee, too, was rather U.S.-bound. But now I had the opportunity to travel and do business with people from other cultures and other ways of looking at the world. It was wonderful, absolutely wonderful." Many Visa hands had similar experiences; the staff was becoming increasingly international in outlook and in its sensitivity to the other regions' concerns and problems.

The energizing of Visa International paid off handsomely for Visa, in terms of growth and image. The perception of Visa as an American-dominated company and product line was erased, and soon Visa was perceived in Italy as an Italian product, in Sweden as a Swedish product, in Colombia as a Colombian product, and so on. Furthermore, each region took Visa's global marketing themes and added their own local flavors and colors, making Visa an integral part of the local landscape. No one directing the operation from San Mateo could make that happen; it had to come from the regions themselves.

During this period of transformation, Dee's own managerial style evolved as well, in some ways at least. According to João and Jim Partridge, Dee did not micro-manage his regional offices. In fact, he left them almost entirely to their own devices. "My job was to build Latin America," Jim recalled. "We had to get out of the red and get out from under California as much as possible. As for guidance, Dee would say, 'Do it! It's your business.'"

Jim faced several problems that were specific to his region. One was a poor telecommunications infrastructure, and initially Jim had no budget to tackle the problem himself. In fact, at the time his region had an operating deficit of $800,000. So he went to member banks in his region and urged them to increase their quarterly service rates, from $125 to $3,000. It was a huge hike, but the added income allowed Visa Latin America to cut its operating deficit and improve the region's telecommunications. From there, Visa and its partners worked together to solve their problems and build their business – and Jim never had to fend off interference from Dee. "It was my show, pure and simple," Jim explained. "Dee knew he couldn't run the world from San Mateo."

The sweeping success of his global restructuring plan helped catapult Dee into a different stratosphere of respect and prestige in the international business community. The illustrious Harvard Business School, for instance, did a laudatory study of Visa's impressive rise and of Dee's guiding vision and leadership. The study, published in 1981, was lavishly sprinkled with wit and wisdom from the man himself. For instance: "Our business schools essentially teach management," Dee opined. "They attempt to teach students that management is a science, and that's a lie. It's an art."

The study portrayed Dee as the creator of a new paradigm for international enterprises. While there was mention of his idiosyncratic style and his tendency to rule with "an iron hand," the Harvard study presented Dee as a man who combined hard-eyed business practicality with a lofty intellect and ideals. "An avid reader, Hock often quoted from literature," the study noted. "His glass-walled office on the 46th floor of the Transamerica Building, with its majestic view of San Francisco Bay, included a library stocked with the books of Yeats, Aurelius, Voltaire, Bacon, Emerson, Khayyam, Lao-tse and others."

Not everyone, however, viewed Dee with such unbridled admiration. In fact, on Dee's staff – and on the four boards of directors he reported to – there was growing discomfort about Dee and his unorthodox ways. Some of the discomfort stemmed from matters of substance; much of it stemmed from matters of style. Harvard research assistants, for instance, might approve of Dee's magnificent view and of the choice of books that lined the shelves of his office. To some of the tight-fisted bankers who paid his salary, though, those suggested a man with airs and an over-inflated ego.

According to several Visa insiders, by the early 1980s Dee and his boards were locked in a troubled marriage, with their relations often marred by bickering and obstinate clashes of will. Phil Giltner, a respected banker from the First National Bank of Omaha, Nebraska, served for many years on Visa's U.S. board, and at board meetings he would watch Dee with an uncomfortable mix of admiration and concern. "Dee had the perfect personality for a start-up," Phil said in an interview. "At board meetings, he dictated from the background. He reminded me of someone with a Bible in one hand and a sledgehammer in the other. If one didn't work, he'd use the other."

Other board members had similar feelings watching Dee at international board meetings. When he was in persuasion mode, pressing his position, Dee would give long, detailed speeches – perhaps "harangues" would be a better description – covering every nuance of every position. Dee no doubt was trying to be thorough and convincing, but some members of his board would bristle at being subjected to these seemingly endless filibusters. In informal gatherings after these sessions, Dee would rarely hesitate to pull board members aside and begin the filibustering all over again. Even fervent admirers like Seymour Fortescue found Dee's approach to be tiresome and overbearing. "If he thought you were going to vote against him, he was relentless," Seymour recalled. "He would talk and talk and just wear you down. He did drive us all mad at various times."

Dee also clashed with his boards over serious matters of policy and direction. One illustrative clash centered on one of America's most prominent nationwide retailers, J.C. Penney. In 1979, Dee and Chuck Russell convinced Penney's to accept Visa cards throughout its network of stores. On the face of it, this was a major coup for Visa. Up to then, Visa had not made significant inroads into the retail chains. Though its business was growing, in image terms Visa was still, to some degree, a second-class citizen. Penney's at the time was considered a top-ranking chain, with an annual sales volume exceeding $10 billion. So Dee and Chuck were ecstatic. They felt the deal would greatly improve Visa's image and give Visa an opening to Sears Roebuck and other powerful retailers. "This was a major, major breakthrough," Chuck recalled. "At that time, no major merchants accepted Visa."

The deal, however, did not conform to the usual Visa model. Penney's had already installed electronic point-of-sale terminals at nearly all its stores, and the agreement called for Penney's to link its terminals directly to Visa's authorization and clearance system. With key support from the BofA's Ken Larkin, who knew the importance of breaking into the big retail chains, Visa's U.S. board endorsed the Penney's deal. But when the terms were made public, the deal sparked sharp criticism from several Visa member banks, including Citibank. They were concerned that Visa, by dealing direct with the retail chain, was straying from its traditional role as an enabling entity between banks and merchants.

The Penney's issue fueled a much deeper concern among some banks: was Visa acting in the best interests of its member banks or was it now intent on building an empire of its own? Dee insisted he was only trying to improve the image of Visa and expand the market for all its member banks, but several influential board members harbored lingering suspicions. In the end, the Visa board decided to allow the Penney's deal to stand. However, to make the limits clear, the U.S. board formally barred Visa from ever again dealing directly with merchants.

There was another episode which illustrated Dee's growing differences with some members of his board, and this involved the debit card. The highly respected business writer Joseph Nocera documented the debit card flap in his fascinating book, *A Piece of the Action, How the Middle Class Joined the Money Class*, which traces the growth of such financial powerhouses as Merrill Lynch, Charles Schwab, and Visa. As Nocera reported, one of the key figures in the debit card dispute was a prominent Colorado banker named D. Dale Browning, himself an early pioneer of the bank card revolution. In an interview for this book, Browning recalled the flap in vivid detail.

As he related, Browning was born in Colorado and did his early bank training at Continental

Illinois in Chicago. In 1966, Colorado National Bank brought him aboard to run their retail banking operation. During this same period, Colorado National became an early licensee of the BankAmericard program. The initial results, however, were disappointing, and the bank asked Browning to take over its bank card program. To learn the ropes of this infant business, Browning said he went to Seattle to look into the card program of the National Bank of Commerce, and in that capacity he met Dee Hock, who was running its bank card operation.

"Dee and I became very close intellectual friends," Dale recalled. "We liked each other professionally." Browning was later a participant at the landmark meeting of the BankAmericard licensees in Columbus, Ohio, when Dee stepped to the fore and began organizing the licensees into a self-governing body. While Dee was building the licensees into NBI and later Visa, Dale was busy building the bank card program at Colorado National Bank. That led him to create a new entity, the Rocky Mountain Bank Card System, a network that processed merchant accounts for some 600 banks in the region. In 1976, when the duality issue was settled and more and more banks began issuing Visa cards, Browning began looking for ways to differentiate his bank's Visa cards from those of their competitors. What he landed upon was the new payment device known as the debit card.

The debit card first came into the marketplace in 1974, via a now-defunct institution named Arizona Bank. The debit card looked almost identical to the credit card, but it functioned just like a check. When presented to a merchant or at an ATM, the debit card reached into the cardholder's bank account and instantly withdrew the money. The cardholder was happy: using the card was easier than writing a check. And the bank was delighted: the cost of processing an electronic transaction was cheaper than processing a paper transaction. There was a bonus for the bank: when a debit card was used in a store, at a point-of-sale terminal, the merchant paid the bank the same fee – between two and three percent – that it paid on credit card transactions. With those benefits in mind, Arizona Bank eagerly issued debit cards to all of its customers with checking accounts.

Browning, too, believed that debit cards held enormous potential, and he eagerly launched them at Colorado National Bank. He did not use them as a means of soliciting new business. He issued them to existing customers, in the hope of cementing the bank's relationship with its existing customer base. "I was a strong advocate of the debit card," Browning recalled. "I saw it as a relationship card and a valuable way for us to differentiate our cards from those of our competitors."

With that same aim, Browning wanted to differentiate the look of his bank's debit cards. Specifically, he wanted to reduce the size of the Visa logo on the face of his bank's debit cards. Visa specified the mandatory size of the logo for *credit* cards, but Browning felt that the debit card was a different animal, and so he had the right to reduce the size of the logo. "I took the position that debit was a non-credit card," Browning explained. "I wanted to issue them to all our existing customers."

Browning's position on debit cards put him on a collision course with Dee Hock. As Dee had often argued publicly, in his view a Visa card was not a credit card; it was a multi-purpose access or payment device that could be tailored to suit the needs of Visa's member institutions. Whether it was tailored as a credit card or a debit card, if it carried the Visa logo, it was a Visa card. That meant that all the Visa rules and operating regulations would therefore apply – including the rules governing the size and the positioning of the logo. Dee strongly objected to Browning's plan to reduce the size of the Visa logo, and in this instance he prevailed. But Browning was undaunted. "I lost that battle," he recalled. "But I didn't give up."

The next round in their conflict involved another tool of modern banking that was just coming on stream in a major way: the ATM machine. The year was 1977, and branch banking was still prohibited in the state of Colorado. In the emerging ATM phenomenon, Browning saw a splendid marketing opportunity. Colorado National Bank had some 400 agent banks throughout the region, and they were already linked via the Rocky Mountain Bank Card Association. So, Browning reasoned, why not create a system whereby customers of Colorado National and any of those 400 other banks could use their debit cards at any ATM machine operated by any of those banks? The banks would put a new identifying logo on the back of these cards – "Plus" – and then customers could access their funds at any ATM carrying the same Plus logo. From that idea, Browning created a five-state ATM network called the Plus System.

The system was an immediate success. Customers with debit cards carrying the Plus logo instantly had access to a wide network of ATM machines. A resident of Nebraska or Iowa could travel to Colorado and access his funds at a large number of ATM machines in Denver – without muss or fuss. The customers were pleased with their expanded freedom, and the Plus banks were pleased that they had an attractive, convenient new tool to offer their customers. It also enabled the banks to greatly extend their areas of coverage – at a time when some states still banned the development of branch banking networks. "The Plus System circumvented branch banking regulations," Browning explained. "At the same time, it told customers with the Plus logo on the back of their debit card that they had additional value because they had access to ATMs in five different states. Up to then, nobody had thought of sharing ATMs."

Still, the creation of the Plus System set the stage for another round of conflict with Dee Hock. Here's the crux of the matter: Colorado National and the other banks in the Plus System insisted that their ATM networks were proprietary, meaning their use was restricted to their own customers. Browning and his colleagues definitely did not want customers from rival banks across the street to have free access to their ATM network. The rival bank, after all, had not spent one nickel to develop or maintain that expensive Plus System ATM network; why should their customers be allowed to use it? Visa, however, functions on the promise of guaranteed acceptance. Dee took the position that any cardholder with a debit card bearing a Visa logo should be able to use that card at any ATM belonging to *any* Visa member bank – including those in the Plus System. Dee wanted that principle to be upheld. Browning refused.

"Even in the first days of Plus, back in 1977, Dee tried to stop me," Browning recalled. "The Plus logo on the back of the card violated Dee's principle that a Visa card is a Visa card is a Visa card. But this time he was unable to stop me."

With Rocky Mountain consumers clamoring for easy access to more and more ATMs, the Plus System grew rapidly. By 1980, it had expanded across 12 states in the central and western United States, and Dale Browning knew he had a very hot venture on his hands. That same year, Browning was approached by Chase Manhattan Bank in New York to start a shared ATM network on the East Coast. Browning had reservations about joining hands with Chase, but the overture encouraged him to take a bold step. With a view to expanding the Plus System nationwide, in 1981 Browning invited 27 major banks to a meeting in Denver. Not coincidentally, those 27 banks included the largest Visa issuers in the United States. They also included most of the banks that sat on Dee Hock's board of directors. Browning's plan was to invite the banks to enter his system – for an up-front fee of $100,000 – and together create a nationwide ATM network. What Visa had done for the bank card, Browning wanted the Plus System to do for the ATM.

"In a way, Hock should have been flattered," Joseph Nocera wrote in *A Piece of the Action*. "Browning's model for the new organization was transparently Visa, from its centralized switching mechanism to its joint ownership by the member banks to its lofty operating principles. But of course Hock was not flattered. He was enraged. He considered Browning's talks an act of treachery."

To press his case, Dee went to Denver with Bennett Katz and Chuck Russell. Browning will never forget that meeting. He and Bruce Rockwell, the president of Colorado National, sat down with the Visa top brass, and then Dee got started. In his usual incisive manner, Dee set forth his objections to Colorado National trying to create a nationwide ATM system. He thought this new proprietary system, relying on cards carrying both the Visa and Plus logos, would conflict with Visa's principle of guaranteed acceptance. "He was very threatening, very emotional," Browning recalled. "He thought what I was doing was very destructive to the Visa brand and the Visa logo. It was very upsetting to Dee. We listened to him for an hour and a half. Then Bruce stepped in. 'We're committed to developing the Plus System,' he told Dee. 'If Dale wants to back off, that's up to him. But I'll back him whatever he decides.'"

With that endorsement from his president, Dale Browning never turned back. Of the 27 banks invited to join the Plus System, 26 agreed to sign on. The only naysayer, he said, was Dee's old bank in Seattle, Rainier. In 1983, the Plus System went into operation as a nationwide ATM network. During this same period, Dee was pressing ahead with plans for Visa to set up a nationwide ATM network of its own. Now it was the turn of Browning and Bruce Rockwell to be upset. In their view, that would put Visa into direct competition with some of its own member banks, namely the partners in the Plus System. In their view, this suggested that Visa was again, as in the Penney's issue, straying outside of its core mission as an enabling entity. Visa initially dropped the idea of developing its own ATM network, and in 1987 it actually became a partner in the Plus System. Later, in the early 1990s, Visa created an ATM network under the Visa logo. Today, most participating ATM machines carry both brands.

Looking back now, Browning sees the episode as a vivid illustration of the inevitable tensions inherent in the Visa concept. As an association that has competing banks under its roof, Visa is naturally a venue where the interests of its individual banks often clash with the interests of the association as a whole. "Everyone at Visa, including Dee, were people acting in good faith, trying to do the right thing for the Visa association," Browning said. "Note that I said 'the Visa association.' I don't think they were trying to do the right thing for individual banks. They weren't bankers, and I'm not sure that Dee and his staff fully understood the competitive problems of commercial banks."

These sorts of flaps are, perhaps, inevitable within the Visa structure. In the view of some Visa insiders, though, Dee's conflict with Browning and Colorado National Bank was rather ill-advised, for at least one simple reason: Bruce Rockwell held a prominent seat on Dee's own U.S. board of directors.

According to Browning and several other Visa insiders, the flap with Colorado National was illustrative of a deepening conflict between Dee and the U.S. board. "There was a growing concern among all the major banks in the United States that Dee and Visa were starting to play roles that were not consistent with the banks' strategic objectives and that deviated from the original intent of creating Visa," Browning said. "There were concerns that Dee and Visa were deviating from their core mission."

There were other issues of contention as well. At Dee's behest, Visa purchased a few companies with new technologies that looked promising for the card industry. On the face of them, these acquisitions looked like smart business moves, and they were approved by the board. According to Visa insiders, however, these acquisitions were expensive and soon failed to fulfill the board's expectations. As their top executives came on board at Visa, payroll costs also soared, insiders said, and the acquired companies ended up adding minimal benefit to the company.

Dee also ran into problems with a venture that old Visa hands refer to simply as "101 California." In 1980, Dee was approached by a leasing company that was looking for clients to rent space in a new high-rise office building planned for San Francisco's financial district. Dee decided to lease the entire 44th floor, something like 22,000 square feet. At this stage, the lion's share of Dee's staff had offices in San Mateo. In addition, Visa maintained a showcase office in the Transamerica Pyramid for important meetings and for greeting foreign delegations. The office suite that Dee envisioned would replace the Transamerica quarters and be a richly appointed corporate headquarters, ideal for his top executives and for welcoming the elite of international banking and finance. "It was part of my long-range plan," Dee explained. "I envisioned a kind of think tank, a place where our top people could get away from their daily operational duties and sit back, reflect, and come up with fresh ideas for Visa's future."

Dee and his team worked hard to turn the new office suite into a sumptuous showcase of refinement and good taste. In every detail it would be

worlds away from the cramped little BofA "garage" where NBI had started a decade earlier, just a few blocks away. The results were splendid indeed. The new Visa offices were open and bright, with palatial hallways, richly appointed meeting rooms, and some 30 executive offices. The boardroom was beautifully equipped for international meetings, with state-of-the-art audio-visual equipment and several translation booths. The offices were also beautifully decorated with antiques and art work from many different parts of the world.

There was only one small detail that Dee had overlooked in his master plan: he never informed his boards of directors of his project – or his planned expenditures. The building was completed in September of 1983, and when his board arrived for a meeting there in November, many of them were aghast. "It offended some of the directors because I didn't ask their approval in advance," Dee recalled. But he said he felt no need to; he had never sought prior approval on his earlier building projects. Dee also insisted that the cost of the furnishings was not outlandish. "I had a few antiques, but by and large it was just good taste. And good taste, darn it, doesn't cost any more than bad taste."

Still, 101 California grated on many members of the board. Surely, some of them had showcase offices that were even more opulent and finely appointed. But to them, the highly visible 101 California venture raised troubling questions. Was this really the sort of image that Visa wanted to project to the world? Why had Dee done all this without the board's prior approval? For some members of the board, the grandiosity of the venture revived a nagging concern: were Dee and Visa self-effacing go-betweens for the banks – or were they intent on building an empire of their own? According to several Visa insiders, several members of the board were mystified by Dee's handling of 101 California. What in the world, they wondered, could he be thinking? How could a man so brilliant be so blind?

Several Visa insiders say the 101 California episode crystallized the board's growing discontent with Dee and his iconoclastic ways. In the view of some members of the board, Visa was straying from its core mission, and Dee's attention seemed to be straying from what should be his central focus. In addition, they felt that Visa's payroll and operating costs had become unnecessarily bloated – at a time when the banks themselves were doing everything they could to cut their own costs.

According to Dee, he was fully cognizant of the storm generated by the 101 California episode and by some of the other contention swirling around him, and he, too, felt the time had come for a change. After 14 years at the helm, he said in an interview, he desperately wanted out – and he had wanted out many times before. "It just seemed like the time," Dee said. "By then Visa was a huge success, and I thought everything was in place for the future. Besides, I was 55 and I had other things I wanted to do with the rest of my life. I thought, 'I've done my best. Let those who can, do better.'"

Lars Piehl, chairman of the board of Visa International, pleaded with Dee to stay on. However, in January of 1984, Dee formally announced his decision to retire. The board accepted his decision, and a few months later they formally turned over the reins of Visa to Chuck Russell. Dee went home to his ranch and disappeared from the world of Visa – to many people, an enigma to the end.

"I think Visa and international banking owe an historical debt to Dee Hock," said João Ribeira da Fonseca, summing up the feelings of many Visa pioneers. "He did something unique. And only he could have done it. Of all the people I've met around the world, no one else had the capacity and the genius to do it."

Since leaving Visa, Dee has devoted himself to a cause that he feels is "infinitely more important" than Visa: trying to bring forth enlightened new models for business and organizations. He works with companies, universities, and foundations in the hope of fostering a new ethos of management, human relations, and living in harmony with the Earth and its over-stressed natural resources.

"I loved Visa and I loved the people," Dee said, and he looks back on those years with some deep satisfactions. As Dee put it, he had a dream, he had the opportunity to pursue it, and ultimately he saw his dream become reality. "How many people can say as much? And who can imagine life today without a Visa card?"

Chuck Russell took over the reins of Visa U.S.A. and Visa International in 1984.

"It's Everywhere You Want to Be"

CHAPTER 18

Chuck Russell had his hands full.

Thanks in large measure to Dee, Visa had a powerful guiding vision, an effective international structure, and a name that was a winner in any language. It also had a strong, reliable product line and a highly respected system of product support. Nonetheless, when Chuck took the reins in 1984, Visa had some urgent problems to address. Financially, the company was struggling with heavy debt, an unhealthy operating deficit, and a bloated payroll. In terms of image, Visa was still widely viewed as a payment device for the local hardware store, not for prestigious dining or luxury travel. The lucrative, high-end travel and entertainment section of the market was still, almost exclusively, the domain of American Express.

Chuck received clear marching orders from his boards of directors: clean up the financial side, cut the excesses, turn Visa into a streamlined, tightly run corporate operation, and put the entire venture on a much more profitable plane. In essence, the board was saying, "The launch and start-up years were brilliant. Now let's solidify the foundation and make this baby really soar!"

Dee's strength had been vision and structure; Chuck's was nuts and bolts. As with the beloved Harley he often rode to work – wearing an orange jumpsuit over his conservative banker's suit – Chuck began tinkering with the machinery. He cut operating costs and staff and scaled back or dropped a few side-ventures that were ill-defined or too ambitious and costly. Chuck saw no need for a complete restructuring of the Visa operation; it was more like he took the company apart piece by piece, cleaned the valves, replaced the spark plugs, boosted engine performance, and added heavy duty shock absorbers for a smoother ride. Then he put Visa back on the road with two clearly defined goals: serve the needs of member banks and merchants better – and make the operation more professional from top to bottom.

Chuck also reshaped the role of CEO. The "big picture" was already in place, so Chuck focussed on drawing the five regions and their boards closer together, to harmonize the whole. He ranged all over the globe as super-salesman, problem-solver, diplomatic firefighter, and choirmaster. "I spend about 50 percent of my time on the road," he said in an interview during those years. "I have to keep the five parts of our world singing out of the same hymnal."

To help keep things running while he was traveling, Chuck turned to his systems chief Roger Peirce. After so many years at IBM and running VisaNet, Roger was a seasoned, tested pro, fully at home with systems and corporate management, and he and Chuck made a formidable team. "I was Mr. Inside; Chuck was Mr. Outside," Roger recalled. "Together we got a lot accomplished."

Indeed they did. "Within a year, we turned the operating deficit into a profit," Chuck said in an interview. "Then it took several more years to pay off the debts."

Early on, Chuck and Roger also made a key decision about the future of Visa's global computer network. In 1982, Dee had initiated a complete overhaul of Visa's hardware and software, an ambitious venture called the Base Systems Rewrite Project. This was to be the next generation of the global payments system that Dee had envisioned. Roger felt it was too much, too fast. "I was really kind of troubled by this approach," he said. "You sort of wilt under the awesomeness of the task ahead. Instead, we felt that Visa needed an evolving strategy. The big-smash approach was just too risky." So Chuck and Roger divided the computer upgrade into more manageable pieces, to be implemented one year at a time. This process was easier to handle financially, and it was flexible enough to accommodate changes in technology, using periodic expansions and updates. Visa has maintained this elastic, evolving approach ever since.

Chuck and Roger set one cardinal objective for their upgrade of the global computer network: no outages, ever. "One year, just before Christmas, we had a 12-minute outage," Roger recalled. "That was enough. Up to then, we had maintained a 99.99 percent standard. We realized that wasn't good enough." Visa has rarely had an outage since; a system of overlapping computer coverage, with backup capabilities, safeguards the system and keeps it functioning nonstop. "We've got to be the dial tone of the financial industry," Roger said. "Part of Visa's success is that you take it for granted."

Chuck and Roger also concentrated on completing the task of "wiring the world." In the mid-1980s, many merchants in the U.S. and abroad were still reluctant to make the shift to electronic point-of-sale terminals. In Chuck's view, this was slowing the pace of the electronic money revolution and it was holding back Visa's growth and the expansion of the industry. But what to do about it?

"One day Roger came to me with an idea," Chuck recalled. "He said the only way we're going to get these terminals out there is to give merchants incentives for doing so," Chuck said. "So we set our interchange fees to favor people with terminals. That put the necessary financial incentives in place." By slashing the fee that merchants with terminals paid per transaction – in some cases down from 3 percent to 1 percent – Chuck and Roger were able to persuade millions of merchants to migrate to electronic terminals. By the end of the 1980s, the old manual zipzaps had all but vanished. This closed the electronic loop between the four elements of the card transaction: the merchant, the merchant's bank, the cardholder's issuing bank, and Visa as the intermediary "switch."

"We, in essence, figured out a way to complete the wiring of the world, by wiring the merchants to the banks," Chuck said. "That made the credit card a real product and an indispensable payment tool."

One of Chuck's strengths was that he knew what he knew – and he knew what he didn't know. Having worked in the bank card industry since its infancy, he knew, down to his fingertips, the intricacies of how transactions were authorized and cleared, how the interchange process between banks worked and how it could be improved. When it came to computers, however, Chuck was no expert and he left that realm to Roger Peirce and B.

Ray Traweek. And with advertising, marketing, and design, Chuck was totally out of his element – and he knew it. But his solution was simple and practical: call in the pros. And stay out of their way.

Enter John Bennett, a skillful, polished, articulate marketing chief with a dream resumé for Visa: he had worked for American Express for 20 years, as well as Citibank and Merrill Lynch. Chuck brought John aboard in September 1984. He was the first consumer marketing professional ever hired at Visa – despite its 14 years in operation. John was astonished by what he found at Visa. "They didn't know the difference between advertising and marketing," he recalled in an interview. "There were lots of former IBM people with systems backgrounds. But marketing at IBM was selling, not talking to consumers. There was little awareness of the need to turn Visa into a consumer brand."

John knew, however, he had an invaluable marketing asset to work with: Visa's credibility in its field. "The operations people at Visa had rules and regulations, created through trials and tribulations, that made their product work," John explained. "Those rules and regulations had generated a set of standards – of operation, behavior, and performance – that had created product credibility." That's a golden word: "credibility." For a marketing pro like John Bennett, it meant that he had the proper base of trust on which to build Visa into a global brand.

Nor did the name Visa carry any negative connotations that would have to be overcome. "The product worked 99 percent of the time or better," John recalled. "There was a security system in place. The banks had built the cost of fraud and counterfeiting into the cost of doing business. That meant, ultimately, that consumers didn't even have to worry about losing their credit card. So we had all the necessary elements for building a brand, with-

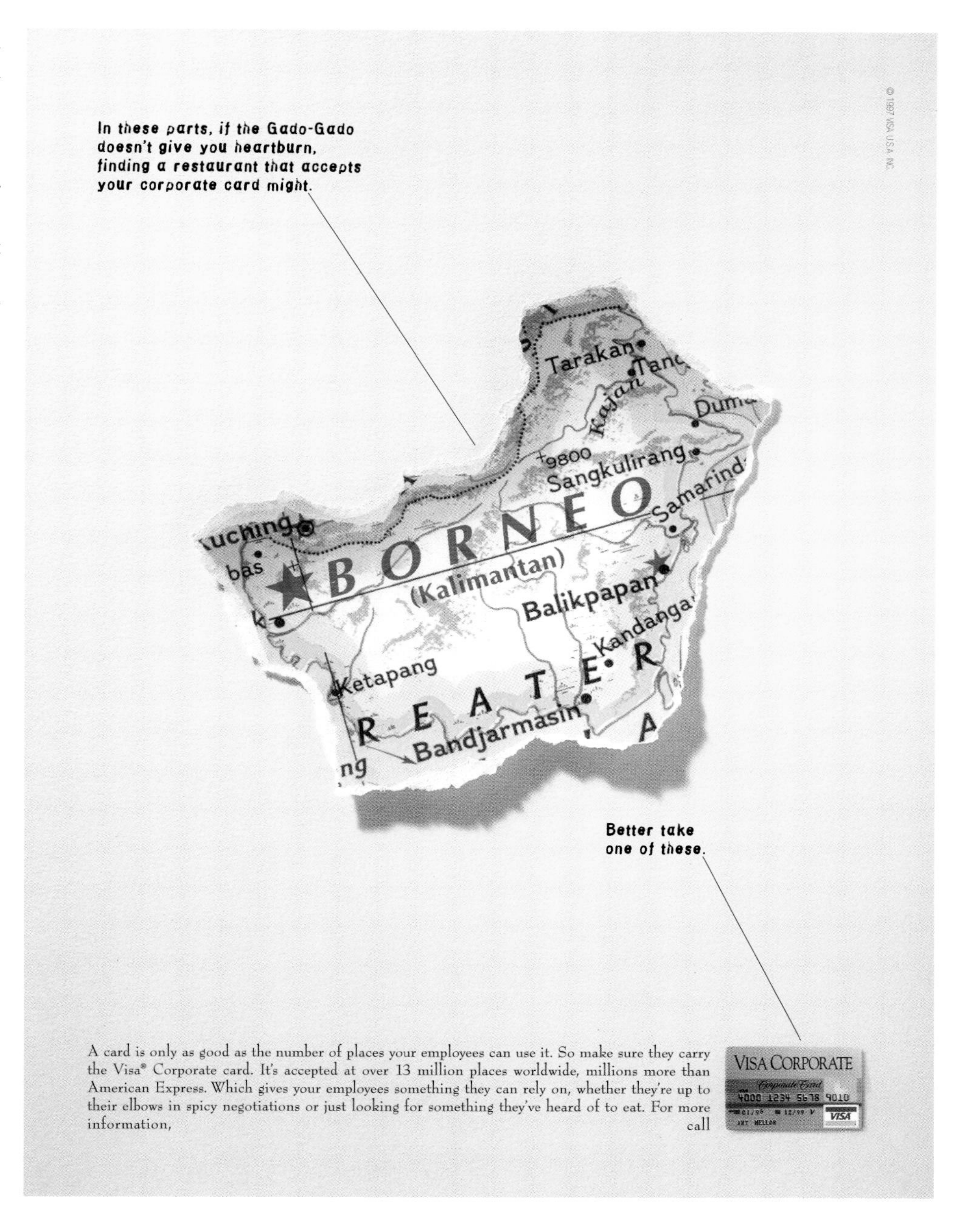

out anyone thinking in terms of brand identity and credibility."

Still, in John's view, he had to start from scratch. When he stepped in, Visa was using two slogans in its U.S. ad campaigns for Visa: "All you need," and, "You can do it. We'd like to help." In John's view, those were symptomatic of a much larger problem. "Up until then, the Visa ads were, frankly, terrible. It was not because they were done in-house. Their focus was wrong. The ads were aimed business-to-business, not to the consumer. Also, they launched a new ad campaign every year. They viewed it like a business plan or a budget – something to be done annually. The idea of consistency of message was not in their thinking."

Early on, John went to Chuck with a recommendation. "We need to hire a top-flight advertising agency to be our marketing partner," John told him. "Visa will never play in the big leagues without one." Chuck readily agreed, provided he would see results in the two numbers he cared about most: market share and members' profitability.

In 1985, John created a search committee and invited bids and trial campaigns from several of the premier ad agencies in the United States. One agency Bennett approached was BBDO – Batten, Barton, Durstine & Osborn – in New York, which handled the advertising for Chrysler, Pepsi, and other leading U.S. and international brands. BBDO was eager to land the Visa account, though it was very small at the time, and it put veteran account executive Gary de Paolo in charge of developing a strategy and some campaign ideas. De Paolo, in turn, asked an eager young ad man named Richard Kronengold to give him a hand. "I knew it was a great opportunity for me, the agency, and for Visa," Richard recalled. "And John Bennett was a great guy. A good, decent human being and a real pro. We all wanted to earn his business."

De Paolo, Kronengold, and a BBDO creative ace named Charlie Miesmer set to work. At first glance, this looked like a classic two-way marketing war, in the tradition of Coke and Pepsi or Hertz and Avis. "Basically, Visa was in a fight with MasterCard and they wanted a knockout punch," Miesmer recalled. "We felt there was something classy about Visa, but that same something had been missed." Kronengold concurred. "Visa was a superior product with inferior imagery," he recalled. "It was not seen for what it was, but as a card pigeonholed for retail, mostly for the middle class or below. American Express was the image leader."

The BBDO team scrutinized the overall card market, looking for clues how to proceed. They saw few differences between Visa and MasterCard that they could exploit. But when they factored American Express into the equation, they found that AmEx did have one glaring liability when compared with Visa: it was accepted at only 25 percent of the places that Visa was. Now the picture was clarifying: rival MasterCard was widely accepted, like Visa, but its image was down-market as well. AmEx was the clear-cut image leader, but its acceptance was limited. So the BBDO team saw an opening and a strategy: simply ignore MasterCard and compete head-on with American Express.

"Our idea was clear," Kronengold said. "By hitching our wagon to American Express, we put Visa in good company and thus raised its image. At the same time, we distinguished Visa from MasterCard." Charlie Miesmer loved the idea. "Why go up against MasterCard? Why not go up against the Mercedes of the industry? And hit AmEx at its weakest point: acceptance."

Now Miesmer and other creative talent at BBDO set out to turn that strategy into an effective ad campaign. This, they knew, was the heart of the matter. Visa would be getting other ideas from some of the best minds in the advertising business;

if their campaign was anything short of brilliant, BBDO could kiss the account good-bye. One of their first tasks was to erase Visa's image as a card only good at the local hardware store. "Visa was seen as *utilitarian*," Miesmer said. "We needed to associate Visa with *aspiration*, things that people want and purchases that make life better. The whole idea was to put aspiration and charm into the Visa card."

Now the ideas started to come. Link Visa to luxury travel. To fine dining. And to dream purchases. Off the sketch board came ad ideas showing Visa cardholders dining at a fine Italian restaurant, motorboating in Bermuda, and buying a vintage guitar at a tiny shop in Texas. Each of the ads took Visa out of the realm of the hardware store and placed it squarely in the realm of travel and entertainment – meaning right in the upscale niche regally occupied by American Express.

Most everyone at BBDO liked the approach, but there were some concerns: were they taking a Ford and saying it was better than a Mercedes? Charlie Miesmer said those fears were quickly dispelled. The primary target, after all, was not American Express, it was MasterCard. "We didn't want to displace AmEx, just make Visa have the same cachet, so you'd use it in great places."

Miesmer and his team then folded all their thinking and creative juice into a set of storyboards for a single TV ad. The ad showed two happy couples dining at a fictional Italian restaurant in Brooklyn. The voice-over would rhapsodize about the Italian dishes and the cheerful ambiance, but then would come the amiable warning: if you dine here, remember to bring your Visa card, because this establishment doesn't take American Express. The ad did everything the BBDO team had hoped: it ignored MasterCard, it elevated the image of Visa, and it stole some of the luster from American Express. And it exploited the harsh fact that AmEx was not universally accepted, even at some upscale venues of travel and entertainment.

BBDO's creative teams actually developed three wholly different campaigns, looking for the best to ultimately present to John Bennett and Visa's top decision-makers. Miesmer's fictional restaurant in Brooklyn emerged as the leading candidate, but the ad was not perfect; something was

Because life has enough limitations, we created the incomparable Visa® Signature card. Visa Signature has no preset spending limit and a revolving line of credit. It boasts a Concierge Service to assist in your travel and entertainment plans, airmiles for worldwide travel, and unsurpassed acceptance, making all of life's limitations not so...well, limiting. For more information, please see www.visa.com/signatureusa or call 1-888-847-2003. It's Everywhere You Want To Be.®

*Individual transactions are authorized by Card Issuers based on factors such as account history, credit record and payment resources. Card Issuers preset upper limits for revolving balances and cash advances. © 1999 Visa U.S.A. Inc.

Introducing Visa® Signature. Whether you're island-hopping across the deep, blue waters of the Caribbean or up to your neck in deep, brown mud at your favorite spa, all you need is the Visa Signature card.

* The only Visa card with no preset spending limit* in addition to a revolving line of credit.
* A personal concierge service for your travel & entertainment needs.
* Valuable air miles redeemable for world-wide travel.

And you can relax because Visa is accepted at over 14 million places worldwide, millions more than American Express.

For the only card you really need, visit www.visa.com/signatureusa or call 1-888-847-2003.

Visa. It's Everywhere You Want To Be.®

missing. "I was struggling for an end-line, something that would be positive, catchy, and affirm all the qualities we wanted to give the Visa card." Like the name "Visa," there are now several people who would love to take credit for finding that now-famous end-line, but Charlie Miesmer said the credit belongs to Gary de Paolo.

"We were sitting around, reviewing the ad, and looking for some magic end-line," Charlie recalled. "And then Gary said, 'Oh, it's clear: *It's everywhere you want to be.*'" At first, Charlie was not thrilled with it, at least not by the way it rolled off Gary's tongue. "It sounded like a corporate statement done by a research guy," Charlie laughed. Soon, however, Charlie and all the others felt that "Eureka" click and the phrase "Visa. It's everywhere you want to be," began winding its way into advertising legend.

First, though, BBDO had to sell John Bennett and David Roberts, Visa's ad manager, on the strategy and the campaign. They, then, would have to sell it to Chuck Russell and the Visa U.S.A. board. When de Paolo's team was ready, John and David went to BBDO headquarters in New York to see the proposed ads and hear their pitch. According to Richard Kronengold, the BBDO team was more than a little nervous. "Visa was new to hard, competitive advertising," he said. "And the campaign we were going to propose had the impact of a punch in the face: we were saying American Express was *not* universally accepted and Visa was. We figured their palms would get a little sweaty."

Right away, however, John Bennett understood the strategy and thought the ad itself was brilliant. But at first he was a little skittish: was the approach too confrontational? Would the ad campaign give too much airtime to American Express? Still, John knew in his heart that if Visa wanted to make a splash and build market share, timidity was not his best ally. Moreover, the BBDO pitch was better than anything he had seen from other agencies. John was ready to go with BBDO. He asked for a finished ad, featuring a real restaurant, to show to Chuck Russell and the Visa board. The BBDO team found a seafood restaurant called "Rosalie's," in Marblehead, Massachusetts. Someone at BBDO called Rosalie's and asked, "Do you take American Express?" The reply was just what BBDO wanted to hear: "No, we only take Visa and MasterCard."

The Rosalie's spot is now the stuff of advertising legend. It showed two happy, prosperous-looking couples enjoying dinner in the inviting Old World atmosphere of Rosalie's, while out of the kitchen came course after course of tantalizing dishes. And then came the tag line: "But if you go there, remember, bring a big appetite and bring your Visa card, because at Rosalie's they don't take no for an answer, and they don't take American Express." Even the voice used in the ad was perfect: it belonged to actor Ed Grover, and he has been the voice of innumerable Visa ads ever since.

John Bennett had little trouble selling the Rosalie campaign to Chuck Russell and the Visa boards, and BBDO got the Visa account, which it holds to this day. The original Rosalie's ad then spawned a series of highly successful ads placing Visa in a variety of romantic locales, from Monterey beaches to French chateaus, from Paul McCartney concerts to the Kentucky Derby, and from Piazza San Marco in Venice to Doyle's famous seaside restaurant in Sydney, Australia. The Rosalie's ad won a prestigious Clio award, the Oscar of American advertising, and it kicked off one of the most successful and long-running campaigns in advertising history.

John Bennett wanted "consistency of message" and the Rosalie's campaign certainly made his dream come true. That campaign and its famous tag-line have remained unshakeable elements of Visa's message in the United States ever

since, and some of Visa's regions have also adapted them for their own ad and marketing campaigns, as we will soon see in detail. There are very few brands, anywhere in the world, that have run a single ad campaign that long and with such positive impact. According to John, every once in awhile Chuck Russell would wander into John's office wondering if they should change the campaign, try out something new. "There's the door, Chuck," John would tell him with a laugh. "Close it on the way out!"

Looking back now, Chuck Russell sees the hiring of John Bennett as one of the best moves he made as Visa CEO. "That was a masterstroke, dumb luck I guess," Chuck said, in his usual modest way. "We hired John and just turned him loose. All you had to do with John was stay out of his way."

The success of the Rosalie's campaign was just the first step, though, for John Bennett. In September of 1985, he added a new member to Visa's marketing team: Jan Soderstrom, a highly respected marketing pro with first-rate corporate experience. Jan had been a senior vice president of marketing with The Gap, and she had also been an executive with Atari. With Jan as his right arm, and with BBDO adding the creative firepower, John began contemplating ways to maximize the impact of the new Rosalie campaign. What could they do that would really put Visa on the world stage? What could they do that would strike a blow straight at the heart of MasterCard and American Express? And then it happened. Two months later, like manna from heaven, a dream marketing opportunity dropped right in his lap.

"It's Everywhere You Want To Be"

US
SILK
8
STRO

Going For The Gold

Chapter 19

It began with a call from out of the blue.

One day in November of 1985, Jan Soderstrom was working in her new office at Visa's San Mateo headquarters. Jan had been on the job all of two months, and she was still getting used to the intricacies of the bank card industry and to helping five different regions with their marketing needs. These were exciting times at Visa. Chuck Russell was streamlining the company, making it leaner and more professional, and Roger Peirce was making substantial improvements on the systems side. The new Rosalie campaign was taking off, and Jan was helping John Bennett look for creative ways to maximize its impact. In the midst of all this, Jan received an intriguing call. Rob Prazmark of ISL had left a message that he wanted to speak with her – urgently.

Who?

Jan did not know Prazmark, but she certainly knew ISL. That was ISL Sports Marketing, a Swiss-based company that was one of the premier commercial powers in the world of sport. But she had never heard of anyone named Prazmark. Her curiosity piqued, Jan returned his call, and during a little preliminary chitchat she found out that Rob Prazmark was a top executive of ISL's U.S. division. Then Prazmark cut right to the point. He was presenting Visa, he said, with "a golden opportunity" – the chance to become a sponsor of the 1988 Olympic Games. For a mere $14.5 million.

Jan did not exactly leap at the offer. Atari, one of her former employers, had once been an Olympic sponsor, and the undertaking had not been a dazzling success. Also, Visa did next to no sports marketing, and Jan knew of no plans to start. More than anything, though, the $14.5 million entry fee was a staggering sum, and Jan knew it was just the beginning. To take advantage of that sort of sponsorship opportunity, Visa would have to spend probably twice that amount – or more – on media buys, ad campaigns, and special marketing programs. The timing was not great either; Chuck Russell was under strict instructions from the Visa board to cut costs – and to cut any initiatives that smacked of empire building. Still, Jan was not about to slam the door. She told Prazmark she would take the idea to John Bennett and get back to him as soon as she could, though she wasn't quite sure when that would be.

Little did Jan know, when she hung up the phone, that Rob Prazmark's call would mark the beginning of a great adventure for Visa, an adventure that would become a landmark in the company's history. Nor did she realize that much larger forces were at work: behind Prazmark's call there was a tinge of desperation – his future was on the line. And across the world in Lausanne, Switzerland, at the palatial headquarters of the International Olympic Committee, the lords of the Olympic Games were also jittery. They had devised a grand plan to transform the politics and the financial base of the Olympic Games and, at that moment, their plan was in serious trouble. And they were hoping against hope that Visa would come running to the rescue.

❀ ❀ ❀

Baron Pierre de Coubertin launched the modern Olympic era on the strength of a noble vision. The French aristocrat dreamed that by reviving the Olympic Games, a popular tradition of ancient Greece, he could bring together athletes from around the world in a great celebration of skill, strength, and courage. On a higher plane, though, de Coubertin dreamed that bringing athletes together in healthy competition would give birth to a new Olympic spirit, transcending national borders and ancient rivalries. Maybe sport could engender, at last, some measure of peace and communion among the disparate nations and peoples of the world.

With that hope, de Coubertin and a group of fellow idealists created the modern Olympic Games in 1894. Two years later, under the patronage of the King of Greece, the first Games – featuring primarily running, jumping, and throwing the discus – were held in a stadium in Athens. From then on, the Games were held every four years, always at a different host city around the world. In those early days, the Olympic Games were the exclusive province of the amateur athlete, and the beauty of the gathering resided largely in the purity of the athletes' struggle to win medals of gold, silver, or bronze. *Citius, altius, fortius,* was the Olympic motto. Swifter, higher, stronger.

Despite their original aims, though, the Olympic Games were often buffeted by war and political conflict. Three times during the 20th Century, world war forced the cancellation of the Games, and in 1936 Hitler tried to turn the Summer Games in Berlin into a showcase for his vile Nazi ideology and propaganda. That was bad enough, but during the 1970s, politics grabbed the Games directly by the throat. At the 1972 Summer Games in Munich, eight Arab commandos sneaked into the Olympic village and murdered 10 Israeli athletes and one of their coaches, leaving the Games soaked in blood and draped in shame. In 1976, a large contingent of African nations boycotted the Games in Montreal, to protest apartheid in South Africa. Then in 1980 Jimmy Carter, then President of the United States, led a massive international boycott of the Summer Games in Moscow to protest the Soviet Union's invasion of Afghanistan. The Moscow Games were crippled, and the boycott put yet another stain on the Olympic ideal.

In the wake of the Moscow boycott, Baron de Coubertin's vision lay in tatters, and the entire Olympic movement was neck-deep in crisis. In Lausanne, the IOC – a private, patrician body that governed the Games – faced an avalanche of problems: political intimidation, declining revenues, and a rising drumbeat of criticism in the world press. Already the Soviet Union was threatening to lead a massive walkout of the Summer Games slated for Los Angeles in 1984. The IOC also faced a more clandestine threat. The Soviet Union, Cuba, and other East Bloc hardliners – all of them eager to break the IOC's grip on the most prestigious sporting event in the world – were pursuing plans to weaken the IOC and shift control of the Games to the United Nations Educational, Scientific, and Cultural Organization, UNESCO, where every nation would have a vote.

All this turmoil provoked palpable fears inside the IOC. Would another boycott cripple the Olympic Games? Could the IOC steer itself out of the deepening crisis? Was there any way for the IOC to create a bulwark against political interference and future boycotts? In those dark days of 1980, no one at the IOC was brimming with optimism, but there was a growing consensus that the time had come to bring radical change to the Olympic Games.

In the midst of the Moscow crisis, the IOC began with a change at the top. Ireland's Lord Killanin stepped down, and the IOC elected a new president, a wily, soft-spoken Spaniard named Juan Antonio Samaranch. In terms of pedigree and diplomatic skill, Samaranch was a natural choice. He had been born in Barcelona in 1920, the son of a wealthy industrialist, and thanks to an upbringing of privilege and the right connections, he had little trouble finding his way into the rarified realm

of international politics, diplomacy, and sports administration. In the 1950s and 60s, Samaranch served on Spain's National Olympic Committee, and in 1966 he was elected to membership in the IOC. From 1974 to 1978, he served as Vice President of the IOC, and during this same period he also served as Spain's Ambassador to the Soviet Union. Now, as President of the IOC, Juan Antonio Samaranch had ascended to the pinnacle of international sport, a post that has been aptly dubbed "Lord of The Rings."

Samaranch knew he had a terrible crisis on his hands and he had to find solutions – fast. He also knew the two root causes of the IOC's predicament, politics and money, were woefully intertwined. Since the 1960s, the IOC had been almost totally dependent on one primary source of revenue: what it received from auctioning the broadcast rights to the Summer and Winter Games. Traditionally, American TV networks like ABC and NBC got into some steep bidding wars to land the Games – and the advertising revenue bonanza that usually went with them. When the Games went well, the networks reaped huge rewards – and so did the IOC. The Moscow boycott led by Jimmy Carter, however, threw that mutually profitable arrangement into turmoil. NBC had paid handsomely to land the Moscow Games, but it took a terrible beating when the United States and other major nations pulled out – and many big advertisers chose to follow suit. Samaranch now feared that the Moscow experience would make U.S. and other broadcasters gun-shy about bidding for future Games. That would drive down the price of the TV rights and further weaken the financial and political position of the IOC.

Samaranch turned for help to his close friend and ally, Horst Dassler, the Chairman of adidas, the sports shoe, equipment, and clothing giant. In 1980 Dassler stood as one of the most powerful men in international sport – and one of the most respected. His father, Adi Dassler, was probably the most celebrated cobbler in the world, with the possible exception of Pinocchio's Geppetto. At the age of 20, Adi began designing gym shoes at his little workshop in Herzogenaurach, a village in western Germany. From there, Adi pursued a novel idea: designing and making shoes for individual athletes, tailoring them to fit their feet and their sporting specialty. Politics and nationality didn't interest him; performance did. In 1936, Adi designed and built the track shoes that America's Jesse Owens wore when he raced to four gold medals in Berlin – putting a thumb in the eye of Hitler and his racist propaganda. After that, Adi's shoes, with their distinctive three stripes along the side, became a mainstay of track and soccer teams around the globe.

Horst Dassler built adidas – the name is a meld of Adi and Dassler – into a $1 billion corporation and a major force in the politics of sport. He did business with the East and the West, and the North and the South. Blending good business and good citizenship, he helped fund and equip youth soccer leagues and training camps in Africa, Latin America, and Eastern Europe. His entrée was legendary. When Mikhail Gorbachev came to power in the Kremlin, Dassler was soon invited in for a chat. In the Olympics and World Cup soccer, insiders viewed Dassler as the real power behind the throne and there are even those who say that he personally engineered the election of Juan Antonio Samaranch.

In the aftermath of the ruinous Moscow boycott, Dassler and Samaranch began working openly to bolster the position of the IOC. Their first aim was to develop a new revenue source for the IOC, to counterbalance the dependency on TV broadcasting rights. Their tool of choice: big-time corporate sponsorship. In the past, Olympic sponsors dealt

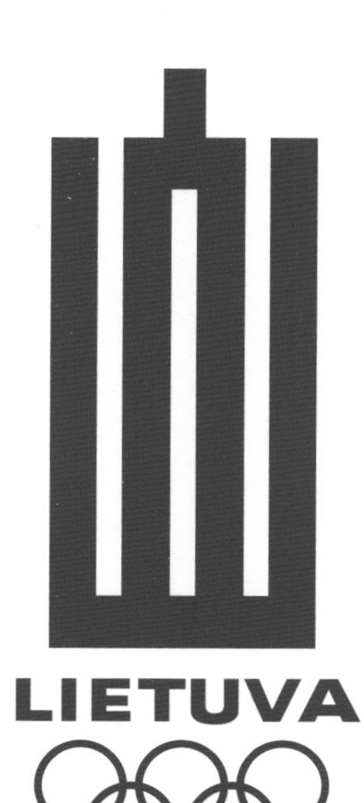

directly with the cities hosting the Games and with the National Olympic Committees.

Dassler and Samaranch wanted to alter that arrangement. Under their plan, all of the National Olympic Committees would cede their individual marketing rights to the IOC, which would then entice prominent international corporations to purchase *global* sponsorship packages, covering the 160 nations in the Olympic family. Under the plan, about two-thirds of the sponsorship revenue would go to the host city; the rest would be spread among the national committees. The IOC would take a small share, about seven percent, for its operations and holdings in Lausanne. Henceforth, one intermediary would negotiate all the corporate sponsorship under exclusive contract with the IOC: ISL Marketing, owned and operated by none other than Horst Dassler.

The Dassler-Samaranch plan was brilliant in its conception, from both a financial and a political point of view. It would give the IOC a strong new source of revenue – initial projections put the potential sponsorship jackpot at $200 million – and it would give Samaranch and the IOC increased political leverage as well. If any nation chose to boycott a future Olympic Games, naturally they would forfeit their sponsorship windfall. Also, Samaranch planned to use some of the new funding to bolster "Olympic Solidarity" programs, which brought badly needed sports equipment and training programs to many Third World countries. At the same time, Horst Dassler's entrée and influence, East and West, would be an enormous asset to Samaranch and the IOC as they tried to head off future political crises.

The linchpin of this entire plan, of course, was money. Big money. And here several critical questions remained to be answered. Was there a sufficient number of large corporations who would see the value of investing huge sums in a global sponsorship package? Could ISL Marketing bring them into the fold? Or would new boycotts put a stake through the heart of the entire sponsorship plan? If that happened, IOC's crisis was bound to go from bad to worse. And Señor Samaranch could wind up holding the bag.

With these ominous possibilities in mind, in March of 1983 Samaranch and Dassler unveiled their grand strategy. In a meeting with select members of the IOC at the lovely Ashoka Hotel in New Delhi, India, they presented TOP, The Olympic Programme, their blueprint for saving the Olympic Movement from future political interference and financial vulnerability. In a smoothly polished video presentation, the architects of the new alliance delivered a stirring message: "You, the International Olympic Committee, own the most valuable and sought-after property in the world. Yet the Olympic rings are possibly the most unexploited trademark in existence. No major international corporation in the world would tolerate such a situation."

The meaning was clear as crystal: it was time for the IOC to shed the tired notions of purity and amateurism and embrace modern commercialism and big corporate money. It was time to take maximum advantage of the marketing and commercial potential of the Olympic Games and the Olympic Rings – not for the sole benefit of host cities but for the benefit of the IOC and the whole Olympic Family. It was time, in sum, to give new meaning to the Olympic expression, "Going for The Gold." The time to start, the video made clear, was now, with the preparations for the 1988 Winter Games in Calgary, Alberta, and the Summer Games later that year in Seoul, South Korea.

The Dassler-Samaranch approach might well have made purists like Baron de Coubertin thrash wildly in their grave, but it earned wide approval among the IOC members gathered in New Delhi.

The truth is, they had little choice. Everyone on the committee knew what was at stake. And everyone knew the IOC desperately needed an infusion of fresh energy and capital. The Dassler-Samaranch plan might not have been an ideal solution, and some critics would surely say it compromised the Olympics' founding ideals, but turning to big-time corporate sponsorship seemed the best way to go. In fact, to many members of the IOC, it seemed the *only* way to go.

If any IOC members came away from New Delhi with lingering doubts, those were put to rest the following year by Peter Ueberroth, the savvy American entrepreneur who was the chief organizer and driving force behind the 1984 Summer Games in Los Angeles. Ueberroth unfurled, for all the world to see, the full potential of big-time Olympic sponsorship. Coca-Cola, McDonald's, IBM, and Levi-Strauss headed his list of star-spangled sponsors – and so did a certain financial services company named American Express.

As everyone feared, in 1984 politics again invaded the Games. The Soviet Union and 13 other socialist countries, including East Germany and Cuba – two traditional Olympic powers – did boycott the L.A. Games, as they had threatened, and they condemned the Games as an ugly display of American flag-waving and raw commercialism. Many sports fans from abroad concurred; they publicly complained that the L.A. Games were not about gold, silver, and bronze; they were more about red, white, and blue. And green, as in U.S. dollars.

None of the criticism, however, affected Peter Ueberroth's bottom line. The L.A. Games generated a record-breaking profit of $215 million, nary a penny of which would go to the IOC or to the 159 National Olympic Committees outside the United States. At the close of the Games, Juan Antonio Samaranch publicly praised Ueberroth's efforts and he proclaimed the L.A. Games a success. But Samaranch surely left the "City of Angels" with a heightened sense of mission. But the question now was this: Could he and ISL replicate Ueberroth's marketing success?

Enter Rob Prazmark. Rob was barely 30, but as a top executive at ISL's U.S. division, he was key to the Dassler-Samaranch plan. It was his job to canvass a select list of U.S. companies and try to sign them on as global sponsors for Calgary and Seoul. Obviously, his first approach was to long-time Olympic sponsors like Coca-Cola. From there, he hoped to build an impressive list of U.S. sponsors. Building that list depended on signing a few star companies and using them to build momentum. Prazmark wanted his candidates to say: "Coke and American Express are on board? That's a group I want to join. Where do I sign?" Other ISL sales teams would be fanning out around Europe, Asia, and Latin America to build the list around the world.

Despite his youth, Rob was well-suited to the job. He was tall, trim, and composed, and he had excellent, in-depth knowledge of the world of sports marketing and its key players. By November

of 1985, however, Rob Prazmark had one tiny problem: after nearly a year at the task, his efforts had come to naught. In fact, he had failed to line up a single new sponsor. Coca-Cola, for years an Olympic mainstay, had agreed to sign on again. But one of his prime candidates – American Express – had turned him down flat. That was not good news. When a respected, prior sponsor like American Express says no, that's a momentum-killer. Other candidates might think, "Whoa, now. Why's AmEx shying away this time around? Sign now? Uh, no thanks."

Prazmark and ISL had done their best to woo American Express. In fact, earlier that month they had Samaranch make a personal written appeal to James D. Robinson, AmEx's chairman and CEO. The reply was still no. From AmEx's perspective, the $14.5 million asking price was simply too high for its potential commercial value, especially since AmEx executives felt that their experience with the Los Angeles Games had not been that successful. The entry fee there had been $4 million, and AmEx's marketing research after the Games revealed that while most consumers remembered Coke, McDonald's, and Levi's as sponsors, few remembered American Express. Given those findings, AmEx was not inclined to sign on for Calgary and Seoul, and surely not for $14.5 million.

The AmEx decision came as a bad blow to ISL and the IOC. It also came as a personal blow to Rob Prazmark. The AmEx decision would inevitably become public, and that could hurt his campaign to sign up other sponsors. As soon as AmEx said no, Prazmark knew he had to pull off some sort of coup – and he had to do it fast. The whole TOP program was on the line and Dassler and Samaranch wanted results. If he couldn't deliver, it would be a bad blow for his reputation – and possibly worse. It was with all this weighing on his mind that Rob Prazmark had picked up the phone and placed that urgent call to Jan Soderstrom.

❀ ❀ ❀

Like Jan, John Bennett did not immediately leap at Prazmark's "golden opportunity." He had his hands full building a marketing and advertising program for Visa, and he wasn't sure he was ready for all the inevitable headaches of mounting a global campaign of the sort the Olympics would demand. Nor was he sure that he could convince Visa's boards to come up with the necessary funding. Still, John was intrigued by the idea, and he called Gary de Paolo, Visa's account manager at BBDO. They then arranged for Prazmark to go to BBDO and make a formal pitch.

Prazmark rose to the occasion. In front of de Paolo, Richard Kronengold, and other tough-minded BBDO executives, he made a fabulous presentation, laying out the case why Visa should become an Olympic sponsor. Visa wanted to move upmarket, he said, and what could be more upmarket than the Olympic Games? What could be more prestigious on a credit card than those five shining Olympic gold rings? Prazmark also added a clincher: this was perfect way to stick it to American Express. One reason AmEx had said no, Prazmark said, was that it figured that neither Visa nor MasterCard would have the gumption or the necessary resources to take on a global sponsorship package.

Gary de Paolo was impressed. He saw a perfect fit with Visa's global ambitions, its five-region structure, and even with its freshly minted Rosalie campaign. How sweet it would be to run an ad showing fabulous Olympic athletes and a festive Olympic venue and then to end the ad with the killer tag line, "...and bring your Visa card, because the Olympics don't take American Express."

As soon as Prazmark was out the door, de Paolo pulled John Bennett out of a meeting with a group of bankers in Miami. "John," he said, "it's a perfect fit for our strategy." The next day, John took the idea to Chuck Russell, who almost gagged on the price tag. "Boy, it's going to cost a lot of money," was his initial reaction. Russell had some serious reservations about the deal – as he did about all such marketing hoopla – but he trusted Bennett and within a few minutes he had the color back in his face. "Put a box around it," he told John, "size it, and let's go for it!"

A short time later, John was at a meeting of Visa's U.S. board of directors, getting ready to present to them the Olympic opportunity. By this time, the entry fee, with everything included, had grown to $17 million, and Chuck Russell was feeling skittish. He took Bennett aside. "Better make this good," he told him. "I've been talking to some of the board members and they don't like it." John then made his best case for becoming an Olympic sponsor. Several members of the board expressed serious reservations. The whole effort would take two years. And with the media buys and special marketing and ad campaigns, the final price tag would hit about $40 million – not a comfortable sum for the board to authorize. In the end, though, John put it over. In retrospect, he said one argument was the clincher: "I told them we were going

to stick the blade into the ribs of American Express." With that, the Visa board approved what amounted to a $40 million gamble. John was elated. Visa was going for the gold.

And so it began. From that point on, John, Jan, Chuck, BBDO, Dave Roberts in advertising, and hundreds of other Visa employees in San Mateo and around the world went a little Olympics-crazy. They convened meetings with member banks and merchants to explain the opportunity and generate ideas. They designed bank card prototypes featuring a Visa logo blended into the Olympic rings, and they created special Olympic tie-ins, contests, and spending programs. "Use your Visa card and support your Olympic team" became a popular way for member banks to convince their customers to sign up for new Visa cards – and to use them. At Visa headquarters, office walls were suddenly lined with splashy Olympic posters for Calgary or Seoul – all of them with the Visa logo standing proudly next to the Olympic rings. The whole staff was energized, and everyone caught the Olympic fever.

As planned, John and Jan bought extensive TV airtime for the new Olympic ads BBDO was crafting from the Rosalie model. They purchased some $7 million worth of U.S. broadcasting time for the build-up to Calgary and another $6 million in time-slots during the Winter Games themselves. The first ads aired in March of 1987 and were they sexy. The ads featured Olympic skiers, bobsled racers, and skaters. And the tag line was a zinger: "But if you go, bring your camera and your Visa card, because the Olympics don't take place all the time, and this time, they don't take American Express."

That tag line did not sit well with American Express. The company, in fact, protested to the IOC, claiming the ad implied that AmEx cards were not accepted anywhere in Calgary, whereas Visa's exclusivity applied only to official Olympic sites. Visa cheerfully refined the tag line, but to John Bennett, the AmEx reaction spoke for itself. "This is a clear signal we're having an impact," he said at the time. "It's a marketing war, and that's new to American Express."

The Olympics opportunity also energized the four other regions in the Visa family and helped them sharpen their competitive edge. Throughout Latin America, for instance, Visa member banks in each country tailored an Olympic message to suit their local markets and to sponsor their local teams. The elasticity of Visa's structure facilitated the process. Carlos Thompson, of BBDO's Miami office, works closely with individual Latin countries, trying to develop ad campaigns that fit their specific language and cultural needs. "It would be very hard to develop one campaign for the entire region," he explained. "You have to understand that each country has its own traditions and flavors. So you want to do a campaign that works for the whole region, but give each country the freedom to add their own particular salsa."

The Olympics opportunity did just that. In

Going For The Gold

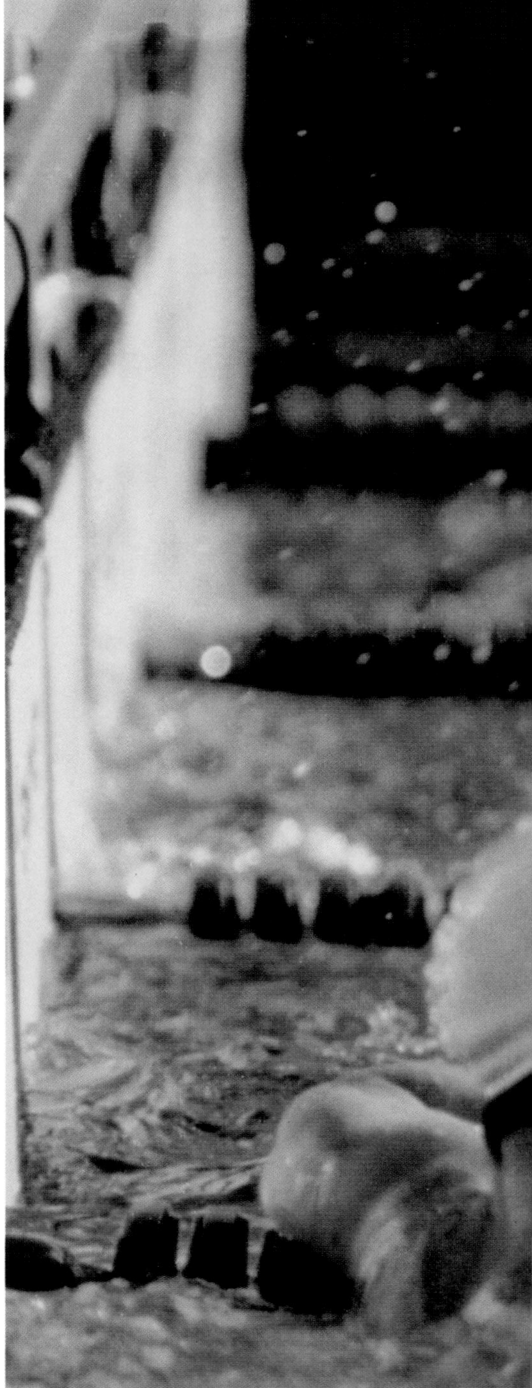

Venezuela, for instance, Visa supported Venezuela's Olympic team with special ads and promotions, and that helped define Visa as a local product, Thompson said. And it did something more for the brand: it gave Visa a huge boost over MasterCard. Prior to the Olympics, there had been "parity" between Visa and MasterCard in many Latin American countries, but the Olympics did wonders for making Visa the preferred brand. At the same time, many Latin American countries made valuable contributions to the larger campaign. This sort of give-and-take quickly became ingrained in Visa's approach to all of its regional marketing.

"Managing a strategy of 'global brand, local usage' presents unique and difficult challenges," Thompson said. Market specifics vary from country to country. Brazil, for instance, is a country where people write a lot of checks, whereas Mexico is a cash-based culture. Visa products and marketing have to be carefully tailored to match those specifics. "You need to talk with people in each country and share what you're doing. We need to have their input and cooperation, so they feel like they're doing something for the Visa family."

Visa markets its products in Latin America in three different languages: Spanish, Portuguese, and English. BBDO helps coordinate advertising and marketing with all the countries except Argentina, which has a long-standing relationship with Young & Rubicam's Latin operation. The tag line "It's everywhere you want to be" is not used in Latin America. Instead, many countries rely on two different slogans: *El Mundo Prefiere Visa.* The World Prefers Visa. And, *Es La Tarjeta.* It's The Card. To complement the Olympics program, Visa in Latin America now also sponsors such popular events as the annual Carnivale festivities and, in many countries, national and regional soccer. The key, Thompson believes, is not finding the right event to sponsor, or the right tag line, it's finding the right *emotion.*

"Cleverness never translates if it's only in the words," he said. "It does if it's in the thought and the emotion. So we emphasize the emotional satisfaction people receive from using a Visa product. What, for instance, would the world be like without romance? Romance is a universal message. It works in any language."

So do the Olympics. But the Olympics work better in some regions than they do in others. Patrick Bowden, who for years served as a marketing strategist for Visa's European operation, was never a great fan of the Olympics sponsorship, especially given its cost. "Outside of a handful of countries, one of which is the U.S.A., I don't think the Olympics has helped very much." Patrick felt that sponsoring World Cup soccer would be a much better investment, especially given the fervor with which European and Latin American countries follow soccer and their national teams. According to Patrick, the chieftains of the World Cup went to Visa's international board with a $10 million sponsorship package, but the board turned it down, a decision he still regrets. "MasterCard grabbed it," Patrick said. "Alas."

In Canada, however, it was a very different story. The Winter Games put Calgary in the world limelight, and Visa banks in Canada used the Games to build the image of the brand. There was extensive advertising linking Visa to the Games and to Canada's ski, hockey, and speed-skating teams. The banks also did several consumer promotions to impel customers to sign up for Visa cards, featuring the Olympic rings, and to increase spending on their existing cards. This was one of Visa Canada's first forays into such consumer promotions, and they proved very effective. The Olympics did so much to elevate the brand in Canada, that Visa Canada formally integrated the Games into their permanent marketing and brand-enhance-

ment strategy.

In Asia, the impact of linking Visa and the Olympics was even more dramatic. Prior to the 1988 Games, American Express dominated the market in Asia, and Carl Pascarella, CEO of Visa, Asia-Pacific, was eager to change that. He had already embarked on an ambitious plan to open offices in China, Japan, Taiwan, India, and Korea. With the 1988 Summer Games to be held in Seoul, Carl saw an ideal opportunity for Visa to improve both its image and its market share. In 1987 he brought in Richard Bush, an advertising specialist who had been working with an ad agency in Tokyo. Pascarella defined their joint mission: use the Olympics to completely reposition Visa in the Asian market.

"Up to then, we had never marketed Visa in Asia; the banks did," Bush recalled. "So American Express had a wide berth here. We were determined to change that. And going into the Olympics, Visa had one distinct advantage. It was seen as a domestic product, with domestic utility, and issued by local banks."

To take advantage of the Seoul opportunity, Visa Asia-Pacific launched a $12 million cooperative marketing venture, with member banks putting up 80 percent of the money and Visa 20 percent. In Hong Kong and Singapore, interest in the Olympics was relatively low, so Visa focused instead on Japan, Australia, and Korea, which were its biggest markets in any case. Working closely with Visa, each country in Asia took the Olympic package and rings and enhanced it with their own marketing programs and slogans. Two slogans were especially effective: "Visa. You are not alone." And, to capitalize on the Olympics and their message of universality, "We are the world."

The campaigns produced dramatic results. In Japan, prior to the 1988 Olympics, Visa stood at No. 3 in the card market, behind MasterCard and the local JCB card. In 1987, though, Sumitomo Bank and several other banks jumped into Olympic sponsorship with great excitement. Sumitomo, in fact, did so with an important shift. Instead of heralding their own name, now the bank's emphasis was Visa, Visa, Visa. The bank put the Visa logo and Olympic rings on their cards and launched a big ad campaign linking Sumitomo with Visa with the Olympics. Suddenly everyone in Japan seemed to want a Visa card.

"Japan was booming at the time," recalled Richard Bush. "Everyone wanted a card to go overseas. They chose Visa. MasterCard had a lot of cards out there in circulation, but no image. Thanks to the Olympics, we just leap-frogged the competition. By 1990, we had become the No. 1 card in Japan, in the space of just three years."

Banks in Australia and New Zealand jumped in enthusiastically as well, sponsoring the entire Australian Olympic team and creating a host of Olympic tie-ins. To take its image upmarket in Australia, Visa began featuring a TV ad cut from the Rosalie cloth. The ad showed happy couples having fish and chips at Doyle's, a legendary eatery in Sydney harbor. "It's the perfect way to spend an afternoon in Sydney," the message went. "But when you go to Doyle's, bring your Visa card, because they don't take American Express." Visa also ran a similar ad featuring Punch Wilson, a charter fisherman in New Zealand. When combined with the Olympic push, these did wonders for Visa's image.

"The Olympics were an amazing tool," Bush said. "They gave us instant credibility across Asia. We were playing with the big boys, Coke, Kodak, IBM, and the rest."

South Korea, as host of the Summer Games, provided the natural centerpiece for Visa's marketing and image-building efforts. Korea Exchange Bank was the official bank of the Summer Games,

and it had a branch on the site of the Olympic complex. To build its image and customer base, the bank launched a Visa Gold Card adorned with the Olympic Rings, and it was a phenomenal success. Merchants throughout Seoul were also eager to associate themselves with the Games, and one of the easiest ways was to post a new Visa sign in their windows, showing the Visa logo and the Olympic Rings. "This sort of promotion was tremendously effective," Bush noted. "The merchants got exactly what they wanted – at no cost. I believe that what we did in Korea in 1988 continues to serve us well to this day. We are now far and away the preferred brand in Korea."

The Summer Games themselves were the crowning moment of the entire Visa effort. Board members from the five regions were invited to the Games and were treated, of course, like royalty by the Koreans – and by their co-hosts, the IOC and ISL. A huge Visa banner was displayed right next to the NBC broadcasting booth, so every time the cameras panned up to the booth, viewers around the world could see a bright, shining image of Visa, under the Olympic flags waving majestically in the breeze. And where was American Express? Where was MasterCard? Nowhere to be seen.

The Summer Games were also a crowning moment for ISL and Juan Antonio Samaranch. With Visa's help at a critical time, they and Rob Prazmark had managed to put together an impressive list of Olympic sponsors: IBM, Xerox, 3M, Coke, Kodak, Federal Express, Philips, Time Inc., Samsung, Japan's Dentsu ad agency, and more. Prior to the Games, North Korea had made all sorts of threats to disrupt the South's moment of glory, but the Games unfolded with no political interference, disruptions, or boycotts.

Samaranch emerged triumphant. With a new measure of political calm, and this huge new infusion of sponsorship revenue, the wily Spaniard could rightfully claim that he had steered the IOC and the whole Olympic Movement back from the brink of disaster. Alas, his friend Horst Dassler, the kingmaker, was not on hand in Seoul to share the triumph. He had died, quite unexpectedly, the year before, in what was a considerable loss to the world of sport.

John Bennett came away from Seoul thrilled by the whole experience. As they had all hoped from the beginning, the Olympics proved to be a perfect fit for Visa and its regions and a perfect fit for the strategy that had been embodied in the Rosalie campaign and the slogan "It's Everywhere You Want To Be." The Olympic Games and the magic of those rings had galvanized Visa and its member banks and merchants, and they had catapulted Visa into the pantheon of global brands. At the same time, the Games had enabled Visa to steal plenty of luster – and market share – from American Express.

"The Olympic Games put us on the world stage and gave us tons of credibility," John reflected a decade later. "We were players. American Express gave up the ball."

The only card accepted at The Sydney 2000 Olympic Games.

© 2000 Visa U.S.A. Inc. 36USC220506

READING IS
RIF

A Spirit of Community

In 1986, when Visa made the crucial decision to "go for the gold," David Brancoli came up with a wonderful companion idea.

Brancoli, a self-effacing, highly respected man who was then running Visa's corporate communications, knew that the Olympic Games were a marvelous way to enhance the image of Visa. It was clear to him that Visa had everything to gain by affiliating itself with world-class athletes and with the international travel and festivities that surround the games. But something else was also clear to him. The games could also showcase Visa's *ideals* along with its brand.

With that in mind, Dave suggested joining forces with the Special Olympics, a widely praised program devoted to helping young people with developmental disabilities. "The idea I came up with," he said in an interview, "was to bring Special Olympians from around the world, at Visa's expense, to the games in Calgary and Seoul. This seemed to me an ideal opportunity to spread the word that Visa is a good corporate citizen."

The idea represented an important departure for Visa. In its start-up years, Visa had not delved into "cause marketing" or charitable sponsorship. In fact, it had rarely embarked on any sort of full-scale public relations effort on behalf of its brand or its member banks. Visa's primary mandate, after all, was to process payments, serve its members and cardholders, and build the card business. Many of Visa's banks and merchants around the world supported various charities and philanthropic endeavors in their own locales; until this juncture, Visa had always been content to leave it at that.

Dave, though, was born and bred in the shadow of A.P. Giannini. He grew up in North Beach, A.P.'s old neighborhood, and after a stint in newspapering, he joined the public relations unit of the Bank of America. After seven years with the house that Giannini built, Dave moved over to the industrial giant, Kaiser Industries. In 1982, he joined Visa in corporate communications, and by 1986 he was running the department and serving as Chuck Russell's chief spokesman to the U.S. and international press. Through all his years in public relations and helping companies mold their image, Dave had become a firm believer in what A.P. Giannini had preached: good business and good citizenship always go hand in hand.

Dave knew, moreover, that Visa had a problem with its corporate image. For all the prominence of the brand, the general public still had a rather hazy and incomplete vision of Visa and what it actually did. Everyone knew Visa was a convenient plastic payment card, but few people had any clue that it was a unique international partnership. And even fewer people knew that A.P. Giannini had endowed it with real ideals about helping people one by one. For too many people, Dave knew, Visa was an organization with no visible heart or soul – an image complicated by the fact that some of its member banks had an unflinching tendency to charge very high interest rates on unpaid balances.

When Visa signed on as an Olympic sponsor, Dave saw an opportunity to mount a public relations campaign that would clarify and enhance Visa's image with a new and very positive dimension. The campaign, if done right, would cast Visa member banks in a very favorable light and it would fit easily into what John Bennett and Jan Soderstrom were doing in marketing and what BBDO was doing on the advertising front. The cost, furthermore, would not be high, while the impact on Visa's image could be immense. "Pre-Olympics, Visa was a pretty low-profile company," Dave recalled. "This was an ideal moment to change all that."

The Special Olympics were an especially good fit. The group was prestigious, of unquestionable merit, and, like Visa itself, was an international effort bridging nationalities, cultures, and languages. Dave also liked that the Special Olympics was not the province of world-class athletes; it was the province of children and adults with disabilities, from all over the world. Dave had little trouble selling the idea to Chuck Russell and to John Bennett and Jan Soderstrom, and Dave himself took the lead in coordinating with the Special Olympics leadership and the IOC.

The Visa program was simplicity itself. The directors of the Special Olympics, through an international canvassing and their own criteria, selected 25 young athletes, each from a different country, to go to the Winter Games in Calgary and another 25 were selected to go to the Summer Games in Seoul. The young athletes attended various Olympic events and were given royal treatment at Olympic venues and functions. They also were able to meet and interact with Olympic athletes. But Visa helped organize an added kick for these courageous Special Olympians.

"It was more than the trip," Dave explained. "In each case, the Special Olympians engaged in their own sporting specialty. In Seoul, for instance, we arranged for a track meet to be held at a local track facility, so the athletes could compete against each other. In each case, we also held a medals ceremony. The kids not only enjoyed the Olympics, they had their own little Olympic competition."

There was another treat as well. "In Seoul, we brought over with us a fellow who works in art therapy in Atlanta, where he has patients draw murals on hospital walls," Dave said. "In Seoul, they painted a giant mural for peace. It was a huge painting of a dove."

The program produced a public relations bonanza for Visa. "The Special Olympians were the media darlings of Seoul," Dave recalled. "This was the first unofficial bringing together of the Special Olympics with the Olympic Games. For us, it was a major success and a wonderful cause for Visa to support."

For the next Winter Games in Lillehammer, Norway, and the 1992 Summer Games in Barcelona, Spain, Brancoli and Visa introduced a different companion program: "The Olympics of the Imagination." This was an international arts competition for youngsters between the ages of nine and 13, again linked directly to the Olympic Games. In the first round, for Lillehammer, children were invited to submit drawings or paintings portraying what they thought the Olympics would look like in the year 2000. To add a special touch, Dave flew to Norway and convinced the Olympic organizers to allow the winners of the arts competition to participate in the opening ceremonies for the Winter Games.

The "Olympics of the Imagination" prompted enthusiastic support from all of Visa's regional offices. "This represented the first time that Visa as an organization globally embraced a public relations idea," Dave said. "Every region eagerly hopped on board and did its own competition."

The "Olympics of the Imagination" sparked a tremendous outpouring of creative activity from kids all around the world. "The response was amazing," Dave recalled. The eventual winners went to the Olympic Games and participated in the opening ceremonies wearing native Norwegian garb. Again, the media showered the Visa program with lavish attention, and it received awards from several important public relations associations. "We had 600 million 'media impressions' from around the world, meaning we reached that many people via newspaper and broadcast outlets," Dave said. "It was incredible exposure."

During later Olympic years, the "Olympics of The Imagination" continued to grow and evolve, turning into a popular fixture of the Olympic gatherings. At the 2000 Olympics in Sydney, the program received one billion impressions in the press worldwide.

Dave retired in the year 2000, but he looks back on the Special Olympics and "The Olympics of the Imagination" as the most rewarding things he did during his 18 years with Visa. "If I had approached some companies with this sort of program, they would have said, 'Are you kidding?' But I was proud to work for a company that would embrace these ideas. They proved to be a wonderful opportunity for Visa to spread its goodwill even beyond the Olympic Games."

Today, Visa's regions and many of its member banks and merchants actively sponsor various good causes and charitable endeavors. As with so many Visa initiatives, these programs are carefully tailored to suit the conditions of the local cultures. One illustrative case in point is a pilot program that Visa sponsored in Indonesia. In the late 1990s, Indonesia's economy and currency were ailing, millions of people were suffering, and Visa did not want to promote consumer spending or increased individual debt. At the same time, Visa wanted to find positive ways to strengthen its brand presence and identity. As a result, Visa launched an innovative promotion to help Indonesia schoolchildren. Called "I will graduate with Visa," the program raised money to subsidize the exams Indonesian children take at the age of 12, to see how they will proceed on to the next level of schooling.

"The program subsidized testing for children in 10 of Indonesia's 26 provinces," said Ellyana Fuad, Visa's director in Indonesia. "With a coali-

Help bring back their smiles.

If you are a Visa cardholder, you can.

A lot of Indonesia's children find it is hard to smile nowadays as their families cannot afford to keep them at school. But it doesn't take much for you to bring back their smiles. Because every time you use your Visa card to dine, shop or make everyday purchases, a percentage of your expenditure will be donated to help the less fortunate 6th graders. So they can stay in school and obtain their elementary school certificate. With this, they will have a more promising future. Visa and these 14 participating banks guarantee a minimum of Rp 400,000,000 towards this fund, co-ordinated by the Indonesian Children's Welfare Society (YKAI) and audited by Prasetio Utomo & Co, a member firm of Arthur Andersen. With your help, we can bring back hope to these little ones. After all, our country's future lies in the hands of these children.

IF THERE'S SKY ABOVE AND GROUND BELOW, ALL YOU NEED IS VISA

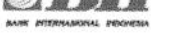

tion of 13 participating banks, we paid the exam fee for 3,000 children in the first round and another 2,000 in a second round of testing." The shipping company DHL and the accounting firm Arthur Andersen helped sponsor the program, while Bank Central Asia, Bank International Indonesia, and the Hong Kong Shanghai Bank played lead roles.

"The program was very effective," reported Adelina Ko, who at the time helped run regional marketing at Visa's Asia-Pacific headquarters in Singapore. "We ran magazine inserts showing happy schoolchildren, and all of them thanking Visa for its support."

According to Adelina, the program helped shape and enhance local perceptions of Visa. "The Indonesians see Visa as an international product, but they know it's issued locally. It helps to have strong local banks issuing Visa cards. We want to be seen as international, but not foreign. We want to make our bigness local. The children's charity program made us look sensitive and caring."

These sorts of "spirit of community" ventures are important mainstays of Visa activities in several other parts of Asia. Leading the way in Japan, for instance, has been Yo Suzuki of Sumitomo Bank, Visa's most prominent partner in the Japanese market. As we will see in a later chapter, Suzuki is one of the great lions of Asian banking, and he played a key role in Visa's emergence in Japan and the Pacific. Suzuki, in the Giannini mold, is a firm believer in supporting substantive initiatives in the arts, culture, and the environment, not just because it's good for Sumitomo's image and business, but because it's the right thing to do. "We support the Red Cross, UNICEF, and the Japanese Olympic Committee," Suzuki said in an interview in his office in Tokyo. "We are happy to contribute a portion of our profits to these good causes."

Visa is Sumitomo's partner in these charitable endeavors. Suzuki's bank issues "co-branded"

Visa cards, with a portion of the sales volume on those cards going to the particular cause highlighted on the face of the card. These ventures have proved very effective in enhancing Sumitomo's corporate image and its card volume, Suzuki said.

Suzuki is an opera lover, and he created a special promotion to help subsidize Japan's Takaraska Opera, again by issuing a co-branded Visa card to supporters of the opera. Here there was a clever twist. Seats to this opera are very difficult to come by, so Suzuki worked out an arrangement with the opera whereby Visa cardholders would get preferential treatment in ticket sales. "Now, unless you hold a Visa card," Suzuki said, "you can't get a good seat!"

During one phase of the campaign, Sumitomo raised $2 million for the Takaraska Opera. The promotion also worked well for the bank: five nights a year, the bank takes over the opera and uses the performance as the springboard for a major membership drive. "The result has been thousands of new Visa cardholders for our bank," Suzuki said. "In exchange, we provide a very good service for these cardholders who love the opera."

Sumitomo's campaign on behalf of UNICEF worked on an even larger scale. Both UNICEF and the Red Cross in Japan have long-standing ties to the emperor's family, Suzuki said, and they are very popular causes for many Japanese people. As a result, the Sumitomo-UNICEF affinity card proved to be very popular among existing customers and helped Sumitomo attract more business.

"The image of bankers in Japan is not good," Suzuki said. "By supporting the arts, education, UNICEF, and the Olympics, we let people know that our concerns extend beyond profits. This sort of marketing I believe will be increasingly important, especially in attracting young people. Through sponsorship in the philanthropic arena, we are now contributing almost $50 million a year to good causes. Everybody wins."

Suzuki believes that banks large and small should do even more, especially in endangered cultural areas such as opera and classical music. The issue, he said, is not money; it's corporate responsibility and leadership. "We can surely say that classical music will rarely generate profits," Suzuki said. "But we believe we should do more to support these art forms and to ensure their continued existence. Without us, they could perish."

Charles Lo, one of the driving forces of China Trust in Taiwan, has also parlayed good citizenship into good business, again with Visa as a privileged partner. Lo spent 17 years in corporate banking but took charge of China Trust's credit card program in the early 1990s, at a time of fierce competition in the emerging card market in Taiwan. Lo restructured the entire card operation to make it more competitive, and then he set out to build the bank's

cardholder base. Key to his strategy was joining forces with a national Buddhist charity comprised of almost 3.5 million members.

"Everybody donates something every month," Lo explained in an interview in his office in Taiwan. "My original idea was to help the Buddhist charity collect those monthly contributions. But the charity did not want that. It preferred to deal directly with its supporters," Lo said. "But then it hit me. Why don't we just propose issuing a co-branded Visa card and we can donate a certain percentage of each transaction to the charity. Then, when people use their card, they'll feel good about it, knowing they're helping support a worthy cause, and one they give to anyway."

The program proved to be a huge success throughout Taiwan. China Trust added 150,000 co-branded cards to its cardholder base, and sales volume jumped. "People like it," Lo said. "Now when they use their Visa card, people have a spiritual satisfaction. They feel like they're doing something good." With this and other creative initiatives, China Trust has become the largest single Visa issuer in Taiwan, with 24 percent of the card market. The joint venture has also worked well for the Buddhist charity. Over a five-year period, Lo said, the program raised over 100 million Taiwan dollars for the Buddhist charity.

"The motivation for people carrying that card is totally different from traditional cardholders," Lo said. "They're religious believers. It shows that doing the right thing, and choosing the right partners, is good business. Very good business."

In recent years, these types of co-branded Visa cards have become very popular in Asia, Europe, and the United States. In each of these regions, Visa has alliances, based on co-branded cards, with many universities, clubs, charities, arts organizations, and sporting associations. Some people want payment cards that offer them frequent flyer miles; others want cards that help them support their favorite cause. In both cases, Visa is a willing and eager intermediary and supporter.

Like Dave Brancoli, Yo Suzuki sees his work in promoting good causes as one of the most rewarding aspects of his entire career. Indeed, he has become a fervent advocate and evangelist on the subject, urging his fellow bankers to do more to leave a lasting and positive mark on their countries and their cultures. When Suzuki stepped down from Visa's Asia-Pacific board a few years ago, his colleagues threw him a farewell party at the Pebble Beach resort and golf course in Monterey, California. Suzuki took the occasion to speak from his heart.

"On that occasion, I told everyone, 'We should not be too selfish,'" Suzuki recalled. "We have to find the right balance between our corporate objectives – profitability – and our civic responsibilities. Sometimes we have to put the good of our communities in front of the good of our bottom lines."

A.P. Giannini would surely applaud.

VISA

Part Five **The Global Revolution**

VISA MAKES THE WOR

LD GO ROUND.

WORLDWIDE SPONSOR
1992 OLYMPIC GAMES

Visa is accepted for more transactions worldwide than any other card.

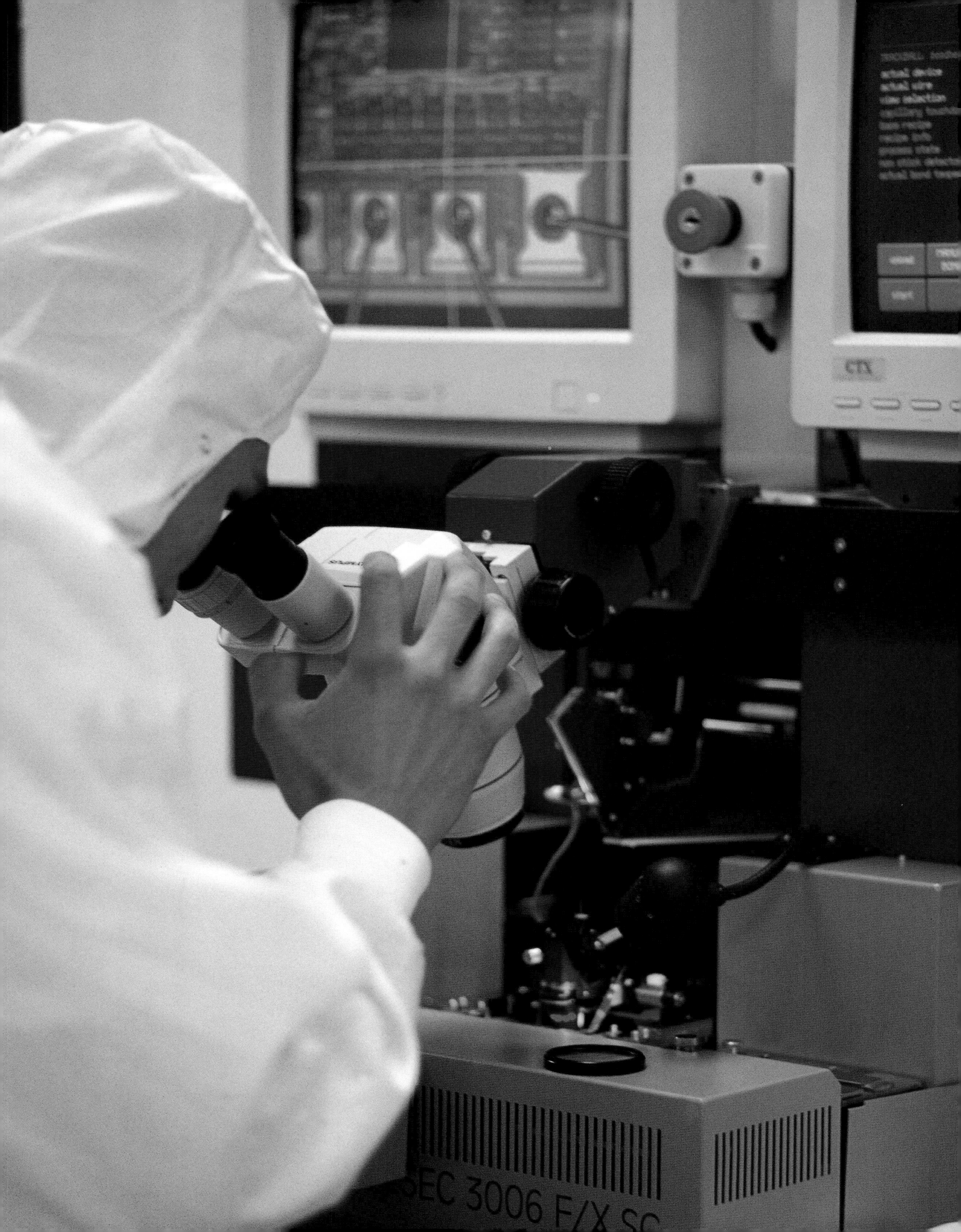
actual device
actual wire
view selection
CTX
EC 3006 F/X SC

Longines
EL MEJOR RELOJ
ENRIQUE SANCHIS
EXCLUSIVAMENTE RELOJES
EL CRONOMETRO
TALLER DE REPARACIONES
GRAN RELOJERIA
ATELIER DE REPARATIONS
19

ROLEX

CRONOMETRO"

RELOJES OMEGA

RELOJES Longines

Europe

Chapter 21

A.P. Giannini would be amazed.

Today, his business philosophy and the little card that carries it are doing wondrous things in many different parts of the world. From Montreal to Lima, from Moscow to Capetown, and from Beijing to Sydney and to Singapore, the world is in a period of profound economic and social transformation, and almost everywhere you look, you'll find Visa hard at work, drawing banks, merchants, and cardholders together in an extremely diverse, yet smoothly functioning global partnership.

To understand the impact that Visa is having worldwide, in large countries and small, the place to begin is with a man we've met before, João Ribeira da Fonseca. João has spent much of his life promoting the credit card as a powerful instrument of economic and social change, and today he can look across the whole of Europe and see the impact of what he and Visa helped set into motion. João can also look back across his own working life and see in it a micro-version of the history of Visa.

In the late 1960s, after a stint with the Portuguese army and with Alitalia, the Italian airline, João joined the Banco Pinto e Sottomayor, one of Portugal's most prominent banks. Banco Pinto wanted to launch Portugal's very first credit card, and it wanted João to help lead the effort. "In 1969, I went to San Francisco to see the Bank of America and began learning about the credit card business," João recalled, relaxing in his office outside of Lisbon. "Then I spent a week at the Barclaycard center in Britain. I had a three-week immersion in how credit cards were working in the more advanced markets. In March of 1970, we launched the first credit card in Portugal. It developed pretty well and we expanded rapidly."

Lisbon is a lovely city, set amidst several cascading hills, and with its tree-lined streets and sophisticated cafes it has the feel of a smaller Paris or Barcelona. In terms of its banking and telephone systems, though, Lisbon and the whole of Portugal in 1970 were anything but modern or sophisticated. As in many cities in Europe, cashing a check was often a lengthy experience, involving waiting in a long line at the bank. Cashing a travelers cheque could take even longer, never mind applying for a small loan. Introducing the BankAmericard represented a very definite landmark in the history of Portuguese banking.

Through meetings of NBI and IBANCO, João spent considerable time with Dee Hock. It was a connection that would change João's life. In 1974, when disgruntled military officers staged a coup in Portugal, João found himself on the outs with the new regime and was compelled to leave his wife and family behind and rush to Paris, with little more than the clothes on his back and only a little cash in his pocket. "I left in March of 1975," João recalled. "I went to Paris looking for a new life."

Once there, one of the first things he did was call Dee in California and ask him if there was some sort of role he could play in his young venture. Dee immediately understood João's plight and arranged for him to come to California. On April 1, 1975, he arrived in San Francisco and became the first non-American to join Dee's team at NBI. Soon he was traveling the world, trying to convince banks to join what was then the IBANCO family. "My strength was that I spoke foreign languages," João recalled. "My mission, basically, was to spread the message."

João took to the task with messianic fervor. At that stage, Base I and Base II were just coming on stream, and all João had to present to prospective banks was a plastic card and the old manual zipzap machine and paper receipts. But João was not selling technology; he was selling an idea. "'This is the future,' I told the banks. 'This is the future of money.'" In his mind, NBI and IBANCO represented a true revolution in banking and consumer payments and credit, and he was determined to spread that revolution around the world. Furthermore, he felt he was trying to put greater financial power and flexibility in the hands of common men and women in every corner of the globe, and he was promoting change in an industry that desperately needed to open its thinking and open its doors.

"I think Visa was the first real global factor in the financial world, a prime factor in what everyone now calls 'globalization,'" João said. "The import of Visa had to be explained to the banks, for they are not known for their creativity and foresight."

João took his message first to Latin and South America, and then to Europe and the Middle East. Whether he met with bankers in Costa Rica or in Teheran, he was always preaching the virtues of change and the inevitable coming of the electronic money revolution. "In the beginning, I felt I was going on a lonely path," João recalled. But he patiently showed banks how IBANCO could help them build a card program, put in place the necessary infrastructure, and then use the payment cards to build revenue for themselves and, at the same time, stimulate economic activity and development in their home communities.

João didn't fully realize it, but he was spreading the same essential message that Woodrow Wilson and A.P. Giannini had spread in the United States more than a half-century before. It was a message of individual empowerment, economic equality and opportunity, and belief in the integrity and resourcefulness of the common man. The credit card looked like a simple piece of plastic, but João tried to make bankers understand that it was the key that unlocked an almost magical formula, one that generated greater profits for the banks – and greater financial power and freedom for their customers. Everybody won.

"In those days, we were the source of creativity and development in the financial world," João said. "Bankers, in their gray pin-striped suits, don't always understand that banking is more about markets than it is about the traditional business of finance. Visa, on the other hand, was a genius on the marketing corner. It took the banks awhile to come around."

But come around they did. By the late 1970s, Dee had to send other missionaries out to help João keep up with the workload. "We realized the world was too big for me alone," João said. "We had to break it up." So Jim Partridge came on to line up banks in Asia and Latin America, while João set up a small office in London's financial district and covered the rest of the world, with a focus on Western Europe. It was a big job, in part because of Europe's wide diversity of cultures, languages, and banking traditions. "We're not countries in Europe, really, we are tribes. We are cultures," João said. "So strategically and culturally, our approach had to be different from country to country."

For João and Visa, though, there was always one common denominator at the heart of their message: Trust. "There is only one way to build trust and credibility, and that is through the show of quality," João said. "And Dee Hock was a master at creating quality and showcasing it." At one international board meeting in Kyoto, João recalled, Dee and his team treated member bankers and guests to a concert played by a young people's symphony, a presentation by a Japanese master of tea, and then a seminar put on by leading economists. European bankers were impressed. "Dee created an ambience of excellence around Visa, and that helped him push his initiatives through the board."

During the 1980s, João and his team in London tried to plant Visa's image and product line throughout Western Europe. In this task, he had some admirable partners. Lars Piehl, a highly respected banker from Sweden, played a pivotal role in the formative years of Visa Europe, and later served as chairman of both Visa International and Visa Europe, when the region also included the Middle East and Africa. Spain's Eduardo Merigo, a distinguished international economist who at one stage served in the Spanish government, also played a key role in the early days of Visa Europe, and he then became head of Visa Spain. Italy's Ugo Scarpetta and France's Jean-Jacques Desbons also played key roles in their native countries and became integral members of the Visa family in Europe.

João and his colleagues had success, but it was far from easy. Germany, Austria, Switzerland, and the Netherlands were always frustrating for Visa executives, due to the strength of the competing Eurocheque/Eurocard system. Britain was not simple either, due to the market dominance of the Barclaycard. France was very difficult, as we will see in a moment, because the French had their own domestic card system. Still, throughout his tenure in London, João participated in startling changes, as the electronic money revolution transformed European banking, consumer payments, merchant operations, and travel abroad.

Today those changes are evident throughout Europe. Thanks to the open borders of the "New Europe," travelers arriving in London, Paris, or Lisbon from other parts of the European Community no longer show their passport on arrival at these airports. Instead, they walk directly into the terminal – and many of them walk directly to a cash machine displaying a Visa logo. There, with their credit card they get enough local currency for their cash expenditures on the trip. Travelers cheques were the anchor of the Visa Europe operation during the early 1980s, but those are rapidly becoming ancient history, just like those long lines at European banks. A glance at any business magazine in Europe will confirm what every traveler can see: electronic money, the digital revolution, and the Internet are sweeping through "Old World" Europe at a furious speed, in some realms much faster than in the United States.

João retired from Visa in 1990 and has returned to his other great passion in life: airplanes. Today he directs one of Portugal's top airlines. But he remains amazed by the speed and depth of change he has seen in European banking and finance. "The final goal of our vision was to make Visa the global Euro, the common currency," João said, reflecting back. "That is still in the offing. But I did see us come a very long way. I was part of something very important. We all were."

❀ ❀ ❀

Visa's London office today bears no resemblance to the start-up it was 20 years ago. Now it's located in large, modern offices in Kensington, near several of London's famous department stores, and it oversees some 500 employees, many of them working in Visa's nine different offices around Europe.

In Visa's lobby, visitors can watch a video featuring Pierce Brosnan, the latest screen incarnation of James Bond. Visa has featured Brosnan as Bond in popular ads shown in Europe and other parts of the world. British music legends Paul McCartney and Elton John have also been featured in Visa ads and in promotional tie-ins with their concerts, all as part of the very high profile Visa maintains internationally and throughout Europe.

While João was an impassioned, do-it-yourself leader in the Dee Hock mold, Hans van der

WHEN THE TRACTOR NEEDS A DRINK you take her to Christina's Bar. She's been serving her customers inside and out for 60 years. It's a way of life on the West Coast of Ireland; there are towns where every shop has its own bar, even the shoe shop. After all, you wouldn't be expecting to make a major purchase without giving it some stout th making up your mind, you'll fin As it is all round the world. Afte

would you? And when you've taken your time
is accepted as readily as a round of Guinness.
ISA MAKES THE WORLD GO ROUND.

Velde brings a cooler, more polished presence to the post of president of Visa "EU," for European Union. He also brings to the job multilingual skills and a wealth of experience in banking and international organizations. Van der Velde, who is Dutch, studied economics at the University of Amsterdam and then joined the managerial staff of the International Labor Organization, ILO, a United Nations agency based in Geneva. When the ILO sent him out to Jamaica to examine ways to develop the bauxite industry there, van der Velde found himself trying to persuade local banks to invest in industrial development. It was an enlightening experience.

Like A.P. Giannini long before him, Hans saw first-hand the amazing potential that banks had to fuel economic development and serve the public interest. So he decided to leave the ILO – and all the politics and bureaucracy that went with it – and go into banking. He went to work first for Citibank in Holland and London and then for the Netherlands Credit Bank, a subsidiary of Chase Manhattan. Then he joined Holland's powerful Rabobank on the corporate and investment side, and helped the bank with several ventures, including international expansion into Germany.

With this unusual mix of experience, van der Velde joined Visa in 1995. The transition was not difficult. Like the ILO and other U.N. agencies, Visa is an international association built on cooperation and governed by discussion and consensus. But unlike the U.N. agencies, Visa has a single focus: the card, plus the vast payments system that supports it. "For me, having that focus was a refreshing change," van der Velde recalled in an interview. "No matter what country Visa operates in, people need the same skills and they have the same concerns."

Still, working in the ILO was excellent preparation for running Visa Europe, with its diversity of languages, cultures, and banking traditions. Visa EU covers 28 countries in all, including the European Union countries, some Scandinavian countries, plus Turkey, Israel, Cyprus, and Malta. In the European Union countries alone, there are some 135 million Visa cards in circulation, generating an annual sales volume of almost half a trillion dollars.

Running the region takes great diplomatic skill. In the whole of the region, Visa member banks compete fiercely for market share, and the region is subdivided by a variety of banking laws and by deep differences of language and culture. "It's an illusion to think that we're now in a global village," van der Velde said. "We're not. I still don't see a united Europe. It will come. But we're a long way from one integrated market."

Under these circumstances, the elasticity of the Visa structure and the company's "think global, act local" orientation are godsends for van der Velde and his team – provided they treat each bank and each country as unique entities inside the association. "In the Visa partnership, your customers are your owners. It's a cooperative," he said. "My job is to balance the interests of everyone involved, and to make it work, you have to understand each of them. We are making people work together who are fierce competitors and would otherwise like to kill each other. It works because the group together can deliver something that none of the banks can deliver on its own."

Van der Velde looks back across history and sees three distinct phases in the evolution of money and payments. The first was the phase of precious metals and coins. Then came paper, in the form of cash, checks, bank drafts, or letters of credit. We are now at the dawn of the third phase, the exchange of information, specifically financial data encoded in digital formats. The electronic money revolution. And Hans believes the traditional credit card was just the beginning.

"The credit card was a nice niche product," van der Velde said. "It created an explosion in the United States. And Barclays was probably saved by it. But in today's Information Age, we all are exchanging more and more financial information. You can do that a lot cheaper and a lot more efficiently with a smart card."

Like João, Hans is amazed at how central credit cards have become to financial institutions around the world. As we will see in coming chapters, Turkey is just one of many countries that have used card technology to leapfrog directly into the electronic money revolution. Throughout much of Europe, the Internet is showing explosive growth and so is business-to-business electronic commerce. In fact, "B2B" commerce is expected to grow exponentially in the next five years.

Smart cards, in van der Velde's view, are inevitably the way of the future, and in Europe the future is rapidly becoming the present. Britain, France, Germany, and Italy moved to chip-based, pre-paid phone cards more quickly than the United States did, and they are now moving to smart cards faster as well. Hans feels the shift will only accelerate, as Visa and other card issuers open the doors to new areas of commercial activity. "We are already using Visa for the Internet and point-of-sale transactions. Soon it will be commonplace in your cellular phone and even for your commuter bus or subway ticket," he said. "Visa is no longer just a credit card. It's a multi-purpose payment tool covering a whole range of activities."

There is another key reason why van der Velde sees the smart card as the way of the future: it almost eliminates fraud. "The security of the mag stripe is coming to an end," he said. "There are now cheap methods of skimming, and it is becoming easier to compromise the mag stripe. The chip offers far more security and can carry hundreds of times more information than the mag stripe. Soon that will be thousands of times more information."

The move to smart cards is already helping to accelerate the existing explosion in Visa Europe's growth and sales volume. "It's not just credit cards," van der Velde said. "It's debit cards, it's business-to-business transactions, and it's smart cards, which allow better integration and usage of financial information. Visa EU's business activity is now double the size it was four years ago. In the year 2000, Visa EU is as big as Visa worldwide was in 1995."

Visa began the shift to smart cards in the mid-1990s with a chip-based, stored-value card called "Visa Cash." It functioned like a phone card, with each purchase immediately deducted from the value stored inside the card. Visa Cash was being introduced on a nation-by-nation basis, but it raised a serious problem: the infrastructures for handling the cards varied widely from country to country, especially in Europe. So Visa took the lead. "We went to major players like Spain and Germany, which issue millions of chip cards, and we said, 'Let's develop the standard,'" van der Velde said. "We then got 22 countries together in one room and our call to them was clear: 'Let's create one standard for the stored-value card.'"

It took some strong diplomacy, but the eventual result was CEPS, "Common Electronic Purse Specifications." This is another of those invaluable initiatives that make the Visa system work but that remain invisible to individual cardholders. CEPS, in essence, is the shared sheet of music that allows each player in the smart card transaction chain to sound the right notes on cue. It covers card technology and software, operating codes, dial-terminal interfaces, cryptography protocols, and other security essentials. It also ensures that the new standards will be compatible with smart cards issued by MasterCard, Europay, and other card issuers. A special consortium was created to implement CEPs and to promote these same standards worldwide.

"We got the members going," van der Velde said. "Initially, MasterCard and Europay didn't believe in it. But the effort gained momentum and we got it done. With the CEPS accord, 90 percent of the smart cards in the world became CEPS-committed. The 22 countries involved simply knew they had to cooperate."

In the defining concept of CEPS, there is one key word to remember: "interoperability." This is the root concept on which the electronic money revolution stands and functions all around the world. Interoperability ensures that all the banks, all the merchants, and all their smart card software fit and function together, for the mutual benefit of everyone concerned. The concept of interoperability is also essential to the next phase of the electronic money revolution: the convergence of the new digital technologies. In the year 2000, there were already examples in the marketplace of what was to come: cell phones offering access to the Internet. Computer keyboards that come equipped with payment card readers. Smartcards that can be used in parking meters, subway stations, public telephones, ATMs, and more. Without interoperability, this accelerating digital convergence would either proceed at a snail's pace or stop dead in its tracks.

Indeed, because the electronic money revolution is moving so rapidly, some analysts and Visa insiders fear the company is not moving fast enough, that its very nature as a member-owned association is keeping it from leading the way in innovation and bringing out new products. Van der Velde thinks some of those fears are misplaced. "As an association, you needn't be the most avant-garde," he said. "When it comes to technological change, what we need to understand is that we're

like a surfer on top of the wave. We can't be behind the wave, but we can't be too far out in front either."

Here, too, Visa performs a delicate balancing act, and van der Velde said that his team works hard to help each country and each banking system develop at its own chosen pace. Iceland, for instance, has become an almost cashless society – a Visa society. There are 275,000 inhabitants in the whole country, and there are 350,000 Visa cards in circulation. Belgium, too, is moving in that direction, and yet card growth in both countries is running at about 20 percent a year, as card usage pushes into new areas of commerce. Turkey has evolved in a different way. On instructions from the ministry of finance, Turkey went straight from cash to payment cards. "The ministry simply decreed there will be no checks in this country," Hans said. "So Turkey leapfrogged an entire phase in the evolution of its payments."

As in many other parts of the world, Europe is witnessing a growth in co-branded cards. In Germany, for instance, the Bayerische Landesbank and Lufthansa launched the nation's first co-branded Visa card in 1999. Through the program, the bank is issuing Visa Classic, Gold, and Corporate cards, with frequent flyer points and a variety of other incentives to promote card usage. In the past, Lufthansa had worked with American Express, MasterCard, and Eurocard, but this time the airline said it chose Visa for its brand strength and superior customer support.

Hans believes that these sorts of high-profile corporate deals are evidence that American Express and MasterCard are not gaining ground on Visa's market position in Europe. In fact, the contrary is true: Visa is gaining market share. "Altogether, American Express has about 40 million cards in Europe," he said. "We're growing by that much each year. So I can't be too worried about

American Express. Their market share is almost negligible."

The rapid development of the electronic money revolution has brought with it a problem: where can European and other banks find the specialists they need to run their card programs and keep on top of the rapidly changing technology? To help fill that need, Visa Europe now runs an innovative yearlong self-study program to train card specialists. Bankers and other students who enroll in the program are given textbooks, videos, and computer-based study materials that take them through five main areas of the card business: strategic planning, marketing, risk management, operations, and progress analysis. This is no lightweight course of study. It's accredited and supervised by the Chartered Institute of Bankers, and at the end there are two three-hour examinations, administered at local centers. In its first three years in existence, some 650 students, coming from as far afield as China, Russia, and Australia, went through the course and earned a graduate certificate. In 1999, the "Bank Card Business School" celebrated the arrival of its 1,000th student. "Member banks need skilled, confident staff who can take their businesses forward into the twenty-first century," said Wendy Martin, head of education services for Visa EU. "This certificate is now established as the best way of filling that need."

Dee Hock would no doubt be pleased. One of his regrets, looking back, was that he did not create, right from the beginning, Visa's own in-house university. In his mind, that would have been the best way to train Visa staff and people from its member banks in the unique complexities of the credit card world. In a larger sense, too, such a university would have been a valuable tool in helping people expand their horizons and learn about the needs and virtues of other cultures. It could have also inculcated in them a far-reaching vision of

CARTE BLEUE. ET TOUT VA MIEUX.

leadership and management in a world of profound social, economic, and technological change. The "Bank Card Business School" is certainly a step in that direction.

Ugo Scarpetta, one of Visa's earliest card pioneers, often thinks of Dee when he considers the profound changes he has seen in European banking and commerce. In 1969, he launched the first BankAmericard in Italy. Today, Italians from Milan to Naples use credit cards routinely when they shop and when they travel, especially abroad. The Internet has been a tremendous success in Italy, with enormous numbers of people logging on every day and using their Visa cards to shop on-line. All this makes Ugo recall some prophetic words from Dee Hock, when he was building NBI and IBANCO back in the 1970s.

"I often think how visionary Dee was when he was preaching throughout Europe that the ideal bank of the future is a telephone company," Ugo recalled. "What he meant was that those who operated a telecommunications network would be in the best position to perform banking operations. Money is now a message that moves through telecommunications lines in digital form. Just as Dee predicted. He saw it all coming, 30 years ago."

The French Exception

Even in the early days, it was never easy with the French.

In the beginning of the 1970s, the BankAmericard's international licensees would schedule one of their regular get-togethers for somewhere pleasant in the south of Europe, and Barclays' Dickie Dale would be asked to perform a special duty. Instead of flying to the locale of the meeting, Dale's mission was to go by car and stop in Paris to pick up a special guest, Bernard Sue. The licensees invited Sue to all their gatherings, for he was a prominent banker at Crédit Lyonnais and, more importantly, he was also the director of the French card consortium Carte Bleue.

Dale would pick up his French colleague and then the two of them would head merrily south, stopping off in the Loire Valley or in Burgundy, or both, for some of the finest food and wine to be had anywhere in the world. Dale's mission, of course, was to put Bernard Sue in the most congenial frame of mind, so that upon arrival at the meeting the other licensees would have a better chance to persuade the Frenchman to join their BankAmericard movement. "We were a huge number of suitors," Ugo Scarpetta explained with a laugh, "all trying to court the one holdout 'lady' among us."

This was anything but an easy seduction. At the time, Carte Bleue was a small organization, but it had an impressive pedigree. It was founded in 1967 by six important French banks, Crédit Lyonnais, Société Générale, Crédit Commercial de France, Crédit du Nord, Crédit Industriel et Commercial, and the newly created Banque Nationale de Paris. By 1970, the consortium counted 437,000 cardholders and 39,000 participating merchants, a modest start for a country of over 50 million people.

Carte Bleue was not a credit device. It was a payment device designed to replace checks. France, at the time, was a check-happy society, and that was costing the banks a fortune. The checks were not only costly to process; by law, French banks were not allowed to charge their customers for their checks. The Carte Bleue was to be a more cost-effective alternative. The group also had strong backing from the French government, which was intent on strengthening French banking through new technology. In 1971, Carte Bleue and its member banks unveiled an important first step, "Distributeurs Automatiques de Billets," the French version of the ATM, and these allowed cardholders to withdraw cash any time of the night

or day. French banking was clearly headed in the direction of cards and automation, and so was much of the rest of Europe. Eurocard, a Swedish credit card initiative, was set into motion in 1967. Nonetheless, Bernard Sue and other Carte Bleue decision-makers were leery of joining forces with Dick Dale and the rest of the BankAmericard group.

They had two main objections, according to French card specialist Jean-Claude Marelli of the Banque Populaire. At that stage, the Bank of America and several other big U.S. banks were losing money with their credit card programs, and the Carte Bleue directorate felt the entire concept might be doomed to fail. That was one reason to stand aside. Another was American control. French bankers saw the BankAmericard licensee program as U.S.-dominated, and they did not want any American bank to have an inroad into their home market, either economically or technologically. With this same concern, Crédit Lyonnais had also rebuffed overtures from American Express and Diners Club to enter into a joint card venture.

Little by little, however, Bernard Sue and Carte Bleue edged away from this hard-line resistance. In 1973, the card consortium took a first step by entering into a formal affiliation with the BankAmericard licensees. The agreement allowed French banks to display the distinctive blue, white, and gold bands on the face of their cards – but only on Carte Bleue cards that were specified "international." Domestic cards would remain wholly French. A few years later, Sue and Carte Bleue went all the way and officially joined the Visa family, but only on the condition that the French card retain the name Carte Bleue. Dee Hock and the board of Visa International agreed to this "French exception," along with a few other "variances" that allowed Carte Bleue to come into the Visa fold without giving up its proud French identity. Today, the consortium insists on having it both ways and taking advantage of Visa's brand strength around the world. Some of its cards are presented as Carte Bleue, while others are presented as "Carte Bleue Visa." In the French view, everybody wins, and Visa is happy to agree.

Edvj Massazza-Gal inherited this complex relationship when she took over as head of Visa France in the mid-1990s, as part of a larger effort by Visa Europe to shift power from London to managers in each individual country. Edvj was well-prepared for the challenge. Italian by birth, gifted with languages, and magnetic in presence, Edvj was a force to be reckoned with, and she knew the credit card industry inside out. She joined Visa in London in 1983 when João was getting Visa up and running in Europe, and she worked there until 1991. Then she went home to Italy to set up an office in Milan. Later, Visa extended her territory to include Turkey, Cyprus, Israel, and Greece. "I feel like a storm trooper," she laughed, during an interview in her office in Paris.

Edvj had a big job to do. After Britain, France is the largest card market in Europe, and usage per card is second only to the United States. France is also one of the most innovative countries in card technology. The French claim fatherhood of the first smart card, and they were among the first to make chip technology the cornerstone of their card industry. With strong financial backing from the government, French banks encouraged merchants to move *en masse* to terminals that could read chip cards. Also, on the strength of their experience in the 1980s and 1990s with the "Minitel," a small computer terminal supplied free to telephone customers, the French have moved gleefully into the world of the Internet and e-commerce. These moves delighted Edvj, and Visa has been France's eager partner in smart card development.

"What we are doing is using the Visa platform

to sustain a French chip that has multiple applications," she said. "Visa has developed credit, debit, and Visa Cash specifications. All applications pertaining to payments have been developed by Visa central and they are being applied by French banks."

For many French banks, the move to chip was an urgent necessity. The reason: fraud. "France was the country with the highest card fraud in the world," explained Jean-Pierre Gervais, a chip card specialist. "Now, thanks to the smart card, it has the lowest rate of fraud in the world. The card is both inviolable and impossible to replicate."

According to Edvj, there was, however, a downside to France's rush into smart card technology: by 1999, the chip they were using was no longer state-of-the-art. She and Visa were working closely with French banks to make sure their next generation of chips would conform to international standards, so they could be used anywhere in the world. "The French need international specifications that can also be applied locally," she explained. "We're helping to facilitate the migration to the new standards."

Early in the year 2000, Edvj returned to London for a new assignment in the Visa family. Edvj, as usual, stood at the ready. "Visa, for me, is first a passion," she said. "Then a frustration. And then, finally, a job. But it's first a passion. And that passion has never changed. I always feel my work has a purpose."

EX-CHEQUERS. INCREASE YOUR BUDGET BY UP TO £300 A HEAD.

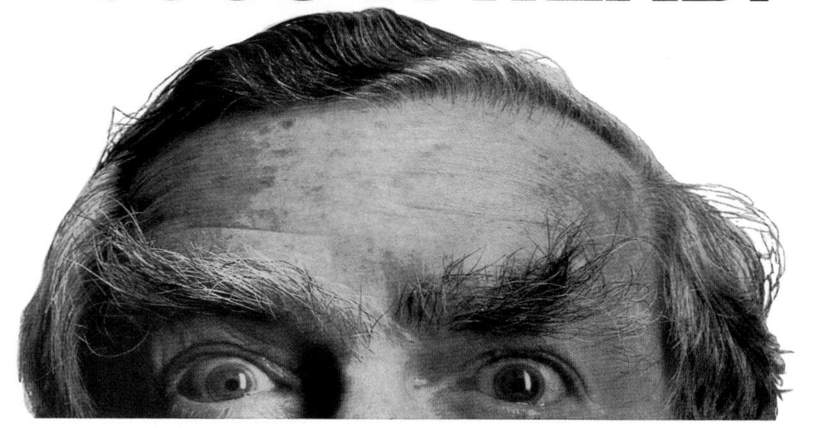

Selected Visa Delta card holders will receive a welcome boost in their February/March statements; details of how to apply for discount vouchers worth up to £300, redeemable at HMV, Tesco, Avis, Pizzaland and Hilton Hotels, to name but a few. That should raise a few eyebrows.

VISA'S DELTA BLOW TO CHEQUES.

Offer applies to existing Visa Delta cardholders of participating Issuers only.

Central and Eastern Europe, The Middle East, and Africa

In December of 1989, the year the Berlin Wall came tumbling down, Chuck Russell received a very important visitor.

His name was Viktor Rajevski, and he was deputy prime minister of the Baltic state of Estonia, which was part of the Union of Soviet Socialist Republics, the USSR. At that moment, like the Berlin Wall itself, communist regimes across Eastern Europe were crumbling. Just the week before, the leaders in the Kremlin had granted economic independence to the Baltic States, and a new era of political and economic freedom appeared to be at hand. The people of Estonia, as in many other countries in Eastern Europe, were starved for basic goods and services. The national cupboards were almost literally bare. The Estonian government was eager to open itself to Western goods and trade, but its banking system was antiquated, and the currency was unstable. Rajevski had rushed to America to put one urgent question to Chuck Russell. What could Visa do to help?

"Rajevsky was looking for a way to move Estonia directly from a barter economy to a system of electronic payments, skipping all the steps in between," Russell explained. In essence, the Estonian leader was looking for a quick, sure way to open his country to the consumer riches of the West, without destabilizing the ruble, and he was pinning his hopes on that magical little capitalist tool, the Visa card.

Significantly, Rajevski was not traveling alone. He had a Soviet official in tow. Clearly, this was a crucial test for Visa, with Moscow watching, and Russell was eager to meet it. In response, he and Visa launched their first major card program in the former USSR, a pilot project that put a Visa charge card, issued through Estonian banks, in the hands of 500,000 Estonians – in a nation of only 1.5 million people.

That was the beginning of a new era for Visa in Eastern Europe. Today, Visa has a wide and rapidly growing presence in Eastern and Central Europe, and its member banks are issuing a variety of card products – including smart cards – which are specially adapted to the needs of their individual countries and their markets. These countries are administered by Visa's largest and most culturally rich and diversified regional grouping, "Visa Central and Eastern Europe, Middle East, and Africa," known by the acronym CEMEA.

With the Estonia pilot and Visa's other efforts to open the markets of Eastern Europe, Chuck worked closely with one of the most beloved men in Visa International, Jean-Jacques Desbons. Born in Paris and trained as an engineer, Jean-Jacques went into banking and participated in the creation of Carte Bleue. In 1981, when Visa created its regional boards, Jean-Jacques was elected to the board of directors for Europe, the Middle East, and Africa. In 1989 he joined the staff of Visa International, and in 1992 he was named president and managing director of the region. Throughout this period, Jean-Jacques worked closely with João, Ugo Scarpetta, Dee, Chuck, and his own staff in London. He, too, was an evangelist and is credited with opening for Visa many markets in Europe and throughout the developing world.

In 1995, the territory Jean-Jacques was covering – from the north of Europe all the way down to South Africa – simply became too big to handle. Also, many of the countries within it were growing at radically different paces. In keeping with the guiding philosophy of "global vision, local roots," Visa decided to split the region into more manageable pieces. This was a very challenging task, both politically and geographically, and much of the responsibility fell on the shoulders of Carol Walsh, the regional general counsel and a respected Visa veteran. "I spent one whole weekend poring over the atlas trying to allocate offshore islands and overseas territories to their correct country and region," Carol recalled. Finally, she brought forth workable blueprints for two regional groupings, one serving the mature markets of the European Union and the other serving the developing markets of Eastern Europe, the Middle East, and Africa. Carol's plan won the approval of Visa members in 1985 and has been in effect ever since. Carol then became regional general counsel for the EU region, and in that capacity she has been an effective advocate for Visa in European policy-making, especially in the fields of fraud control and electronic commerce.

Under the new division, Jean-Jacques Desbons took on responsibility for the countries of the European Union, plus a few others, and a dynamic woman named Anne L. Cobb was handed responsibility for the newly created CEMEA.

Cobb has a cultural heritage that is almost as diverse as the territory she manages. Her mother is Belgian, her father was American, and she was born in Germany but carries a French passport. After university, Anne went into banking and worked for 12 years at France's Crédit Agricole. There she began an immersion in electronic money, helping the bank develop its ATM network, manage its travelers cheques, and launch a Eurocard program. In 1983, she joined Eurocard in Brussels as general manager. A decade later, with this wealth of experience in banking and payment cards, Anne joined Visa as executive vice president, with responsibilities for strategic planning and new product development.

Today, as head of the CEMEA region, Anne

oversees Visa operations in 92 countries, on three different continents. From Moscow to the tip of Africa, the business landscape is changing dramatically. In many CEMEA countries, the card industry is in its infancy, but Anne has seen dramatic changes in just the past five years. In the mid-1990s, there were 2.5 million Visa cards in the region. In a period of four years, the number jumped to 14 million and growth is continuing to boom. By the standards of Europe or the United States, those numbers may be small, but not by CEMEA standards. "In some ways, we remain very, very small," Anne said in an interview. "But we are bringing payments systems – and Visa above all else – into countries where they hadn't even been heard of before."

Running CEMEA, with its geographic reach and deep differences of culture, language, and economic development, is an especially delicate balancing act. When the region was split off, for instance, some countries in Eastern Europe were not happy with the division. They wanted to remain with the countries grouped as the European Union, even though those markets were far more advanced. Anne and Visa stepped in with a workable compromise. They promised to change the status of Poland, Hungary, and the Czech Republic once their own card markets had matured and these countries had joined the European Union.

In CEMEA, there are huge structural and technological differences as well. In several countries, Anne and Visa are not just building card programs; they're actually helping to build retail and corporate banking from the ground up. "We're helping our member banks build their infrastructures and their banking practices," she said. "Progress sometimes takes a long time and the learning curve is steep. We are working with banks that need computer systems, links with their branches, ATMs, and point-of-sale terminals.

”السرعة،
المرونة والإعتماد.
ما الذي تريده أكثر
من رفيق الفريق
والطريق؟“

عندما ألعب مع زملاء فريق يتصفون بالسرعة والمرونة والإعتماد، فإن النجاح سيكون حليفنا الأول. أما خارج أرض الملعب فلقد وجدت في بطاقة فيزا كل هذه الصفات. فهي تلبي كافة إحتياجاتي المالية على وجه السرعة. ويمكنني إستخدامها للدفع بمعظم العملات المالية ومن ثم السداد لاحقاً بالريال السعودي وبأقساط شهرية مرنة. وفي الحالات المالية الطارئة فإن بطاقة فيزا هي خير رفيق يمكنني الإعتماد عليه. فهل أطلب أكثر من رفيق مثالي في الفريق ورفيق مثالي في الطريق؟

IF THERE'S SKY ABOVE AND GROUND BELOW,
IT'S THE PLACE FOR VISA.

Often patience is what we need most."

These sorts of issues, plus the sheer enormity of the territory she covers, make Anne Cobb's one of the toughest jobs in Visa. But Anne likes the challenge. "We don't need to invent or reinvent the wheel here," she said. "We can use what's worked elsewhere. And that's the beauty of it. That said, we're dealing with banking systems that are neither mature nor stable."

Her patience, though, is starting to pay off. Hungary, for instance, issued its one millionth Visa card in 1999, representing a 10-fold increase in a period of just three years. Visa's most popular card product in Hungary is Visa Electron, a debit card that gives people an easy way to pay and instant access to cash and bank services at local ATM machines. In the Czech Republic, too, Visa Electron is the hot product. The Czech Savings Bank alone has issued one million debit cards. In both these countries, Visa Electron is enabling cash-based societies to leap directly into cards, bypassing paper checks completely. As many other countries follow the same pattern, Visa Electron is one of the most rapidly growing products in Visa's worldwide family.

The recent success of these Eastern European countries marks an important shift within CEMEA. "When we created the region in 1995, our main business came from South Africa," Anne said. "They represented more than 50 percent of the cards and more than 55 percent of the sales volume. South Africa is still growing, but the rest of the region is growing much faster."

The Visa country that Anne is proudest of is Poland, and the story there is not just about card products, brand strength, and new technology. It's about a young Polish woman named Gosia O'Shaughnessy. After graduating from university in Warsaw, Gosia moved to London and went to work for Visa as a junior assistant. Gosia learned the card business from the ground up, became steeped in the Visa philosophy, and along the way she married an Irishman who gave her that jaunty last name. In 1995, when Visa decided to open an office in Warsaw, Gosia was chosen to run it. She proved to be the right choice.

"Our success story today is Poland," Anne said. "When we opened the office, Poland had 30,000 cards. Today it has 5 million! Business is booming. We have 40 member banks in Poland, all of them pushing the business, and they're starting to move toward smart cards as well."

Visa's activity is having a catalytic effect on Poland's banking industry and its economy. "This

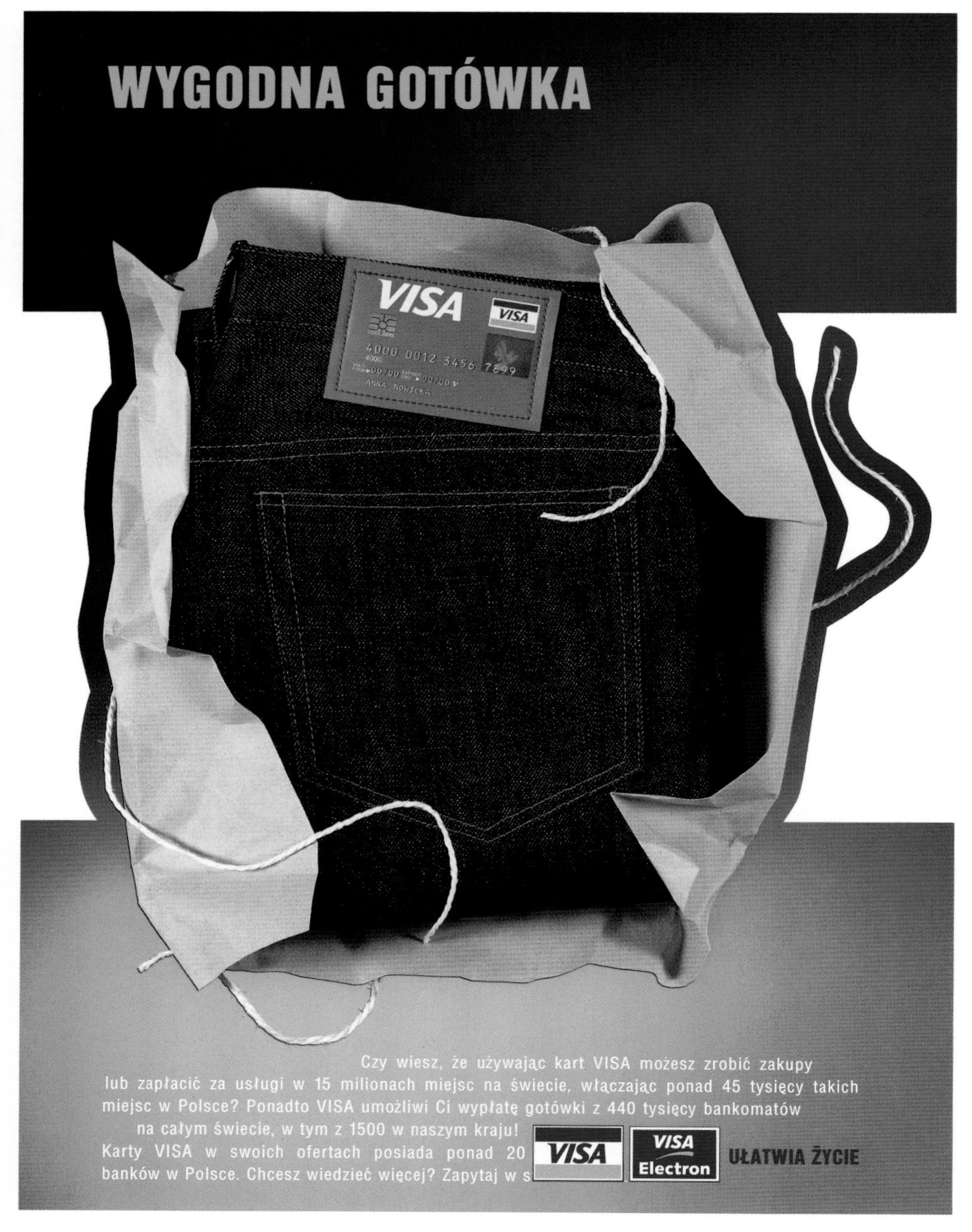

society is coming from money under the mattress to a growing belief in banking," Gosia said in an interview. "Banks are bringing people in, using the Visa card as a lure, and showing them the convenience of a modern payment system."

Visa is working closely with its member banks in Poland to help them modernize their industry and formulate retail banking strategies. "We are making important investments here in bank card education and technology. We have equipped all our members with Visa computers that link them to VisaNet. We've also shown the banks how to market cards and use them to gain new customers and build the brand and product loyalty."

This close working relationship with the banks has generated enormous goodwill for Visa in Poland, illustrating once again that being a good partner is very good business. "We are aiming at growth of just under 100 percent per year, and there is a growing gap between Visa and our competitors," Gosia said. "The main reason is Visa's long-term approach. Opening an office here really showed local bankers the depth of our commitment. Since we opened the office, we've seen significant growth, and I can see a tremendous difference – thanks to operating close to our customers."

The banks, in turn, are stimulating increased commercial activity throughout the country. As consumers flock to payment cards, Polish banks have been busy installing point-of-sale terminals and signing up merchants and retail chains. In the third quarter of 1999, the total card volume processed by one merchant bank jumped by $250 million. "More and more Poles are using cards," reported *Puls Biznesu,* a national business daily, and the headline on the story summed up the market configuration: "Visa dominates the card operations market." Gosia puts it a little more modestly. "We're making progress," Gosia said. "We started with very little, but Visa is very popular here, and we are moving forward in great leaps. It's very exciting for all of us to see."

The arrival of smart cards has also been big news in the Polish press. LOT, the Polish airline, is at the front of the line, bringing out a co-branded Visa smart card. Three large banks have joined forces with major retail chains to join the smart card movement. ATM networks are also rapidly expanding. With smart cards, ATM networks, and spending incentive programs based on the frequent-flyer model, Polish banks anticipate an explosion of economic activity in the coming years. "The true revolution may be the introduction of chip cards," the *Puls Biznesu* speculated. "If the current programs are successful, this will pave the way for creating co-branded programs on a mass scale, where points collected by clients will be stored on the chip."

Poland's success story carries a much larger lesson for Visa, in Anne Cobb's view. "Periodically, people question if being structured as an association is the best thing for Visa. In our region, it is," she said. "We're not perceived as a threat. We're not perceived as ugly Americans coming to eat their markets. Immediate success – that's the demand of traditional business. But we can afford to look two, three, ten years down the road. Today, people say, 'Oh, Poland is very interesting.' But five years ago, who would have put a nickel into Poland?

"The beauty of Visa is that there's a core system that works, and it is applicable in every country," Anne continued. "And from there it can be adapted to each country's individual needs and special demands. But the basics can be applied anywhere. They're universal."

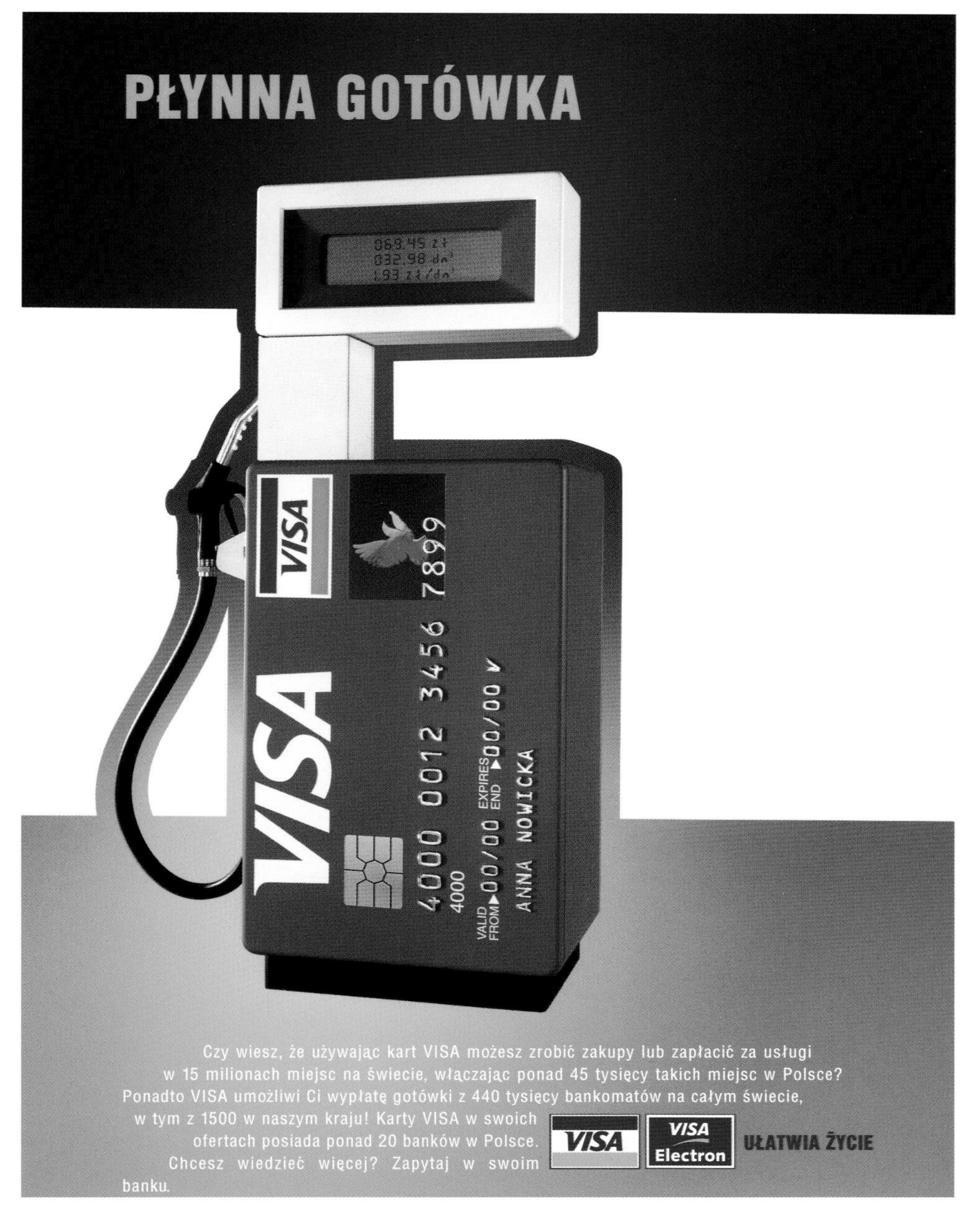

Chapter 23

Latin America and The Caribbean

If Jim Partridge cut his hand, you might well find blue, white, and gold running from the wound.

As with João, Jim's life has been a mini-version of Visa history. His father was American, his mother Venezuelan, and Jim was born in New York, where his father worked as an executive of a steamship company. When Jim was 10, the company was sold, and the family moved to Puerto Rico, where Jim finished high school. After a stint in the U.S. Army during the Korean War, he returned to Puerto Rico and went to the local university in business administration.

"I needed a job in the evenings," Jim recalled as he sat in his office in Miami. Through a family connection, he went to see the head of Puerto Rico's Banco Popular. He liked Jim and felt that one day he would be a strong addition to the bank. "Look," the bank chief said, "we'll give you $150 a month during college. No obligations." Jim happily accepted the offer, finished his studies, and then went to New York University for a master's degree in business administration. While in New York, he also worked in the operations department of Morgan Guaranty Trust, learning banking from the inside out. Once he earned his degree, Jim returned to Banco Popular and soon found his calling.

"My passion was automation," Jim said. He set out to find ways to streamline the bank's operations and improve its bottom line using new technology. His poked into every corner of the bank and his scrutiny settled on one department: personal loans. "We had 150,000 personal loans on the books, and it was incredibly costly," Jim said. "Most were 12-month loans, but after six months, many people were coming back to renew them. The process was very expensive."

Jim began to look at a new banking tool: credit cards. He was impressed by what he saw. "This was exactly what I thought the bank should do," Jim said. "So I designed a card program." But when he took the plan to the president of Banco Popular, Jim ran into a stone wall. "He thought the plan was unworkable. He feared the whole idea of credit cards and unsecured lending. He was probably right at that given moment."

Jim, though, was convinced that credit cards were the way of the future; in fact, he had become passionate about their potential. So he took his ideas to another bank in Puerto Rico, the Banco Credito. The bank chiefs liked what they heard and offered him a job and a jump in salary. Jim accepted, but it was not money that dictated his decision. "We struck an agreement. Once I had begun to automate demand deposits, they would let me do a credit card. One Monday, several months later, we signed an agreement to become a BankAmericard licensee."

And so it began. From there, Jim went to San Francisco, met with Ken Larkin, and soon thereafter he began his long personal odyssey as a globe-trotting evangelist for Dee Hock, Visa, and the electronic money revolution. In his early years with Visa, Jim focused on Asia, meeting bankers across the region and laying the foundation for Visa business there. But Jim's real legacy is to be found in Latin America. For more than two decades, Jim Partridge embodied Visa all over Latin America and in the Caribbean. On first encounter with Jim, many Latin bankers found him to be a big, gruff, blunt-spoken, no-nonsense American. But as they got to know him better, those bankers discovered that behind that gruff exterior, Jim Partridge was a passionate, temperamental, deeply committed man, in his words, "a true Latino." That proved to be a tremendous asset.

"The core of this business is not plastic, it's *relationships,*" Jim said. "In the beginning, some people in Latin America viewed Visa as an American product. But as our relationships deepened, the idea that Visa was a U.S. company was quickly put to rest. Today Latins view Visa as a Latin American company."

That feeling emerges directly from Jim and his staff. Jim speaks fluent Spanish, thanks to his Venezuelan mother and his schooling, and so does most everyone else at the Miami headquarters of the regional grouping known as "Visa Latin America and Caribbean." The *feel* of the office is also Latin – open, warm, and hopping, thanks in part to some powerhouse Cuban coffees. Also, in his 20 years of building the operation, Jim brought in many top bankers and card specialists from around Latin America, including some with deep family roots in the region's banking and financial institutions and with historic ties to the Visa partnership.

Eduardo Eraña, for instance, is like family to Jim. His father, Eugenio, was a founder of Mexico's Banco de Comercio, known as Bancomer, and he served with Jim on the board of Visa International. In 1968, young Eduardo went to work for Bancomer, in a little branch the bank opened in the Olympic Village during that year's Summer Games in Mexico City. Soon thereafter, he was given a new post, one that he feared was a painful demotion: he was put in charge of the bank's fledgling BankAmericard program. At the time, Bancomer was the leading bank in Mexico, but its card program was weak, and Eduardo was doubtful it would ever grow. "No, no," his boss assured him. "This is going to be big. You just wait and see."

Eduardo's boss was right. "We grew from 400,000 cards to over one million cards in nine months," Eduardo recalled. "We became the largest card program in Latin America." According to Eduardo, the owner of Bancomer had initially wanted to do a card venture with American Express, and he was a bit skeptical about Visa. "But then he began to understand the Visa philosophy," he said. "You can be your own boss. You use the Visa brand, but you manage your own accounts. I think this is one of the most important things about Visa. Each bank can develop its own strategy within the framework of Visa's international rules."

The success of the Bancomer program enhanced Visa's standing throughout Latin America, and it transformed Eduardo's career. By 1984, Eduardo was a proven card manager and an articulate true believer in the Visa mission. So Jim Partridge brought him aboard to help him spread the word throughout Latin America. Eduardo welcomed the challenge, and in his mind the Visa partnership had two assets in particular that made the overall Visa message very compelling for regional banks. "The name was growing, but that was only one key to Visa's success in Latin America," Eduardo said. "The other key was principle."

The principle Eduardo was referring to was this: open membership. Visa is open to any bank, large or small, provided it meets certain basic requirements and agrees to operate its card program according to Visa standards and regulations. In practical business terms, this meant that when Jim and Eduardo visited a Latin American country, they would knock on as many doors as they could, trying to sign up as many banks as possible. The more, the merrier. MasterCard followed a very different strategy.

"Visa gave no exclusivity to any bank in the region," Eduardo said. "MasterCard did. Visa went to all the banks. MasterCard chose an exclusive partner in each country and targeted the customers

Sí Puedo.
VISA
Para Llegar Adonde Quieras.
www.visalatam.com

of *one* bank. Visa, by contrast, educated and targeted the whole population of a given country. There is here a fundamental difference of philosophy."

To Jim Partridge, the principle of open membership was sacred and inviolable – and in 1986 he saw that principle put to the test in a very dramatic way. It happened in Brazil, one of the biggest markets in Latin America. In the early years, Visa had great difficulty in trying to sign up banks in Brazil; in fact, by 1986 only one group had signed on. The group consisted of three banks led by Citibank and was known as "Credicard." This was no small account for Visa; Credicard represented 20 percent of Visa's card base in the region. Then the Chase Manhattan Bank's affiliate in Brazil came knocking at Visa's door, eager to start a card program. Jim was all for it. "Visa was founded on open membership and universal acceptance," he said. "So our reaction was, why not? They met all the necessary criteria."

John Reed, then chief of Citibank, did not see it quite that way. One Sunday, on a cruise up the Hudson River on Malcolm Forbes' yacht, Reed ran into Visa's Chuck Russell. According to Partridge, Reed did not mince his words: "You get the hell out of Brazil! The hell with Chase! That's my country!" Reed went so far as to issue an ultimatum to Visa: give Citibank exclusive rights in Brazil, just as MasterCard did in other countries, or else he would yank all of Credicard's business out of Visa's hands.

Needless to say, the following morning Chuck reported the encounter to Jim Partridge. The stakes were exceedingly high for Visa, but Russell had full confidence in Partridge and was not about to interfere. "Chuck, to his eternal credit, let me make my own decision," Jim said. And there was really no debate in Jim's mind: he had to honor Visa's ideals and its guiding principle of open membership – even if it meant losing one of Visa's biggest customers.

So Visa went ahead and signed an agreement with the Chase affiliate. As threatened, Credicard promptly pulled out of Visa, cracking the foundation of Visa's entire operation in Brazil. Jim knew this was a terrible blow. It damaged Visa's revenues and its reputation, and it could hurt Visa business throughout Latin America. So Jim went into full-scale crisis mode. "Basically, I moved to Brazil and camped at a hotel in Rio," he recalled. "We knocked on every door in Brazil. Then we hit a stroke of luck. Banco do Brasil was interested in starting a credit card program." With that new partner in the fold, Jim and Visa were able to begin rebuilding the business they had lost, and from there they never looked back.

"Today we're No. 1 in Brazil, the top of the heap. It's our largest market, with 20 million cards," Jim said. "Even Credicard is back in the fold."

When Jim recounts this episode, you can hear the conviction steeling his voice. "That's a story of principle," he said. "Open membership is one of the principles Dee Hock set from the beginning, and I felt we needed to defend it. If it meant we had no more business in Brazil, so be it. You have to have principles and you have to live by them, or else you do yourself terrible harm. Your word is your bond."

A.P. Giannini would bow in admiration.

❁ ❁ ❁

Jim's passionate, family-style leadership has helped make Visa the undisputed market leader throughout Latin America and the Caribbean, a region covering over 44 countries and territories and representing a combined population of 480 million people. In terms of sales volume, Latin America has topped the $100 billion mark, and the number of cards in circulation has been climbing about 25 percent a year. The region has also been upgrading its telecommunications networks and moving into e-commerce.

As in other regions, Visa's marketing team in Miami develops overall themes and campaigns, and then each individual country is free to use them, ignore them, or adapt them to their own markets. The aim, though, is coherence of message. "Our job is to create something that can work regionally so there don't have to be campaigns in each individual country," explained Lane Atkins, a BBDO veteran who now plays a key role in regional marketing and advertising. An added difficulty, though, is that some countries push credit cards, while others push debit cards and other Visa products. "Different countries have a different level of maturity with the various Visa products," he said, "and we have to be sensitive to that." They also have to be attuned to the wide variety of cultural, political, and linguistic traditions in this delightfully diverse region.

As in Italy, France, and Poland, Visa has catalyzed profound economic and social changes in many countries in Latin America. Venezuela is an interesting case in point. A nation of 22 million people, Venezuela has rich petroleum and natural gas reserves, a high rate of literacy, and since 1958 it has been a relatively stable democracy. For many generations, though, the banking industry focused mainly on wealthy people and the business community, not the common man. For the vast majority of Venezuelans, getting a loan was difficult or impossible.

In 1968, however, a contingent from the Bank of America made a visit to the Banco Union in Caracas, the second largest bank in Venezuela. "They invited us to join the BankAmericard program," recalled Henry Benacerraf, whose father was then vice chairman of this private commercial bank. "So we went to San Francisco to see the card program, and then we went to Mexico City to see how Bancomer's card program was working. We

Visa pioneer Jim Partridge, longtime head of Visa Latin America.

CONFIA en MEXICO
VISA
CUNHA-SILVA
CAMPBELL
Sprite
CONFIA en MEXICO
VISA
PATROCINADOR OFICIAL
DOUGLAS

were impressed and decided to join."

Banco Union's card program – with the celebrated Italian actress Gina Lollobrigida on hand for the launch – got off to a good start. But there was no overnight revolution. The bank used the BankAmericard as a credit device, and it followed very conservative lending practices. "We started slowly and gave it mainly to customers with good credit," Henry said. Soon, though, the card attracted new customers, and the bank began expanding its retail side. As business grew, the bank opened branches all over Venezuela. According to Henry, this brought new customers flocking to the bank, including many people who had never set foot in a bank before. The BankAmericard program became the hottest growth sector in the bank.

Up to then, Banco Union had been a traditional commercial bank, focusing on medium and large-sized business accounts. Now the emphasis shifted to retail banking and serving the needs of individual customers, no matter how modest their account. For 16 years, Banco Union was the only bank in Venezuela that issued Visa, and MasterCard was making few inroads into the country. So if anyone in Venezuela wanted a credit card, they usually went to Henry's bank. "It helped us a lot. The card was very important for the way Banco Union was perceived throughout the country," Henry said. "We led the way, and now all the banks in Venezuela are issuing credit cards. And Visa is the most popular brand in the country."

Through all this, Henry became a devoted convert to the credit card gospel, and in 1974 he served as one of the 12 founding members of IBANCO. Later, as head of his bank, he became one of Visa's most prominent supporters in Latin America and served for 15 years as chairman of the Latin American board. What happened in Venezuela then happened in dozens of other Latin countries. The collective impact was enormous. "From the beginning, we were very conscious that Visa was going to radically change our way of banking," Henry said. "Dee Hock was a true leader and visionary and one of the brightest men I've ever met. He was very sharp and clean in his ideas. And from the beginning, he was global in his thinking."

Today, Venezuelan banks are moving into e-commerce and the newest card technology. Henry himself is in the vanguard. Though he has retired from the bank, he keeps in constant touch via e-mail. He keeps an apartment in New York and loves to go to restaurants in the city, always paying with Visa of course. Henry also keeps in touch with the people at Visa; they're family after all. At one stage in the 1970s, Jim Partridge got caught in a political struggle inside his bank in Puerto Rico; Henry promptly hired him in Caracas and today they remain close friends. As Jim said, the core of Visa is not plastic, it's relationships.

Visa also had a profound impact on banking in Colombia. In 1968, Banco de Bogota was invited by the Bank of America to become a BankAmericard licensee. At the time, only one other local bank, Banco Industrial Colombiano, offered credit cards and it offered MasterCard. Instead of taking the plunge alone, Banco de Bogotá joined with five other banks and formed a card consortium called "Credibanco." The Credibanco brand is now strongly linked to Visa, and there are 30 banks in Colombia that issue Visa cards. The blue, white, and gold has 53 percent of the card market, while MasterCard has only 30 percent. Diners Club has a 17 percent share of the market.

According to Orlando Garcia, president of Visa Colombia, Visa's influence extends far beyond market share. In the late 1980s, for instance, Visa wanted to launch a gold card, aimed in particular at Colombian businessmen who travel abroad. At the time, however, the Colombian government had strict currency controls in place, and it opposed the launch of Visa Gold. Visa began working closely with the central bank to find a solution, and finally they worked out a formula that brought in the gold card and gave new freedom – and a $3,000 credit line – to Colombians traveling abroad.

In the latter half of the 1990s, Jim Partridge spent a lot of time thinking about how his corner of Visa should work in the future. In fact, he tore his Miami operation apart and examined it piece by piece. During the late 1980s and throughout the 1990s, Visa had enjoyed phenomenal growth in the region, and Jim's staff had grown to keep pace. Now he feared his operation had become too big and too corporate. The passion and missionary zeal that had propelled Visa in its start-up years had given way to a cool, nine-to-five professionalism. That had its merits, of course, but Jim missed the fire that he and the other pioneers felt in the beginning, and he wanted the young people coming aboard to understand the ideals, principles, and deep sense of purpose that together formed the core of Visa and its mission.

One of Jim's biggest concerns was internal communication. In the Miami office, as in so many big corporate offices – including Visa headquarters and some of its regional offices – most of the staff had private offices or work cubicles, what Jim referred to as "silos." These did not engender the openness and spirit of cooperation that Jim treasured. "We didn't talk to each other," he said. "Those silos were barriers to communication."

Jim feared that something else was slipping away: that all-important pull-together, family feeling. In the early days, Jim and the other Visa pioneers worked 60- or 70-hour weeks, whatever it took to get the job done. And they did so willingly, whether it was building Base I or opening new markets in Europe, Asia, or Latin America. Jim was not advocating 70-hour workweeks, but he did want his staff to have that same sense of fire and commitment. He wanted them to understand that Visa wasn't a job, it was a calling. He wanted them to feel like they were part of something larger, a great movement and an extended global family. "I wanted to rekindle," he explained, "a sense of belonging."

After a period of intensive study and reflection, Jim decided that it was time to make some changes, time to re-energize the whole operation. "The time to reorganize and make fundamental changes is when you're on top of the world," Jim said. "You shouldn't have to do it under duress. I had this terrible feeling that we were getting fat, that we were losing touch with what had made us great. And I knew I had to act."

So Jim launched an overhaul, starting with the physical set-up of the Miami office. He called in a crew and ripped down the silos. He tore down walls and opened up the work areas. Anything that looked like it might be a barrier to openness and communication came down. Then the crews began to rebuild according to a very different philosophy and plan. Where once there had been cubicles, Jim created big open spaces for his various teams. His marketing and public relations people had large, open working spaces to themselves, where they could see each other easily, talk, and exchange ideas. His risk management people had their own open space. Jim then grouped the directors of his various departments together in one large, open, visible area, creating the equivalent of a captain's bridge on a ship. Jim wanted his top lieutenants to work side by side, keeping Visa on course. Under this new physical arrangement, e-mail was out; talk was back in. "You have to be able to see each other and talk to each other," Jim said. "I like personal communication, pressing the flesh. It works."

Jim also tore down invisible walls. Corporate hierarchies, "glass ceilings," traditional career tracks – all these went out the window. In their place, Jim set in motion a novel experiment: he would shake up all the jobs in the Miami office and each employee would be allowed to apply for any position in the company, including his. Each staffer could specify three different jobs that he or she really wanted to do and felt capable of doing.

In essence, Jim was trying to revive the spirit of the old "Dirty Coffee Cup System" of the BASE I days, when the tech staff came to work every morning and volunteered for whatever tasks needed to be done. Jim wanted to generate that same kind of energy, fervor, and creativity. He wanted his people to come to work excited, eager to do their job, and feeling that they not only belonged, but that their personal talents were appreciated and being put to the best possible use.

The impact of Jim's initiative was startling. When the dust had settled, everyone on the staff was jubilant, and almost everyone was assigned one of their three choices in jobs. A small handful of people, unhappy even before, fit nowhere in the new scheme and were asked to leave the company. Through this process, a few surprises emerged. Jim and his managers found out that several of their colleagues had theretofore hidden talents – and they were not using them at Visa. One person, for instance, had a talent for computer programming; another had a gift for design. With their hidden talents revealed, they were given new assignments at Visa. The employees won, and so did the company.

Looking back now, Jim sees the overhaul as a significant success. The communication is back and so is the fire. "No more silos, no more turfs. Now our teams sit together, our team leaders sit together. And there are no barriers to communication," he said. "At first, people thought I was out of my mind. But we created a better team. And now we're back on track."

Through this process of reflection and reorganization, Jim realized there were two essential

qualities on which he could henceforth evaluate each person on his staff: values and performance. Jim was crystal clear about which was more important. "If someone's performance is not up to snuff, I can give them another chance. Or move them to a different job where they'll have a better chance to succeed. But if someone's values aren't there, they're out."

Like Dee Hock, and like A.P. Giannini long before Dee, Jim prizes one value above all others: personal integrity. For Jim, this is the bedrock on which all other values rest. Another key value Jim preaches is self-reliance. He wants each person on his staff to show initiative and follow-through; you take on a job and then you do whatever it takes to get it done, just as in the old "Dirty Coffee Cup System." That goes for the Miami office as a whole. He does not want his staff shoveling problems to Visa International in California; he wants them to use their ingenuity and find their own solutions. In Jim's view, integrity, self-reliance, and personal responsibility all flow together into a single guiding ethic. And he has now come to understand that one of the most important responsibilities of any business leader is to clearly set forth a company's values, principles, and ethics – and to work to instill them in everyone on the staff.

For years, Jim did just that with a man named José Smith. José's roots were Cuban, and by all accounts he was a smart, very personable man who shared Jim's missionary zeal and understood the intricacies of the credit card industry. Jim was grooming José to be his successor, but in 1996 José suddenly, shockingly, keeled over in the middle of a business meeting and died of a heart attack. For Jim, José was family, and he took it very hard. So did everyone else in the Miami office.

In his mind, too, Jim had lost the perfect successor. After three decades of pioneering work in the credit card business, Jim was eager to step aside, but his top priority was to find the right person to carry forth Visa's mission in Latin America. There were two or three Visa executives in Miami that he could have turned to, but Jim was eager to bring in fresh blood and fresh ideas. Then Jim suddenly realized it: in a sense, he had already hired just the right man.

His name was Jonathan Sánchez-Jaimes. Jonathan is a tall, refined, very personable young man, and he came to Visa with an impressive mix of academic and business credentials. He was born in Caracas in 1961 and had grown up in Miami. He studied government and economics at Dartmouth

College, and later he earned graduate degrees from both the Harvard Law School and the Harvard Business School. In 1980, while attending graduate school, he joined a management training program of Aetna Life and Casualty and began learning the practical side of running a business. He spent 11 years with Aetna, learning and polishing his management skills, and then in 1992 he joined the highly respected Boston Consulting Group, BCG, working there with a variety of Fortune 100 corporations. In 1996, when Jim wanted to rethink the mission of Visa Latin America, he hired Boston Consulting to help, and Jonathan arrived as the head of the local BCG team. "It was a fascinating time to come look at Visa," Jonathan said in an interview. "Visa saw its mission as almost evangelical. It was building the world's premier payments system. Along the way, it had built an incredibly powerful brand."

Jonathan and his team delved deep into the interior of Jim's operation. Like Jim, the consultants concluded that this was an ideal moment for Visa to make serious changes. New technology was coming on stream, and that would inevitably bring enormous change to the credit card industry. Visa had to be ready. Moreover, Visa had been in a period of rapid expansion for two full decades, and worldwide it was now larger than all its competitors. "This was exactly the time to make changes," Jonathan said. "We were all in agreement on that."

The Boston Consulting Group also came up with a more startling conclusion. "We ended up," Jonathan said, "exactly where Dee Hock had started: devolution." In 1981, when he gave Visa a unique global structure, Dee was convinced that the future of the organization depended on devolving more authority and responsibility to *regional* centers around the world. Now Jonathan and his team concluded that it was time to take Dee's formula to the next level: Visa Latin America should give more authority and responsibility to *national* Visa entities or to "sub-regions" covering different parts of Latin America and the Caribbean. Jonathan foresaw a lean, efficient headquarters in Miami overseeing the whole. His reasoning echoed Dee's: each country in the region was so different in its traditions, markets, and needs that key decisions were best made by people with local knowledge and local roots. The guiding philosophy of "global vision, local roots" had stood up well for two decades. Now it was to put even more emphasis on those local roots.

In their work, Jonathan and his team strongly reaffirmed the ideals and principles that Dee, Jim, and the other early pioneers had shared from the beginning. Visa, they concluded, had to be "open and inclusive" in its membership. Its pricing and finances had to be completely transparent. And its member banks, large or small, had to have a definite "sense of ownership" in the partnership. Small and large member banks both needed a proper voice in Visa governance, albeit with the clear understanding that larger members account for the lion's share of Visa sales volume. Dee and the "founding fathers" had articulated these principles in Sausalito in 1969, and Jonathan believed

they were no less valid today.

That said, Jonathan and his team were still prescribing some rather stiff changes for how Visa Latin America was run, and they were quite surprised by Jim Partridge's reaction. "We were messing with the organization that he built," Jonathan said. "But he never took it as a personal criticism. He was always looking forward, never back. And Jim was not just open to this, he was *insistent* that we press forward with new ideas."

During this process, Jim became convinced that Jonathan was the man to lead Visa Latin America into a new era of growth and innovation. He had the right background, the right training, and the right feel. One person was not so sure: Jonathan. It's one thing to be a freewheeling consultant; it's quite another to take the controls of a major enterprise like Visa Latin America. "It was a long courtship," Jim laughed. "But I got my man."

Still, Jim was not about to push Jonathan directly into the top job. In 1997, Jonathan formally came on board as executive vice-president in charge of business development and support. Over the next two years, his responsibilities expanded to encompass such areas as human resources and legal issues, as well as operations in two of Visa's biggest markets in the region, Mexico and Brazil. Finally, in 1999 Jonathan took the reins as president. By then his earlier misgivings had vanished, and Jonathan had eagerly taken up the Visa mission.

"This region is very complex and challenging," he said. "Uruguay is different from Peru, and both are different from Brazil. There is no way to use a cookie-cutter approach here. Visa needs to show leadership, but we can't impose. We have to bring fresh ideas, not models."

Jonathan believes that Visa Latin America – and Visa as a whole – now stands at a critical crossroads. The year 2000 marks the 30th anniversary of the creation of NBI, and in that time Visa has grown from an idea into a global giant, a financial power that has transformed banking and commerce all around the world. Visa now finds itself at the nexus of three converging industries: financial services, telecommunications, and computer processing. At the same time, the speed of change in the business world is accelerating, and new technologies such as the Internet and e-commerce are just beginning to show their promise. Jonathan believes this is a time for Visa to be nimble, entrepreneurial, innovative, and bold. It is a time for Visa to explore new frontiers and generate a fresh sense of mission.

"There's a free market," he said. "Use it!"

Visa sponsors many cultural events across Latin America, including an opera here at the Municipal Theater in São Paulo, Brazil.

Visa Screening Rooms.
Where outstanding directors get their credit.

Visit **www.visa.com/filmfestivals** for all Visa Screening Room listings at the Montreal, Toronto & Vancouver Film Festivals. **In life, as in art...Visa.® All you need.™**

Visa. All you need.

Exclusive card of the Montreal, Toronto & Vancouver Film Festivals.

®/TM Visa Int/lic user

Chapter 24

Canada

The amazing story of Visa Canada really begins with a quiet, self-effacing man named Roger Woodward.

Roger was born and raised in the town of Peterborough, Ontario, and in 1950, at the age of only 18, he went to work for a nearby branch of the Canadian Imperial Bank of Commerce, a national bank headquartered in Toronto. Roger initially took the job as a prelude to university studies, but he enjoyed the work so much he never left. During his first years with Canadian Imperial, Roger worked in the auditing division, one of the more lackluster corners of any bank. By 1968, however, he was moving up the ladder, and the bank sent him to San Francisco to take a close look at that newfangled banking tool, the BankAmericard.

Roger was excited by the potential of the card, and he returned to Toronto with a license for his bank to issue the cards throughout Canada. That seemed, at the time, like a very big gamble. "At that point, almost everyone else except the Bank of America had dropped out of the card business because it was a money loser," Roger recalled. "But we were determined to give it a try."

Canadian Imperial faced a daunting challenge: creating a bank card market from scratch – and doing so in a country that was both vast and diverse. Roger's bank figured it could not build a nationwide market alone, and so it joined hands with three other banks – Royal Bank of Canada, Toronto Dominion Bank, and Banque Canadienne Nationale in Montreal – and created the Canadian Bank Card Association. Each bank had its own non-exclusive license with the Bank of America, and each bank was free to customize their cards with their own name and logo. The banks would also compete for merchant accounts and the profits that went with them. To facilitate marketing, advertising, and card processing, though, the banks agreed to issue their cards under a single name: Chargex.

The formula worked – beyond anyone's imagination. In the space of a few short years, the card association had enlisted thousands of merchants and cardholders, and the card quickly became a centerpiece of retailing and consumer life in Canada. The concept of interbank cooperation also took hold in the financial community. "It was a bit difficult at the beginning because each bank had to subjugate its way of doing things and take on a larger perspective," Roger recalled. "But we developed a good system of cooperation. Collectively, we found we could cover the territory and solve problems like marketing and risk management better than any of the banks could have done on their own. From there, we rapidly became the No. 1 country in cards per capita."

There were three main reasons for the card's phenomenal success in Canada. One was that Canada's banks were national in reach and had effective branch networks. Another reason was that there were was no duality. The U.S. Justice Department's position in favor of duality did not apply in Canada, so banks were not compelled to issue MasterCards, and they could pour their resources into promoting Visa. The third reason was the name change. In 1977, as we've seen, the association dropped the name Chargex in favor of the new global brand Visa, a change that boosted the card's popularity and consolidated Visa's hold on the rapidly developing Canadian market. "The adoption of the name Visa worldwide was the smartest thing we did, apart from the creation of the card," Roger said. "The name Chargex was working well in Canada, but when our cardholders went abroad, they were having problems. The name meant nothing, for instance, in Ireland or Scotland. When we went to the name Visa, those problems simply disappeared."

With these advantages and strong support from member banks, the little wonder tool performed brilliantly, and time after time it defied everyone's expectations. "I remember when the Bank of Nova Scotia came into the card association," Roger recalled. "All the other banks feared they would lose market share. No! The reverse happened! The Bank of Nova Scotia came in with fresh advertising and marketing, and that generated fresh excitement about Visa cards. Usage jumped. Later, the Bank of Montreal introduced a MasterCard and guess what? Visa sales continued to jump. Whenever someone new comes into the marketplace, the rest of us wake up and say, 'Hey, that's good,' and we expand our products and services."

For the next dozen years, Roger served on the board of Visa International, representing the Canadian bank card association. During this same period, the Canadian banks made heavy investments to develop the market and strengthen the Visa brand. By 1989, Canada was home to a booming credit card market, and Visa and its partners in Canada felt it was time to make another important shift. To further expand the business, the association turned the management of the card program over to a newly created entity, Visa Canada, and Roger came aboard as its first president. In the early days, he had one other person on his staff: Pran Bahl, a former teacher who had been in Canadian banking since the 1960s. "In the early days, Roger and I couldn't go to lunch at the same time because someone had to watch over the phones," Pran recalled. "Today we have more than 60 people working here." Pran wrote the original operating regulations for Canadian banks, and he continues to keep member banks up to date on changes to the operating regulations.

Roger led Visa Canada until he retired in 1996. He now serves on the board of one of Visa's member banks, and he often steps back and marvels at how credit cards, ATMs, and all the other attendant technology have transformed Canada's banking industry and much of its retailing and commerce. "Look at ATMs," he said. "For a long time they weren't paying for themselves. And look now. We'd be lost without ATMs today. These things have become a part of our ordinary life."

As important as the card concept and technology were, Roger believes that the real key to Visa's success was its people, starting with Dee Hock and Chuck Russell. "In the very beginning, Dee saw a lot of things that could happen and he set out to make them happen," Roger said. "He wasn't always popular. And it wasn't always easy to work with Dee Hock. But it took someone like Dee in the beginning because we were a group of bankers that sometimes found it very difficult to compromise. And it took someone like Chuck to follow Dee and mend all the fences and fill out all the details. Because the devil is always in the details."

"Visa has to be one of the best success stories in the world today. We started from nothing and today it's known the world over," Roger Woodward said. Though not one to boast, Roger can't help but feel a touch of pride. "For me, it was the most stressful, the most exciting, and surely the most rewarding activity of my professional life. We changed the way people live."

How do you build on that sort of success?

That task now rests on the shoulders of Roger's successor, Derek Fry, an affable, articulate, very capable banking pro who took over from Roger in 1996. Derek arrived with a wealth of experience in running bank card associations and in marrying money and new technology — two key qualifications for running Visa Canada, with its 24 member financial institutions.

Derek was born in Britain, and in the early 1960s, fresh out of school, he joined National Westminster Bank in London. His first job inside the bank, aptly enough, was with a traditional credit device. "I was involved in letters of credit, documentary letters of credit for finance of foreign trade," Derek said. "Then I transferred into the automation division." At the time, "Nat West" was introducing computers into its check-sorting operation, and soon Derek was building computer centers and installing terminals and accounting systems in Nat West's many branches, an assignment that put him on the ground floor of the revolution to come.

In February of 1977, Derek moved to Canada and joined the Bank of Montreal, again to develop big computer systems and automate the bank's system of branches. Soon he was running a division devoted to developing new technology. A decade later, Derek took over the bank's electronic banking business, which included a MasterCard program, debit cards, and an ATM network. Now Derek found himself at the center of the credit card world, serving on various MasterCard committees and also serving for six years as the unpaid chairman of the board of Interac, Canada's debit card system. Visa was a logical next step.

Thanks to his experience in both British and Canadian banking, Derek came to Visa with an acute sense of the social and economic impact of the credit card revolution. Not so long ago, he noted, "it was a privilege to have a bank account and only people of means could have a bank account. During the 1970s and 1980s, in developed countries, we put a lot of spending power into the hands of people who historically had found it difficult to get credit. Visa has been the tool to do that,

Olympic gold medalist Pierre Leuders, pilot of the Canadian bobsleigh team (left), with Derek Fry, chief of Visa Canada.

and it unleashed a lot of people who, given the history of Europe and other parts of the world, did not have such discretionary spending power. Here was the tool to put the wheels on the wagon."

Derek also came to Visa Canada with a keen sense of the strengths and limitations of an association that operates on the principle of consensus. "My first real exposure to associations was Interac," he said. "There we found the way to incorporate the desires of big organizations and small organizations. For six years I brokered deals that would be okay with the big guys and would let the small guys survive. You have to find the roads where you can move forward and win the support of most of the people around the table."

Leadership is key to running an organization like Visa Canada, he said, and so is creating a sense of shared loyalty and responsibility. "Associations don't win anything by getting down to vote," he said. "Our job is to craft the ways that are good for all. Then we have to make those ways attractive to our members." In Canada, as in all the other Visa regions, careful diplomacy is an absolute must. "Boards are, by nature, teams, and you need to create among the members a feeling of loyalty to each other," Derek said. "So you encourage. You cajole. You get them to feel good about compromise."

With Visa Canada already holding the commanding heights of the credit card market, Derek does not feel he needs to craft a new vision or strategy for the next five or ten years. "I'm personally not high on elegantly crafted strategies," he said. "Before, vision was key. But now that we are up and running well, the question is, 'How do you fine-tune the engine?' 'How do you push Visa into new areas of business?' Also, we live in a rock-and-roll world that is constantly changing. We need to be able to act quickly and manage that change."

In his first years at the helm, Derek placed his emphasis on leading Visa Canada into previously untapped market segments such as supermarkets, health care, government payments, and the Internet and e-commerce. With his strong backing, Visa Canada has also run several pilot projects featuring smart cards, a technology which Derek sees as an exciting cornerstone of Visa Canada in the years ahead. "I think we have to face the reality that the magnetic stripe, on which so much of our success has been built over the past 25 years, is not strong enough to last another 25 years," he said. In his view, smart cards will be multi-purpose electronic passkeys into the emerging world of e-commerce, electronic banking and payments, and a range of new realms that we cannot yet imagine. By the summer of 2000, a new consensus had formed: Canadian banks were ready to move to chip technology, aiming to phase the technology in over the next eight to ten years.

To help position Visa at the forefront of e-commerce and these new frontiers, in 1999 Visa Canada underwrote the creation of a handbook showing Canadian entrepreneurs how to set up websites and begin doing business via the Internet. Visa helped launch the book, appropriately enough, with a press conference broadcast live over the Internet. As exciting as these new vistas are, Derek believes that Visa's strength resides first and foremost with the trust that people feel toward the Visa brand. "Visa has a good image and an image of reliability," he said. "On the Internet, where there are issues of security, there are many customers who eagerly grab at Visa as a talisman they can trust."

Visa Canada works hard to maintain that cardholder trust – in what is often a very challenging environment. In the past few years, for instance, Canada has been hard hit by criminal gangs adept at the high-tech practice of "skimming." According to Mike Hayes, head of Visa Canada's risk management team, the problem is

not confined to any particular criminal element. In recent years, the criminals have hurt several member banks and compromised many points of sale.

To fight skimming, counterfeiting, and other types of fraud, Visa Canada is helping member banks to transform the emphasis of their fraud programs from detection to prevention. "Detection is about criminal investigation, while prevention is about stopping fraud before it happens," Hayes said. "Preventing fires is better than detecting fires." With that in mind, Visa Canada redesigned its fraud management program in 1999 and now works with each member bank to tailor a fraud prevention program to suit their par-

NO HASSLES IN HOLLYWOOD.

NO WORRIES DOWN UNDER.

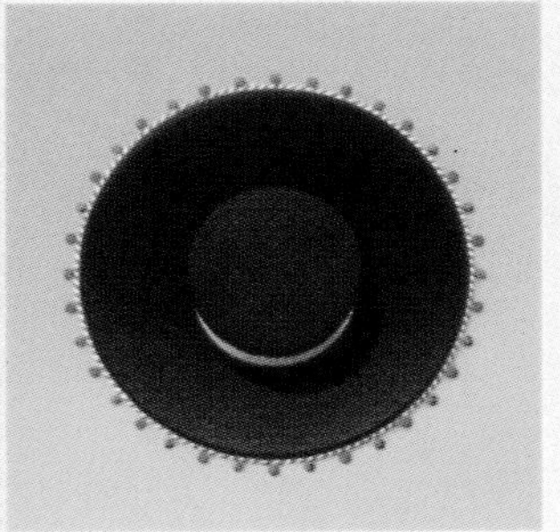

NO BULL IN BARCELONA

NO PROBLEMS WITH REFUNDS...PERIOD

ticular needs and concerns.

Technology is key. Visa has developed what it calls a High Risk Fraud Analysis database to gather and store confirmed fraud reports from its member banks. Visa Canada scrutinizes that data base on a daily basis and alerts members to potential new attacks. Using projection models developed by Visa, the risk management team issues monthly "leading indicator" reports for each member bank, helping them to track trends and prevent problems. "Before developing this projection model, we relayed to our members data that was months old," Mike said. "The reports were useless history for a program intended to prevent fraud. The projection model provides timely insights. Now we're doing something about fraud, not just reporting it."

Early results from the program have been excellent. The first member to use the program reduced its number of fraudulent transactions by more than half, and Visa predicts similar results for its other members. That was very good news; fraud hits banks right in their bottom line. "Cutting fraud in half means half as many calls from cardholders, half the investigations, fewer cards to reissue, and fewer fraud-related chargebacks," Hayes said. "Members save expense in all areas of their business. Our primary goal is to maximize cardholder and merchant confidence in Visa payments, while minimizing the crooks' return on investment."

Despite their concerns about fraud, Visa's member banks in Canada feel very confident about the future. Mark Tonneson of Royal Bank, for instance, applauds Visa Canada's move toward smart cards and the way Derek and his team stay in close touch with their members' needs and concerns. Mark examines Visa's position in Canada from a unique perspective. He formerly ran the credit card division of Bank One in Columbus, Ohio, but now he is the top executive in the credit card division of Royal Bank. He sees several fundamental reasons why Visa is significantly stronger in Canada than it is in other countries.

"In the United States, credit cards were the first way banks had to reach outside their local geography," he said. "City, state, or regional banks could issue cards as a *national* product. In Canada, all the banks are national to begin with. Therefore, reaching outside geographically was neither necessary nor effective." The size of the banking community also works in Visa's favor. "The management of Visa Canada is in constant personal contact with its members," he said. "In the United States, with so many members, customer contact can be very difficult."

In Canada, furthermore, Visa has long emphasized co-branded cards, which have double marketing power behind them. Canadian banks, Mark noted, also held onto both sides of the card business: issuing cards and signing up merchants, and that made deploying Visa nationwide far easier – not to mention far more profitable for the banks.

When it comes to chip cards, Mark is a true believer. He sees them as essential in the fight to cut card fraud, especially in this era of high-tech skimming. "The economic case for chip is directly linked to fraud," he said. "My fraud losses are equal to one-third of my total credit losses. And my fraud losses at times run 50 percent higher than those of U.S. banks. When we deploy chip-reading capabilities at all points of transaction – ATMs and points of sale – the incremental cost of adding new functions will be small and those new functions will be high value. It's also a strategic issue. If we don't deploy the chip, someone else will and then we'll be running just to get our credit function on their card."

For the future of Visa, and of credit cards in general, Tonneson believes the key goes all the way back to a cornerstone principle of Woodrow Wilson and Dee Hock: interbank cooperation. "What's relevant," Mark said, "is how we all move forward and secure a place for our cards in a multi-function future."

For the nearer term, Derek Fry and his team are working hard to keep the Visa name front and center in the Canadian consciousness. To do this, Visa focuses on two of the nation's favorite pastimes: sports and cinema. Visa continues to be the title sponsor of the Canadian National Bobsleigh Team, and in 1997 Visa became a major sponsor of the annual Toronto International Film Festival, one of the premier events for screening quality films in North America. That sponsorship proved so successful that Visa decided to become a prime sponsor of the Montreal World Film Festival and the Vancouver International Film Festival.

With the Toronto festival, Visa is much more than a passive sponsor. Unlike the festivals of Cannes or Venice, Toronto's is not an industry event; it's a 10-day revel for a movie-loving general public. Visa worked with the festival to provide a one-week advance purchase opportunity for all Visa cardholders and to develop exclusive ticket packages for its gold and platinum cardholders. These packages have become a crowd favorite because they feature the festival's best movies, reserved seating, and access to events that are not usually available to the general public. One of the festival's most prized settings is Toronto's Elgin Theater, an exquisite Edwardian "double-decker" theater complete with royal boxes, red balconies, and elegant gilding. The theater was declared a national historic site in 1982. During the festival, held every September, the Elgin is designated "The Visa Screening Room," and Visa also maintains a special lounge where its premium cardholders can relax before and after the screenings.

This collaboration has paid off handsomely – for Visa and for the festival. Visa gets great public

exposure and high usage on its cards, and the festival, which is run on a non-profit basis, gets Visa's help in promotion and selling tickets. "It's a true partnership," said Michele Maheux, managing director of the festival. "We think we've got the most amazing partner we could have. Visa has the marketing acumen to take our message and our brand much further than we could on our own."

At many festivals, one part of the viewing public is often left out: kids. Not in Toronto. In conjunction with the main events, the festival runs "Sprockets," the Toronto International Film Festival for Children. Each year this program provides free tickets and bus services to "children in need," kids who would otherwise not be able to take advantage of Sprockets activities. The festival raises money for this program through what it calls the "Sprockets Pocket Fund." Visa now matches dollar-for-dollar most contributions to the Pocket

Fund, a "spirit of community" activity that has enabled hundreds of kids to join in the festival fun and the learning experience that goes with it.

"Visa now underwrites this entire program," Michele said. "And that has encouraged our staff, our board, and the general public to contribute to the fund. Thanks to their support, kids from poor areas of Toronto and many outlying areas are able to come enjoy the festival. It's a phenomenal thing that Visa has done."

Visa Canada stands today as one of the Visa family's greatest successes. In a nation of 31 million people, there are 23 million Visa cards in circulation – an exceptionally high level of penetration. Usage per card is also exceptionally high, and annual sales volume is expected to top 100 billion Canadian dollars in the year 2001. At the same time, Visa has built a prominent and very positive public image in Canada. All this translates into another revealing statistic: Visa's share of the Canadian bank card market is an astonishing 72 percent, making dwarfs of all its rivals in one of the most highly developed card markets in the world.

"We aim to keep it that way," Fry said. "We're working closely with our members to develop new technologies to meet the changing needs of consumers and business. We think Visa has a very exciting future in Canada."

April 15,

Dear Piers Handling,
Thank you for donating money to the school so we could go to the Flim Festival. Everyone liked the movies. The best one was First Daughter. It was sad when the grandmother died. I also liked Strange Friends, because it was exciting and it had a lot of action in it. I'm sorry for writing with red pen.

Sincerely Keisha

The Sprockets Film Festival, sponsored in part by Visa, was a big hit with Canadian youngsters.

HOSPITALITY

Asia-Pacific

Chapter 25

Singapore has an amazing pulse.

Walk around the downtown area and almost everywhere you turn there is new construction: office buildings, apartment complexes, and elegant shopping arcades. From dawn to dusk, the city hums with commerce and trade, people go to lunch with cell phones to their ear, and you don't have to look far to find electronic billboards featuring the latest stock prices or hawking the hottest websites, e-trade specialists, or electronic gear. Two decades ago, Singapore was a sleepy little Asian backwater; today the whole place seems wired, booming, and cutting edge.

What's happening in Singapore is emblematic of the profound social, economic, and technological changes that are transforming the whole Asia-Pacific region. What you feel today in Singapore you can also feel, in varying degrees, in Bangalore, Bangkok, Seoul, Shanghai, Taipei, Manila, Sydney, and Tokyo, of course. For many years, Japan was the primary engine driving the Asian economy, but now several other nations have emerged as economic powers, and the entire region is entering into an era of dramatic change and development. Just consider these simple facts: China and India each have over one billion people, the nations of the Asia-Pacific account for more than half of the world's population, and there is no place on the planet where the middle class is expanding so rapidly.

The credit card revolution is expanding in kind. Independent research predicts that the payment card market in Asia will expand by a mind-boggling 600 percent over the next ten years – and that means hundreds of millions of new credit card holders. Smart cards are already in use in Singapore, and several countries that were tradition-bound, cash-based societies are now bypassing checks and paper billing and leaping directly into the age of digital payments and electronic commerce. This makes the Asia-Pacific region an important proving ground for the latest innovations in payment technology, and it also makes the region one of the most exciting in the entire Visa family.

Visa is no newcomer to the region. In the early years of IBANCO and Visa, evangelists like Jim Partridge, João Ribeira da Fonseca, Chuck Russell, and Tom Honey went to Asia, knocked on doors, and established a small, tentative foothold throughout the region. In country after country, though, Visa faced numerous roadblocks and frustrations, as the credit card industry remained in its infancy. In January of 1983, however, Visa sent a new man out to Asia, Carl Pascarella, and his mandate was clear: break open the markets, build the card business, and turn Visa into the uncontested market leader.

"I walked into a very interesting situation," Carl recalled. "We had just been thrown out of Australia, so we had absolutely no presence at all in what was our second largest market. In our largest market, Japan, we were number three or four. In terms of the whole region, when you added everything up, we probably ranked third or fourth, clearly behind MasterCard, behind the local JCB card in Japan, and way behind American Express in some markets. The perception of Visa was actually below Diners Club in some of the Southeast Asian markets. We had virtually no market penetration in Taiwan, next to none in China, and we were the secondary or tertiary card in all the rest of the market. I guess you could say we were the best-kept secret in Asia."

Carl faced a daunting challenge: re-energize Visa and lead it into the upper echelons of Asian business – in a vast, diverse region with rituals of business that to a newcomer can resemble the Dance of the Seven Veils. Was he up to the task? Sometimes Carl had his doubts, but he was eager to test his mettle. "When it came to Asia, I was a complete neophyte," Carl said, "and I had very little experience with Visa. But give me the brand and the infrastructure and I'll get results."

Though his experience with Visa was limited, Carl did come to the task with some very impressive credentials. He was born and raised in the little town of Salamanca, New York, about 60 miles south of Buffalo. He went to public schools and then studied at the University of Buffalo. Carl did brilliantly at Buffalo and went on to earn a Masters of Science in Management at the prestigious Stanford Business School. Carl then set out to build a career in the world of banking and finance. While still in school, Carl had gotten his feet wet at the Buffalo Savings Bank, and after Stanford he worked at the Flagship Banks in Florida.

In 1974, Carl moved over to what was then NBI, still in its formative years. Working under Dee Hock and Aram Tootelian, who was running the systems side, Carl traveled around the United States doing a strategic study of the banking industry and the growing competition in the payment card market. He also studied the existing telecommunications systems being used by the banks to clear and settle transactions. After a year at NBI, though, Carl's ambition drew him back to banking, first with Banker's Trust and then with Crocker Bank in San Francisco. At Crocker, he worked on the retail side, then the wholesale side, and finally he moved into Crocker's international division. There he ran the bank's office for trade finance and made a few brief trips to Asia. By this time, Carl's varied experience and proven reputation as a first-rate manager had marked him as a young executive on the rise.

Now Visa again came calling. Visa International was looking for a new head of its Asian operations. Would he be interested? To the surprise of some of his bosses at Crocker, Carl said yes; the post in Asia sounded challenging, and it fit his longer-range ambitions. "The thing that I wanted was some actual international exposure living overseas," he said. "I planned to work there for two or three years and then come back and get a job running a bank. So I suppose I went over there for all the wrong reasons."

Once on the ground in Asia, Carl made several important moves. Visa had only a skeletal staff, so he began recruiting and hiring. He also took steps to revitalize and strengthen his board of directors, to bring aboard bankers with more experience and seniority in their member banks. He also decided to move the regional headquarters from Singapore, which had not yet become an economic powerhouse, to Tokyo. "I looked around and said, 'I don't think Singapore is the place to be,'" Carl explained. "Clearly, the engine for Asia is Japan. Japan is the center for productivity, and it is the center for finance. That's where we need to have our headquarters."

So Carl set up shop in Tokyo and began looking for ways to gain a stronger foothold in the very difficult Japanese market. As Carl was new to Japan, Chuck Russell took him in hand and together they made the rounds of Japanese bankers. They went from bank to bank, introducing Carl, preaching the Visa gospel, and trying to cut whatever roads they could into a system of banking and finance that seemed almost totally closed. "What we had to do was virtually break open the market," Carl said. "We were knocking on doors until our knuckles bled."

Visa had one important ally in Japan,

Sumitomo Bank, which had secured an exclusive license to distribute Visa cards during the early days of the BankAmericard program. But Sumitomo was an uncompromising ally; it did want to build the card market – but for its own benefit and no one else's. In fact, Sumitomo held about 30 percent of the card market, which was fine for Sumitomo but prevented Visa from building the Japanese market as a whole. But how to break that Sumitomo lock-hold? Carl spoke no Japanese, he had little knowledge of Japan's delicately nuanced business customs, and he had yet to forge a close working relationship with any of the top people in Japanese banking and finance. He knew he had to find a Japanese ally – and a Japanese approach to tackling the problem.

His starting point was the eminent Bank of Japan, the government's central bank. Carl hoped he could befriend people there, enlist their support, and through them recruit a respected Japanese banker they could all work with and support. "I had three meetings with the personnel director," Carl laughed. "I had to pass a virtual sniff test with the Bank of Japan."

Carl did make some inroads, but finding the right person to recruit was a daunting task, especially given what Carl could offer candidates for the job. "The people at the Bank of Japan had status, good pay, and tenure for life. I'm thinking, 'I don't have a house to offer. I don't have a company car to offer. How am I going to recruit a top-quality Japanese banker?'"

Pascarella did manage, however, to find just the sort of person he was looking for: Kuhachiro Furuya, a highly respected banking insider who had served 25 years with the Bank of Japan. Furuya seemed an ideal choice to head up Visa's new Tokyo office. He was experienced, discreet, spoke good English, and his wife was also an asset: she was a highly respected professor and author in Japan. But there was one slight problem: Furuya was not eager to make a move.

"I had a very happy career at the Bank of Japan," Furuya recalled. "I had also been fortunate enough to study at Yale for one year and to spend four years on loan to the International Monetary Fund, overseeing projects in Kenya, Tanzania, and Uganda. From there, I came back to the central bank and worked mainly in international finance. I was in no hurry to leave."

Pascarella tried for months to entice Furuya to join Visa, without success, so then he called in reinforcements: Dee Hock and Chuck Russell. Dee invited Furuya and his family to come to California and see Visa headquarters. "I spent two days there, and Dee and Chuck took me around," Furuya recalled. "Upon returning to Tokyo, I decided to join Visa. I was 48 years old, and I had spent 25 years as a public servant. If I was ever going to do it, it was probably time for me to go into the private side. Also, I saw Visa as a chance to better know the real world of business."

Once he had joined forces with Carl, Furuya began trying to pry open the Japanese market. "I started talking to Japanese banks and trying to persuade them to join Visa," Furuya recalled. "It was very, very hard." The main reason: Sumitomo Bank. Yo Suzuki, the head of Sumitomo, kept throwing up roadblocks and trying to prevent Carl and Furuya from seeing other banks. On one occasion, Furuya said, they made some headway with the highly respected Mitsubishi Bank, only to hear later that Suzuki had spoken with Mitsubishi directors in a rather intimidating way. "Visa is controlled by Sumitomo Bank," Suzuki purportedly told them. "You can't join!" When Mitsubishi executives related the episode to Furuya, he was so shocked by Suzuki's fury and tactics that he had to stay home a day to recover.

For Carl, the situation was very frustrating.

With Furuya, he knew he had found a fine partner with excellent connections and entrée. "Nobody dared confront Furuya-san," Carl said. "And we worked well together. I could be the aggressive foreigner and he could be the quiet insider. But we weren't making a dent." If the two men failed to crack the market, Carl feared that his entire effort across the Asia-Pacific region could crumble. "If we couldn't break into Japan," Carl recalled, "it's over. Turn out the lights."

After a full year with no progress, Carl and Furuya made an overture to a pillar of Japan's public sector: the Postal Savings Bureau, part of the government-run Post, Telephone & Telegraph. The Postal Savings Bureau was a huge organization, the size of six major banks, and it boasted 60 million customers. Again, though, the door refused to open. The PTT decided it could not join a private organization like Visa. This was another depressing blow. "By now, the picture was clear," Furuya said.

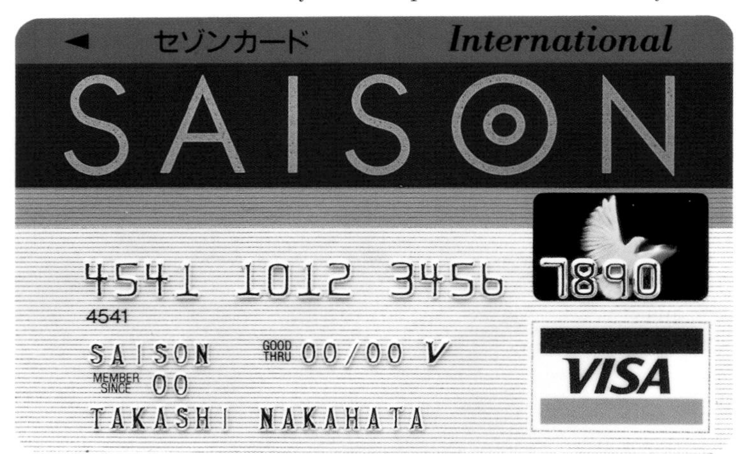

"No private banks were going to join Visa because of Sumitomo, and the PTT wasn't going to join either, because of the government. It was very frustrating."

At this stage, running out of options, Carl and Furuya found one more door to knock on: Nippon Shimpan, a finance company that issued a huge number of proprietary payment cards. Here they received an encouraging reception, but there was a problem: Nippon Shimpan was not a banking institution, and there was a question of its eligibility to join the Visa family. Enter Visa lawyers Bennett Katz and Dave Wagman. They crafted a solution that allowed Nippon Shimpan to join Visa as a special "non-bank licensee," with no voting rights, no equity in the company, and no seats on the board. With those restrictions, Nippon Shimpan agreed to join the Visa family – to the delight of Carl and Furuya. At last, they had a larger foothold in Japan – beyond the reach of Sumitomo.

Their next challenge was to expand that foothold. "Nippon Shimpan had a co-branded card they issued with the PTT," Furuya recalled. "So we wondered, could we put Visa on that joint card?" The PTT agreed, in effect meaning it would begin issuing Visa cards. The banks, though, had a stiff rivalry with the PTT, and when they heard of the planned joint venture, they went to the Ministry of Finance to complain. Sumitomo also vehemently objected to the PTT deal with Visa. The next thing he knew, Furuya was being called onto the carpet by the deputy governor of the central bank. This was a tense moment, but Furuya stood his ground. "I told them, 'Competition is a good thing for consumers,'" he said. "They listened, and the Ministry of Finance then rejected the appeal of the banks."

With that official green light, in 1986 the PTT and Nippon Shimpan began issuing a joint, co-branded card with a Visa logo. The program was a success, and a year later Nippon Shimpan began converting its own proprietary cards to Visa. With these breakthroughs, the huge Japanese market now flung its doors open to the blue, white, and gold. Soon Visa signed on two big department store

Gondo Shopping Mall

chains, and Carl and Furuya were really on their way. As we've previously seen, Japanese member banks then took full advantage of the Olympic sponsorship opportunity in 1988 and used it to catapult Visa into the No. 1 slot in the market – just five years after Carl Pascarella came out to Asia.

Through these and many other episodes, Carl learned a valuable lesson about doing business in Asia: it wasn't just the quality of your product or the brilliance of your strategy. Business in Asia was, first and foremost, personal. "It's all about personal relationships," Carl said. "You have to pass the rite in Japan and in Southeast Asia. And it requires that you care. In America, business is lawyers and contracts. It's litigious. In Asia, business is the handshake. Your word is your bond."

This understanding was invaluable to Carl as he set out to replicate his success in Japan in other Asia-Pacific countries such as Taiwan, Thailand, India, and Australia. It was also invaluable as Carl set out to repair the damage done to Visa's relationship with its historic ally in Japan: Yo Suzuki of Sumitomo. That damage was severe. Suzuki felt that both Furuya and Carl had been going behind his back in their effort to broaden Visa's member base and market share. He also objected to the granting of Visa licenses to institutions like Nippon Shimpan that were not traditional banks. In an interview, Suzuki said these disputes raised a fundamental question in his mind: "Is Visa a servant of its banks – or an autonomous body working to lead the banks in the direction Visa wants to go?"

Looking back now, Suzuki said that many of the initial conflicts stemmed from the inevitable tensions he felt serving two masters: he was a loyal member of the Visa board, but he also was eager to protect and promote the interests of his bank. In time, though, he came to understand the wisdom embodied in Dee's famous formulation, "The will to succeed, the grace to compromise." Sumitomo, headquartered in Osaka, for years had maintained a hammerlock on the Visa brand in Japan, while most of the big banks in Tokyo had gone with MasterCard. From that position of strength, those banks were able to block Visa from building the market. Suzuki came to see that the constricted market did not serve either Visa's interests or Sumitomo's. The best way to build the market, Suzuki realized, was not through self-interested exclusivity but through open membership and interbank cooperation.

"For Sumitomo," Suzuki said, "it might have been fine to have the Visa brand to itself. That meant we could have a large part of a small pie. But I came to see that Sumitomo could no longer go it alone. We needed the help of other banks to build the market. I saw that it was a good idea to make it a much, much larger pie, even if we shared our portion with other banks. We now have 40 banks in the Visa system in Japan and we are bigger than JCB, our biggest competitor. So looking back, I feel the option we took, to go for a larger pie, was a success."

Through these heated and tumultuous times, Carl, Furuya, and Suzuki were able to forge a strong working relationship, and Suzuki became an effective champion of the Visa cause and guiding philosophy. Their initial conflicts gave way to deep bonds of friendship and deep mutual respect. "Suzuki and I went through fire and hell together," Carl said. "Now we'd kill for each other." From that point on, friendship and business always went hand-in-hand. In Tokyo, Carl fell in love with a lovely Japanese woman and when they went to the Stanford Chapel to get married, Carl asked Suzuki to stand beside him at the altar. He also asked Chuck Russell to be at his side. Carl loves to tell the story that as his bride, Yurie, came walking down the aisle, Suzuki was still grousing to Chuck about his treatment by Visa.

As the Suzuki story again illustrates, Visa is not a product that is easy to package and bring out in new markets. Rather it's a whole concept and philosophy that must be carefully tailored to each individual country, market, and culture. It must also be carefully explained to local governments, member banks, the press, and the public. In each new country, member banks also have to learn the Visa philosophy and see for themselves the benefits of joining the Visa partnership and cooperating with other banks, even their fiercest competitors. To facilitate this process, Visa executives like Carl Pascarella had to be more than evangelists and capable businessmen; they had to be teachers of extraordinary patience and skill.

Visa's unique regional structure and system of governance were invaluable assets in adapting to new cultures. "The regions governed themselves," Carl said. "So we could go out and say we're an Asian company. We are Asians making Asian decisions." This was extremely important when Carl set out to extend Visa's success in Japan to other countries in the Asia-Pacific region. While Carl and his senior staff provided the overview, the strategy, and the goals for each market, he hired and relied on local managers to get the job done.

"The people on the ground have to drive the market," Carl explained. "So in each country we set up an executive committee to handle the issues in that country. They would then coordinate information and share their knowledge via the regional boards. The idea was to push the governance down, so it becomes a sales, marketing, and relationship tool."

The island of Taiwan is a revealing case in point. In 1989, the Taiwanese government opened the country to foreign credit cards, and Carl sent in Raymond Chan and Werner Thalen, both based in Hong Kong, to assess the local market and build a card program on the island of 22 million people. Soon Visa began issuing cards in Taiwan, but with only limited success. After three years, Visa had only 200,000 cards in circulation. In a move to boost Visa's presence on the island, Carl and his colleagues opened an office in Taipei in July of 1992, and then they set out in earnest to build the market.

As always, Carl was eager to forge a relationship with the best possible local partner, and the man he settled upon was Dr. Jeffrey Koo, the highly respected head of the bank China Trust. "Taiwan had some of the largest foreign exchange resources in the world," Carl said. "It also had big state banks, filled with lifetime bankers, and it had some smaller, privately owned banks. Jeffrey Koo's bank was private, nimble, and it already issued cards, but with no affiliation. Most important, Jeffrey Koo was a man of extraordinary intelligence and vision."

Chinese society in Taiwan and elsewhere puts enormous value on education and intellectual accomplishment, and with Dr. Koo as an adviser and partner – and later as president of the Asia-Pacific board – Visa sought to establish its presence in Taiwan with an approach that could be described as education, education, education. "In the beginning, we had quite a task," Dr. Koo recalled. "We had to educate the government about the credit card industry and how to regulate us. We had to educate consumers about how to use credit cards, and we had to educate the banks in Asia-Pacific. Early on, some scholars criticized the concept of plastic money and thought its arrival in Taiwan would spell disaster. We had to address that in a very persuasive way."

The process of education was deliberate, ongoing, and carried out at several levels. "I invited prominent people to give lectures and speeches," explained Dr. Koo, who has been a longtime adviser to the Taiwanese government on matters of banking, finance, and trade. "Fortunately, about 60 percent of the cabinet members of our government hold Ph.D.'s from major international universities, and they were quite quick to catch on to this idea. People in Taiwan are basically conservative. But once they found the convenience of the card, they came along quickly. Banks, at first, thought this was chicken feed, but they caught on quickly as well."

To help formulate a program of consumer education, Visa turned to George Yi, a respected reporter, public relations pro, and professor of communications. George came aboard in 1991, and he was not pleased with what he found. "From 1989 to 1991, Visa was not aggressive in Taiwan," George said. "There was not even a Visa office here. The Visa program was being managed from Hong Kong." In one of his first moves, George drew together all the information he could on credit cards and the payment market and made it available to local reporters. "If you want to develop your market," he explained, "you have to have strong, open communications with the press." MasterCard, he said, was not doing well in this regard. "In the space of a very short time, MasterCard changed public relations agencies three times."

One of the first aims of the consumer education program was to build trust in the credit card tool. This was especially important because for thousands of years Taiwan had been a cash-based society. "The Chinese people love to keep cash in their pocket. They also felt more comfortable with cash, and we had to change that," George said. "So our first job was to educate people about the convenience and safety of credit cards."

This was no easy task, in part due to an unusual tradition among the Chinese. Because of the nature and complexity of the written language, many Chinese were not trained to sign their name. As a result, they conducted their banking and other official business with something called a "chop," a seal that served as the equivalent of a signature. Also, very few people in Taiwan had checking accounts, and few understood the concept of a line of credit. So to most Taiwanese, credit cards were a totally new and somewhat suspicious concept.

To build the necessary trust and confidence – and to help catapult Taiwan into the modern era of electronic payments – Visa developed brochures that explained in clear, easy-to-understand terms what credit cards were and how to use them. These brochures also answered such questions as what to do if your card was lost or stolen. To stimulate public usage of these brochures, Visa came up with a clever promotional tool: public quizzes. Using various magazines and newspapers, Visa would set forth a list of questions about credit cards and then invite readers to send in their replies. Winners received free air tickets to Hong Kong. The quizzes brought forth a huge and very positive response. "The quizzes generated growing awareness of the Visa brand," George said. "They also helped educate the public and build the necessary base of trust. We also issued co-branded cards with local universities, aimed at young graduates eager to establish their credit. With these programs, we created a lot of stories in the press and built respectability for the brand."

Visa also came forth with a masterstroke in Taiwan. It was not enough to put out explanatory brochures; Visa wanted to find a way to put an appealing human face on its payment tool. "No matter how practical and convenient Visa was, it had no emotional component," George explained. "So we decided we needed a person to represent the brand. Ideally, we wanted a respected intellectual who could become the public face of Visa."

Enter Albert Shiung. For 20 years, Albert had been an engineer with IBM, and he was a man of

VISA

great personal warmth and intellectual stature – a perfect fit for George Yi's strategy. Visa made Albert its personal spokesman, its resident professor, and its roving ambassador of goodwill and good cheer. "This was a new technique for Taiwan," George said. "No other companies had personal spokesmen completely identified with the brand. We had Albert sign articles published in the press. We had him pose for photos while using an ATM. Albert became the public face of Visa in Taiwan."

But Albert was not just an amiable face or an attractive talking head; he brought real credibility to the brand. "I tried to present Albert as just what he was: someone who was smart, well-educated, and knowledgeable about money management and payment systems," George said. "We always kept him very serious and distant from reporters, to make him appear very authoritative. He was like the professor of payments and money management."

For Albert, the role was a natural. He was born in mainland China in 1947, and his parents brought him to Taiwan in 1949. In college he studied electrical engineering, and in 1971 he went to work for IBM. That was the beginning of a distinguished career. In 20 years at IBM, Albert held jobs in many corners of Big Blue: sales, marketing, programming, and more. For a time, he headed up the sales office in Taiwan, but he also worked for IBM in Westchester, New York, and in Palo Alto, California, IBM's main outpost in the Silicon Valley. In the late 1980s, as IBM went through some dramatic down-sizings, Albert decided it was time to make a move. "Everybody was talking about the next century belonging to Asia," Albert recalled, "and I was eager to return."

He joined Visa as head of the Taiwan office just as it opened in 1992. His timing was felicitous. "We entered the market early, ahead of the competition," Albert said. "And starting from day one, we did two things. One, we educated the public about consumer credit, which was extremely new to the Chinese people. Two, we created a lot of educational coverage in the press – not necessarily advertising – showing people what a credit card is and how to use it. Naturally, in that coverage the brand name was used and so was my name. In this way, we created the market and the demand for Visa."

The arrival of Visa and other credit cards in Taiwan helped catalyze major changes in the business community and the travel industry. "Until 1987, Taiwan had foreign exchange controls in place," Albert explained. "If you wanted to travel abroad, you needed central bank approval to buy foreign exchange. Passports were also tightly restricted. You needed an exit permit to leave the country. With the lifting of those restrictions and the arrival of credit cards, the Taiwanese realized they could leave the country and take money with them on foreign travel, just by using their cards. They could go to a hotel or a car rental and pay with a credit card. So there was a huge increase in outbound travel. And soon people realized that a credit card was not a luxury, it was a necessity. That helped us build the market."

Build the market they did. In January of 1989, the first Visa card was issued in Taiwan. By 1999, a decade later, Taiwan had 9.6 million Visa cards in circulation. "This was unbelievable growth," Albert said, "and all in the space of seven and a half years. There was a true explosion in the market."

Those numbers delight Alex Chen, the dynamic young executive who replaced Albert as chief of Visa Taiwan in 1999. "The market is mature, but it is by no means saturated," Alex said. "By the end of 1999, Visa had 67 percent of the market in terms of card numbers. But card transactions represent only 10 percent of what people spend for personal consumption. So we have plenty of room to grow."

Alex also has first-rate credentials. After earning both a bachelor's and a master's degree in computer science, he joined IBM as a systems engineer in 1990. After two years with IBM, he joined Visa Taiwan and helped set up its card center and train its staff. He left briefly to work as a director of marketing in a computer firm but returned to Visa in 1995 as chief of member services, a post that made him the right arm of and heir apparent to Albert Shiung. Alex credits Albert, George Yi, and Raymond Chan with not only creating a credible, highly visible image for Visa but also with forging strong links to Taiwanese banks and merchants.

Linda Kao is a case in point. For years, Linda was a major figure in the credit card division at BA Merchant Services Inc., a subsidiary of the Bank of America and Visa's first acquiring bank in Taiwan. Linda said Visa got off to a roaring start and never looked back. MasterCard, by contrast, has never been able to gather similar steam. "It was always Visa out in front. Afterwards, the banks joined in," she said. "Here, the banks did not have the skill to use credit cards to build their image, but Visa showed them how. MasterCard was a year late. They never caught up."

Linda has seen first-hand the impact of the credit card revolution in Taiwan – right in her own office. When she first joined her bank's merchant services in 1991, there were only 12 people handling merchant accounts and helping with transaction processing. "Now we have a whole floor dedicated to credit cards," she said. "Merchant services has more than 100 people."

Linda expects Taiwan's card market to continue to grow at a phenomenal pace. With more and more Taiwanese traveling abroad for business or pleasure, Linda's bank has had great success with a co-branded Visa card it issues with China Airlines. "We did a buy-one-ticket, get-another-free promotion on the card and that was a big attraction," she said. "Taiwanese people who emigrate to the United States like to travel on China Airlines, and they loved that program."

There is nothing down-market about Visa's image in Taiwan or the rest of Asia. Ten years ago, American Express had a commanding hold on the top hotels and restaurants, especially those that cater to foreign travelers. No longer. The Hotel Imperial in Tokyo, one of the most luxurious and well-managed hotels in the world, is seeing a significant jump in its clients' preference for Visa. Kiyohito Minoshima, the managing director of the Imperial, said that in years past American Express was the card preferred by 50 percent of his clientele. Now that number has slipped to 37 percent. "Visa's image is coming up in Asia, and the transaction is very easy," Minoshima said. "We see more Americans using Visa here. Visa is getting more popular among Japanese as well." Minoshima-san is always happy to see Imperial clients use their Visa card to pay for their room, a day of special spa treatments, or for the hotel's famous "Marilyn Monroe Breakfast" – the Hollywood goddess once stayed at the Imperial with her husband Joe DiMaggio. "I have a preferred rate with American Express, but Visa still takes 0.35 percent less per transaction," Minoshima said. "Visa saves me money."

While Alex Chen mans the store in Taiwan, Albert Shiung is now working hard to spread the Visa gospel on the rapidly evolving Chinese mainland. In a nation of 1.2 billion people, this is a hugely challenging and exciting endeavor. Albert received a major boost in his efforts in 1999 when China's central bank authorized local banks to issue credit cards. "I said, 'Wow, this is like Taiwan in 1988. We're at the very beginning of the credit card business,'" Albert said. "It's a great potential market. And I have to do the same two things I did

The fabulous Hotel Imperial in Tokyo, like many other fine hotels around the world, has seen a significant jump in its clients' preference for Visa.

in Taiwan: create a demand side in a culture that still prefers cash and does business with the 'chop,' and work with the government to liberalize its foreign exchange controls and exit permits. I can see changes and I can see things starting to repeat our earlier experience in Taiwan."

Still, there are several complicated problems facing China as it builds its credit card industry. The currency is not yet fully convertible outside the country. The necessary computer infrastructure is not yet ready to handle massive traffic. Also, the government has been tightening up its credit policies, and some people who have not paid their bills have been sent to jail. So for a company like Visa, there are some serious risks in pushing too fast. If it advertises a set of products and services, but cannot deliver them effectively, that could cause credibility problems and hurt the brand. So Albert is moving cautiously.

"I bumped into the Taiwan market at the right time, and I saw it explode," Albert said. "Now I'm seeing the same thing in China on a much larger scale – in terms of both potential and challenges. We're trying to replicate the business and media experiences that worked so well in Taiwan, but we have to be careful to maintain our credibility." If history does repeat itself, China could rapidly turn into a colossal card market and one of most important partners in the Visa family.

In Japan and China, personal relationships have been key to Visa's success, and that is true in the Philippines as well. One day, back in the early years of Visa International, Jim Partridge was passionately preaching the Visa gospel at a meeting of Asian bankers that Visa was hosting in Kyoto. At the meeting, he was approached by a personable young man named Tony Go. Tony came from a prominent family in Manila, and he was at the meeting representing Equitable Bank, then a small, privately run bank controlled by his family. Tony was very

impressed by Jim and his message and was eager to know more. "I had talked to American Express and MasterCard about starting a card program, but they didn't want to talk to me," Tony recalled. "Jim listened."

Jim did more than listen. On the spot, he canceled all his appointments in Kyoto and Tokyo and flew right back to Manila with young Tony Go. The flight was three and a half hours long, and the whole way Jim tutored Tony in the intricacies of the credit card business and how to set up a profitable card program. It was a Ph.D. course taught by a master instructor. "I asked intensive questions and Jim gave me intensive lessons," Tony said. "I will always remember that flight. The others wouldn't even see me. We were too small. But Jim dropped everything to help me. I was impressed. Without him, today I'd probably be pushing some other brand."

Today, Equitable Bank is a major credit card power in the Asia-Pacific region. It offers Visa credit and debit cards, and it runs a very extensive ATM network. Its card and sales volume growth are both in double digits. It took a little time to set up the necessary infrastructure, and as the bank invested heavily to boost volume and introduce cards into a cash-loving society, the early years did not generate profits. ("My father almost disowned me," Tony said.) But in July of 1999, Visa recorded its one millionth cardholder in the Philippines, and for Tony Go and his bank, the Visa program now stands as a huge success. And, of course, it has also been a success for Visa, which has several prominent banks in its fold. "Visa now has a very strong presence in the Philippines. We have a dominant market share," Tony said. "Almost all merchants are Visa merchants. Now, of course, the other card companies come knocking. But I remain loyal to Visa."

In Australia, Rob Hunt tells a similar story.

First, though, a bit of background. As Carl Pascarella noted earlier, at the start of the 1980s Visa was unceremoniously thrown out of Australia. The action resulted from a complicated dispute with the Bank Card Association of Australia, a consortium of four of the nation's leading banks. The consortium had its own card called Bank Card, which it wanted to use exclusively in the domestic market, while keeping Visa only as an international card. Visa insisted it did not work that way. The dispute escalated until the banks effectively kicked Visa out of the country.

Back in California, the expulsion stirred the ire of Dee Hock. "We are not getting thrown out of any country!" Dee thundered. "I want a task force! I want a strategy! I want a game plan to get back into that market! I don't want to have a card that is accepted worldwide *except* in Australia! Who here has ever been to Australia or New Zealand?" Dennis Wlasichuk, a veteran systems man at Visa, spoke up. "Good! You're going back!"

Thus it was that Visa sent a repair team back to Australia, to sign up merchants on its own and to find inroads back into the banking community. At the very least, Dee and Carl Pascarella wanted the team to sign up a few hotels and restaurants, just to plant the Visa flag back in Australian soil. Since the top-tier banks were closed to Visa, the team set its sights on different financial institutions: Australia's "building societies," which function like savings and loan houses. Rob Hunt worked for a building society called Bendigo Bank, and in the dispute between Visa and the big banks, Rob saw an opportunity. "At that time, nothing much was being done regarding merchant acceptance," Rob recalled. "We saw that as an opportunity to talk with Visa. We thought we could make that card work for us. And we felt confident that Visa was going to be a big winner in our market."

Rob and Visa representatives sat down to talk. "Our role was, first of all, to convince Visa that we could use the card to help our customers access their money. And we would work with Visa to sign up merchants and bring other building societies into the fold," Rob said. "I was only a small player, coming from a small building society. I could have been completely dismissed. But I wasn't. I was listened to."

Like Tony Go, Rob was impressed with the openness and receptivity of the Visa team. He was also impressed by what he called "the Visa ethos," specifically its belief in the importance of interbank cooperation and the democratization of credit. Indeed, this was the beginning of a beautiful partnership. Bendigo Bank helped ease Visa back into the Australian market, and Visa in turn helped Bendigo build its business and give its customers an invaluable payment tool. "The association we've had with Visa makes me pleased and proud," Rob said. "Visa managed to pick up a bit of assistance from us and other building societies, and we were all very strong in issuing Visa cards into the market here. It's been a very positive development for us, and it helped launch Visa in Australia."

From the momentum generated by Bendigo and other building societies, Visa was able to join forces with the highly respected ANZ, one of the premier banks of Australia and New Zealand. This was a big feather in Visa's cap, but the relationship was by no means an instant success. During the 1980s, ANZ struggled mightily to get its card program off the ground, with little success, and by 1989 some ANZ executives wanted to shut the whole operation down. Charles Carbonaro, who had just taken over ANZ's card program, disagreed. "It was a dog's breakfast of a business," Charles recalled. "It was losing a lot of money. But I gave an indication to the bank that it was worth saving."

At that time, ANZ had a card processing center in every state in Australia. The entire system was bloated, disorganized, and lacking credible market data and analysis. Charles slashed the staff by one third, consolidated data processing in a single building in Melbourne, introduced new products and services, and began expanding the card program internationally. "Within three years, we came to a break-even situation," he said. "Now we've become very profitable. Our card business is now in 17 countries across Asia, and obviously in the coming years, Asia will be an increasingly strong part of our business." ANZ issues Visa, MasterCard, and the local Bank Card, but, Carbonaro said, it's really no contest. "The growth has been 90 percent Visa."

The big phenomenon at ANZ and across Australia and New Zealand, as in so many other countries, is co-branded cards. "In the mid-1990s, we heard that the U.S. was going into co-branding, and we thought, 'No doubt that will come here. How can we do it?' We picked the best partners any company could have." The first of those partners was Telstra, the local phone and telecommunications company. It quickly proved to be a brilliant choice. "It provided us with the ability to communicate with Telstra's vast customer base. That was a great coup for us," Charles said. "Subsequently, we realized that what people really wanted to do was fly free. That led us to Qantas, an international airline and a great brand." The result was a card with the names Qantas and Telstra on the front and ANZ on the back. Some banks might balk at having their name on the back, for ego or prestige reasons, but not ANZ. "I'm interested in the bottom line first," Charles said, "and recognition later."

Within a short time of its launch, ANZ had two million of those co-branded cards in the market. And spending on those cards runs almost double the industry average. "That's incredible business for us," Charles said. "Ten years ago, people were telling us the card business was kind of saturated in Australia. But our co-branded cards have been a phenomenal success."

ANZ's success has been a powerful locomotive for all of Visa Australia. "Five years ago, Visa and MasterCard were neck-and-neck," said Hilton Sack, who headed Visa Australia during the latter half of the 1990s. "Now, Visa is three times bigger. We are doing unbelievable business, and it is growing faster than it has ever grown before."

Australians are rather adverse to credit, so at Bendigo and many other banks the preferred Visa card is debit. With this in mind, Hilton Sack positioned Visa as a payment card, not just a credit card, and targeted cash and checks as the biggest area of potential growth for Visa. His argument to the banks was drawn directly from Dee Hock, and it was clear and persuasive: by positioning Visa as a payment device, it could move into non-traditional but high-volume payment sectors such as telephones, utility companies, and supermarkets. Also, he reminded the banks that while checks cost in the neighborhood of $1.50 to process, it only cost a few cents to process a Visa digital transaction. Of all expenditures in Australia, cards represented only 13 percent, Hilton said, and that left a handsome 87 percent of those transactions for Visa's member banks to target.

Visa made another very shrewd move in Australia. To take advantage of the huge popularity of loyalty and frequent flyer programs, Visa entered into a formal alliance with a creative venture called Pinpoint Marketing, which specializes in putting together and managing attractive loyalty programs. Pinpoint recruited major retailers to be "bonus merchants" in the program, offering cardholders additional goods and services and putting a percentage of their profits into a common pool to fund marketing and special campaigns and rewards programs, such as for the 2000 Olympic Games in

Sydney. In addition to charging the banks to run these programs, Pinpoint gets a percentage of the profits generated. "They have a stake in our success," Hilton said. "They profit from our loyalty programs. So the more the volume increases, the more their profits increase."

Kim Harding, the brain behind Pinpoint, is very pleased with this unusual alliance. She ought to be: Pinpoint has grown into an $80 million marketing company, making it one of the largest such companies in the Asia-Pacific region. But it was not easy building the business. "The relationship with Visa began 10 years ago," Kim said. "At that time, Visa was small. Its market share was only 10 percent. You have to be a facilitator, an agent of change, and you're dealing with members in competition with one another. But once you get everyone on board, the members see the growth – and their own increased profits. Now, Visa's market share is over 60 percent."

Kim describes herself as a "simple marketer." She worked in Australia for Kimberley Clark in the 1970s, and from 1980 to 1985 for American Express. "We grew the card base from 100,000 to 550,000 in that period," she said, but it was far from a happy experience. In her view, American Express failed to build a proper relationship with banks and merchants in Australia and other parts of Asia, and they became too far removed from the everyday concerns of consumers and people in the marketplace. "American Express should be the size of Visa today," she said, "but they made some serious mistakes. With Visa, the members provide a constant reality check. It can't get too self-important or impressed with itself. AmEx did."

If there's one thing Aussies don't like, it's self-importance. Kim has built a very strong, impressive business, and she plans to expand across Asia, but she describes her company with

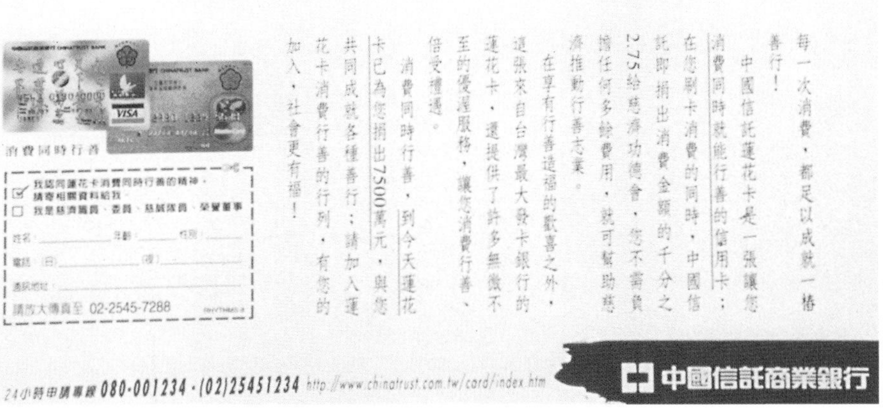

wit and self-deprecation. "We're a marketing company and we pride ourselves on innovation and being customer-oriented. And we have fun. We call it 'Profit with pleasure and dignity.'"

Carl Pascarella could adopt the same motto. During the decade he spent there, Carl fell in love with Asia, met and married Yurie, and had what Kim Harding might term "a modest little success" with Visa. From 1985 to 1993, card sales volume in Asia climbed from $3 billion to $50 billion. Cards in the market increased from 6 million to 58 million. By 1995, in its head-to-head competition with MasterCard, Visa's market share had topped 60 percent.

Looking back now, Carl believes that his success in Asia flowed from something he shared with Chuck Russell, Jim Partridge, Roger Woodward, João Ribeira da Fonseca, and all of Dee Hock's other original evangelists. "We didn't have much money. We didn't have much prestige. We had no structure. No common business model. I think all of us brought a different mindset and a different skill set. But we all shared this: we believed so deeply in what we were doing."

His own business formula, he said, was not rocket science. "When you go into a different environment, you have to be a jack-of-all-trades. You have to go into your individual markets, with a supportive board, and find out what works in that particular market. Your inclination is to go in there and immediately drive to become No. 1. But that is not always the right approach. You have to first build the infrastructure. You have to make sure that people understand what unsecured credit is, how it works, and how they have to guard against impulse buying. You have to make people understand how powerful this little tool is, how it can transform economies and transform societies. We had a tremendous, tremendous responsibility to these countries, young and old, as well as to Visa, to build the business and do it in a careful, cooperative way."

The times have changed, and the details vary from country to country, but when you strip it down to its essence, what Carl and the other evangelists preached had one common root. "We're using absolutely the same business model as A.P. Giannini," Carl said. "He empowered the farmer, and the Bank of America is still the biggest agricultural banker in California. His bank gave the common man a piece of plastic – with a logo – to use as an unsecured line of credit. Now, thanks to Visa, we can all use an unsecured line of credit – anywhere in the world and for anything we want. We do what A.P. Giannini did. We empower the individual."

TAXI
해외 여행에 현금이 필요하다?
PLUS
해외 여행을 할 때 비자 카드를 지참해보세요. 현금 걱정이 사라집니다. 88개국에 설치되어 있는 250,000개 자동 현금인출기에서 비자/플러스 카드를 사용하시면 현지 통화를 가장 유리한 환율로 편리하게 인출하실 수 있습니다. 환전상과 입씨름할 필요도 현금을 많이 가지고 다닐 필요도 없습니다. 비자카드를 기억하세요. 비자카드－세계 어디에서든지 당신과 함께 합니다.
VISA
The world's most preferred card.

U.S.A.

Chapter 26

For the past 40 years, Phil Giltner has had a front-row seat at the credit card revolution.

Phil was born in the American heartland, in the little town of Joplin, Missouri. His father was a banker for 50 years, and his father's father had also been a banker. Phil had a star-spangled boyhood in the Midwest. He loved sports and was a student athlete in high school. Then came World War II. Phil served in the U.S. Army, in the infantry, and was wounded in the Battle of the Ardennes. He was later decorated for his battlefield heroics.

After the war, Phil returned home and earned a business degree at the University of Missouri. After a detour practicing law for several years, he found that banking was calling him back. It was in his blood, it was in his genes. So in 1955, Phil went to work for the United Missouri Bank in Kansas City, and later he moved to a bank in North Dakota for a couple of years. Finally, his apprenticeship complete, Phil moved to Nebraska in 1964 and joined the First National Bank of Omaha. First National was not in the mold of J.P. Morgan; it was in the mold of A.P. Giannini. "We were the blue-collar, dirty-neck people," Phil recalled. "We didn't do silk stocking work."

Located in the heart of the farm belt, Omaha was a major hub of economic activity, and its banks fought fiercely to win the loyalty of the area's farmers, cattlemen, transporters, suppliers, tradesmen, small businessmen, and laborers. The competition was rugged and relentless, and while it was very hard on the banks, it was good for the people of Omaha and the surrounding communities. "We did everything we could think of to get deposits," Phil said. "In one of our best promotions, we gave away football blankets. People in Nebraska are crazy about football."

Then came credit cards. In the late 1950s, just as the Bank of America was launching BankAmericard, First National decided to take the plunge. Many banks had fallen flat on their faces with credit cards, and even the Bank of America was still working to find the key. But in the fiercely competitive environment of Omaha, First National felt compelled to give it a try; if a rival bank beat them to it, the result could be disaster. So First National launched its own card, "First Charge," and while it was a convenient payment tool, a revolution it was not. "It was a real Mom and Pop thing," Phil said. "It had a tough time getting started. And we were alone. We processed our own transactions."

In 1964, the year Phil came aboard, First National shifted course. It sent Fred Hoffman, its in-house counsel, out to San Francisco to meet with Ken Larkin and the BankAmericard team. The big city boys showed Hoffman a very good time. "They took him to a comedy club," Phil said, "and Fred drank clam juice for the first time in his life." Hoffman negotiated a contract and returned to Omaha with the BankAmericard franchise for the whole state of Nebraska. Phil moved into the card program, and for a while he and the team at First National thought they were in clover, as their customers embraced this new tool of unsecured credit. The bank suddenly had a new way to attract customers, and thanks to the card's fees and interest rates, the bank had a brand new revenue stream as well.

First National plunged in whole hog. "We had a relatively high appetite for credit cards," Phil recalled. "Soon we had a sales force covering four different states." The early years, though, were anything but profitable. "We suffered a bloodbath

Carl Pascarella, the man at the helm of Visa U.S.A.

about the third year out," Phil recalled. "People said, 'Wait a minute. This is a disaster.' We found out in a hurry you have to weed out the bad credit risks as you go."

Still, the competition was not far behind. Soon, First National Bank of Lincoln, a bank not far away in Lincoln, Nebraska, went to the Bank of America and acquired a BankAmericard license of its own, with a card territory overlapping First National's. Now the interbank competition got even fiercer. "We went into an all-out war," Phil said. This time, though, the marketing wars were not fought with football blankets or free toasters for opening an account. They were fought with lower interest rates, reduced fees, and special card promotions. No-fee cards, loyalty programs, and frequent flyer incentives would not be far behind. Again, the competition was hard on the banks but good for the consumer.

Soon, Phil and his colleagues at First National came to a startling realization. They were out on a "new frontier of banking" and the old norms and assumptions of banking were being swept away, as those plastic cards catalyzed changes that few people fully understood. For instance, the credit card war between First National of Omaha and First National Bank of Lincoln produced a surprise; it was proving good for both banks. Very good. "We started to expand – rapidly," Phil said. "There was a boom in cards. And that became one of the elements that really helped the bank to develop." Phil watched his bank's earnings grow from a modest $685,000 a year to their present levels of between $70 million and $85 million a year. Phil knew he was witnessing a true revolution.

"The impact of those cards was almost unbelievable," Phil said. "We were the conventional bank, clanking along, and when that little card arrived, everything changed. Our customer base grew. Our assets grew. Our earnings grew. And our rival banks grew too. For us, the credit card was the wave of the future. Now we have built a whole culture around the credit card."

Phil went on to serve on the boards of both Visa U.S.A. and Visa International. First National was still a "blue-collar, dirty-neck" working man's bank, a fraction of the size of a Citibank or a Chase Manhattan, but now Phil found himself sitting at the same table as the presidents of those banks – and being treated as an equal. He and his wife were also able to travel the world with Visa and to get to know eminent international bankers like Lars Piehl of Sweden, Peter Ellwood of Lloyd's Bank in London, and Dr. Jeffrey Koo from Taiwan. All this was quite an experience for Phil, the down-home banker from Omaha, Nebraska. "These guys were the heavyweights, the elite. They were bright, capable men," he said. "It was a privilege being with them."

Chuck Doyle's experience was similar to Phil's. Chuck is an Oklahoma country boy, born and bred in the little town of Mangham, where his family was in the brick business. He moved to Texas as a young man and worked for Union Carbide there for more than a decade. Then in 1973 he and a group of partners bought a little bank in Hitchcock, south of Houston. In a relatively short time, Chuck turned that bank into a booming little empire called Texas First Banks, with four banks in the fold. Visa played a very big role in Chuck's success. "Visa gives a local bank international language," he said. "It allows our customers to feel that big as well. It's a product that you brand globally and market locally, through big banks and small banks like ours. As the ads say, 'It *is* everywhere you want to be,' and to have that universal presence and universal acceptance, you have to have all the banks – big and small, big city and country – participating, working together to build the market and make the system work."

U.S.A.

How pleased Woodrow Wilson would be. In 1908, when the American banking system was in crisis, Wilson urged the nation's bankers to join forces and set up a national branch banking system. Through interbank cooperation, he said, the banks could stimulate economic growth across the American heartland and give increased economic freedom and opportunity to the common man – and build their own profits at the same time. With Visa's tools and its system of interbank cooperation, Phil Giltner and Chuck Doyle could apply Wilson's thinking in their own banks and heartland communities – with astonishing results. The economic activity in their towns and villages is growing right along with the increased economic freedom and opportunity for their customers – provided they are responsible in the way they use the card – and increased profits for their banks. And the bankers have grown their profits and a little added wealth, status, and excitement for themselves. Everybody wins.

Phil and Chuck are not isolated examples. There are some 22,000 financial institutions in Visa's global family, and each one of them has a comparable story to tell. Dee Hock and his followers laid the foundation, created the tools, and showed the way. But it was up to the banks and credit unions to use their experience and ingenuity to design the card programs they needed and build their own success. It is impossible to tell all their stories here, but the real, day-to-day heroes of this global revolution are Visa's member institutions – and the men and women who make them great.

❀ ❀ ❀

On January 1, 1994, Chuck Russell resigned as the head of Visa International. In many ways, it was the end of an era. With Dee, he had helped build the enterprise from scratch, and after Dee's departure Chuck and his team built Visa into a streamlined, smoothly functioning organization.

With John Bennett as his head of marketing, Chuck hired BBDO to add thrusters to Visa's image and trounce the competition. Then they took the historic decision to become an Olympic sponsor and used that opportunity to catapult past their rivals, MasterCard and American Express. Chuck steered Visa into an era of accelerating profitability, credibility, and international expansion, and while Visa was no longer a start-up, it retained a start-up's can-do verve.

"The spirit we had in those years was amazing," recalled Madeleine Socash, who served as the personal assistant to Dee, Chuck, and two subsequent chiefs of Visa International. "We had the right people in the right positions to create that spirit and pass it down through the ranks. People really felt so proud. Everybody wanted to work here. We were going head-to-head with MasterCard and American Express and we were winning. We were going after new markets. There was real pride. American Express was a very powerful company, and we were the little guy. It was very exciting."

Several years before he retired as chief of Visa International, Chuck had stepped down as head of Visa U.S.A. Like Dee before him, Chuck had held the two posts concurrently for several years, but then he decided it was just too much for one person to handle. John Christofferson, an able banker from Southern California and a member of the U.S. board, ran Visa U.S.A. for a few years. Robert Heller, a highly respected figure in the financial world, with long experience as a governor at the U.S. Federal Reserve, then came aboard for a similar period. When Heller left, the board of Visa U.S.A. decided to turn to a Visa insider with long and proven experience in the highly specialized credit card field: Carl Pascarella.

When Carl came back from Asia to lead Visa U.S.A., he felt the operation had begun to stagnate. Faced with a massive market buffeted by constant changes in technology and products, Carl felt that Visa's decision-making had become too sluggish. The reigning mentality, he decided, was too clubby and not enough of a lean, hard-driving, fiercely competitive financial services company. He was

also surprised by what he saw as a worrisome shift of the pendulum: Visa U.S.A. was putting so much emphasis on technology and systems that it was not giving proper emphasis and resources to marketing and brand development. To redress that, Carl hired Michael Beindorff, a marketing and product management whiz from Coca-Cola. To re-energize the advertising side he hired Becky Saeger, an ad and product launch specialist from Foote, Cone & Belding.

Carl also took steps to remold his board of directors to fit the demands of a market in the throes of upheaval. There were some 12,000 institutions in the Visa U.S.A. system, but unprecedented consolidation in the banking industry had resulted in 25 banks controlling 60 percent of all U.S. banking assets. Moreover, five or six banks now controlled 70 to 80 percent of Visa's volume in the U.S. market. So Carl shrank his board of directors from 26 member banks to 17, and later from 17 to 10. With these moves, Carl felt he could better serve his primary partner banks while still maintaining the highest possible commitment to the other banks in Visa U.S.A., especially with stronger marketing and advertising.

By shrinking his board down to a more manageable size, Carl was returning to a lesson he had learned in Asia, working with Yo Suzuki, Dr. Jeffrey Koo, and others: the key to this business is not plastic cards or performance numbers. It's the quality of the *relationships* you forge with your partners and customers. If they win, you win. Just as A.P. Giannini had concluded during his own business apprenticeship.

Carl's approach paid off handsomely. From 1993 to 1998, the number of Visa cards in circulation jumped from 157 million to more than 308 million – almost double. In 1993, Visa cards represented 48 percent of the market's all-purpose cards (Visa, MasterCard, Discover, American Express, Diners Club); by 1998 that figure had climbed to over 53 percent. In the critical head-to-head competition with MasterCard, by 1998 Visa's combined product line – credit, debit, and commercial cards – was outpacing MasterCard's by a margin of 67.5 percent to 32.5 percent. Finally, what did all of this add up to in terms of transaction volume? In 1993, Visa's sales volume was just over $200 billion. By the end of 1998, it had *tripled,* to $610 billion. The numbers have continued to rise since then, and in the year 2000 there was no sign of a slowdown in America's payment card revolution.

"To me, the success is not just Visa," Carl said. "We are governed by our owners, the banks. Our job is to help them do well. And if they do well, we do well. It's a unique mix. What we do is all interlocked."

Because of that, Carl puts great emphasis on working closely with his board of directors. Visa U.S.A. is now a huge enterprise, operating in a healthy, growing market. In Carl's view, it no longer needs visionaries blazing new trails; it needs close cooperation between Visa and its member banks. "I can't bring the tablets down from the mountain," he said. "I have to work with my board to define our mission, vision, tactics, strategy, and parameters of success. Then the entire organization has to connect the dots and make that strategy work."

Carl also emphasized something else that he had seen work phenomenally well in the Asia-Pacific region: debit cards. The logic here seems unassailable. While Visa may have the largest share of the U.S. card market, the fact remains that 80 percent of all payments are still made by cash or check. "Our real competition is not American Express or MasterCard, it's cash and checks," Carl said. "Those are our new targets of opportunity." Thanks to the new push on this front, by the year 2000 debit transactions had grown from 2 percent to 25 percent of Visa U.S.A.'s total volume. He also backed the development of a whole line of cards designed specifically for businesses large and small. These are to facilitate purchasing, large lines of credit, and business-to-business online transactions.

On the marketing and sponsorship side, Visa U.S.A. has built on its Olympic experience and become a major sponsor of NFL football, NASCAR, and horse racing's fabled Triple Crown. It also sponsors a huge variety of other national and regional sports and entertainment events. NFL greats Steve Young and Jerry Rice have starred in some delightfully witty Visa ads, as has Jason Alexander, the inimitable "George Costanza" from the hit TV comedy series *Seinfeld.*

Jerry Yang-Chief "YAHOO! Yes, that's my real title.

Visa® Purchases: Yahoo! Shopping
Most of my friends seem to be getting married. Go figure,
I usually get them hi-tech gadgets for presents.
$93.72Hi-tech Thingamajig.
$88.95 Hi-tech Thingabobber.
$134.87 Hi-tech Whatchamacallit.
$78.20 Hi-tech Whoozeewatzit.
$1,493.55Taiwanese food – well, after
I bought a $1,450 plane ticket.
I even applied for my card online.

No cash.
You don't need it when
you're always online.

One of the few
times you'll ever
find me in a suit.

I started Yahoo! with my partner David
when we were at Stanford. I never did
get that Ph.D. Maybe someday, I mean,
Dr. Yang does have a nice ring to it.

Yahoo!'s first servers were named
after sumo wrestlers. This big guy
reminds me of when we started.

It's In Your Wallet.
It's In Your Life.®
It's Everywhere You Want To Be.®

RANKIT www.rankit.com©1998 Visa U.S.A. Inc.

For Carl and his team, one immediate challenge is the world of the Internet and e-commerce. Carl is determined to be leading edge, but he knows that the changes being generated by these new domains are going to be tumultuous and ongoing. "Traditional banking and marketing are either going to be obsolete or they will undergo significant change. In these new environments, how do you brand? Where do you brand? Now everything is up for grabs. We have to redefine ourselves and reinvent ourselves for the Internet and e-commerce. Nonetheless, our brand strength gave us a strong head start on the Internet. It's ours to lose."

Carl has no intention of losing. Visa has maintained a long and profitable alliance with the Internet power Yahoo!, and Visa U.S.A. has set up "e-Visa," an electronic commerce unit they hope will make Visa the undisputed leader in transactions and payment security on the Internet. In addition to Yahoo!, Carl has already developed strong relationships with such Silicon Valley and e-commerce powerhouses as Intel, Sun Microsystems, Cisco Systems, and Amazon.com.

Some leaders of industry and finance fear the Internet and all the uncertainty it has been generating. Not Carl. In fact, he sees this as a huge new opportunity for Visa and even something more: another giant step toward a consolidated global payments system, just as Dee Hock envisioned three decades ago.

"Paper checks and paper forms of payment in general are high-risk, low-return areas," Carl said. "Therefore, I say let's make them high-priority targets of opportunity." Sending out and then processing a simple monthly electricity bill, for instance, costs the utility company well over a dollar – in paper, stamps, and time – whereas processing that same bill via an electronic payment system costs only pennies or less. "I think that in the years ahead, we will be taking the labor-intensive, high-risk, and high-cost elements out of the payments process. I'm not sure that money or currency as we know it today will have the same value as what I call 'info-money.'" Translation: hold onto your hats, folks. The revolution has just begun.

In the end, though, Carl Pascarella believes the future of electronic payments will be determined by the people and the companies who hold to and inspire certain core principles and values. "To me, the keys are: trust, education, infrastructure, credibility, privacy, and, finally, the power of the individual. In this new Information Age, the consumer has the power. It is the marketplace that will ultimately choose the winners."

Visa headquarters, south of San Francisco.

Chapter 27

The New Frontiers

What a long road we've traveled.

We began the Visa story with A.P. Giannini, and we saw how his simple idea of what a good bank should be revolutionized American banking and gave birth to an ingenious new tool of consumer credit, the BankAmericard. We met Dee Hock and saw how he and a group of fellow believers seized the BankAmericard concept and machinery and built them into the unique global partnership that Visa is today. We saw how Visa developed new technology to facilitate and coordinate the daily transactions of people and businesses, and we saw how Visa built itself into one of the most prominent and trusted brands in the world. And finally we saw how the little Visa card – with the Giannini philosophy embedded inside it – has taken root, flowered, and changed the economic and social landscapes of countries and cultures in every corner of our globe.

Where does this road lead now? Where does the Visa revolution go from here?

These questions now sit on the capable shoulders of Malcolm Williamson, the president and chief executive officer of Visa International. Williamson is a tall, gentle, soft-spoken man who came to Visa at the peak of a long and distinguished career in British banking. He was born in 1939 in the north of England, near Manchester. He began his career there with Barclays Bank and then moved to London, where he helped Barclays set up its first computer system. Later he returned to the Manchester area and began an immersion in bank cards, issuing cards, and signing up merchants for the Barclaycard program. Williamson then went back to Barclays headquarters in London, serving first as head of strategic planning, later treasurer, then as director of lending and marketing, and finally as regional general manager.

In 1985, with his star on the rise, Williamson was named Managing Director of Girobank, the banking arm of the British Post Office. There he set up an embryonic card business and, under the watchful eye of then-Prime Minister Margaret Thatcher, he prepared Girobank for privatization. It was a difficult mission, but under Williamson's guidance Girobank was streamlined and then sold in 1989 to the Alliance & Leicester Building Society, as part of Mrs. Thatcher's radical overhaul of Britain's overburdened public sector.

When that was done, Williamson joined the board of the London-based Standard Chartered PLC, an international banking group with a strong presence across Asia and an esteemed history dating back to 1853. He rose to managing director of Standard Chartered in 1991 and to chief executive in 1993. As at Girobank, Williamson faced a difficult task. "Standard Chartered was in trouble," he recalled. "Profits were abysmal. The challenge was to turn the situation around. It thought it was an international bank, but its international operation was failing. It was regionally governed and its management procedures were old-fashioned. There was no coordination and no proper strategy."

His success or failure, Williamson knew, would hinge on one thing: his ability to "manage change." As he did at Girobank, he restructured the company, trimmed staff, and reoriented the bank's business strategy. Instead of focusing on Europe and other regions with well-developed economies, Williamson pushed Standard Chartered to place its emphasis on the emerging countries of Asia and other parts of the developing world. He also pushed forward with the development of new technologies – with smart cards at the top of the list.

Within five years, the bank turned around.

Malcolm Williamson, an esteemed British banker, charts the future of Visa International.

Today, Standard Chartered has an international network of over 500 offices in 40 countries and a staff of some 24,000 people worldwide. Through its hubs in Hong Kong and Singapore, the bank has become one of the most powerful banks in the whole of Asia. It has also become a leader in smart card technology and programs. "We managed to transform the place quite considerably," Malcolm said. "When I left, we were turning out consistent profits, and I felt I'd achieved practically everything I could achieve."

Williamson came to Visa International in the autumn of 1998, following the very successful tenure of Edmund Jensen, who led Visa International from 1993 to 1998. Under Jensen's tenure, Visa's worldwide market share climbed to 58 percent, and global volume rose by more than 24 percent annually. In that time, Visa also launched 70 different chip card programs in 29 countries and began establishing itself as the premier payment card on the Internet. On his watch, Visa also made considerable headway in opening China and helping it lay the groundwork for the creation of a credit card industry. Ed, an able, congenial banker from U.S. Bancorp in Portland, Oregon, was one of the best-liked leaders Visa ever had, and his quiet competence and self-effacing manner were lauded by member banks around the world. "Ed led Visa to its greatest level of success and positioned it for continued growth into the next millennium," said Peter Ellwood of Lloyd's Bank, then-chairman of the board of Visa International. "He can take great pride in having created the environment that has led to this historic success."

That said, Jensen's years as chief of Visa International coincided with enormous tumult in the credit card industry. The U.S. telecommunications giant AT&T had entered the card market via an alliance with MasterCard, and that posed problems for Visa in the United States and abroad. High-tech companies like IBM, Microsoft, and Netscape were also nosing around the banking and card industries, looking for a way into the realm of processing and dispersing financial information and services. Online banking and electronic commerce were also making their debuts, and on top of all this, there was some friction among the component regions of Visa International.

"Even before I came on, the Europeans were upset about potential U.S. domination of Visa," Ed recalled. "They felt it was time for a European to be CEO of Visa International." That attitude persisted throughout his five years at the helm, and at times it made his job uncomfortably difficult. "The political side of leadership in that company was so much more pronounced than I had expected," Ed recalled. Because the international umbrella has such diverse countries and regions under it, Ed said, it was very difficult for the CEO to articulate one vision that would apply to the whole Visa family. "As a leader, you have to nudge, rather than say, 'This is it.'" As Ed discovered, there were also inevitable tensions between Visa International, with its global reach and broad range of member banks, and Visa U.S.A., with its very high transaction volumes and its powerhouse member banks.

While he was proud of his success at Visa, Ed said he felt a measure of relief when he stepped down in 1998 to return to private business and to pursue community-based philanthropic work in Portland and the San Francisco area. "Every day we faced problems without evident solutions, and sometimes the frustrations were enormous," Ed said. "But Visa has a greater number of highly intelligent people than anywhere else I've ever worked. I will miss the challenge, the energized atmosphere, the relationships, and the many victories."

In many ways, Ed Jensen was a tough act for Malcolm Williamson to follow, especially since

Malcolm was facing growing turbulence in the bank card market. "Visa is now facing a very challenging period," Williamson said during a chat in his office at Visa International's headquarters, south of San Francisco, where it moved to from San Mateo in 1993. "First of all, there is a wave of banking consolidation which threatens to go on and on. This, of course, has a direct impact on Visa. The needs of a small group of extremely big banks are very different from the needs of smaller banks." Also, at a time when they were aggressively cutting costs, some member banks felt that Visa International was not properly following suit. This created, Williamson said, a certain "noise level" that had to be addressed when he took the helm.

Another source of turbulence was the speed of change on the technology front. Some of Visa's regions were eager to press forward with smart cards and a common approach to e-commerce and the Internet. Many U.S. bankers, though, were reluctant to make the costly changeover to smart cards, arguing that the cost would be huge, the magnetic stripe was still viable, and that the pace of technological change was so fast that chip cards could be outdated even before they were implemented.

There were other sources of turbulence as well. Because of its unparalleled success in the bank card market, Visa was a tempting target for political, legal, or regulatory challenge. In the United States, Europe, Asia, and Australia, some governmental regulatory agencies were separately questioning Visa's business model and practices. In the year 2000, a case brought by the U.S. Justice Department against both Visa and MasterCard highlighted the unique and complex nature of the entire bank card industry.

Williamson, no stranger to this sort of turbulence, said that from his earlier experience he knew exactly what the key would be: "managing and catalyzing positive change." As a first step, he established what he called the "President's Projects," a number of in-depth studies of the major challenges facing Visa International. He wanted to examine the internal structure of the company, how it priced its services, and how it charged its member banks. He also wanted to take a hard look at the future of the card market and identify potential growth areas. In addition, he wanted to have a clear assessment of how best to secure Visa's commanding role on the Internet, how VisaNet was handling the explosive growth in global transactions, and what could be done to further enhance the value of the Visa brand. Williamson hoped this process would provide a clear picture of where Visa International stood as it entered the new millennium. He also hoped it would stimulate an open and vigorous dialogue with all of Visa's member banks.

The results generated by the "President's Projects" were revealing. "When I listened to members, there were a number of recurring themes," Williamson said. "One was, 'We pay too much for our transactions. You're not as cheap at processing as you should be.' The second theme I heard was that Visa was not responsive enough to our banks. They said, 'We're customers. We don't feel we're getting what we want.'"

Through an in-depth analysis of the way Visa charges its banks, Williamson found that over the years, as Visa kept adding on new services, it tended to bundle the costs of those services together, and eventually they were passed on to the regions and to member banks. The result, he said, was a complex "mishmash" of charges that was extremely hard to decipher. "I came to the conclusion that 'bundling' had outlived its usefulness," he said. "We had to unbundle those charges and look at each service individually, and then compare our costs to the marketplace." The aim, of course, was to find ways to clarify and streamline the cost structure and then charge members accordingly. Also, by unbundling the charges, banks could then better decide what services they really wanted from Visa – and were willing to pay for – and what services they might want to drop or cut back. The aim was to provide member banks with a menu of services that they could tailor to their own needs – and their own budgets.

This line of thinking led Williamson to a larger question. "We needed to identify what the head office of Visa ought to be," Williamson said. "What is it that the center should do on behalf of the regions?" Answering this question led Williamson to readjust the division of responsibilities between Visa headquarters and the regions. "Our guiding principle now is to do everything we can in the regions, and only do at the center the things that cannot be done effectively by the regions."

Williamson thus decided that Visa headquarters should be responsible for the control, protection, and enhancement of the Visa brand. It should also be responsible for building common platforms for Visa products, to ensure their "interoperability" throughout the Visa family and their compatibility with other card systems. The center should also control financial management and auditing, as well as key elements of information gathering, global corporate communications, and personnel management. Once he had redefined the role of the center, Williamson trimmed the staff in Foster City by 270 jobs and made important staff changes in the regions.

Perhaps his boldest decision was to create a new company within Visa International called "Inovant," a for-profit, stand-alone entity to process credit and debit card transactions. In essence, Inovant was to become an enhanced version of the VisaNet processing network, handling Visa's transactions on contract. In Williamson's view, the new company would bring commercial discipline to Visa's core processing function.

"I see this as Phase III of Visa as a company," Williamson explained. "Phase I was the start-up period. Phase II began with the international organization of Visa in 1981, when there was a formalization of the regions. Then Chuck Russell came in and essentially said, 'We've got to run this like a modern corporation.' That, to me, is the beginning of Phase II. Now, 15 years later, we are saying, 'So far, so good.' But now we need to sit down and really look at where we're making our money. We also need to ask how we can better serve our members and how we can cut costs. At the same time, though, we need to do this in ways that give us the flexibility that we need to expand and expand rapidly. I see this as a different way of running Visa. I want to give Visa a new ethos, determined not by cost but by the market."

In terms of business goals, in the year 2000 Williamson was pushing Visa to expand its debit card volume, given that cash and checks still accounted for the lion's share of consumer and business transactions. He was also pushing Visa to expand its share of business-to-business and business-to-government transactions. Like everyone else at Visa, he was also placing a very high priority on making Visa the preferred means of payment on the Internet and in all forms of e-commerce.

"There's no doubt that companies are changing their way of doing business, thanks to the Internet and e-commerce," he said. "We need to have a major role on the Internet, and we're in a strong position to do so."

Williamson, having been an eager pioneer of smart cards while he was at Standard Chartered, was also eager to see Visa take the lead in the smart card movement. "Visa International undertook a cost/benefit assessment of multi-function smart

cards," he said. "We took into account the unique product and service opportunities they could produce – including boosting purchases by as much as 10 percent in the world of electronic commerce. What did we find? The investment on necessary infrastructure to shift to the multi-function smart card over the next decade would equal just 1.3 percent over and above what member banks would spend on the normal operations of their card programs. Over the same 10-year period, through the chip, member banks would stand to reap five to seven billion dollars in new or incremental revenue – and build customer relationships – by bundling a variety of products and services on a single card and tailoring them to each customer's needs."

Williamson said that by the end of the year 2000, there will be some two billion chip cards in circulation around the world – and less than one in 16 will be issued by banks. If the banks now fail to take the lead in smart cards, he warned, "others will – and leave us behind. We cannot afford to let chip cards just fall where they may. The sooner banks make a prudent investment to create the next generation of payments, the sooner we stake our place ahead of the curve in the financial services marketplace."

Still, in the year 2000 no one knew for certain exactly what form the smart card movement would take – Williamson included. To demonstrate the point, he opened the back of his cell phone and revealed a small chip inside. That chip turns his cell phone into a payment instrument that is powerful, mobile, and increasingly popular. In Asia in the year 2000, cell phones with chips were selling faster than traditional PCs or handheld computers. "Cell phone eclipses PC as e-commerce platform," was the headline on one report from Japan. But whether e-commerce would proceed via PCs, cell phones, hand-held computers, computer keyboards equipped with card readers, or via some other device, Williamson was determined that Visa lead the way.

Maintaining consumer trust is, as always,

absolutely essential. To ensure Visa's security on these new frontiers, Visa International launched a double-pronged initiative to curb fraud and payment disputes in e-commerce. One component of the plan was the "Payment Authentication Program," a set of protocols and technical tools designed to reduce the risk of unauthorized use of a cardholder's account on the Internet. This program gives online merchants effective ways to authenticate cardholders and their payments. It also protects the privacy of transmissions, and ensures that data transmissions remain secure – whether the consumer is working with a PC or chip card, mobile phone, or hand-held computer. The second component of the plan was the "Global Data Security Program," a set of standards and a certification tool designed to protect online buyers and merchants. Both these components were designed to protect Visa's strongest asset in e-commerce: the Visa brand.

Just how strong is the Visa brand? To find out, in 1994 Visa International launched a comprehensive study of the Visa brand worldwide. "It was astonishing what that study showed us," said Caroline McNally, who heads up the brand management unit. "We found that in the public's mind the brand has a remarkable set of attributes. First, Visa was perceived as a global, yet local brand, something that few brands can claim. Second, we found that people see Visa as safe and reliable. Finally, and perhaps most surprisingly, the study revealed that many cardholders had formed an *emotional* connection to their Visa card." In essence, Caroline explained, some of the attributes of the Visa card often rubbed off on the individual cardholder. For instance, since the Visa card was universally accepted, the cardholder had a tendency to feel widely accepted as well. Visa's image as the recognized leader in the payment card field also made many people all the more proud to carry it. "We found that it's a very personal connection people have to their Visa cards," Caroline said. "People don't feel that way about cash or other cards."

So as Visa moves onto the new frontiers of the payment card revolution, it does so with a powerful brand, a revitalized corporate structure and mission, and continuing innovations in the field of global payments. Just as Dee Hock had dreamed 30 years ago, Visa today is the world's premier system for processing and clearing digital payments, and it seems set to lead the revolution for many years to come. In the end, though, perhaps its greatest asset is the trust and confidence it inspires in its cardholders, plus that emotional connection that Visa has forged with hundreds of millions of people around the world.

One person who firmly believes that is Takahiro Miyamoto, the creative director of the Asatsu advertising agency in Tokyo and one of Visa's most compelling image-makers. Miyamoto is a quiet, reflective man, and the various campaigns he has created for Visa suggest a subtle, finely tuned intelligence and wit. Clearly, he has peered deep inside Visa and what it stands for, and he has been able to distill out the essence and convey it in print ads and on screen. Few people in the Visa family can communicate that essence so clearly or so winningly.

"When I think of Visa, the first theme that comes to mind is independence," he explained. "With this card, you can make dreams come true. It is a card of empowerment."

To illustrate these themes in one particular ad, Miyamoto turned to one of his personal heroes: Ernest Hemingway. "Many Japanese men, when they're young, dream of living a life like Ernest Hemingway's," he said. "I know I did. He lived without borders, the whole world was his home. He was so free. And he had freedom of mind and spirit. He lived the life he wanted to, he went everywhere he wanted to go. I'm not sure if he was happy or not, but to us in Japan, living in crowded cities, working nine to five everyday, under terrible pressures from our bosses, Hemingway's lifestyle looked very free and very open-minded."

Out of this contemplation, Miyamoto created a 60-second ad using Hemingway as a symbol of independence, freedom, and more. The ad showed a young man – prototypical and not discernibly Japanese – living in the United States and dreaming of becoming a novelist, a novelist known and respected all over the world. The young man worked hard, writing every day, but one day he hits a wall. To overcome it, he gets on a plane and flies to the Caribbean, in search of the liberating spirit of Ernest Hemingway. He makes his way to an old Hemingway haunt, a bar where the daiquiris are strong, the men rugged, and the women enticing. Of course, the young man comes away from his dream adventure energized, inspired, and ready to write. All made possible, of course, by the power of his Visa card.

"The ad was targeted at a younger audience,

Forget magnetic stripes and PIN numbers. Biometric fingerprinting could be one security device of the future.

THE
OLD MAN
AND
THE SEA

from 20 to 34," explained Hiroko Shiokawa, who manages the Visa account for Asatsu. "The response to the ad was huge. It really touched a chord with young people in Japan. We do dream of studying abroad. We do dream of careers that are big and international. But the average young Japanese person feels stuck, boxed in. Visa is the tool to get out."

Miyamoto created a companion ad aimed at young women, this one featuring an aspiring dancer who dreams of becoming a world-famous ballerina. When she becomes blocked, she pulls out her Visa card and heads to the American South, in search of the liberating spirit of Scarlett O'Hara, the celebrated heroine of Margaret Mitchell's *Gone With The Wind*. This ad, too, conveyed freedom, dreams, and individual empowerment – in a world where walls and borders are disappearing, a world where young people now travel without hesitation, where they learn to speak foreign languages, and where people of all ages and colors share increasingly close bonds of culture, opportunity, and aspiration.

For the 1998 Winter Olympics held in Nagano, Japan, Miyamoto and the Asatsu team were able to take these themes onto an even larger plane. They created print ads and posters of great artistry and power, showcasing Visa as an Olympic sponsor but also reaching for a more universal message. "Visa," one ad said, "Your Ticket To The Global Village."

Freedom. Dreams. Individual empowerment. A global village. These are not new ideas. These were the ideas that inspired the Wright Brothers in their quest to conquer the skies. These were the ideas that inspired Henry Ford in his quest to build motor cars that millions of ordinary men and women could afford and would be excited to drive. These were the ideas that inspired A.P. Giannini to create a new kind of bank, devoted to the public good and to giving the little fellow the financial tools and freedom he needed to spread his wings and soar. And these were the ideas that inspired Dee Hock and his colleagues to create Visa and turn it into a universally accepted payment card. In the process, of course, they created more than a card. They forged a revolutionary tool of astonishing power and reach, and they created a unique example, for all the world to see, of what can happen when greed and self-interest give way to cooperation and partnership.

In developing a new campaign for Visa, Takahiro Miyamoto gave voice, in a simple, eloquent line, to what he hoped would be the next step in this noble, uplifting march of freedom and progress:

"Visa. The World Is One."

PHILIPS
AGL
Canon
TECO
NEC

Acknowledgments

Some books spring forth whole from a lone writer's talent, inspiration, and area of expertise. Not this one. Over a period of two and a half years, I received exceptional help from the staff of Visa International. At the outset, they made available to me 34 boxes of historical material and internal correspondence, and this formed the necessary foundation of research and understanding.

To bring the story to life, I then conducted more than 100 interviews with Visa executives and specialists, past and present, and with several top executives of Visa member banks and financial institutions. My reporting took me to nine different countries, and I had extensive telephone interviews with members of the Visa family in a dozen countries more. Finally, in order to guarantee the accuracy of Visa's history and of my understanding of the workings of the bank card industry, more than three dozen Visa staffers pored through the manuscript, fixing my mistakes and adding clarity and depth. Those staffers are too numerous to name here, but I extend my thanks to them all.

I must, however, single out a few people for special thanks. At the top of that list is David Brancoli, who recently retired from Visa International. For years, old Visa hands had been discussing the idea of putting Visa's history into book form, but Dave took charge and put this project onto the rails. I also want to tip my hat to Ed Jensen, who approved the project when he was running Visa International.

Once we were on the road, I was given enormous support and guidance by a Visa task force chaired by Jim Partridge, one of Visa's original pioneers. I consider Jim to be the true godfather of this book, and I am deeply indebted to him for sharing with me his wealth of knowledge of Visa and its creators. Jim was ably assisted on the task force by Bennett Katz, Win Derman, Tom Cleveland, Ron Schmidt, Bob Miller, and many others, and my thanks go out to all of them. I also salute Malcolm Williamson and Carl Pascarella for their ongoing support for this book.

I also want to give special thanks to Dee Hock, the founder of Visa. Dee met with me for several hours and followed that with several lengthy conversations on the phone. Dee also reviewed large portions of the manuscript and made dozens of pertinent suggestions and amplifications. The book is no doubt stronger and more accurate as a result of his cooperation.

I also want to salute Ugo Scarpetta, a Visa pioneer in Italy and a lifelong admirer of A.P. Giannini. Amazingly enough, in all those 34 boxes of official Visa material, there was next to no mention of Giannini or his revolutionary banking philosophy. Ugo brought this dimension of the story to light and helped me understand its historical importance in the creation of Visa.

I also want to highlight the contribution of Duncan Knowles, a highly cultured man with long experience at the Bank of America. Under the able direction of David Demarest, head of global corporate relations at Visa International, Duncan served as my project coordinator, copy reader, sounding board, and occasional wailing wall. Thanks, Duncan; thanks, David. I also received invaluable input and professional editing from Walt Bode and Stephanie Kartofels of Harcourt, two of the best editors any overburdened writer could have. I also want to thank Libba Cooperman, Katherine Papp, and Cheryl Heinonen of Visa International for patiently guiding me through Visa's many administrative corridors. A warm salute, too, for Keir Walton of Harcourt, for his invaluable help.

While the telling of the Visa story was a truly collaborative effort, one woman alone is responsible for the dazzling look and feel of this book: Yumiko Nakagawa. Yumiko selected the visuals and brought her unique artistry to every page. The cover is hers both in concept and design, and I feel it gives bold and elegant expression to what I defined as the soaring theme of the Visa story: "The Power of an Idea." Thank you, Yumiko, for sharing your gifts with all of us and for giving color and wings to my leaden, earthbound prose. Thanks, too, to Margaret Ensley, our photo researcher, and to Jan Martí, our indefatigable typesetter.

Finally, I want to thank Tom Hummel and his colleagues at Toppan Printing in Tokyo and Los Angeles. Our delays and our demands for perfection no doubt gave them fits, but everyone at Toppan rose to the challenge and produced a beautifully printed book, one we can all admire for many years to come. Tom, to you and everyone at Toppan I say, from the heart, *"Arigato!"*

– Paul Chutkow

In chapters one through four, much of the material regarding A.P. Giannini is drawn from *Biography of a Bank, The Story of Bank of America,* original copyright 1954.

Excerpts from Dee Hock's memoir, *The Birth of the Chaordic Age,* copyright 1999 Dee Hock, are reprinted with permission of the Berrett-Koehler Publishers, Inc., San Francisco, CA. All rights reserved. 1-800-929-2929.

Page No	Credit
2	Corel Professional Photos
4	Visa Archives
5	Visa Archives
6	David Kohl/Visa
8	Matthew Klein/Visa
14	Scala/Art Resource, NY
18	© Bettmann/CORBIS
20	From the collections of Henry Ford Museum & Greenfield Village
22	Courtesy of The Mariners' Museum, Newport News, VA
24	Courtesy of Bank of America Corporate Archives
27	William A. Wulf Historical Collection
28	Courtesy San Francisco Maritime NHP, HDC#A12 152n
29	William A. Wulf Historical Collection
30	San Francisco History Center, San Francisco Public Library
33-38	Courtesy of Bank of America Corporate Archives
39	Courtesy San Francisco Maritime NHP, HDC#A12 30155
41	Courtesy of Bank of America Corporate Archives
42	Golden Gate Bridge, Highway and Transportation District
44	Courtesy of Bank of America Corporate Archives
45	Courtesy of Woodrow Wilson House Museum, a National Trust Historic Site
46-49	Courtesy of Bank of America Corporate Archives
50	California History Center Foundation
52-53	Courtesy of Bank of America Corporate Archives
55	© 1946, Time Inc. Reprinted by permission
56	Used with the permission of Boeing
59	Visa Archives
63	Courtesy of Bank of America Corporate Archives
64-65	Visa Archives
66	NASA
68	Courtesy of Bank of America Corporate Archives
69-71	Visa Archives
74	© Bob Krist /CORBIS
76	Courtesy of The Grand Hotel des Iles Borromées, Stresa, Italy
78	Giraudon/Art Resource, NY
80-89	Visa Archives
90	© Mystic Seaport, Rosenfeld Collection, Mystic, CT
95-97	Visa Archives
99	© James Rigler, Sausalito, CA
100-107	Visa Archives
110	Raanan Lurie/Life Magazine, © Time Inc.
112	Visa Archives
113	Courtesy of Bank of America Corporate Archives
115-122	Visa Archives
125	Courtesy of Bank of America Corporate Archives
127	Visa Archives
128	Courtesy of The Grand Hotel des Iles Borromées, Stresa, Italy
132	© Michael S. Yamashita/CORBIS
136-143	Visa Archives
146	© Dario Campanile, Eric's Studio, 18x24 Oil Canvas, Corte Madera, CA
148-152	Matthew Klein/Visa
157	Courtesy of Tom Schramm
161	Courtesy of Tom Schramm
162	Visa Archives
164	Graphics: Margaret Ensley, Ensley Consulting, Alameda, CA; Information Design: Randall Choo
165	Card Imprinter, Courtesy of Bank of America Corporate Archives
165	Card Scanner, Visa Archives
167	Visa Archives
169	Matthew Klein/Visa
170	Visa Archives
173	Matthew Klein/Visa
174	Visa Archives
177-179	Matthew Klein/Visa
183	Visa Archives
184	Matthew Klein/Visa
186-190	Visa Archives
192	© 2000 Robin Smith/Stone
196	Visa Archives
200	© 2000 Hugh Sitton/Stone
206-218	Visa Archives
220	Matthew Klein/Visa International
222-245	Visa Archives
246	Visa Archives
248-250	Public Domain
251-261	Visa Archives
262	Chuck White/Visa
265-274	Visa Archives
275	Matthew Klein/Visa
276	© Paul A. Souders/CORBIS
278-289	Visa Archives
292	© Adam Woolfitt/CORBIS
294-299	Visa Archives
300	© 2000 Ary Diesendruck/Stone
303-313	Visa Archives
314	Colin Fulkner/Visa
317	Courtesy of Mike Ridgewood, Calgary, Alberta, Canada
318	Shin Sugino/Visa
320	Roger Hill/Visa
322-343	Visa Archives
344	Matthew Klein/Visa
347	Mikki Ansin/Visa Archives
348-349	Dean Hendler/Visa
350-351	Chuck White/Visa
352	Visa Archives
353-359	Matthew Klein/Visa
360	Visa Archives
361	Matthew Klein/Visa
362	Visa Archives
364	Matt Turner/Allsport

officers doing business on an unwalled, raised platform in the middle of the bank – a Giannini innovation. "Everything was open to public view," Ugo recalled. "Physically and in spirit, the bank was open, wide open. It was amazing."

Ugo had another surprise: all the bankers on the platform were Italian-American! But the business they were conducting was nothing like banking Italian-style. The BofA bankers were busy issuing loans. Auto loans, home improvement loans, student loans, and all sorts of installment loans. Italy had no comparable instruments of consumer credit. Ugo was also astonished by the bank's lending policy. The bank didn't care if a loan applicant was rich; it cared if the applicant was reliable and made payments on time. "You can be rich and be a bad payer," Ugo explained. "But if you had established your credit-worthiness, and shown yourself to be a good payer, the Bank of America would loan you money."

Traditional bankers, in Italy as in America, judged loan applicants on three basic criteria: capital, capacity to pay, and character. At the BofA, these same three criteria were applied, but their order was reversed. In the bank Giannini built, character always came first. *Carattere.* "Giannini's lending parameters were often no more than the calluses on a man's hands," Ugo said. "He worked on trust. And there was a surprise dividend: fidelity. If you gave a man his first bank loan, you earned his business for life."

Ugo returned to Italy full of excitement and eager to promote similar changes at BAI. "In 1965, I set up a new service for Italy: personal loans. This was a revolution. Up to then, banks in Italy did no consumer financing. Vendors gave you credit to purchase a Fiat or an Alfa Romeo, not banks. The same was true in the furniture business. We changed all that, and personal loans became the No. 1 profit-maker of the bank."

Ugo and other BAI chieftains inspired the same reaction that Giannini had early on: they infuriated their competitors. "It was a sort of scandal in Italy, and we were viewed with contempt by many people in the Italian banking community," Ugo recalled. "England and France were already doing personal loans, but not Italy. 'Are we becoming money-lenders?' Italian bankers asked. 'Are

Ugo Scarpetta helped bring A.P. Giannini's philosophy – and Dee's – to Europe.